The Economic Consequences of Immigration

Other Books by Julian L. Simon

Population Economics

The Effects of Income on Fertility (1974)
The Economics of Population Growth (1977)
The Ultimate Resource (1981)
Theory of Population and Economic Growth (1986)
Population Matters: People, Resources, Environment, and Immigration (1989)
Essays on the Effects of Population Growth in LDC's (forthcoming)

Other

(with Herman H. Fussler) *Patterns of Use of Books in Large Research Libraries*
Basic Research Methods in Social Science (1969; 3rd edition, with Paul Burstein, 1985)
How to Start and Operate a Mail-Order Business (1965; 4th edition, 1986)
Issues in the Economics of Advertising (1970)
The Management of Advertising (1971)
Applied Managerial Economics (1975)
Effort, Opportunity, and Wealth (1987)
Good Mood: The New Psychology of Overcoming Depression (1989)

Books Edited by Julian L. Simon

Research in Population Economics, vol. 1 (1978); vol. 2, with Julie daVanzo (1980); vols 3 and 4 with Peter Lindert (1981, 1982)
The Resourceful Earth, with Herman Kahn (1984)

The Economic Consequences of Immigration

Julian L. Simon

Basil Blackwell
Published in association with
The Cato Institute

British Library Cataloguing in Publication Data

Simon, Julian L. (Julian Lincoln), 1932–
    The economic consequences of immigration.
    1. United States. Economic conditions.
    Effects of immigration, to 1987
    I. Title
    330.973

        ISBN 0–631–15527–9

Library of Congress Cataloging in Publication Data

Simon, Julian Lincoln, 1932–
    The economic consequences of immigration.

    1. United States – Emigration and immigration –
    Economic aspects. 2. Immigrants – United States.
    I. Title.
    JV6471.S54 1988   304.8'73   88–10401
    ISBN 0–631–15527–9

Typeset in 10 on 11.5 pt Ehrhardt
by Setrite Typesetters HK
Printed in Great Britain by T.J. Press (Padstow) Ltd, Padstow, **Cornwall.**

To the memory of
Simon Kuznets

And for Friedrich Hayek
May he live to be 120

And also for Milton Friedman
Their younger colleague

When in the Course of human events, it becomes necessary for one people to dissolve the political bands which have connected them with another ... a decent respect to the opinions of mankind requires that they should declare the causes which impel them to the separation ...

The present King of Great Britain ... has endeavoured to prevent the population of these States; for that purpose obstructing the Laws of Naturalization of Foreigners; refusing to pass others to encourage their migration hither.

The Declaration of Independence
July 4 1776

Summary

Contents

Figures

Figures

Tables

Preface

I am grateful that it is my lot in life to write a book about immigration into the United States. People's lives and personalities, their creations and tragedies, can be seen and felt more clearly amidst immigration data and analyses than when writing about most topics in economics.

Immigrants' voyages to this land, following upon preparations that required extraordinary effort and often pain, have been among the most exciting and noble of human endeavors. Women and men and children have been strong and brave. They have undertaken their inevitably-frightening transits to a new place for the best of motives: the desire to improve their own lot and that of their families; the urge to leave countries whose governments they could not abide; and the willingness to help build another country where persons can live in freedom and dignity. Perhaps most noble of all have been those immigrant families who, while themselves still struggling to keep together body and soul — a particularly apt description of so many — drew upon their meager resources to help relatives and friends pay for passage and then become established so that they, too, could share the blessings of liberty and opportunity. And our country has often acted with generosity beyond what it conceived to be its national self-interest, even though its self-interest was thereby served better than most citizens imagined.

I am blessed to have known two cohorts of immigrants — my grandparents and their kin who came early in this century, and recent arrivals from Vietnam and from the USSR. This acquaintance surely has influenced the questions that I ask about immigration, and it may also have influenced the answers at which I arrive.

The professional reader may ask which ideas and data in this book are new. My answer: Too much is new. I began the book intending mainly to review the existing literature using a standard theoretical framework, including modest amounts of my own research. But as I proceeded I found large lacunae in the literature that I felt I had to fill with my own work before proceeding further. Therefore, the theoretical frameworks are largely new, with the most important exception being the short-run capital-use theory of Yeager, Borts and Stein, and Berry and Soligo. Perhaps most notable theoretically are the comparison in chapter 2 between the received theory of the international movement of goods and the movement of people, far less similar than commonly supposed; the analysis in chapter 8 of the cost of the use of capital by immigrants; and the queuing theory of the effect of immigration upon native unemployment in chapter 12. Perhaps most novel empirically are (a) the assessment of the effects of immigrants on the public coffers (chapter 4); (b) the across-city estimate of the effect of immigrants upon unemployment (done jointly with Stephen Moore in chapter 12); and (c) the estimate of the cost of the use of demographic capital (part done jointly with A. J. Heins in chapter 8). The discussion in chapter 16 of selling admission to the country as an immigration policy is serious intellectually, though it is not a plausible suggestion at the moment; our world is not ready for such dispassionate schemes even though they may benefit everyone concerned. The quasi-philosophical analysis in appendix A of the ethics of a closed border exercised my faculties to the full but arrives at a conclusion that many will find obvious. The simulated overall assessment of the effect upon the standard of living (chapter 10) is original, but simulations tend to excite little intellectual interest even though they may be useful for policy decisions.

The writing which I most enjoyed doing – the collection in chapters 3 and 4 of a wide range of data on many characteristics of immigration and immigrants in the US and abroad – will probably strike readers as the work of a crazed pack rat. I wish I could have found more such data, especially for Singapore, Hong Kong, and Argentina. Properly there should be an entire volume of such data, but alas, such an inelegant activity is not a popular art form or work tradition in the academic community today, though it needs saying that my fellow demographers are outstanding in their care for data.

Topics are sometimes introduced with a statement by the organizations that lobby[1] for reducing immigration into the US, such as FAIR (Federation for American Immigration Reform), The Environmental Fund (TEF), or Zero Population Growth (ZPG). (There are no organizations that lobby for more immigration.) My purpose is to show that there is controversy about the issue in question, and that the discussion is not just an assault upon a straw man, as some of these issues might otherwise seem. In my judgment, inquiry into incorrect popular beliefs is a valuable scientific activity even if it does not also lead to important theoretical discoveries – though in fact it often does come to be a rich source of theoretical advance.

Newspaper accounts are cited from time to time as anecdotal evidence in support of the general argument. I hope that the reader does not conclude from this that the book is not serious scholarship. Such a conclusion may be warranted on other grounds, of course, but in my view the use of such casual material is not a failing. Rather, it seems to me that social scientists should use whatever materials are at hand to advance our knowledge about the subject. Theory, together with samples of data which are sufficiently homogeneous that they will support statistical generalizations, does not constitute the only evidence that a reasonable person will admit as having weight. Here I stand with physicist Percy Bridgman who, when asked about the nature of scientific method, answered that "The scientific method, as far as it is a method, is nothing more than doing one's darndest with one's mind, no holds barred" (1945, p. 450).

Immigration is a controversial topic that arouses strong emotions. Nevertheless, I hope that the book is a reasonably objective and comprehensive scientific inquiry into the economic consequences of immigration. Most of the research described by this book — others' work and my own — is "pure" or "basic" science in the sense that it was done mainly out of curiosity about fundamental economic questions, though of course the economic and political importance of immigration also stimulated the research. If advocacy is understood to be the pointing to a conclusion that seems warranted by fully presented facts and data and analyses, joined with explicitly stated values (necessarily part of any point of view about a social decision), then one may regard this book also as partly advocacy. It is so partly because I conclude from the facts presented here that immigration is in most ways economically beneficial to US natives, and partly because my values and tastes[2] favor having more immigrants. I find no contradiction or inconsistency in these two roles. And I do not consider this duality of roles a defect or a frailty, except insofar as a person's inevitable human interest in, and preference for, one cause rather than another necessarily challenges one to be fair. The person who could write about a topic such as immigration without an emotional tinge one way or another would be both rare and peculiar. The most to ask and hope for, I think, is that the writer try to remain aware of his or her own preferences, and to be as honest as possible with the evidence — which includes adducing all the relevant evidence, even if it does not further the cause that the writer prefers.[3] Perhaps I am fooling myself, but such a course of conduct seems easy in the work at hand, because the more widely and deeply I inquire into the facts and the theory, the more evidence I find of the economic benefits of immigration for US natives, and the stronger seems the case in favor of more immigration. (This is just the opposite of the view with which I began my study of population economics two decades ago.) I hope, however, that the book will not be considered a debating argument, if debate is understood to be a selective marshalling of evidence that is favorable to one's point of view without mention of opposing evidence, and without indicating how one's personal preferences enter into the argument and conclusion. I have struggled to be even-handed and complete.[4]

When weighing the possible effect of the author's views upon the content of this book, the reader might wish to take into account that (as noted above) I began work on the economics of population in the 1960s with the belief that additional people are economically deleterious for the world and for the US. It was my reading of the literature, and later my own study of the data and theory, that influenced and reversed my belief, rather than my original beliefs influencing what I wrote and write.

I hope that readers inclined to worry about fairness of presentation will notice that this book introduces, apparently for the first time, a weighty factor which militates against a policy of immediately-opened borders. This is the concept of human capital externalities, which suggests that the effects of immigrants may be different when immigrants make up a large proportion of the population than when they make up a small or moderate proportion of the population. The implication is that if the rate of immigration is to be increased very greatly − that is, by a considerable multiple of the present rate − it would make sense to bring about such a change in several increments rather than all at once, so that there will be time to examine the extent to which there are negative effects upon natives from the interaction between the present population and a large number of persons who come from countries with lower levels of economic activity. It was consideration of this new theoretical element which first persuaded me away from the policy of open borders to which I had previously been attracted because there seemed to be no economic theory or evidence against it. (But it should be emphasized that this notion of negative human externalities does not pertain to immigration levels of the size that are being considered by any of the sides in the national debate now going on.)

Several chapters of this book, especially chapters 8 and 9, draw heavily from my 1981 book, *The Ultimate Resource*. That book, and my 1977 book, *The Economics of Population Growth*, analyze the effects of additional people upon various aspects of the economy. Immigrants are people, *inter alia*, and therefore the earlier book's analysis applies to them. I hope that the reader does not find the treatment here unnecessarily redundant; the only option would have been frequently to refer readers to the earlier writing, which is to ask for more effort than is reasonable or likely.

The book sprawls too much. It might be better to reduce the data for foreign countries, eliminate coverage of some fringe topics, and cut the number of citations from the newspaper and other non-standard sources. But that comprehensiveness helps us understand the subject; I also believe it will assist the next person who tackles the subject.

The following excerpts from a letter by a new immigrant (with blemishes in English left intact) may be appropriate here:

Your article about the economic impact of immigrant reprinted here on *The State Record* in Columbia [South Carolina] has encouraged me a lot. [It] has really relieved my doubt about being a burden for this country. I am Vietnamese refugee arriving on 1976.

If the American public has a supporting and fair attitude ... the immigrants would be able to be more productive. A negative and false opinion about our situation really discourage the young generation to stand up with dignity and to contribute to build up our society ... somehow, the American public expects to hear another kind of message such as: truly the immigrants are burdensome, but the great country of U.S.A. will make sacrifices to help out.

It is unhealthy. I think all immigrants should renounce to the idea of charity. Nobody can maximise the potential without being recognized and expected to do so (C. Le, 9 July, 1980).

I am glad I could encourage Mr Le. And in turn a letter like this encourages *me* a lot.

I hope that you will now share with me the excitement of examining the economic effects of migration to the US, from countries all over the world, of men, women, and children who come here to improve their material life as well as to enjoy liberty and other spiritual benefits. They struggle for their own sakes and for the sakes of their loved ones, but inevitably they benefit the rest of us, too.

Julian L. Simon
Chevy Chase, Maryland
July 4 1989

NOTES

1 FAIR disclosed that it hires an expensive Washington lobbying firm.
2 Perhaps a few words about my tastes are appropriate. I delight in looking at the variety of faces that I see on the subway when I visit New York, and I mark with pleasure the range of costumes and the languages of the newspapers the people are reading. When I share a cab from the airport to that city with two visiting high school girls from Belfast, Ireland, and I tell them about the Irish in New York — and about the other groups, too — I get tears in my eyes, as I again do now in recalling the incident. I remember the contribution that my grandparents made to their new country in which they arrived with little except their hopes and their willingness to work hard and take chances, as I also remember the contribution of opportunity and freedom that their new country gave to them. I find no important difference between then and now that makes the process more difficult for either the immigrants or the country than it was then.

3 William James saw it this way:

> [S]cience would be far less advanced than she is if the passionate desires of individuals to get their own faiths confirmed had been kept out of the game ... if you want an absolute duffer in an investigation, you must, after all, take the man who has no interest whatever in its results: he is the warranted incapable, the positive fool. The most useful investigator, because the most sensitive observer, is always he whose eager interest in one side of the question is balanced by an equally keen nervousness lest he become deceived. (1962, p. 52)

Many writers on immigration differ, I believe, not in whether they are passionate, but whether they allow the passion to show. I hope that the reader does not equate the existence of passion with the existence of prejudice, and will not in turn prejudge this work because of a distaste for this aspect of my style.

4 Much of the professional literature on immigration *seems* technical and impartial while actually making an unbalanced and technically-unwarranted argument in favor of an immigration policy preferred by the author or the agency. For example, two of the most prominent writers on the economics of immigration (let them remain unnamed, though the citation may be found below), in an article entitled "Immigration and Employment: A Need for Policy Coordination," arrive at the statement that "30 to 45 percent of the annual growth of the labor force may consist of newly arrived aliens." On these grounds they urge that, with respect to US immigration and labor market policies, "Logic would seem to suggest that there should be a close relationship between these policies." But by their own estimates as of the time of their writing in 1980, legal immigration made up only 15 percent of the annual growth of the labor force, with the percentage expected to decrease at least through 1985. They arrive at an upper limit of 45 percent by projecting a drop in native labor force entrants together with the assumption of a high level of illegal immigration. And the writer of the blurb for the article then converts their statement quoted above, which does not pertain for about a decade after the date of publication, into "In coming years, immigrants may constitute as much as 45 percent percent of US labor-force growth; efforts are needed to ensure that national goals for immigration and employment are complementary."

That is, a tenuously projected upper limit is converted into a seeming central-tendency forecast through the use of the weasel words "as much as." And the policy conclusion is stated as fact rather than as speculation or personal preference, even though the connection which underlies the conclusion — the proposition that immigrants adversely affect native employment — is simply the authors' "logic" and is unsupported by any evidence. Furthermore, this kind of writing finds publication in the US Department of Labor's *Monthly Labor Review* (October 1980, pp. 47–50), an official publication obliged to be factual and impartial. It is relevant that the Department of Labor consistently reflects much of organized labor's view that immigration, and especially legal and illegal immigration from Mexico, should be reduced or eliminated, and it is also relevant that the Department of Labor has been supporting the work of the senior of those writers for many years. So much for the patina of objectivity in supposedly "objective" analyses of immigration. Open and frank advocacy would seem preferable.

Acknowledgements

A grant from the Sloan Foundation hastened and eased the preparation of this book. The book would eventually have been written even without the grant, but the work went better and more happily with it.

Dah-Nein Tzang, Richard Sullivan, and Stephen Moore were, in that order, diligent and capable research assistants. They wrote and ran the computer programs, and wrestled successfully with refractory tapes.

Jeremy Atack wrote the excellent computer program to make the Census Bureau's SIE tape usable for my purposes.

David Simon suggested the quotation from the Declaration of Independence which is the epigraph.

Helen Demarest typed corrections and did a dozen other secretarial tasks with care and clear-headedness; she works with a diligence and dedication that awes me.

Annelise Anderson and Ivy Papps generously read the entire manuscript, and both made many useful suggestions.

A. James Heins and Yew-Kwang Ng were kind enough to allow me to use the fruits of our joint work here.

Helpful comments on one or another chapter were received from Stanley Engerman, Fred Giertz, Thomas Mayer, Richard Lambert, Nathaniel Leff, Nadav Halevi, Charles Kindleberger, Richard McKenzie, Melvin Reder, Warren Sanderson, Dan Usher, and Robert Warren.

Clarifications, references, and other sorts of help were received from (among others) Frank Bean, David A. Bell, David Boaz, Edward Crane, Wilfrid Ethier, Gregory deFreitas, Gordon deJong, Ray Marshall, Richard Mines, and T. John Samuel, M. J. Sattler, Christopher Smith, Lois Sparkes, and Paul Wonnacott.

Several sections of chapters have appeared as articles in journals. These include: Chapters 3 and 4 as "Basic Data Concerning Immigration into the

United States," *The Annals of the American Academy of Political and Social Science*, September, 1986, pp. 12–56; Chapter 5 as "What Immigrants Take from, and Give to, the Public Coffers," in *U.S. Immigration Policy and The National Interest*, Staff Report of the Select Commission on Immigration and Refugee Policy, Appendix D (Washington, DC: GPO, 1981), revised version published as "Immigrants, Taxes and Welfare in the United States," *Population and Development Review*, 10(1) (March 1984); Chapter 7 as "The Effect of Immigrants on Natives' Incomes through the Use of Capital," *Journal of Development Economics*, 17, 1985, pp. 75–93 (with A. J. Heins); and Chapter 10 as "The Really Important Effects of Immigrants upon Natives' Incomes," in Barry Chiswick (ed.), *The Gateway* (Washington, DC: American Enterprise Institute, 1982). I appreciate permission of these journals to use the material in book form here.

Thank you all. I am grateful for your help.

Julian L. Simon
Chevy Chase, Maryland
July 4 1989

1 Introduction

The Parable
Beyond the Parable
The Scope and Viewpoint of the Book

Each chapter's conclusions may be found at its end. And the main conclusions are summarized in chapter 17. Here I shall try to present the key ideas in the form that economists have come to call a "parable", that is, a simplified analogy. I hope this mode of presentation will illuminate the logic of the analyses as well as the empirical assessments which together are the fruit of the book. After the parable, some of the other key ideas are stated in simplified form.

The Parable

Consider an idealized farming "nation" composed of 100 identical farmers, each with the same amount and quality of farmland, each working the same hours and producing the same output. Along comes a foreigner who offers himself as a hired laborer to the first farmer he meets. (For now this is entirely a male community, with no other family members.) The "rational" farmer is willing to hire the foreigner as long as the wage will be even a bit less than the value of the increase in output that the foreigner produces. Being a shrewd bargainer, however, the farmer offers the foreigner a wage considerably less than the amount the foreigner asks. Not less shrewd, the foreigner proceeds to offer his labor to all 100 farmers, going back and forth until he can strike the best deal. He eventually settles for just a tiny bit less than the value of the additional output if the "market" works well. This is his "market wage."

Let us assess the economic impact of the entry of this immigrant into the community. The farmer who employs the immigrant increases his own income by just a tiny bit, but that tiny bit is preferable to no increase at all. The "nation's" citizens as a whole are better off, because 99 farmers have their incomes unchanged whereas one has his income increased slightly, and hence the average income goes up just a tiny bit. If we include the immigrant "laborer" in the calculation, computed mean income goes down, however, because the immigrant laborer's income is lower than the average farmer's; in the very short run, and assuming the number of hours worked per person stays the same, the incremental output of the second person working on the farm is not as great as that of the first worker − the famous "law" of diminishing returns. But that decline in the average masks the fact that *each person's* income has gone up − including the immigrant's, because we assume he would not immigrate here unless his income is higher than in the country which he left.

The parable so far portrays the logic of the Yeager−Borts−Stein−Berry−Soligo theory set out in chapter 7.

A word about the impact during the first moments that the immigrant is in the hypothetical society: Any simpleton can − and a great many do − show conclusively that a new immigrant or a new baby has an immediate negative effect upon the country's standard of living. Before the new person begins to work, s/he reduces per person income purely by arithmetic. (To paraphrase Peter Bauer, when a new calf arrives, per person income automatically increases, but when a new person (baby or immigrant) arrives, per person income automatically decreases.) Of course the changed statistical measure does not necessarily hurt the rest of us, but it surely sounds bad. And if the new entrant gets any help from the society before he or she goes to work, then there is a real negative effect upon the rest of us, as well as the apparent effect.

Now let us move ahead in the story to a moment after considerable immigration has occurred, when there is one immigrant laborer working for wages on *each* farm, 100 in all. The wage of each will be just about the same as the market wage that the first immigrant received. And let's say that each immigrant now has been made a new citizen. But the new citizens have not yet had time to buy any land, so the old citizens still have higher incomes than the new citizens.

Now along comes still another foreigner looking for a job. He goes back and forth until he strikes the best deal, which will be for a wage just a tiny bit below the value of the increase in output his employer will obtain from the *third* person working on his farm. And then another 99 more foreigners follow. On each farm we now have one native-citizen owner (who also does farm work), one naturalized-citizen laborer, and one new-immigrant laborer.

But now something else happens, too: the wage of the naturalized-citizen laborers falls to the level of the new-immigrant laborers. The reason is that all 200 of the landless laborers are now competing for the same jobs, and no owner needs to pay more than the incremental output of a *second* laborer on the farm in order to hire two laborers, because the amount of work done by all the laborers is the same. And the farm owners are now making a bigger profit than before, because they only have to pay the "first" laborer the value of the "second" laborer's output; the fact that some laborers are citizens while others are not does not affect their wages.

The overall results of the second wave of immigration may now be seen as follows: the native owners are better off than before. The new-immigrant laborers are better off than in the country from which they came. The naturalized-citizen laborers are better off than in the old country, but worse off than before the second wave of new-immigrant laborers came. And therefore, the naturalized-citizen laborers will (in advance of the event) surely make a political protest against letting the second wave enter the country, although some of them will, for sentimental reasons, wish to have more of their compatriots enter the country even though the wage does fall.

Let us again change the facts. Assume that the 100 naturalized-citizen laborers have been in the country long enough to buy half-ownership in each farm from the native-citizen original owners. The total yearly proceeds from each farm are now split between the native citizen and the naturalized citizen. Along come the 100 new-immigrant laborers. Assume that all three workers on each farm receive as *wages* only the value of the incremental output of the third worker. The native-citizen and naturalized-citizen owners are no worse off, however, because the drop in their "wages" is equal to their gain in "returns to capital." If this is so, the naturalized citizens are not injured by the entry of the second wave of immigrant laborers.

It seems, then, that whether the existing stock of workers is or is not injured by the new wave of immigrants depends upon who gets the returns to the capital with which the workers work. And here we may refer back to the realistic world of the US in 1989. The "workers" − that is, people who earn wages and salaries − own a very sizable portion of the productive capital of the country, to a considerable extent through pension funds. This means that the situation is not simply one in which "labor" loses and "owners" gain by immigration. The extent to which a working person gains or loses by immigration depends upon the actual facts about the extent to which that working person has an ownership stake in the capital of the country.

Now let us complicate the situation just one bit more before we leave this analysis of the effect of immigrants through the labor market. There is also some additional benefit to natives from immigrants because the immigrants do not arrive in such neat one-to-a-farm waves as assumed above. If a given farm successively employs two new immigrant laborers at a wage equal to the incremental output of the "last" of the two (the "marginal" worker), then the citizen owner(s) of the land will obtain the difference between the wage of the next-to-last immigrant − which now equals the incremental output of the last immigrant − and the incremental output of the next-to-last immigrant. But this quantity is not of much practical importance and therefore can be disregarded, though it is theoretically neat.

The main conclusion to be drawn from the parable so far is that in the short run, additional immigrant workers do not damage the welfare of citizens taken altogether by diluting the capital stock, but may damage "workers" if as a class the workers do not get most of the returns to capital. This effect is transitory, however, and in the long run it is likely to be dominated by many other dynamic effects — especially the effect of immigration upon productivity, and the effect through welfare transfers from, and tax transfers to, the public coffers — even for classes of people who might be hit hard by this particular effect.

This model (as is the propensity of such models) has operated frictionlessly and instantly. But real markets do not operate so perfectly, and this leads us to the question of unemployment. Instead of assuming all the original 100 citizens to be farmers producing the same output, let us assume that they constitute a self-contained community producing a variety of goods and services which they then consume — grain, laundry service, transportation, religious services, meat, and the like. Each business is composed of one citizen owner and one citizen laborer.

Along comes an immigrant looking for a job. But there are no laborer's jobs open. So the immigrant goes to one of the farmers whose barn needs painting, and says, "I'll paint your barn for cheap, and do a good job." The farmer thinks about it for a few minutes, and decides that at the price the immigrant has set, the farmer's own time is more valuable — either for other work or for recreation — than that amount, and he therefore tells the immigrant to go ahead. So unemployment is not increased by the immigrant's arrival.

The immigrant spends her resulting income for goods and services in the community, while the farmer spends an equal amount less because he has that much less to spend. So total income to businesses remains the same, though some businesses will lose as others gain if the immigrant buys different goods than would the farmer. If the farmer uses the time to paint a picture instead of the barn, *average* income of the community (including the new immigrant who is now included in the calculation) goes down because *total* income remains the same, and now is divided among more persons. But everyone is better off, or at least no worse off, than before the immigrant came. (The reader will note that the pictures the farmer paints are not counted as income even though the farmer is getting benefit from them.) If instead of painting the barn the farmer uses the time to paint pictures that he sells to others, total income goes up, and average income might either go down or go up.

But perhaps one of the citizen laborers is out sick, or meditating in the woods on unpaid leave, at the moment the immigrant arrives. The immigrant latches onto that citizen's job. When the previous occupant of the job gets back, he cannot immediately find another job and classifies himself as unemployed. Another possibility: The immigrant arrives, goes to the nearest business, and says: "I'll work harder and cheaper than the laborer you now employ." And the owner promptly fires the citizen and hires the immigrant. These are the cases that the labor unions worry about most, and which constitute the strongest political objection to immigration now and always. It undoubtedly does happen this way sometimes.

Another possibility: After she finishes the farmer's barn, the immigrant goes around to all the other farmers, points to the fine job that she did, and makes deals to paint four other buildings. She realizes that she cannot do all the work by herself, so she hires three footloose citizens, and brings over her cousin from the old country as well. Presto, a new business, and increased total employment; unemployment might then be either less or more than before.

As noted above, some "displacement" of particular natives from jobs by immigrants takes place, just as some new creation of jobs by immigrants and on account of immigrants surely takes place. But the job-creating forces must typically operate at least as strongly as displacement, because on balance immigrants cause little if any native unemployment (see chapter 12). The newest immigrants themselves do at first suffer from relatively high unemployment when times are bad, but that suffering by immigrants provides something of a buffer for natives.

Now let us add to the original farmer parable that each farmer has a wife, two aged retired parents, and two dependent children. Each farm family pays (say) 20 percent of its income in taxes to provide stipends for the aged and schooling for the children, along with standard family welfare services. The immigrant laborers come without aged parents, though wives, single women, and some children do come with them. The immigrants also pay 20 percent of their income as taxes at first. But it is soon found that there is a surplus in the public coffers because most of the taxes go to support aged people, the cohort of which remained the same while tax collections rose as the immigrants arrived. So the tax rate to natives (and to immigrants) would thereby be reduced below 20 percent. Hence the tax-and-transfer mechanism results in benefits to natives because, as the data show (and contrary to popular belief) immigrants use less rather than more of the standard family welfare services than do native families (see chapter 5).

Beyond the Parable

What about the supply of farmland and other natural resources as immigrants swell the population? Will that phenomenon not eventually cause income to be lower than otherwise? The answer is clear-cut, though difficult to explain. The short answer is that the element of land and other capital in the production process benefits the owners of capital when more immigrants arrive because the value of their capital goes up. And natives benefit even if they sell some of their land to new immigrants because the sale price is higher than it would otherwise be; that higher sale price reflects the expected higher demand for food and fiber in future years due to the presence of the immigrants. The land sales give the natives wealth in other forms from which they benefit later on. And the new immigrants who buy a share of the land are better off than in the old country.

But will not *average* income fall over the years due to the restricted supply of land and other capital, if immigrants swell the population larger than it would otherwise be? This is the heart of the Malthusian nightmare. And the nightmare will become reality, at least in part, if the society does not quickly expand the supply of capital. But countries *do* expand the capital base, as did even China throughout much of her millennia (Perkins, 1969; Jones, 1981).

Throughout earlier history, communities have responded to tightness of the land supply mainly by reclaiming wasteland through a variety of techniques. And the new land has not been poorer than the old, on balance, just as the Midwest of the US after it had been developed was not poorer land than was New England. Of course there were heavy costs to be paid in building the land. But the "new people" paid the price while their descendants reaped the benefits, and eventually all persons were better off because the price was paid by the early comers and a bigger and better supply of capital was built. This resource-creating mechanism is a central element in the history of humanity. It is part of the story of problems being caused by additional demand flowing from more people and higher income, with the solutions leaving us better off than if the problems had not arisen.

The story is different – and less problematic – in a modern economy such as the US is today, where land and other natural resources are relatively unimportant. (Consider the small share of agriculture and other natural resources in total national output, even though the US is the greatest agricultural producer in the world; the incredulous may consult Simon, 1981a, chapter 6.) Even more astonishing to some – but an indubitable economic fact – natural resources are increasingly *less* important with each passing decade (Barnett and Morse, 1963). The crucial capital nowadays is "human capital" – people's skills plus the stock of knowledge – and migrants bring this human capital with them. Furthermore, nowadays much physical capital is created sufficiently quickly so that, even considering only the effect through the supply of such capital (apart from the beneficial aspects of immigration), an immigrant with average skills and earnings probably has a negative (partial) effect on natives' computed per-person income for only a short time. And the longer-run dynamics of the creation and replacement of physical capital are such that the whole community is eventually caused to be better off by additional capital being needed, and the newest capital being bought and inventions made; this process causes the stock of capital to be more up-to-date than it otherwise would be.

In short, whatever the relevance of the Malthusian production-capital nightmare in earlier times and other places, in a modern country the concern lacks reality and should not disquiet natives. Human capital is the main element of production in a modern country, and the supply of physical capital is normally expanded relatively easily and quickly.

The availability of wilderness is not essentially different from the supply of productive capital and natural resources; in the short run more immigrants mean more people visiting existing parks, but in the long run more people create more wilderness areas and greater access to them, as the history of the US throughout this century illustrates.

Immigrants do burden natives through increased demand for schools and hospitals, and also through the use of public production capital by government workers, though to a considerable extent immigrants finance their share of the facilities through the pay-as-you-go bond system used by most localities. These are exceedingly complex issues, and the interested reader can struggle with them in chapter 7. I conclude that these negative effects upon natives are relatively small compared to the positive tax-and-transfer public-coffers effect, as well as compared to the productivity effect.

If *some* immigrants are, on balance, a benefit, then why shouldn't even more immigrants – and a completely open door – be even better? There are two possible negative effects of immigrants that could come more strongly into play with much higher immigrant levels: congestion, and negative educational externalities. We do not have experience with these effects at very high levels of immigration – that is, levels much higher than the rates at the turn of the century, which were much higher than now – and therefore, prudence would dictate moving up to much higher levels slowly rather than all at once. But in any case, a jump to much higher levels of immigration is most implausible politically, and hence not deserving of much attention. Nevertheless, these two negative effects are interesting theoretically, and worth a bit more mention now.

It is reasonable that a billion, or even ten million or two million immigrants in a year, would on average be absorbed more slowly than one million or 100,000 immigrants, simply because at any given moment there are a fixed number of potential employers looking for workers, a fixed number of empty stores looking for new shop-owners, and a fixed amount of housing. During the period that capital and organizational structure are relatively fixed – that is, before they have a chance to adjust – more people working with the same capital leads to less output per person.

Additionally, there is congestion. Additional people make it more difficult for the original persons to do the work they were doing before, just as a great many additional trucks in a market place may prevent all of them from moving except with extreme difficulty. This gridlock congestion effect is different than Malthusian capital dilution, which does *not* operate more strongly at higher levels of immigration than at lower levels.

A second possibly important drawback to very large-scale immigration – which has not appeared in previous technical discussions of immigration – is a force which we may call "human capital externalities." A person's output depends not only on the person's own skills and the quality of the machines one works with, but also on the quality of the skills of the people one works with. Immigrants from poor countries possess poorer productive skills than do people *with the same amount of formal education* in richer countries; this is almost definitionally true, and the effect can be seen in the lower incomes of those immigrants in the countries from which they have come than in the incomes they expect in the US (which is exactly why they come). So until they improve their *informally* learned skills – handling modern communications systems, for example, or getting used to doing things by telephone and computer rather than in person and with pencil and paper – they represent lower-quality human capital for American workers to cooperate with. And this would reduce the productivity (and growth of productivity) of American workers until the immigrants – in perhaps 2 or 5 years – pick up the informal learning, after which time they likely forge ahead of natives.

(There also is a linked positive effect, the beneficial impact of working with someone from a different culture. Immigrants cause new ideas to arise, even when higher-skilled persons are exposed to more "primitive" ways of doing a job.)

The size of the negative human-capital externality effect must depend upon the proportion of immigrants that natives work with. If your work companions are 1 percent new immigrants, the negative effect surely is small, and outweighed by the positive effect. But if you work with immigrants 50 or 90 percent of the time, the outcome might be quite different. Such scenarios are wholly unlikely, however.

The most important effect of immigrants almost surely is their impact upon productivity. This occurs partly through increased demand, which leads to learning-by-doing productivity increases. Even more important is the gain in productivity through the immigrants' new ideas which enlarge technology and thence improve production technique. This productivity effect cannot be captured in simple theory. But we should not allow difficulty of description to cause us to slight the phenomenon. It is this phenomenon that literally makes our world go round, and advances our civilization. It is this contribution to our nation and to the rest of the world that enters when the US opens its doors to immigrants. And it is thus that we inadvertently do so well while our intentions are mainly to do good. This progress is a happy unintended consequence of our better impulses. It is a product of the skill, courage, and humanity of the immigrants who bless us with their presence and the fruits of their work, as we bless them with freedom and opportunity.

The Scope and Viewpoint of the Book

The book does not discuss refugees, in small part because they are likely to differ in nature from "economic" immigrants in ways that affect their economic performance, but in larger part because the political discussions concerning the admission of refugees adduce different sorts of arguments than discussions of non-refugee immigrant admission; decisions of refugees are apparently affected by "humanitarian" motives instead of, or in addition to, the effect upon natives' economic lot. The book also does not discuss the effect of immigration upon the immigrants themselves. Neither of these matters affect the policy decision about how many immigrants to accept, which is the book's central interest.

The book attempts to address both interested laypersons and professional students of immigration, which makes for some difficulties. The technical material that is necessary to persuade professionals of the validity of the arguments and of the conclusions tends to make a book unattractive and inaccessible to the layperson. But writing separate books for lay and professional audiences would not be feasible. Therefore the tactic chosen is to present the occasional block of technical material in smaller print. These few sections may be omitted by the reader unless more support for the argument is desired, or unless the reader has a professional interest in the scientific procedures used. This technical material is presented mainly in those chapters where the analysis is the author's own research rather than others' research that is already available in the professional literature. I hope this device proves to be only a minor inconvenience.

Though the discussion is framed to apply to the US, most of the theory and much of the empirical material should apply to other developed countries as well. There are, however, some differences among countries that heavily influence the analysis and conclusions. Two examples should suffice: (1) The relative level of family assistance for children is much greater in European countries such as West Germany than in the US. This must affect any cost–benefit analysis of additional immigrants. (2) Ethnic variation is now much greater in the US than in most other developed countries. This mostly relates to social rather than economic adjustment, but it can also affect the benefits as well as the costs of an additional person coming from a given area, e.g. the value of having an additional immigrant citizen who is a native speaker of another country's language is less for commercial purposes when there already are many such persons.

The findings may be more relevant for Canada and Australia than for other countries, even for Great Britain. These countries seem to share many common cultural elements with the US, including being traditional countries of immigration. The fact that so many of the data in chapters 3 and 4 are similar for these countries likely is the result of this common culture, and is testimony to the existence of the commonality. (The uncanny correlation in the ups and downs of their fertility behavior over the years also is evidence of this commonality.)

A crucial analytic element is the time horizon that we apply. If one asks only whether additional immigrants today will help us economically tomorrow or next month, the answer probably is "no", just as a baby is a burden at first. But if we extend our time horizon so that we put heavy weight on the longer-run economic future of the country – months and years and decades in the future – then the answer is the opposite of the answer for the short run, and more immigrants can then be seen to be good for the standard of living. Often in a discussion of whether immigrants are good or bad for the standard of living, one arguer focuses upon the long run whereas the other focuses upon the short run, in which case different values are at the root of the disagreement – though of course the disagreement might also be about facts, as we shall see.

Though the book focuses on the economic welfare of US natives, this does not imply that the author believes that the welfare of a country's citizens ought to be the be-all-and-end-all of economic and immigration policy. The "sovereign" nation is just one among many possible communities whose members one might reasonably wish to consider – the neighborhood, the city, the state, the region, or humanity at large. To elevate the nation to a pre-eminent position is either implicitly to make a nationalistic value judgment or to err by equating what is with what ought to be. It is true that nations can control who crosses their borders, and there is international sanction for nations doing so in what they believe to be their own self-interest. But that does not mean that nations *ought* to try to maximize the economic or other welfare of their present or future citizens. The book focuses on the nation for practical reasons rather than as a matter of principle.

The book aspires to consider all of the important economic mechanisms by which immigrants affect natives, while paying little or no attention to theoretical developments which are elegant but bear little upon the contemporary situation. Yet it is an open question whether *any* of these factors have much influence in national decision-making, even though they are often given as arguments for and against immigration. It may be that non-economic factors really are most influential; certainly they enter as strongly into discussions of immigration policy as they do into almost any other economic policy issue. For example, one of the most powerful non-economic elements is the desire that one's society not become less homogeneous. As a case in point, Prime Minister Margaret Thatcher of Great Britain declared in a television speech that the British fear "being swamped by people of a different culture", and she said that Great Britain therefore "must hold out the clear prospect of an end to immigration" (Population Reference Bureau, May 1978, p. 3; see further discussion on p. 363). This illustrates how non-economic factors can predominate in immigration policy – even in a situation where net migration is negative, as it was in 1977 when Thatcher gave the speech quoted above. True, this particular non-economic factor probably is more important elsewhere than in the US, where the society is relatively heterogeneous ethnically.[1] But this and other non-economic factors cannot be dismissed as irrelevant or irrational. If we believe that people's tastes are important in social decisions, then tastes about national culture can also claim attention. It would, however, seem reasonable for people to at least make clear their real motivating reasons when they argue for or against immigration, rather than putting forth economic reasons as apparently-acceptable justifications for the policies they seek for other reasons.

NOTES

1 It would be a grave error, however, to believe that non-economic issues are not of enormous importance in the US, too. Appendix B shows how powerful an issue this was in years past when people felt free to speak of it publicly. Nowadays the references are more oblique, usually phrased in terms of *other* people's thinking rather than the writer's, as, for example, this introduction to testimony before the Joint Economic Committee by Governor Richard D. Lamm of Colorado:

> [M]assive immigration involves serious and profound risks. Ethnic, racial and religious differences can become a wedge; they can grow and eventually splinter a society. (29 May 1986, p. 1)

2 Some General Theory of Immigration's Consequences

An Introductory Note on the Literature
Trade Theory versus Immigration Theory
Discussion

An Introductory Note on the Literature

The economic literature on the effects of immigration upon natives is remarkably sparse, as may be confirmed by inspection of standard texts on international trade. Rosenzweig (1982) avers that the complexity of the subject, and the large number of factors that may enter into the analysis, may explain the paucity of work on the topic.

The only systematic treatise is that of Isaac (1947), which canvassed and organized what had been written on the subject four decades ago. Competent as it is, to the present-day reader that book seems lacking in several respects. It devotes considerable attention to a great many topics we now consider unimportant. It does not consider many of the issues we consider important, including most of those examined at length in this book. It contains almost no empirical evidence bearing on any of the topics discussed. And it attempts no integrated assessments offering answers to policy questions about the quantity of immigration. These deficiencies are not a criticism of Isaac's valiant effort, but rather an indication of how long ago in the history of economics the work was done. And since then, despite the manifest social and political interest in the field, the literature has continued to be thin, as the reader will see in the discussion of individual topics that follow.

More generally, the literature in this century on the economics of population is not well-developed. In previous centuries there was much greater interest by economists, however. It was the economics of population that led Petty, perhaps the first great economist, to the study of economics in general. As Hayek notes:

[T]he science of economics may well be said to have begun when in 1681 ... Sir William Petty ... [became] fascinated by the causes of the rapid growth of the city of London. (1989, chapter III)

The best single review of the conventional theory still is Reder's 1963 article, in which the standard issues are stated clearly and sensibly. For our purposes here, however, that article has two drawbacks: First, it proceeds on the assumption that immigrants to rich countries from poorer countries have less education and skill than the rich-country workforce and therefore compete with the lower-income natives, which is not the representative case in the US on average, though it fits much of the European experience in recent decades. Second, it does not consider such dynamic and trans-formational forces as the effects of immigrants upon workplace productivity and economic flexibility, forces which are of great importance.

In an article that I regrettably did not read until after this manuscript had gone off to the publishers (and that seems not to be mentioned anywhere, because of its obscure publication; James Buchanan referred me to it by a happy confusion), Yeager (1958) either solved or made considerable progress with several of the key issues discussed in this book. Most notably, he provided a clear statement of the capital-utilization effect of immigrants, the discussion of which in chapter 7 follows the lines of later work by Borts and Stein, and Berry and Soligo. He also raised the question about the similarity of trade and immigration in a fashion somewhat similar to the discussion in the latter part of this chapter, though his mode of dealing with the question is somewhat different; further consideration of that matter must be deferred to a later technical paper. The main point of this paragraph is to draw attention to Yeager's considerable achievement, and to hope that others follow up on some of the issues he raises in that paper.

Other general treatments of the topic include an article by Spengler (1956) which sensibly set the problem in the context of standard economic theory. Grubel and Scott (1977) deal with international migration in a wide-ranging fashion; by being willing to go outside the standard frame-work they provide us with many rich insights. Jones and Smith (1970) attacked the subject in a sensible and useful fashion, in the context of a pathbreaking empirical study of New Commonwealth immigration into Great Britain. The recent policy-oriented review of the topic by Cafferty et al. (1983) is capable and reasonable. The Select Commission on Immi-gration and Refugee Policy also should be mentioned because it produced much useful material. And with respect to data and governmental reports, Canada and Australia lead the world in quantity and quality.

Ethier (1984) systematically examined migration in the light of pure trade theory. His work helps establish the potential contributions of that body of theory, as well as the limits to those contributions. A point to be developed below should be noted immediately with respect to Ethier's analysis: he deals only with people who work at producing goods that are internationally traded — the canonical cloth and wine. He does not analyze either (a) the case of people who work at producing non-traded goods such as bus travel and restaurant food or work in organizations such as IBM where the organization as a whole cannot easily move, yet who may be thought of as an input to production just as are the people in Ethier's analysis; or (b) the case of people whose persons embody the goods, such as entertainers and journalists and medical workers, and who are therefore best thought of as outputs rather than inputs. A large proportion of immigrants would seem to fall into these two categories; the analysis given by Ethier does not apply to them, in my view.

In Ethier's analysis of people as inputs to the production of traded goods, the reason that people move between two countries is either that the countries have (by assumption) recently opened trade and hence are not yet in equilibrium and therefore the relative endowments of capital and labor differ between the two countries, or else there is an absolute production-cost difference between the countries which causes different wage rates. (The Ricardian model may here be seen as a special case of the Heckscher–Ohlin–Samuelson model.) For the most part, such analysis of people as labor input is the same as the analysis of capital as input. The migration occurs in response to the difference in wage rates, and continues until a wage-rate equilibrium is reached (at wage-rate *equality* under most sets of assumptions). Migrant agricultural labor in the states of the US bordering Mexico would seem to fit this model, although the same crops might just as well be grown on the Mexican side of the border, and the causes of the location of production in one country or the other are not immediately obvious.

There has, however, been considerable time for pairs of countries such as the US and the UK to move most of the way toward such an equilibrium between them. One might argue that immigration restrictions prevent an equilibrium from being reached. But prior to 1924 there were few restrictions on immigration into the US, and quotas from the UK to the US have not been a tight constraint. Yet migration has not equalized wages across the two countries in such fashion as to remove the reasons that cause some persons to migrate from the UK to the US.

Ethier (1985) has also offered an interesting analysis of European-style temporary migration which makes sense of the fact that guestworkers are said to be complementary to native workers when they are desired, but are said to be substitutes when they are no longer wanted. Because he deals with labor as essentially composed of large homogeneous sectors, however, his analysis is not helpful in understanding the sort of international migration envisaged in this book.

In contrast to the study of its consequences the study of the *determinants* of migration — a topic which is mostly outside the purview of this book — has received considerable scholarly attention (Ravenstein, 1889; Lee, 1966; Sjaastad, 1962; plus a large volume of recent empirical work. But see Thomas, 1954, chapters 1−3, for a review of the major writings of Classical and modern economists with respect to such questions as whether free trade and innovation lead to international migration, and the importance of mobility between occupations and between "classes". He concludes that the subject was not much advanced by those writings.) And the topic seems sure to receive even more attention in coming years as economists interested in the family and in labor shift their attention to this issue and away from studies of the determinants of fertility and mortality, topics which share common theoretical and empirical investigative methods with immigration studies. Whether the increasing study of determinants will turn out to be a complement or a substitute for the study of the consequences remains to be seen.

The explanations of migration boil down to the proposition that the expected gains from the move outweigh the expected costs of the move. That is, the market value of the individual must be greater in one place than in another, over and beyond transaction costs. It follows, then, that to understand inter-country migration we must know why people are different in value in one country rather than in another. And we require an explanation which does not require that the countries be out of equilibrium due to the recency of trade or migration opening up between them.

Most of the research on the determinants of migration does not speak to this question, however, but rather simply assumes some set of characteristics of the individual, and of the origin and destination countries, that make a move profitable. That is, most research concerning the determinants of migration focuses on the reasons that randomly chosen *individuals* move, rather than the reasons why there may exist *systematic* gains to migrants, and hence *net* migration from one place to another. Most of that body of research is composed of microeconomic studies of individuals moving from one part to another of a country such as the US or Canada.

Immigration and modern domestic migration differ greatly in their respective ratios of net to gross migration. For example, the rates of in-migration and out-migration for a sample of cities are as shown in table 2.1. The ratio of gross to net migration obviously is very large internally, whereas international immigration is mainly one-way. (These remarks do not pertain to black migration from the rural South, or earlier white migrations from farm to city.) These data fit with the variations in price structures being relatively small among various regions of countries such as the US, compared to the variation in price structures among countries.

The determinants of domestic migration are largely those that reflect imperfect matching of individuals' specific abilities with the characteristics

Table 2.1   Annual rate of in-migration and out-migration per hundred
             residents

Metropolitan area	In-migration	Out-migration
Akron	6.9	7.4
Albany	7.0	6.2
Albuquerque	14.4	14.8
Allentown	5.7	6.1
Atlanta	11.4	11.4
Bakersfield	15.1	15.1
Baltimore	5.3	5.9
Birmingham	8.6	10.4
Boston	5.8	6.3
Bridgeport	8.0	8.0
Buffalo	4.8	5.9

Source: Morrison and Wheeler, 1978, table 1

of specific jobs; the match can be better west *or* east, north *or* south, for most persons in most occupations most of the time, in addition to such extraneous factors as climate. That is, even if the net migration between two areas of the US is zero, gross migration in both directions may still be considerable. And the causes of that gross migration are the search for, and the execution of, improved matching. Individuals A and B may exchange jobs in two states and thereby produce a better match of individuals with jobs, but this sort of migration and its determinants – which constitutes most of the contemporary internal migration in the US, as shown by the fact that gross migration is large relative to net migration – is not of interest from the point of view of this book, because the citizens of neither place are affected except by a general increase in efficiency produced by the improved matching. This explains why almost all research on internal migration focuses upon the personal characteristics of the migrants, and upon distance, which is symmetrical rather than one-directional.

A by-product of the theory presented below is that it helps distinguish between international migration to the US, and contemporary internal migration within the US (as distinct from the rural-to-urban migration of the past). Broad factors such as differences in average income, as related to the structures of prices and wages, help us understand international migration. This is in contrast with the myriad of relatively small "random" factors related to individual employers and prospective employees, rather than to the economic environment generally, which explain internal migration. This is why individual characteristics have not been the focus of past research on international migration.

The next section of this chapter examines what the "pure" economic theory of trade has to say about the effects of immigration upon natives. The surprising conclusion is that the standard theory of international trade – almost the only brand of "pure" theory that apparently bears upon the matter – is not at all relevant. Migration does not confer the sort of benefits to the consumer that trade in goods and capital movements provide. This section is offered as a new theoretical contribution. (But see Yeager, 1958.)

Other theory is brought to bear upon more specialized topics in other chapters. For example, in chapter 7 marginal productivity distribution theory enters into the analysis of the effects of immigrants through the utilization of capital. Some new theoretical approaches to the effect of immigration upon unemployment may be found in chapter 11. And the effect of remittances is analyzed in an afterword to chapter 7. Some other theoretical issues are touched on in the discussion section of this chapter.

Trade Theory versus Immigration Theory

The aim of this section is not to develop theory upon which we shall build later, but rather to clear the decks of theory that is thought to be useful but is not. The common view is that international trade and international migration are similar phenomena, to be analyzed with the same general theory, the Heckscher–Ohlin–Samuelson theory of factor-price equalization that considers movement of workers and movement of capital to be alternative routes to the same production end. But the analogy is not sound. International trade and international migration are theoretically different phenomena rather than similar. Trade theory is necessarily silent about migration, as is confirmed by texts on that subject. The gains from trade are quite unlike the gains from migration. Consumers do not obtain the same sort of gains from the international movement of people as they do from international exchange of goods, though there are important gains from immigration to the countries of destination through mechanisms other than trade-like effects. And the "explanation" of why people move is different from the explanation of why goods move.

A numerical example helps illuminate the issue. Consider first the more difficult case of an "occupationally unbalanced" migration, that is the immigrants not in the same proportions as the workforce in the country of destination. Let just a single barber move between countries ("US" and "India") which have only barber and chicken-farming sectors. The analysis proceeds in two stages, the first stage before the destination economy fully adjusts, and the second stage after it reaches its new equilibrium.[1]

Assume that initially the "US" and "India" each have 400 man-hours per week available to the economy and that they produce chickens and haircuts as in table 2.2. One man-hour produces 1 haircut in both countries, but produces 3 chickens in the US and 2 chickens in India. One haircut is worth 3 chickens in the US and 2 chickens in India. Now let one barber migrate, shifting 40 man-hours per week of barbering.

In the first adjustment stage, the migrant barber forces US haircut prices down enough to create demand for his services, but as yet no native barbers have left the trade. The opposite happens in India. Production in the two countries is as shown in table 2.3. Total world production is the same as prior to migration, so there clearly is no total gain in consumer welfare. The barber is better off, however, because he/she is paid at a higher price than before — more than 80 chickens-worth though less than 120 chickens-worth — which explains why the migration takes place.

After some time, the shift in prices leads to occupational adjustments. There is no reason to expect the fully adjusted occupational proportions to be different than before the migration. Hence the structure of production will be as shown in table 2.4, and prices should therefore return to what

Table 2.2   Production prior to migration

Source of income	US	India	Total
Haircuts	200	200	400
Chickens	600	400	1,000

Table 2.3   Production after migration but before adjustment

Source of income	US	India	Total
Haircuts	240	160	400
Chickens	600	400	1,000

Table 2.4   Production after adjustment to migration

Source of income	US	India	Total
Haircuts	220	180	400
Chickens	660	360	1,020

they were prior to the migration. Now there is an increase of 20 chickens in total world production, but all the increase goes to the migrant barber, in connection with the higher price of haircuts that he gives in the US, and represents the increase in his/her standard of living. But everyone else's standard of living is as before. So we distinguish three groups − the natives of the origin country who do not move, the natives of the destination country, and the immigrant. The first two groups do not benefit from the move, whereas the immigrant does benefit. This is the key point.

To repeat, trade-induced shifts in prices and production benefit consumers in both countries, whereas the shifts due to international migration benefit only the migrant. And after full adjustment, international migration leaves prices as before, whereas trade in goods alters the price structure. Capital has been omitted from the model for simplicity.

If migrants come to the destination country in the same proportion as the existing labor force − not wildly different from reality in the US − the entire process can be seen as a single stage. Prices then simply remain unchanged, the total economy expands in proportion to the migrants, natives' incomes are unchanged, and immigrants obtain a higher standard of living. This discussion does not answer the question of why production of the tradeable good is higher in the destination country. There are many possible explanations, just as in trade theory. But this question is not part of the matter at issue here.

Trade theory refers to goods − oranges, chickens, autos, computer programs − which can be sold separately from the services of the persons who own the means of production of these goods. In contrast, the benefit which the migrant confers upon the person or organization that pays the migrant for her/his services cannot be delivered at a distance. That is, trade theory deals by definition with internationally traded goods, while international (economic) migration is a response to the fact that that person's output cannot be directly sold at a distance. It should not be surprising, then, for trade theory to be silent about the immigration that takes place.

Standard trade theory does explain why migration *need not* take place under certain conditions. But it does not explain why the migration that *does* take place *should* occur. To put the point differently, people either migrate internationally or they do not. One class of people who (in trade theory) do not immigrate are those engaged in the production of internationally traded goods, whose wages are thereby equalized in all relevant countries (at least the wages are equalized in principle, though by another principle the equality of wages is not testable empirically); they therefore have no motive to move. Another group of people choose not to migrate because their earnings are greater in the country of origin than in the country of destination. But some people do migrate internationally, even some whose skill in their professions is average. Factor-price-equalization theory provides no motive for these people to migrate. And most important, there is no gain to non-moving natives similar to the Ricardian wine-and-cloth increase in total production whose benefit is realized by native consumers in both countries.

The statement above seems very unconvincing at first, and requires a long paper (Simon, 1988a, available upon request) to carry the argument. Because the issue is not central to this book, the matter may safely be left at this point.

Discussion

1   One may question whether there will not inevitably be some changes in relative prices due to the immigration of a disproportionate number of barbers, say, because of the very argument adduced here − that some occupations need not immigrate because there are no gains to their immigration. Inevitably some such distributional effect will occur, and it is especially obvious in the case of self-employed immigrants who work alone, e.g. doctors and domestics. The market for medical services in the US in recent years has undoubtedly been affected by the influx of foreign physicians. And this is not welcome to US physicians; there will be an obvious loss to the previous sellers of that service who were previously sufficiently efficient to reap some producer surplus, as well as the more difficult-to-calculate loss to the previously marginal producers who are forced out of the business. (And the benefits gained by the immigrants are not an offset to the latter's loss, given that the context of our discussion is the welfare of natives.)

2   Another "conventional" channel through which immigrants can affect the welfare of nationals is the dilution of capital. This effect is discussed in chapter 7. In private industry, the Borts−Stein−Berry−Soligo analysis points to gains to "owners of capital" being slightly larger than losses to "workers," for a slight net social gain, but these effects are small compared to gains to trade, and also compared to other effects of immigration. As the stock of capital per worker returns to what it would have been in the absence of immigrants, the situation will be exactly what it would have been without the immigrants. That is, the immigrants would then cause the economy to be larger, in proportion to the amount of immigration, but all other magnitudes would be the same. Theory for publicly-used capital also is given there, a larger effect than the above but still much smaller than other effects of immigration.

3   Another "classical" channel through which immigrants have temporary distributional effects is consumer prices. For simplicity imagine a self-

employed immigrant who works alone, e.g. a doctor or domestic. By increasing the supply of labor in a given industry, the immigrant pushes down the price of that service. This bestows some additional consumer surplus upon all consumers down to the marginal person who would not have bought at the old price. This situation might profitably be analyzed more carefully, but I will not pursue it here because the size of the effect is likely to be small relative to other effects analyzed in this book.

If immigrants are distributed evenly throughout the occupations, and if their consumption patterns are similar to those of natives, the wages and prices of goods will be exactly what they would be without immigrants, aside from the effects due to the temporary dilution of the stock of capital. And as the per-worker stock of capital and the occupational mix return to what they would have been in the absence of immigrants, the situation will be exactly what it would have been without the immigrants.

NOTES

1 The numbers and some of the language in this example are adapted from a letter by Ivy Papps, who kindly granted me permission to do so, though the argument was different from mine.

3 The Demographic Dimensions of Immigration into the United States

The Volume of Immigration
Age and Sex Composition
Education and Occupational Skill
Number of Aliens Illegally in the United States
Countries of Origin
The Demand for Immigration

The aim of this chapter is to supply demographic data relevant to discussion of the consequences of immigration into the US. Unfortunately there is not now available a reference volume presenting immigration statistics. Therefore, subject to constraints of space the chapter presents as wide a variety of data as I could find, covering as long time spans as possible. Closely related subjects dealing with immigrants' behavior (such as fertility, and labor-force participation) rather than with immigrants' demographic characteristics at entry, are treated in chapter 4. Data on the quantity and characteristics of illegal immigrants are presented in chapter 15.

The Volume of Immigration

Gross annual immigration since 1820 – the total numbers of immigrants arriving each year – is shown in figure 3.1.

The proportions of emigrants to immigrants, a magnitude which has received little attention, are shown in figure 3.2.[1]

Net immigration – the difference between arrivals and departures, shown in figure 3.3a – produces a different impression than does gross immigration. Sometimes, as during the 1930s, emigration has exceeded immigration. This has been the case even more dramatically in other

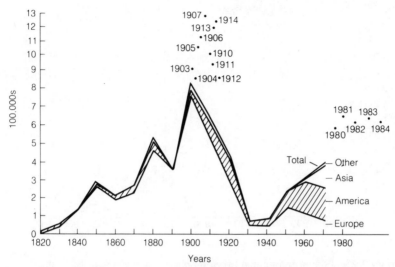

Figure 3.1   Average annual number of US immigrants per decade by
continent, 1820–1979, plus ten highest individual years and
individual years since 1980 (in 00,000s)
Sources: US Department of Commerce, *Statistical Abstract for the United States*
(Washington, DC: Government Printing Office, 1981), p. 85. 1980–4 data from US
Immigration and Naturalization Services Annual Reports, 1981–5

countries of immigration such as Canada and Australia (see figure 3.3b for
Canada). Emigration data make clear that gross immigration data are
misleading when used to estimate population growth and labor force
growth.[2]

The data on immigrant flows refute widely held ideas. For example, the
anti-immigration organization FAIR says, "Immigration to the US is at
record levels" (fund-raising letter signed by Roger Conner, no date, p. 2).
And a recent Commissioner of the US Immigration and Naturalization
Service (INS) wrote: "The United States is probably undergoing now the
greatest surge of immigration in its history" (Chapman, 1976, p. 2). The
INS statement included illegal immigrants, who are excluded from the data
underlying the figures shown above. But the data on legal immigration are
such that no plausible assumption about the rate of illegal immigration
could justify such a statement, as we shall see below.

Figures 3.1 to 3.3 demonstrate that immigration into the US is not an
inexorable force, but rather depends upon people perceiving that circumstances in the US are relatively favorable for new immigrants and for
residents. The large scientific literature analyzing the determinants of

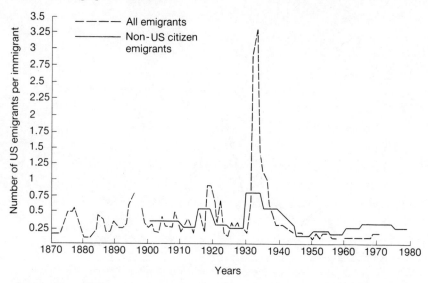

Figure 3.2   US emigration as a proportion of immigration, 1870−1980
Sources: Data for 1870−1907 are male steerage departures per male immigrant
   arrival, originally described in Harry Jerome, *Migration and Business Cycles* (New
   York: National Bureau of Economic Research, 1926); see Thomas Kessner,
   "Repatriation in American History." Appendix A of *U.S. Immigration Policy and the
   National Interest*, pp. 287−388. Data for 1908−57 are from US Department of
   Justice, Immigration and Naturalization Service, *Annual Report* (Washington, DC:
   Government Printing Office, various years 1908−57). Data for 1960−70 are originally
   described in Ada Finifter, "Emigration from the United States: An Exploratory
   Analysis," mimeo, 1973; see Passel and Peck, 1979. Data on non-US citizen
   emigration from Robert Warren and Ellen Kraly, "The Elusive Exodus: Emigration
   from the United States," *Population Trends and Public Policy*, 8 (March), 1985, p. 5

international and domestic migration mentioned in chapter 1 shows that
the volume of immigration is heavily affected by conditions in the receiving
country, and (less heavily) by conditions in the sending country. (The
number of countrymen in the potential receiving country also has a large
effect on whether immigrants come (Bartel, 1982), and if they come, where
they settle. Distance and the cost of transportation also have important
effects, of course.)

   To be meaningful in discussion of immigration policy, a statement about
the volume of immigration must be a comparison of some sort. Inappropriate comparisons cause misleading and frightening conclusions. For
example, one frequently comes across statements about the *proportion* that
immigration bears to total population *growth*. That proportion may seem to

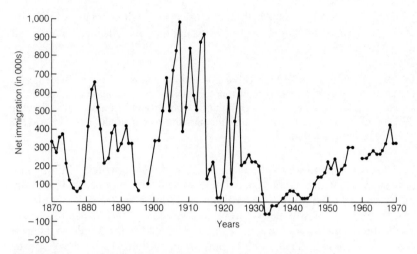

Figure 3.3a Net immigration to the United States (in 000s)
Note: This figure has been prepared by applying the percentages in figure 3.2 to the
gross immigration data in figure 3.1.
Sources: For data 1870–1907 see Thomas Kessner, "Repatriation in American
History." Appendix A of *U.S. Immigration Policy and the National Interest*,
pp. 287–388. For data 1960–70 see Passel and Peck, 1979.

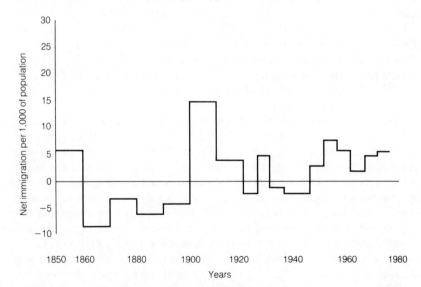

Figure 3.3b Net Canadian immigration relative to population, 1851–1980
Source: Peter Lindert and Charles P. Kindleberger, *International Economics*, 7th edn
(New York: Irwin, 1982)

be rising, even rapidly, especially if one uses very high estimates of the rate of illegal permanent immigration. For example, The Environmental Fund (TEF) says:

In 1980, the proportion of U.S. population growth due to natural increase (births minus deaths) was 59%, while population growth due to net immigration was 41%. By the year 2000, if current levels continue, natural increase would account for only 29% of U.S. population growth and immigration would account for 71%. (*The Data*, May 1982, no. 1, p. 1)

Historian of immigration Graham (a FAIR director) writes: "Immigrants now supply half the nation's population growth, the proportion is steadily rising, and at some point, between the year 2000 and 2035, *all* population growth in the US will derive from immigration" (*The Center Magazine*, 1978, quoted in an advertisement of the Center for the Study of Democratic Institutions). Again, unless one assumes there to be a volume of illegal immigration far beyond anything warranted by the scientific literature (see discussion below), these statements were quite wrong in 1978 when Graham wrote; births that year were 3.3 million, deaths were 1.9 million, legal immigrants were 0.6 million (*US Statistical Abstract, 1980*, pp. 61 and 94), so legal immigration was perhaps one-fifth of total growth excluding emigration, perhaps one-sixth including immigration, and perhaps a maximum of one-fourth including illegal immigration. Nor could the TEF 1982 statement have been anywhere near close to true even for the peak recent immigration year, 1980, when legal immigration was 0.8 million.[3] By contrast immigration accounted for about 39 percent of total population increase during the decades 1881−90 and 1901−10 (Easterlin et al., 1982, p. 3); even earlier, from 1830 to 1885, it was "almost a quarter" (Kuznets, 1977, p. 4).

Even if the quoted assertions about the proportion of total US increase represented by immigration *were* correct, such a measure does not tell anything meaningful either demographically or economically, because the proportion depends heavily upon native fertility. For example, if the native population were growing by exactly one human being per decade − that is, at one person above zero growth − and exactly one immigrant came, immigration would then account for fully half of the two-person population growth. Two immigrants would then account for two thirds of growth, and so on. As fertility has fallen in the US, immigration inevitably constitutes a larger proportion of natural increase. This measure is not useful for any demographic−economic purpose I can think of, except perhaps to indicate just the opposite of what those who have constructed this comparison have in mind. It shows how much scope there is for immigration to make up a shortfall in case one worries about low fertility leading to population decline. The measure *is* meaningful, however, if one cares about maintaining racial homogeneity (which, we must note, is no more illegitimate logically than wanting your children to look like you, even if some of the rest of us do not share your concern; morality is another matter). If immigration bears a high proportion to total population growth, there will be a relatively rapid rate of change of population composition by country of origin, assuming that the present composition of immigration differs from that of the native population.

Immigration should also be seen in the context of native fertility. Births are projected to be around four million in the foreseeable future; immigration will be closer to 500,000 than to a million if present policies continue − something more than only a proportion of one to eight compared to fertility.

A more meaningful ratio − demographically, economically, and sociologically − is the flow of immigration as a *proportion of the yearly resident population*, shown in figure 3.4a. Immigrants who arrived in the decade 1901−10 constituted 9.6 percent of the population at the end of that decade; by comparison, those who came in 1961−70 and 1971−80 constituted 1.6 percent and 2.0 percent of the population, respectively. That is, relative to resident population the rate of gross immigration − the latter being more relevant from the point of view of *absorption* problems than is net immigration − was five or six times greater in the earlier period than recently. In the recent years 1980−3 the ratio of immigrants to population was three or four times as large in Australia as in the US (Ozdowski, 1985, p. 3).

Another relevant comparison concerns *stocks* of people rather than flows: In 1910, 14.6 percent of the US population was foreign-born, but in 1970 only 4.7 percent of the population was foreign-born, and in 1980 only 6.2 percent. That is, the recent proportion of foreign born is less than half of what it was in peak periods in earlier decades. (The data from 1900 to 1980 are shown in figure 3.5.) In 1850, in the "large" cities outside the South, foreign-born whites constituted 39 percent of the population, and by 1920 66 percent (cities over 500,000; Kuznets, 1977, p. 3). In Canada in 1981, 16.1 percent of the population was foreign-born, compared to the 6 percent in the US (Samuel and Woloski, 1985).

Woodrow, Passel, and Warren show that the relative stock was rising rapidly around 1980. And the rise continued through the Current Population Survey in June 1986, at which time the proportion was perhaps 6.4 percent (1987, table 3). The proportion was rising less rapidly during the period from 1983 to 1986 than from 1980 to 1983, however (1987, table 4).

In some flourishing countries there are very high proportions of foreign workers to total workers (see figure 3.6). (US data are not easily available,

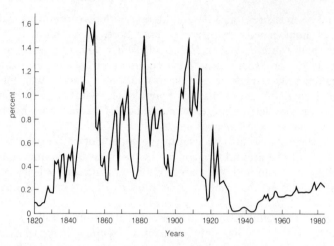

Figure 3.4a Immigrant arrivals as a percentage of US resident population
population

Source: Council of Economic Advisors, *Economic Report to the President* (Washington, DC: Government Printing Office, 1985), chart 7-1, p. 216

Figure 3.4b Immigrant arrivals of working age as a percentage of civilian labor force, 1870–1980

Note: For 1920–80, immigrants 16 years old and over; for 1900–15, immigrants 14 years old and over; for 1870–90, immigrants 15 years old and over.

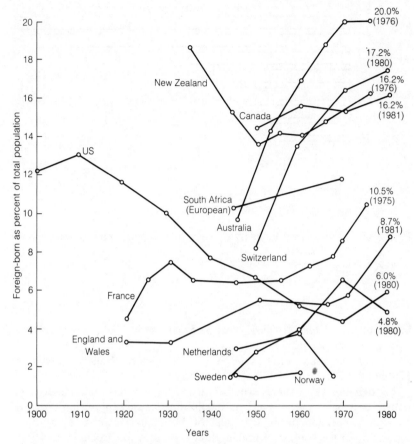

Figure 3.5   Foreign-born as percentage of total population, in selected
countries, 1900–70

Sources: Select Commission on Immigration and Refugee Policy, 1981, p. 3, based on
a chart in Kingsley Davis, "The Migrations of Human Populations," *Scientific
American*, 1974; 1980 Census of US Population, vol. 1, chapter D, "Detailed
Population Characteristics," part 1, P680–1–D1–A, March 1984, table 253; and
United Nations, *Demographic Yearbook, 1983* (New York: United Nations, 1983)

and in any case, official data would understate the proportion due to the
presence of illegal workers.) The data for Germany are particularly startling
when one adds in (the numbers of) displaced persons, refugees, and
immigrants from East Germany into West Germany after World War II.
The proportion of the West German labor force that was either foreign or

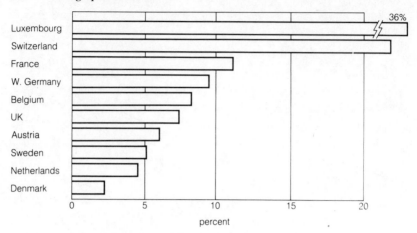

Figure 3.6   Foreign workers as percentage of total employment in host
country, 1977
Source: Select Commission on Immigration and Refugee Policy, 1981, p. 24

in one of these other categories was 31.5 percent in 1970, and must have
been even higher in earlier years (Neal, 1983, pp. 7, 9). In the US in 1860,
26 percent of white adult males were foreign-born (Soltow, quoted by
Gallman, 1977).

Though the key issue is whether an additional person, immigrant or
native, is a benefit or a burden, stabilization of the population size has
apparently become an implicit goal of US policy, expressed even (or
especially) in the context of immigration decisions. For example, the Staff
Report of the Select Commission said that if certain immigration flows
would occur, then immigration would reach "the figure for new entrants
which would bring the US to a stable population of 274 million ... by the
year 2050. ... The Commission's recommendations ... would allow
negative population growth within 80 years" (p. 423, 424). The Commission
did indicate some doubt about this goal when it continued the discussion
quoted above with "without the alleged deleterious effects of continuous
growth," especially with respect to natural resources and the environment.
But the Commission certainly treated population stabilization as a serious
goal in its deliberations. In contrast, I do not consider the relationship of
flows of immigrants to projected stabilization to be a relevant comparison.
Stabilization has no demographic or economic meaning in itself. As someone put it in the 1960s, the desire for zero population growth is simply a
non-rational preference for round numbers.

In brief, comparisons of proportions of immigrants to natives, as a flow during any given period and as a stock at any given time, appropriately measure the relative burden upon the native community as a whole, and upon individuals, of absorbing the cohorts of immigrants arriving at particular times. In contrast, absolute numbers of immigrants are of little economic interest. Nor is immigration as a proportion of total population growth of economic importance, though it may be of interest to those concerned about perpetuation of national and ethnic character. The ratios that are relevant indicate that the burden of refugee absorption has been relatively low in recent decades.

Age and Sex Composition

From the point of view of US residents, the most important characteristic of immigrants is their age composition. As has been true of migrants in all times and places, contemporary immigrants typically are young adults just beginning their work lives. Their age composition is the key to their economic contribution to the native community, especially because immigrants lighten the burden of supporting the aged through Social Security, as will be discussed in more detail later.

The reasons for the concentration of immigrants in the young-adult ages are easy to discern. Compared to an older person, a young person has before him or her a larger number of future earning years during which to recoup the costs of the investment in transportation, and of learning the ways of a new environment. An older person has already made various investments in the home country, such as developing a network of personal contacts and developing various other capacities necessary to make a living, that cause the additional costs of earning a living in any future year in the home country to be lower for the older person than for the younger person; furthermore, for psychological reasons these sunk costs often exert more influence than sensible present-value calculations would suggest they should, causing the person to abjure change in personal circumstances.

Let us consider the age-composition data for some representative countries.

United States

The age distribution of legal immigrants is heavily concentrated in the prime labor-force years, much more so than the distribution of the resident population, as figure 3.7 shows. A key element is the proportion that persons of ages 25–34 bear to total population: 16.3 percent for natives, and 26 percent for immigrants. For Asians who entered between 1970

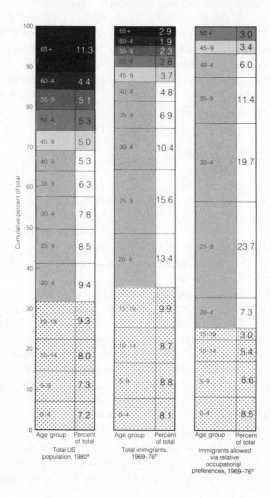

Figure 3.7 Age distribution of total US population, total immigrants, and immigrants allowed under occupational preferences, 1969–76 and 1980

Notes:
[a] Ages 50–4 = 1.7 percent; ages 55–9 = 0.9 percent; ages 60–4 = 0.3 percent.
[b] Columns do not sum to 100 percent due to rounding.
Source: Select Commission on Immigration and Refugee Policy, 1981, Appendix D, p. 23

and 1980, the proportion was 31 percent. (US Department of Commerce, Bureau of the Census, 1984, pp. 1−7). For those admitted under the occupational preference category, the proportion aged 25−34 entering 1969−76 was 43.4 percent; this proportion is a reasonable expectation of what would happen with a system of economic criteria rather than the existing family-connections system.

The story has been much the same throughout US history, as figure 3.8 indicates. In earlier years there was a heavy predominance of males (figure 3.9), among whom the labor-force participation rate is higher than among females. And if we generalize from the available data for Mexican immigrants, illegals are especially concentrated in the prime working ages of 16−44; additionally, they are disproportionately male and many are single; illegally entered married men usually do not take their wives and children with them to the US (see chapter 15).

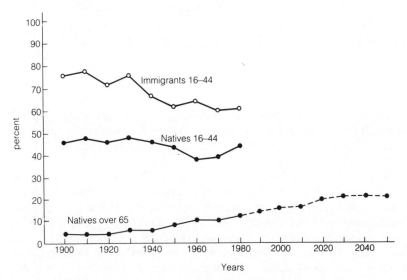

Figure 3.8   Percentages of US immigrants and natives between the ages of 16 and 44, and the percentage of natives over 65 (with projections through to the year 2050)

Sources: US Department of Commerce, Bureau of the Census, *Historical Statistics, Colonial Times to 1970* (Washington, DC: Government Printing Office, 1975), pp. 10, 112; US Department of Commerce, *Statistical Abstract for the United States* (Washington, DC: Government Printing Office, 1981); idem, *Statistical Bulletin*, January−March 1984, p. 19

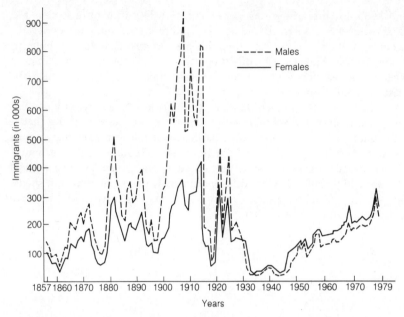

Figure 3.9 Immigrants to the United States, by sex, fiscal years 1857–1979
Source: Houstoun, Kramer, and Barrett, 1984, p. 914

The heavy concentration of immigrants in the younger working ages is especially important in light of the expected US increase in the proportion aged 65 or over among natives (see figure 3.8), who will need to be supported by working persons.

Data on the recent distribution of immigrants by sex and by country are peculiar. For example, 72.4 percent of the immigrants from Finland in the fiscal years 1972–9 were female, a higher proportion than among immigrants from any other country. Unlike the data for some other countries, these cannot be explained by the presence of US military forces. It would seem that there is an "importation" – or perhaps "exportation" from Finland – of blond mates for American men. Economics assumes that there is a welfare gain to American men thereby. But what about the effect on American women? All kinds of interesting questions are raised thereby that will not be explored herein.

Experience in other developed countries confirms the US pattern. (One reason why the following examples come only for developed countries is that one of the goods which richer countries buy is social science research on the nature of their societies.)

Canada

Parai (1974, p. 43) found that about 75 percent of immigrants were of labor-force age (15 plus) compared to about 60 percent for Canadian-born residents. Among immigrants who came between 1947 and 1972, 52.9 percent were classified as "workers", versus the 33 percent of Canadian-born residents classified as "workers" in the 1961 census (p. 92). Higher labor-force participation among immigrant women than among native women aged 25−44 accounted for part of the difference (p. 44), but the main cause of the higher proportion of "workers" among immigrants is the difference in age distributions.

Great Britain

Among the "New Commonwealth" immigrants (that is, from the British Commonwealth other than Australia, Canada, and New Zealand) whom Jones and Smith studied, the proportion of persons in the prime working ages from 25 to 44 was considerably higher than in the population at large: 46 percent versus 26 percent in 1961, and 47 percent versus 25 percent in 1966. (The 44 percent proportion for *all* immigrants in 1961 is similar to that for the New Commonwealth immigrants, confirming that the New Commonwealth immigrants are a fair sample of the larger group.) The proportion of immigrants who were 15−24 was also somewhat higher among immigrants than among natives, while the proportions 0−14, 45−64, and 65 and over were lower among immigrants (Jones and Smith, 1970, p. 19).

Israel

Among the Soviet Jews (Israel's largest recent immigration wave, and the group that has been studied most intensively) who came to Israel in 1973, 68 percent were between the ages of 15 and 64, in comparison with 60 percent in the Israeli Jewish population. For the age group 15−44 the percentages favored Soviet Jewish immigrants 47 percent to 42 percent. The differences arise chiefly from the smaller proportion of children among the Soviet Jews. The Soviet Jewish immigration contained a slightly larger proportion of persons over 65 than found among the Israeli Jewish community, 10.5 percent versus 7.3 percent.[4] This unusual characteristic for a wave of immigration was due to the Soviet Union's policy of allowing many elderly persons to leave in order to save on their pensions.

Australia

Goddard, Sparkes and Haydon (1984) have provided a detailed comparison of the age compositions of immigrants and natives. In figure 3.10a, the bars representing immigrants are wider in the prime labor-force years and narrower in the late middle-aged years than are the bars representing natives.

Goddard et al. (1984) also divide total immigration into the groups that arrive in various admission categories — categories which correspond closely to US preference categories (except for the "special eligibility" category, which is a small hodge-podge including children of Australian citizens born abroad; this category may be left out of the discussion). Figure 3.10b shows that migrants who arrive in order to reconstitute families do not have a favorable age distribution relative to natives; and to the extent that female immigrants have a lower rate of participation in the labor force than do males (see chapter 4), immigrants in this category also do not have a favorable sex distribution, though of course the relatively high proportion of females in the nubile ages cannot be considered separately from the age and sex distribution in the other categories.

Figure 3.10c shows the age distribution of immigrants who are admitted on the grounds that their occupations, including entrepreneurs, are in high demand. Such persons are concentrated in the 30−45 age brackets. Much the same is the case with the "independent" migration (figure 3.10e), people "who have outstanding achievements in an occupation which is not necessarily in demand"; it takes some years of adulthood to attain such status, which explains their being older than other economic immigrants.

The "labor-shortage" and "independent" groups are young, but not as young as immigrants who come from those places from which people are entitled to enter Australia as through an open door with "no preference restriction." This may be seen in figure 3.10g, relating to New Zealand citizens, who may enter Australia freely; they are concentrated heavily in the 20−5 age bracket. The New Zealand-to-Australia pattern presumably is as close as one can get to a modern immigration totally free of special requirements, though it probably is somewhat more heavily weighted in the older age categories than would be a totally free immigration from poorer countries, because the age pyramid in New Zealand is much less heavily skewed toward the young ages than is the pyramid in poorer countries. (Migration among the Scandinavian countries is also very free. It would be interesting to study the patterns of behavior found in that context.)

The age distribution of refugees (figure 3.10f) is particularly interesting because it contradicts the common idea that refugees are less desirable immigrants than are "economic" immigrants. To the extent that economic

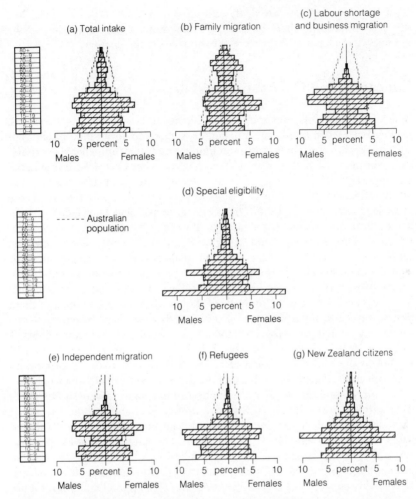

Figure 3.10   Age and sex distribution of Australian settler arrivals by intake category, 1982–3
Source: Goddard, Sparkes, and Haydon, 1984, p. 14

desirability depends upon age, the refugees admitted to Australia are seen to be relatively desirable, though not so much as the wholly-free immigration from New Zealand.

The pattern of immigrant labor-force participation within age and sex categories reinforces the effect of age composition of immigrants. Data on labor force participation are dealt with separately in chapter 4 because they describe behavioral characteristics of immigrants rather than the demographic characteristics which are the subject of this chapter.

Education and Occupational Skill

The distribution of immigrants by skill, as measured by education and occupation – commonly but infelicitously referred to as the "quality" of the immigrants – strongly influences immigrants' effect upon natives through their earnings, as well as through a variety of other channels. Immigrants' earnings largely determine their tax contributions, and also have a very strong effect on the amounts of transfer payments that they receive, as we shall see in chapters 5 and 6. Other effects of skill and knowledge – such as the amount of innovation immigrants cause to happen, the extent to which co-workers are able to learn from them, and the way they function as citizens – are harder to document but probably are very important, also.

A common belief is that immigrants are poor in the sense of not having much all-important human capital in the form of education. For example, W. Fogel (1978) writes: "Hundreds of thousands of people – most of them poor – are now immigrating to the United States." This is wrong. Contemporary immigrants have a bi-modal educational and occupational distribution relative to natives. As table 3.1 shows, there is a disproportion of natives in the lowest education category. But there is also a disproportion – much more important both numerically and economically than the low-education disproportion – in the highest educational categories. In 1980, 16.1 percent of employed natives were professional and technical workers; the corresponding figure for immigrants who entered between 1971 and 1979 was 26 percent; in 1970 the figure for natives was 14.2 percent, whereas it was 23 percent for immigrants between 1961 and 1970. That is, a *much* larger proportion of immigrants than natives are in professional and technical occupations (*US Statistical Abstract, 1981*, pp. 89 and 401). Figure 3.11 shows the comparative pattern for the year 1975. This paragraph refers to all permanent immigrants, legal and illegal. Given the relative size of net illegal immigration – perhaps one-third or less of legal immigration, and perhaps even zero – their educational and occupational distribution apparently is not such as to render incorrect the statements about immigration overall that are made in this paragraph.

We may also compare the average educational level of the immigrants arriving each year with that of the stock of native workers, not holding any factors constant. Such a comparison tells us whether immigrants on balance raise or lower the education level of the US labor force and its average productive capacity. Data come from the 1976 Survey of Income and Education (see appendix to chapter 5 for information on this survey). Adult immigrants who arrived between 1965 and 1974 had three-quarters of a

Table 3.1 Percentage of the population with high and low education: US natives, all immigrants, and Asian immigrants, 1980

Education attainment	Native	Immigrated 1970–80	
		Total immigrants	Asian immigrants
Percentage with 4 years' college education (persons 25 years and older)	8.7	9.7	17.6
Percentage with 5 or more years' college education (persons 25 years and older)	7.5	12.5	19.8
Percentage with less than 5 years' elementary school education (persons 25 years and older)	2.9	12.8	7.4

Source: US Department of Commerce, Bureau of the Census: *1980 Census of Population;* Detailed Population Characteristics, March 1984

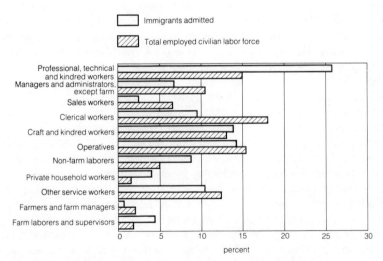

Figure 3.11 Occupational distribution of US immigrants and of all employed US civilian workers, 1975
Source: US Department of Commerce, Bureau of the Census, 1976

year less education on average than the average of natives in the labor force. Before 1965 the amounts of education were probably about equal for immigrants and the stock of natives, but there were probably somewhat larger proportions of immigrants in the highest education categories, in accord with the data on recent occupational distribution presented above.

A similar pattern may be seen for Canada in table 3.2. Among immigrants who arrived between 1946 and 1961 the proportions in professional and technical and skilled work were far greater than the overall proportion of immigrants in the population. And in table 3.3 we see that the proportions of both Asian and UK immigrants who arrived after 1960 with more than secondary schooling are vastly larger than the proportion of the stock of the Canadian-born. The high proportion of immigrants from the UK with advanced training other than university training is of particular interest, since it is likely to indicate technical skills. And the decline in the incidence of university training among the Asians from the earlier to the later period − though it was still high in the later period − probably was a result of many more persons in the later group arriving via family reconstitution rather than via the point system (and perhaps there was some influence of Vietnamese refugees, too).

A similar pattern may also be seen for Australia in table 3.4. The data collected by Miller (1983, appendix, in Harrison, 1983, table 7) show this pattern for South Australia even when the data are adjusted for age. Those data also show similar average amounts of education for natives and for immigrants in South Australia. Not only does the stock of immigrants contain a share of educated persons larger than among natives, but the most recent cohort also contains a *much* larger share than the share among natives (see also Baker, 1986, p. 18). As in the United States, the Australian distribution is somewhat bi-modal, the proportion of immigrants apparently being greater − or at least not smaller − at the lowest educational levels than among natives (see also Boyd, 1980, p. 2, re Canada).

The offspring of immigrants are a consequence of immigration. Hence their educational attainments in Canada and Australia are seen in table 3.5. In both countries, having one foreign-born parent leads to more education than having both parents natives. Having *both* parents born abroad leads to more education in Canada (excluding Quebec) but less in Australia.

Another interesting piece of Australian evidence: a survey of General Eligibility Migrants − those who are not refugees or relatives of persons already in Australia − showed the following proportions in the various occupational groups: Professional and technical, 29 percent; skilled metal and electrical, 28 percent; skilled mining, building and construction, and other, 15 percent; clerical, commercial, 14 percent; semi-skilled, 8 percent. This is a remarkably desirable occupational profile, the result of the economic criteria used in selecting this group (Northage & Associates, 1983).

Table 3.6 shows the New Zealand distributions of immigrants, emigrants, and natives among various occupational-skill groups. Both migrating groups

Table 3.2   Occupational distribution of Canadian postwar immigrants relative to total labor force, 1961

Occupation	1946–61 immigrants as percentage of the total at 1961 census
Professional and technical	
Engineers	
Civil	25.3
Chemical	20.6
Electrical	25.1
Mechanical	32.9
Professors and college principals	16.0
School teachers	4.7
Physicians and surgeons	19.2
Dentists	4.9
Graduate nurses	13.0
Lawyers and notaries	3.0
Architects	34.5
Skilled workers	
Plumbers and pipe fitters	12.7
Sheet metal workers	17.1
Bricklayers, stonemasons, tile setters, cement and concrete finishers	45.4
Carpenters	16.5
Plasterers and lathers	31.1
Painters, paper hangers, glaziers	22.4
Aircraft mechanics and repairmen	23.0
Motor vehicle mechanics and repairmen	13.6
Toolmakers and diemakers	36.0
Barbers, hairdressers, manicurists	20.9
All occupations	12.4

Source: Louis Parai, *The Economic Impact of Immigration* (Ottawa: Manpower and Immigration, 1974), table A-12, p. 106

Table 3.3 Educational attainment of Asian- and UK-born Canadian immigrants, by sex and period of immigration, and of the Canadian-born population, 1981

Sex and period of immigration	Immigrant group	Population aged 15 and over: educational attainment (percentage)					
		Number	Elementary	Secondary	Non-university[a]	University	Total post-secondary
Males							
1960–9	Asian	46,425	6.7	22.1	17.8	53.5	71.3
	UK	90,175	2.1	36.4	35.7	25.7	61.4
1970–4	Asian	66,605	7.5	25.6	16.8	50.0	66.8
	UK	32,165	2.2	32.5	41.5	22.8	64.3
1975–9	Asian	68,080	13.0	32.3	16.8	37.9	54.7
	UK	26,090	2.9	27.5	45.4	24.2	69.6
	Canadian-born	7,387,060	18.9	40.5	23.7	17.0	40.7
Females							
1960–9	Asian	46,510	18.4	26.7	18.9	36.0	54.9
	UK	93,610	3.2	51.1	30.0	15.8	45.8
1970–4	Asian	61,340	16.6	29.5	17.4	36.5	53.9
	UK	32,010	4.0	49.3	32.2	14.4	46.6
1975–9	Asian	76,205	24.4	32.6	14.6	28.4	43.0
	UK	26,830	4.9	48.4	33.7	13.0	46.7
	Canadian-born	7,638,180	18.4	45.9	22.2	13.4	35.6

Note:
[a] Includes college diploma, trade certificate, etc.
Sources: Basavarajappa and Verma, 1985, table 4; originally from Statistics Canada, 1981 Census of Canada, Special Tabulations

Table 3.4 Educational attainment of Australian labor force: Australian-born versus foreign-born arrivals between 1970 and 1974, and total labor force versus Australian-born arrivals between 1981 and 1986

Educational attainment	Percentage of total excluding those still at school	
	Born overseas	Born in Australia
	Arrived 1970 – November 1974	As of 1970–4
Males with post-school qualifications		
Degree level	7.3	4.3
Nondegree tertiary	5.7	4.5
Technician level	5.7	5.0
Trade level	16.7	16.8
Other	2.7	2.6
(Total)	(38.1)	(33.2)
Males without post-school qualifications		
Martriculation, n.e.i.	7.9	4.8
Left school at:		
17 years or over	9.5	6.6
16 years	8.5	12.6
14 or 15 years	26.3	37.3
13 years or under	9.7	5.5
Still at school	–	–
Total excluding those still at school	100.0	100.0
Females with post-school qualifications		
Degree level	6.4	2.6
Nondegree tertiary	6.7	5.5
Technician level	7.3	7.8
Trade level	3.2	1.5
Other	9.0	8.1
(Total)	(32.8)	(25.4)
Females without post-school qualifications		
Martriculation, n.e.i.	7.9	4.0
Left school at:		
17 years or over	9.2	6.4
16 years	10.4	17.6
14 or 15 years	28.8	43.0
13 years or under	10.9	3.5
Still at school	–	–
Total excluding those still at school	100.0	100.0
	Arrived 1981–6	As of 1986
Total labor force with post-school qualifications	53.5	42.5

Sources: Miller, 1983, appendix, table 7, in Harrison, 1983; originally in Australian Bureau of Statistics, *Migrants in the Labour Force: 1972–1976*, 1977, pp. 13–14; Baker, 1986, p. 18

Table 3.5 Distribution of native-born population 15 years and over by educational attainment, controlling for birthplace of parents and own birthplace in Canada (excluding Quebec, etc.) and Australia, 1971 (standardized percentages)

Birthplace of parents	Educational attainment completed							
	University degree		Other tertiary		Secondary		All other	
	Rest of Canada	Australia	Rest of Canada	Australia	Rest of Canada	Australia	Rest of Canada	Australia
Males	6.3	2.7	12.0	3.4	13.4	12.3	68.4	81.5
Both born in Canada	5.8	2.7	11.5	3.4	12.6	12.2	70.1	81.7
Both born outside Canada	6.7	2.1	13.1	2.5	14.0	10.8	66.3	84.7
One born in Canada	8.0	3.4	13.7	4.1	16.2	13.7	62.1	78.8
Females	3.1	1.0	13.8	3.3	17.1	10.0	66.0	85.7
Both born in Canada	3.0	1.0	13.6	3.3	16.3	9.9	67.2	85.8
Both born outside Canada	3.4	0.8	14.4	2.3	17.9	9.3	64.4	87.6
One born in Canada	3.8	1.3	15.5	3.8	20.2	11.2	60.6	83.8
Total	4.7	1.8	12.9	3.3	15.3	11.2	67.2	83.7
Both born in Canada	4.4	1.8	12.5	3.3	14.4	11.1	68.6	83.8
Both born outside Canada	5.0	1.5	13.7	2.4	15.9	10.0	65.4	86.1
One born in Canada	5.9	2.3	14.6	3.9	18.2	12.4	61.4	81.4

Note: Percentages are standardized with the age composition of the total population of Canada, 1971. The standard total population 15 years and over is 15,187,181.

Sources: Lakshmana, Richmond, and Zubrzycki, 1984; originally from Statistics Canada, *1971 Census of Canada*, 1 percent Public Use Sample Tapes, Individual File (excludes Prince Edward Island, the Yukon, North-west Territories and Quebec); Australian Bureau of Statistics, Special Tabulations (SP042)

Table 3.6 Proportions of immigrants, emigrants, and natives in various occupational groups, New Zealand, *circa* 1961

Class of worker	Immigrants	Emigrants	Natives
Professional	0.131	0.187	0.107
Semi-professional	0.105	0.150	0.144
Skilled	0.353	0.346	0.279
Semi-skilled and unskilled	0.411	0.316	0.469

Note: Native data are from the *1961 Census of Population.* Migrant data are for the combined fiscal years 1960−1 and 1961−2.
Source: Lane, 1970, table 1

are more heavily concentrated in the high-skill groups than are natives as a whole.

Particularly interesting is that even throughout the early history of the US, immigrants did not arrive with less education than natives had − contrary to popular belief and contrary to the famous poem by Emma Lazarus at the base of the Statue of Liberty.

> Give me your tired, your poor,
> Your huddled masses yearning to breathe free,
> The wretched refuse of your teeming shore.
> Send these, the homeless, tempest tossed, to me:
> I lift my lamp beside the golden door.

And of course the same "refuse" belief led to very different recommendations when the belief was held by another sort of person:

> Wide open stand our gates
> And through them passes a wild motley throng . . .
> O Liberty, white Goddess! Is it well
> To leave the gates unguarded?
> (Thomas Bailey Aldrich, quoted by Morrison, 1980, p. 353)

Hill (1975a, p. 31) calculated a measure of the "labor force quality" of immigrants relative to that of natives, roughly equivalent to a percentage. The estimates are: 1870, 0.97 (e.g. in that year immigrants had 97 percent the labor force "value" of natives); 1880, 0.99; 1890, 0.95; 1900, 0.97; 1910, 0.95; 1920, 0.93. And according to Hill's (1975a, 1975b) analysis of the wages and occupations in censuses and other data sources, covering the period 1840−1920 but with special emphasis on the decade just before the turn of the century

almost all the empirical evidence leads one to a conclusion in direct opposition to that reached in most of the historical literature . . . immigrants, instead of being an underpaid, exploited group, generally held an economic position that compared very favorably to that of the native born members of the society. (1975b, p. 48)

Bailyn's research on the Colonial-period Registry of Emigrants from Great Britain reveals that way back then, too, immigrants had excellent economic characteristics, being composed mainly of young "useful artisans" and farmers. Based on his data, he characterized as follows two groups of migrants, one from the "metropolitan" population center of Britain in the Thames Valley, and the other from the provinces:

The metropolitan pattern, which characterizes the central migration from the Thames valley, is typified by a young man, in his early twenties, acting individually. He is not, characteristically, drawn from among London's most desperate, destitute slum dwellers; nor is he from the more stable or substantial segments of the population. He is, rather, an impecunious young artisan or craftsman who has served all or some part of his apprenticeship, or in a less formal way, learned something of a trade, found employment irregular or nonexistent, and, still un-married and without family encumbrances, has decided to head out to the colonies alone.

At the other extreme, there is a different pattern altogether. In this provincial pattern the characteristic unit is not an isolated male worker in his early twenties, a bondsman for several years of unlimited servitude. It is not even a person. It is, rather, a family, and a family that contains not only mature women but also small children, including a remarkable number of young girls.

Few of these family members were indentured servants; in one way or another — often by liquidating all their possessions, real and personal — they had raised enough money, often just enough, to retain their freedom. (Bailyn, 1986, p. 31)

Another way to measure the economic "quality" of immigrants is according to earnings level, which is an indication of productive capacity as judged by the market. Within a few years in the US, the average contemporary immigrant male head of a family comes to earn more than does the average native male head of a family (e.g. Chiswick, 1979; Simon and Sullivan, forthcoming). (Of course much of this superior earnings performance, and the relatively high education level, is due to the simple fact that immigrants migrate when they are young, and education levels have been rising all over the world. As I repeat many times, it is hard to overestimate the importance of the age distribution among immigrants, which is the source of so many of their economic effects.)

In Canada, table 3.7 shows that within ten years or so immigrants earn as much on average as do natives. And natives with both parents born in Canada earn less than do natives of immigrant parentage, and less than even recent immigrants.[5]

Table 3.7   Median earnings of current experienced labor force, 15 years and
over, in 1970, by sex, controlling for birthplace of parents for the
native born and period of immigration for the foreign-born,
Canada (excluding Quebec, etc.) (standardized parcentages)

Birthplace of parents/period of immigration	Males	Females
Birthplace of parents of native-born		
Both born in Canada	$6,635	$3,218
One born in Canada	7,391	3,444
Both born outside Canada	7,369	3,258
Period of immigration of immigrants		
Before 1946	7,251	3,316
1946−60	7,212	3,466
1961−5	6,701	3,333
1966−71 (first five months only of 1971)	5,923	3,061

Notes: Percentages are standardized with the age composition of the total population
of Canada, 1971. The standard total population 15 years and over is 15,187,181.
Median earnings are given in dollars, excluding negative and zero earnings.
Sources: Richmond and Zubrzycki, 1984, pp. 105, 107; originally from Statistics
Canada, *1971 Census of Canada*, Special Tabulations

Number of Aliens Illegally in the United States

The number of aliens illegally residing and working in the US enters into
the discussion of immigration in many ways, and therefore must be discussed even though the measurement of illegal alien flows and stocks is
necessarily fraught with uncertainty, and even though estimates are more
specific and transient than the rest of the scope of the book is intended to
be; the topic is discussed in chapter 15, which is devoted to the entire
subject of illegal immigration.

Countries of Origin

The national origins of immigrants have little or no economic implications
for natives once immigrants' education and occupation are taken into
account. Differences in economic performance related to ethnic origin are
relatively small by any measure that I would consider meaningful. There
may be some difference in the first generation between, say, Japanese and
Haitians, but such differences tend to disappear after the first or second

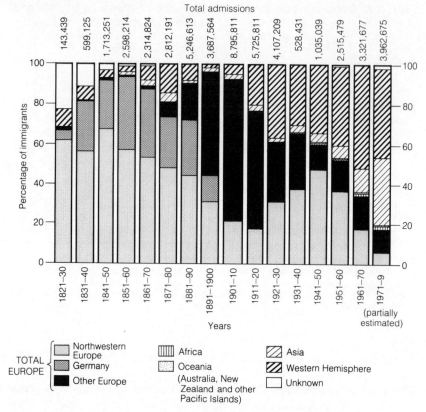

Figure 3.12   The origins of US immigration, by region, 1821–1979
Source: Select Commission on Immigration and Refugee Policy, 1981, pp. 172–3

generation. A likely explanation for some of the differences is the distance that one must travel to reach the US, together with the political possibility of being able to return. These factors may explain the only reasonably large difference in performance which is observed, that between Mexicans and others.

Despite the lack of economic importance of the matter, readers are likely to be interested in the ethnic composition of immigrants. The continents from which they have come are shown in figure 3.12 (and also in figure 3.1). The change in the immigration law in 1965 led to a major shift in pattern.

The Demand for Immigration

Immigration policies make implicit assumptions about the number and types of people who would like to immigrate to the US. Often the assumption is that the supply of potential immigrants is almost infinitely large. Perhaps typical is this letter in *The Wall Street Journal*: "We cannot make it easy for the millions of potential immigrants to come to this country. We would be overwhelmed" (Herbert N. Woodward, 1 September 1983, p. 25). Or another letter in the same newspaper: "We are faced with the fact that some large percentage − and it could be a very large percentage − of the earth's 4 billion non-U. S. inhabitatants would opt, if they could, to leave where they now live and come to this country. If that happened, Lifeboat U. S. would quickly sink" (Roger Lewis, 30 November 1981, p. 23). The Staff Report of the Select Commission spoke of "the huge demand to immigrate to the United States" (p. 374), and the then-commissioner of the INS asserted that "a survey taken by the government of Haiti ... revealed that 40 percent of the persons interviewed wished to migrate to the United States. Their motivation is economic" (Chapman, 1976, p. 11).

There does not seem to be solid evidence for so large a supply of potential immigrants. One reason given for belief in a large supply is, as the first letter writer quoted above puts it, the assumption that immigration now is at an "incredibly high rate," but the early part of chapter 3 refutes this assumption. There seems to be very little relevant evidence, a few scrappy pieces of which will now be mentioned. The most important conclusion implied by the review to follow is that systematic research into the topic would be exceedingly welcome.

1   The number of persons on the official lists waiting for immigration visas is astonishingly low, little more than one million as of 1980 and 1981 (Select Commission, Staff Report, p. 377). Of course, this set of lists does not constitute a fair estimate of the numbers who would come from the various countries if they were allowed to immigrate freely; many persons are undoubtedly discouraged from applying because of their knowledge that the wait for admission is at least many years, and might be forever.

2   A very large number of Turks registered for positions as temporary workers in West Germany. There were 1.25 million persons in the queue as of 1971, at which time the Turkish government placed restrictions on applicants (such as that unskilled workers could not be over 25 years of age when applying, or skilled workers over 40). But the queue rose again to 1.2 million by 1973, representing a ten-year wait (Payne, 1974, p. 67). It should be noted, however, that the travel expenses were paid by employers

in most cases, and jobs were provided in advance; both of these factors certainly increased the demand for migration. Also, this program was not intended to lead to permanent family migration, the latter being a much more drastic step than is temporary migration by a single family member; this tends to lengthen the Turkish waiting list.

3   Most Puerto Ricans remain in Puerto Rico despite the absence of administrative barriers and the low cost of travel to mainland US, though average earnings in Puerto Rico are considerably lower than in the mainland.

4   A relatively large number of Europeans immigrated to the US in the years before World War II even though the passage was relatively more costly and difficult than now. Some of this large inflow probably was occasioned by worry that the US would soon pass restrictive immigration laws, however.

5   Most blacks remained in rural areas in the South until World War II opened up many job opportunities in northern cities. This suggests that there will not be a large influx of ill-educated immigrants unless there are available attractive jobs which they think that they can obtain. Only in this fashion can one explain the observed low rates of internal migration in places such as Colombia, where income on the coast is much lower than in prosperous inland areas.

6   Most Mexicans do not enter the US, despite the ease of entering illegally and the relatively low cost of the trip. And most who do enter illegally return home later, after a relatively short time; this phenomenon is detailed in chapter 15, and it is also evidenced by the extremely low rate of naturalization of Mexicans (and also of Canadians), as may be seen in table 3.8. This point should be kept in mind even though the statistics concerning the number who do enter illegally arouse so much interest. If the US were as universally attractive as so many Americans think it is, one would expect to find more illegal immigrants than there are now.

7   During the 1930s, when labor market opportunities were poor, emigration exceeded immigration, as seen earlier in this chapter.

Table 3.8   Comparison of naturalization rates of US immigrants from all countries and four major sending countries (by percentage of total admitted who were naturalized by 30 September 1979)

Years in US (as of September 1979)	All countries	Mexico	Canada	Philippines	Korea
3	1.6	0.2	0.6	5.3	6.2
4	3.6	0.5	1.5	11.5	11.8
5	5.9	0.6	2.5	16.6	17.8

Source: Immigration and Naturalization Service, Annual Reports, 1967–79

Table 3.9   Percentages of emigrants by age group

Ages 1960	Percentage emigrated 1960–70
20–4	7.8
25–9	8.7
30–4	4.1
35–9	5.8
40–4	4.7
45–9	4.6
50–4	3.1
55–9	2.6
60–4	3.2
65+	2.6

Source: Warren and Peck, 1980, p. 78

8   A body of studies, and especially the studies of trans-Atlantic migration mentioned earlier, generally find that the rate of immigration is most heavily influenced by the "pull" of employment, and only secondarily by the "push" of unsatisfactory labor market conditions in the country of origin.

Recognition of the pull factor makes explicable the very large immigration to the US in the decades before World War I, and it also implies that that episode is not necessarily a good predictor of future immigration rates if entry were free. The US represented an extraordinary opportunity for many Europeans between 1850 and 1914. There were great quantities of land to be acquired easily, and jobs seemed easy to come by. Credentials were not needed. To potential immigrants it seemed as if the streets were "paved with gold", even for those with relatively little skill. This also explains why so many fewer immigrants went to Canada and Australia and to some other places in the world where entry was also quite free.

Under the present system, the effective demand for immigration is necessarily effected by the number of relatives of new immigrants. These numbers, categorized by elegibility and likelihood of immigrating, are discussed in chapter 16.

NOTES

1 Perhaps this is because it is never flattering to feel that people wish to depart your country and prefer to live elsewhere. It may cushion the blow to remember that some emigration occurs for financial reasons, such as taxes and the cost of living, especially after the age of retirement, and some other emigration is due to failure to adjust to the US.

2 Contrary to my (and probably others') impression, emigration is not concentrated among older persons. Rather, among adults, the 20−29 group has a higher rate than any older group. The data for 1960−70 are as follows, calculated as a percentage of the 1960 census count.

3 For many years, a large proportion of Australia's natural population increase has come from immigration. From 1946 to 1975, 39 percent of the total population increase derived from immigration. That is, immigration was almost two-thirds as large as natural increase (*Australian Immigration*, Consolidated Statistics no. 8, 1976, p. 8). Yet this phenomenon has not had any noticeable economic ill effects.

4 Israeli data used in this and other sections of this chapter are mainly derived from a follow-up study of a sample of 1360 immigrants who arrived in 1969−70, and similar samples up through 1972, done by the Central Bureau of Statistics (Israel) and the Israel Institute of Applied Social Research. The survey data are supplemented by Israeli census and national-income data. This report describes the immigrants from Russia, though data on other Eastern European immigrants are used to enlarge the sample where necessary.

5 A large body of research based on comparisons of the earnings of immigrants who arrived at different dates has suggested that immigrants rapidly catch up with the earnings of comparable natives, and then pass them. Recently, however, Borjas (1985a) has presented evidence suggesting that the observed recent results are due to a decline in "quality" of immigrants during recent decades, rather than due to assimilation. It will likely take some years of thrashing out the matter to arrive at a satisfactory understanding, and to know whether the currently accepted generalization, based on data in other eras and places, is faulty.

4 Behavioral Characteristics of Immigrants

> Tom [Thomas Corcoran, adviser to Franklin D. Roosevelt] was the grandson
> of an Irish immigrant. His mother used to point to the immigrants who were
> still pouring into America from Ireland when he was a boy. "The cowards
> never started," she would tell her son. "The weak died on the way."
> (Straight, 1983, p. 136)

This chapter reviews evidence on a range of immigrant behavior related to
immigrants' economic contributions. These characteristics include the rate
of labor-force participation, the rate of unemployment, the propensity to
start new businesses, the propensity to save, the propensity to exert work
effort, geographical mobility, fertility, and the propensity to commit crime.

Because the data are derived from a wide assortment of countries, the
samples differ from country to country by age, education, and category of
entrance (family reconstitution, needed skills, etc.). If these background

characteristics were held constant, comparisons would be improved, and it is hoped that research along these lines will be done. The best we can do now is to keep these problems in mind as we draw conclusions from the available data.

Similarity of Behavior in Different Countries

Figures 4.1a and 4.1b show that the adjustment of immigrants to their new societies is strikingly similar in Canada and Australia even though these data are unadjusted for background and though the composition of immigrants into the two far-distant countries is quite different. This is strong evidence about the value of data for one developed (and perhaps English-speaking) country for understanding the effects of immigration in another country, especially when sufficient data for the country of interest are not available. Other data for Australia or Canada in this and the preceding chapters strengthen this point.

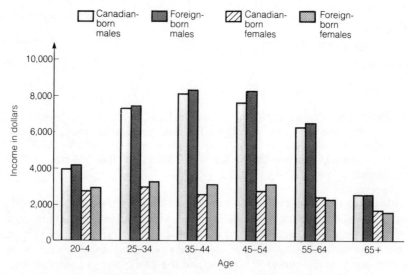

Figure 4.1a   Median income by sex and age in Canada: Canadian-born versus foreign-born

Source: Richmond and Zubrzycki, 1984

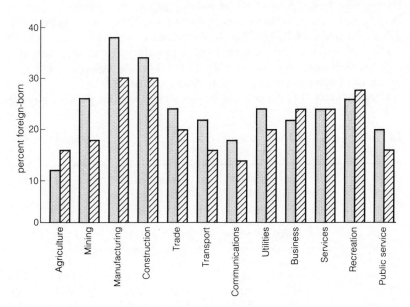

Figure 4.1b Percentages of foreign-born workers by industry
Source: Richmond and Zubrzycki, 1984

Labor-Force Participation of Immigrants and Natives

The differences in age composition discussed in chapter 3 are important mainly because of the effect that they have upon labor-force participation. But even within particular age-and-sex categories there often are differences between immigrants and natives; this is especially true among women, where there is more slack for group differences to appear. Among men in the prime years, the overwhelming proportions are in the labor force among natives as well as immigrants, and hence there is little possibility of group differences. In the youngest and oldest male cohorts, however, where there is possibility of variation, immigrant participation tends to be higher than among natives.

All the readily available data will be presented, even those that lump together the age composition and the participation rates, because all help illuminate the general issue at hand. These data should be understood as reinforcing the data on age composition alone in showing relatively high proportions of working persons among the immigrant populations.

United States

Historically, larger proportions of women and young persons at each age have been in the labor force among immigrants than among natives. This may be seen in Hill's (1975a) data reproduced in table 4.1a for 1890. Additional evidence comes from table 4.1b, which shows that this effect, together with age-compositional effects, led to much higher overall participation rates among immigrants than among natives.

Contemporary data for the US do not show the same pattern, however.

Table 4.1a   US labor-force participation rates, native and foreign-born, by age, 1890 (percentages)

Age	Native white with native parents		Native white with foreign or mixed parents		Foreign-born	
	Male	Female	Male	Female	Male	Female
10−14	7.4	2.5	7.5	3.7	15.6	9.8
15−19	49.4	15.8	63.8	33.7	81.7	58.8
20−4	89.2	19.9	92.6	36.6	96.6	45.4
25−34	97.1	11.4	97.2	19.2	98.3	19.8
35−44	97.6	9.2	97.7	12.1	98.3	12.0
45−54	96.2	9.8	95.4	10.9	97.0	10.5
55−64	93.1	9.9	91.6	10.7	91.4	9.4
65+	74.2	6.7	71.7	7.2	69.0	6.1
Age unknown	69.2	22.2	73.3	31.1	90.0	37.6

Source: Hill, 1975a, table 23

Table 4.1b   US labor-force participation rates, native and foreign-born, 1870−1920 (percentages)

Year	Foreign-born	Native
1870	46.6	29.7
1880	52.3	32.0
1890	55.2	32.8
1900	57.8	35.5
1910	57.8	36.7
1920	55.6	36.9

Source: Hill, 1975a, p. 11

Table 4.2 US labor-force participation rates for immigrants, natives, and native children of foreign-born parents, by sex, 1970 (percentages)

Age	Males			Females		
	Native of native parentage	Foreign-born	Native of foreign or mixed parentage	Native of native parentage	Foreign-born	Native of foreign or mixed parentage
14–24	53	57	53	38	43	41
25–44	94	94	96	48	46	46
45–64	86	88	90	47	47	49
65–74	31	32	34	14	12	14

Source: US, Department of Commerce, Bureau of the Census, *National Origin and Language*, publication PC2–18, appendix to *1970 Census of Population* (Washington, DC: Government Printing Office, 1973), and tables 6, 7, pp. 36, 46

Rather, the labor-force proportions among the foreign-born, natives of native parentage, and natives with at least one foreign-born parent, are similar (see table 4.2).

Canada

Many more data are available for Canada than for the US. Since World War II, markedly higher labor-force participation is seen for immigrants than for natives in every age–sex category (tables 4.3 and 4.4). Overall age-adjusted participation rates for the Asian and UK immigrant groups that entered during various periods (see table 4.5) reveal little difference among males between those groups and the Canadian-born; among females, participation is higher among the immigrants, even the most recent immigrants.

The *children* of a foreign-born parent also have a higher rate of labor-force participation than do the children of Canadian-born parents; age-standardized data are shown in table 4.6. Among males, having just one Canadian-born parent is correlated with the highest labor-force participation rate of all; this observation is verified by the similarity of patterns for males and females in each area shown.

Israel

Whereas in the early 1970s some 53 percent of the civilian Israeli population aged 18 and over was in the labor force, about 65 percent of the immigrant

Table 4.3   Canadian labor-force participation rates for selected age−sex cohorts of the 1946−60 immigrants versus native-born population, 1961 and 1971

Age and sex	1961		1971	
	1946−60 immigrants	*Native-born*	*1946−60 immigrants*	*Native-born*
Males				
5−14	−	−	−	−
15−24	67.5	59.8	70.3	61.2
25−34	96.3	93.4	94.7	91.5
35−44	96.7	93.6	96.3	91.3
45−54	94.5	91.3	95.3	88.5
55−64	85.7	80.7	89.2	78.2
65+	35.6	29.2	40.4[a]	30.2[a]
75+			15.8	10.3
Females				
5−14	−	−	−	−
15−24	46.3	39.9	57.0	45.0
25−34	39.3	27.7	47.1	42.2
35−44	39.9	29.3	49.1	41.4
45−54	41.0	32.3	51.0	42.3
55−64	27.9	24.5	38.7	34.0
65+	7.7	7.1	12.0[a]	10.8[a]
75+			4.2	5.0

Note:
[a] For 1971, ages were 65−74.
Source: Richmond, 1980, p. 103

Soviet Jews in that age group were in the labor force two years after their arrival. (During the period of adjustment up to that two-year point, fewer of the Soviet Jews had as yet entered the labor force.) That is, a fifth more of the Soviet Jewish immigrant adults were in the labor force than among the existing Israeli Jewish population − which is a huge difference in economic terms.

Great Britain

Partly because the immigrants included a disproportionate number of males, Jones and Smith found that "72% of coloured adults were economically active compared with only 62% of the (adult) British population" (1970, p. 30).

Table 4.4   Labor-force participation rates by birthplace, age, and sex for
Canada (excluding Quebec, etc.) and Australia, 1971

Age and sex sex	Canada		Australia	
	Natives	Immigrants	Natives	Immigrants
Males				
15–19	50.2	52.6	55.7	55.6
20–4	88.9	88.9	89.8	87.7
25–34	94.3	95.4	95.4	93.2
35–44	94.4	96.6	95.2	94.2
45–54	91.7	95.1	92.8	93.5
55–64	81.7	84.3	82.2	83.7
65+	25.1	23.3	22.6	21.1
Standardized: all ages[a]	78.3	79.9	79.6	78.8
Females				
15–19	38.1	46.0	51.7	53.6
20–4	62.9	66.0	58.5	59.5
25–34	44.9	51.9	36.4	45.4
35–44	46.4	51.9	41.8	51.4
45–54	47.4	51.6	33.7	47.0
55–64	38.1	35.2	22.1	24.4
65+	8.5	7.3	4.2	3.9
Standardized: all ages[b]	41.5	45.3	36.6	41.9

Notes:
[a] Percentages are standardized with the age composition of the male population of
Canada, 1971.
[b] Percentages are standardized with the age composition of the female population of
Canada, 1971.
Source: Richmond and Zubrzycki, 1984

Australia

The pattern for Australia, seen in table 4.7, is similar to the patterns for
other countries seen above. Women immigrants age 25–54 participate in
the labor force considerably more than do native women of the same ages.
Older immigrant men − those 55–9 and especially those 60–4 − participate more than do native men.

In a paper summarizing much useful data about immigrants and labor
markets in Australia, Baker (1984) shows that the ratios of immigrants' to
natives' participation rates in most sex and age categories fell from 1972 to
1983 (see his figures 4.2 to 4.10).

Table 4.5 Canadian labor-force participation rates of Asian- and UK-born immigrants, by period of immigration, and of native population, 1981 (percentages)

| | | Period of immigration | | | | | |
| | | 1960−69 | | 1970−74 | | 1975−9 | |
	Native	Asian	UK	Asian	UK	Asian	UK
Crude rate							
Male	78	88	88	88	89	81	89
Female	52	68	66	66	63	59	59
Age-adjusted rate							
Male	78	79	82	76	81	76	79
Female	52	61	60	56	58	53	56

Note: Immigrants and Canadian-born residents were aged 15 or older.
Source: Basavarajappa and Verma, 1985, p. 29

Table 4.6 Canadian labor-force participation rates of native population by birthplace of parents, 1971 (standardized percentages)

	Participation rate
Males	
Both parents born in Canada	74.1
One parent born in Canada	80.3
Both parents born outside Canada	77.8
Females	
Both parents born in Canada	37.0
One parent born in Canada	43.6
Both parents born outside Canada	43.6

Note: The participation rates are standardized with the age distribution of the population of Canada by sex, 1971. The Canadian-born males and females were aged 15 or older.
Source: Richmond, 1980, p. 284

Table 4.7 Australian labor-force participation rates by age and marital status for natives and immigrants according to period of residence, 1981 (percentages)

Age, status, and sex	Native	Immigrants' period of residence (years)			
		11+	6–10	2–5	Less than 2
Males, not married					
15–19	61.8	60.0	46.7	38.5	52.5
20–4	89.0	86.8	87.5	80.0	77.4
25–9	89.8	92.3	92.6	91.6	87.0
30–4	90.4	90.2	94.6	96.3	85.7
35–9	89.6	88.3	95.1	–	78.6
40–4	83.0	86.0	88.2	–	–
45–9	81.3	87.0	86.1	–	–
50–4	75.5	84.7	–	–	–
55–9	67.7	75.1	–	–	–
60–4	41.6	47.9	–	–	–
Males, married					
15–19	90.6	–	–	–	–
20–4	96.9	100.0	96.8	91.8	91.9
25–9	97.8	96.6	97.1	92.9	83.0
30–4	97.7	96.2	95.8	96.1	86.2
35–9	96.7	95.9	96.0	93.8	89.9
40–4	97.3	95.8	95.2	94.8	83.3
45–9	96.1	94.6	95.0	95.0	89.5
50–4	91.3	88.5	87.1	91.2	–
55–9	82.7	83.5	85.0	90.6	–
60–4	53.5	63.5	79.2	62.5	–
Females, not married					
15–19	56.4	60.3	47.9	39.3	56.0
20–4	81.2	79.4	75.3	79.0	80.7
25–9	72.1	79.0	87.7	83.0	62.5
30–4	66.0	67.7	76.8	88.5	–
35–9	61.3	64.6	75.0	–	–
40–4	67.9	64.0	–	–	–
45–9	62.5	52.6	–	–	–
50–4	51.8	42.3	–	–	–
55–9	38.3	35.6	–	–	–
60–4	18.0	17.2	–	–	–

Table 4.7   Cont.

Age, status, and sex	Native	Immigrants' period of residence (years)			
		11+	6−10	2−5	Less than 2
Females, married					
15−19	48.6	−	−	−	−
20−4	58.6	54.3	54.8	56.4	48.3
25−9	46.9	48.5	52.5	51.2	41.7
30−4	49.0	50.9	61.9	54.5	41.1
35−9	55.7	59.0	66.1	63.1	50.0
40−4	60.5	62.4	66.1	56.9	46.4
45−9	57.1	59.7	57.2	46.1	42.3
50−4	42.1	47.2	45.6	−	−
55−9	30.3	33.5	25.9	−	−
60−4	16.9	18.1	−	−	−

Note: No data are shown in cells where the number of persons is fewer than 25.
Source: Inglis and Stromback, 1984, p. 14

The overall Australian age-adjusted participation rates for native and immigrant males in 1972, 1976, and 1981 show much the same patterns. But for women the age-adjusted participation rates are significantly higher for the overseas-born, with married females being the cause of most of the difference; as Australian-born women moved more heavily into the labor force between 1972 and 1981, however, the difference between natives and immigrants narrowed somewhat (Baker, 1984, table A4.2).

Table 4.7 contains more recent data categorized by both age and length of time in Australia. It shows much lower labor-force participation rates for immigrants in Australia less than two years than for those longer in Australia, but after the two-year mark the rates for female and older male immigrants are generally higher than for natives. (Please note the small sample sizes for the immigrant groups which make particular cell estimates unreliable, especially cells close in the table to other cells having less than 25 observations and therefore without estimates.) Among males in Australia less than two years and not in the labor force as of June 1981, 60 percent were attending an educational institution, indicating that low participation was not necessarily due to inability to find a job. Of that group, 58 percent had been in residence less than one year, an indication of increase in participation within the two-year period (Inglis and Stromback, 1984, p. 14). The fact that 40 percent of this group had poor English is further explanation of the observed low rate of participation; it should be noted that normal economic immigrants tend to arrive with good English, unlike the refugees who constituted a considerable part of this sample.

The data for multiple job-holding in Australia (table 4.8) show a mixed pattern by arrival date, with generally lower rates for immigrants than for natives. This runs against the general pattern of the other data presented here.

Table 4.8   Holders of multiple jobs in Australia (percentages)

As of 1975		As of 1983		
Period of arrival	Males	Period of arrival	Males	Females
Before 1955	2.4	Before 1961	2.2	–
1955–61	3.1	1961–70	1.8	1.5
1962–7	3.0	1971–83	1.7	1.6
1968 – August 1975	2.6			

	As of stated date					
	Males			Females		
Birthplace	1973	1975	1983	1973	1975	1983
UK and Ireland	3.0	3.6	2.4	2.3	2.4	2.0
Other overseas countries	2.9	2.3	1.6	1.5	1.6	1.1
Total overseas countries	2.9	2.7	1.9	1.8	1.9	1.5
Australia	4.3	4.4	2.7	2.2	2.3	2.7

Sources: Australian Bureau of Statistics, *The Labour Force, 1977*, p. 32; and adopted from *Multiple Jobholding, Australia, August 1983*, 1984, table 8, p. 9.

Summary

The similarity in patterns of labor-force participation among these countries of immigration is striking. This consistency provides confidence that the experiences are sufficiently alike so that we probably will not be far wrong if we generalize from data in one or more of these countries to the US, when data for the US are not available. Taken as a whole, the data tell us that labor-force participation is substantially greater among immigrant women and older men than among natives in those categories, the differences being quite sizable from an economic point of view. The reasons for these differences are still a matter of speculation, and are in any case outside the scope of this chapter.

Unemployment

Great Britain

In Great Britain the unemployment rates for the New Commonwealth immigrant labor force in 1961 and 1966 were difficult for Jones and Smith (1970) to estimate because of spotty coverage of the relevant categories in the census. The 1961 unemployment level in the "conurbations" (large, densely populated, urban areas) was considerably higher (4.3 percent) for the immigrants compared to 1.6 percent for the *total* native labor force (p. 39), but Jones and Smith did not consider this a representative comparison. They had more faith in the 1966 all-Britain figures of 1.63 percent for immigrants and 1.37 percent for the total labor force (p. 40; yes, rates were once that low!). This difference between immigrants and natives is apparently due to the much higher unemployment rates for New Commonwealth women (1.52 percent) than the rate for all women (0.76 percent), which they interpret as being the result of immigrant women having a greater propensity to be in the labor force than native women.

Canada

Data on the length of time it takes immigrants to find a job are interesting even without comparison to natives. In Canada, in the early 1970s, the average period between arrival in Canada and starting work was 4.2 weeks (p. 19). Unemployment after six months was 10.1 percent, but then dropped

to 4.8% by the end of their third year (1972) — the final level being higher than the Canadian control group's 3.7% but below the average of 6.8% for the male Canadian labour force. At the same time, the duration of unemployment diminished until by the end of the third year after arrival the immigrant sample as a whole, at 2.8 weeks on average, was within striking distance of the control group on this measure. Altogether, considering that average levels of unemployment in Canada remained high during this period, it can be concluded that immigrants were very successful in finding employment in Canada. (Manpower and Immigration, 1974, p. 8)

United States

Chiswick's analysis of the 1970 Census of Population, and of the 1976 SIE survey, produced these results:

In 1969, a year of tight labor markets and very low unemployment, adult male immigrants in the U.S. for less than five years worked three fewer weeks during the year than native-born workers with the same demographic characteristics. This implies that the immigrant unemployment rate was higher or the labor force participation rate was lower by a combination of 6 percent of the labor force. The work-year of those who had been in the United States for five to nine years was only one week shorter than that of the native-born, implying that the immigrant unemployment rate was higher or the labor force participation rate was lower by a combined 2 percent. There was no difference in the number of weeks worked between those who had been in the United States for more than ten years and the native-born. A similar pattern occurred in 1975, a year of very high unemployment, although the intensity of unemployment for those in the U.S. less than five years was greater in the recession.

Shorter work years are not necessarily proof that the immigrants were looking for work, but a direct examination of unemployment rates shows similar results. In the 1970 Census reference week, the last week in March 1970, immigrants in the United States for up to five years had a significantly higher unemployment rate than that for the native-born; for immigrants in the country a longer period of time, there was no difference in unemployment rates.

It is important to note that both shorter work years and higher unemployment rates are short-term characteristics of immigrants that virtually disappear after the first five years in the country. (in Cafferty, et al., 1983, pp. 17, 18)

Among Vietnamese refugees the employment ratio for males aged 16 and over rose from 67 percent in August–September 1975 (it is not clear how long they had been in the country at that time) to 86 percent in July–August 1976. This is a rapid rise to a high rate of employment, compared to native-borns, especially when one considers that some of the males over 16 are in school or retired.

DeFreitas (1986) found in a micro-sample from the 1980 census that among "Anglos" who work in industry, the 1975–80 immigrants work slightly more hours per week but suffered slightly more unemployment per year than the native-born. With respect to Hispanics, the 1975–80 immigrants do worse than the native-born in all respects (and have a far lower proportion with twelve years and more education – 29 percent compared to 62 percent). Recent female immigrants do less well than the native-born in all categories.

Israel

Within two months of arrival, 66 percent of the Soviet immigrants who came to Israel in 1972–3 and were in the labor pool had found jobs.

Within one year of arrival, 90 percent of those in the labor force who came in 1971—2 were employed. For males, the available figures are even more impressive: 95 percent of the men in the labor pool who came in 1971—2 were employed in less than a year.

Australia

Among persons in the labor force, the unemployment rate in 1977 was slightly higher for immigrants who had been in Australia 16 years or less, and much higher for the first year or so until the immigrants become adjusted (table 4.9), compared to natives. After 16 years in Australia, unemployment is lower among immigrants than among natives. Similar data for 1972 through 1975 show the same pattern (Australian Bureau of Statistics, *Migrants in the Labour Force, 1972—1976*). Data for 1983, when

Table 4.9 Australian unemployed persons, by birthplace and period of arrival for the foreign-born, 1977

Birthplace and period of arrival	Percentage of labor force unemployed
Males	
Born in Australia	4.2
Born outside Australia	
Arrived before 1955	2.8
Arrived 1955—61	3.2
Arrived 1962—8	5.2
Arrived 1969—75	5.2
Arrived January 1976 to survey date	15.5
Total born outside Australia	4.5
Females	
Born in Australia	6.3
Born outside Australia	
Arrived before 1955	5.2
Arrived 1955—61	5.4
Arrived 1962—8	7.4
Arrived 1969—75	8.4
Arrived January 1976 to survey date	22.4
Total born outside Australia	7.4

Source: Australian Bureau of Statistics, *Migrants in the Labour Force, 1972—1976*, 1977, p. 62

economic conditions and general unemployment were somewhat worse than earlier, show much the same pattern but reveal considerable diversity in unemployment rates (and in participation rates) among groups from different countries of origin. (The educational–occupational mix also varies greatly among such groups.) The authors of the latter study could find no satisfactory explanation for the differences among countries of origin, though they noted differences in proportions of elderly persons within the various ethnic communities; that compositional difference could contribute to the apparent overall differences in unemployment rates (Victorian Ethnic Affairs Commission, 1983). Harrison (1983, tables 8 and 7) shows considerable differences between persons from English-speaking and non-English-speaking countries.

Table 4.10 shows more detail on the relationship of age and period of residence to unemployment in Australia, as of June 1981 when native unemployment was relatively high and immigrant unemployment was even higher. (For an explanation, see chapter 11; see also figure 4.1. Baker's data (1984) for the younger age-and-sex categories in various years from 1972 to 1983 show much the same pattern as does the aggregated figure 4.2.) Unlike participation, which tends to level off within a few years, unemployment continues downward over the entire observed period for married men, who are the most important segment of the labor force; this

Table 4.10   Australian unemployment rates, by age and marital status for natives and immigrants according to period of residence, 1981 (percentages)

| Age, status, and sex | Native | Immigrants' period of residence (years) | | | |
		11+	6–10	2–5	Less than 2
Males, not married					
15–19	12.8	18.2	16.1	13.5	32.3
20–4	9.1	11.1	8.0	12.5	22.2
25–9	7.8	12.9	11.5	11.9	17.0
30–4	6.7	7.6	8.6	7.7	16.7
35–9	5.2	6.4	7.7	–	–
40–4	8.4	7.6	6.7	–	–
45–9	8.5	7.6	9.1	–	–
50–4	7.6	8.1	–	–	–
55–9	7.0	10.6	–	–	–
60–4	7.4	7.1	–	–	–

Table 4.10 Cont.

| Age, status, and sex | Native | Immigrants' period of residence (years) | | | |
		11+	6−10	2−5	Less than 2
Males, married					
15−19	13.8	−	−	−	−
20−4	5.1	5.3	6.7	4.4	17.7
25−9	3.5	3.8	4.4	5.1	12.2
30−4	2.5	2.3	2.4	4.8	6.7
35−9	1.9	1.9	2.6	2.7	3.2
40−4	1.7	2.8	3.7	5.5	4.0
45−9	1.6	2.1	4.0	6.7	8.9
50−4	2.0	3.1	5.1	11.3	−
55−9	2.3	4.5	5.9	24.1	−
60−4	2.8	4.1	5.3	10.0	−
Females, not married					
15−19	17.9	20.7	16.3	20.0	34.0
20−4	10.6	10.5	8.2	13.9	18.0
25−9	6.6	10.9	6.3	4.5	20.0
30−4	5.5	8.0	7.6	13.0	−
35−9	6.2	9.7	6.7	−	−
40−4	4.3	5.8	−	−	−
45−9	5.1	3.9	−	−	−
50−4	7.3	5.9	−	−	−
55−9	5.0	6.4	−	−	−
60−4	5.4	2.8	−	−	−
Females, married					
15−19	22.7	−	−	−	−
20−4	4.4	8.2	5.0	8.8	35.7
25−9	3.2	4.5	10.3	9.5	14.3
30−4	3.0	2.5	3.6	8.1	30.0
35−9	2.6	3.5	5.0	9.2	23.1
40−4	1.5	2.9	1.2	9.1	23.0
45−9	1.4	2.7	5.1	12.7	41.2
50−4	0.6	2.9	10.2	−	−
55−9	1.2	2.8	14.3	−	−
60−4	3.8	1.3	−	−	−

Note: No data are shown in cells where the number of persons is fewer than 25.
Source: Inglis and Stromback, 1984, table 3.2

latter phenomenon is less marked for the other three groups for the crucial 25−44 age groups. It also is much less marked among those from the UK and Ireland, and somewhat less marked among those from New Zealand, the most "economic" of all immigrants; additional evidence for the latter is seen in table 4.11 (Inglis and Stromback, 1984, table 3.2).

A more aggregated analysis sheds additional light from a policy point of view. In table 4.12 we see that for the decade from 1973 to 1982, persons in Australia 17 months and more (the category which contains the bulk of immigrants) have unemployment rates not substantially different from that of persons born in Australia. This suggests that the rate of unemployment among immigrants is not a critical factor except insofar as the high rate among new immigrants indicates that help in finding work for them might be appropriate.

Among General Eligibility Migrants − those who are not refugees or relatives of families in Australia − "In *the first six months* only 10% had not found employment," a rather remarkable record which speaks once more

Table 4.11   Australian unemployment rates for immigrants aged 25−44, by birthplace and period of residence, 1981 (percentages)

Period of residence (years)	Birthplace		
	UK and Ireland	New Zealand	Other countries
Males			
Less than 1	11.8	21.1	10.2
1−2	2.4	5.6	9.5
3−4	4.7	11.6	8.5
5−6	0.0	6.5	3.8
7−9	3.2	10.2	5.0
10−14	2.2	2.9	4.9
15−19	6.0	3.7	3.6
20 or more	3.4	0.0	3.4
Females			
Less than 1	26.7	45.5	41.7
1−2	2.0	8.8	17.0
3−4	5.6	10.5	11.7
5−6	4.5	5.3	5.3
7−9	6.9	6.7	5.0
10−14	6.0	2.5	5.3
15−19	5.6	0.0	4.9
20 or more	3.2	0.0	4.3

Source: Inglis and Stromback, 1984, table 3.1

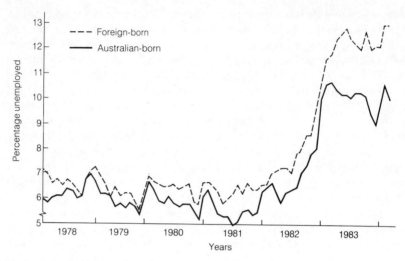

Figure 4.2 Australian male immigrant and native unemployment rates, 1978–83

Source: Cooper and Constantinides, 1984

Table 4.12 Australian unemployment rates for immigrants, by length of residence, and for natives, 1973–82 (percentages)

Date of survey	Overseas-born by period of residence				Native	
	Less than 17 months		17 months+			
	Males	Females	Males	Females	Males	Females
May 1973	3.0	10.8	1.5	2.7	1.2	2.4
May 1974	3.0	4.5	1.3	2.3	1.1	2.5
May 1975	7.3	12.7	3.8	6.2	2.9	4.7
May 1976	6.2	16.5	3.7	6.0	4.1	6.8
May 1977	15.4	22.4	4.1	6.7	4.2	6.2
May 1978	9.2	27.7	5.4	8.1	5.0	7.6
May 1979	13.4	18.9	4.8	8.0	5.1	7.9
May 1980	15.4	19.8	5.1	8.1	5.1	7.7
May 1981	13.4	27.6	4.6	7.3	4.3	7.0
May 1982	17.5	30.3	5.7	8.5	5.3	7.8

Source: Harrison, 1983, p. 30; originally from Australian Bureau of Statistics, *The Labour Force*, 1973–82

to the desirability of allocating admission by economic criteria (Northage & Associates, 1983).

The association between the general unemployment level and unemployment among immigrants is strongly seen in figure 4.1. It is also shown by the fact that when the average duration of unemployment increases for the Australian-born, the duration increases even more for immigrants who are not from the main English-speaking countries, as may be seen in table 4.13.

Table 4.13   Average weeks of unemployment in Australia, by birthplace, 1979—84

Birthplace	1979	1980	1981	1982	1983	1984
Australia	25.9	26.6	29.1	26.9	30.0	39.3
Foreign-born	24.8	28.8	31.5	32.2	32.5	44.6
Main English-speaking countries	22.2	27.0	29.0	27.4	31.5	35.2
Other countries	27.0	30.2	33.6	35.9	33.2	50.6

Note: Surveys were taken every February, 1979—84.
Source: Cooper and Constantinides, 1984, p. 77

Summary

Immigrants do not remain long on the unemployment rolls drawing unemployment compensation. Rather, they find jobs, stay employed, and have unemployment rates that compare favorably with the rates for natives.

Propensity to Start New Businesses

United States

A large proportion of new jobs in the US arise in small businesses. Several studies show that firms with fewer than 20 employees, which employ about 33 percent of all working persons, create somewhere between 51 and 80 percent of the net new jobs. The data for firms with fewer than 100 employees, and those with fewer than 500 employees, show the same high propensity to create new jobs (US Small Business Administration, 1984b, p. 3). Immigrants apparently have a high propensity to start their own businesses; this seems obvious to the casual observer. For example, the proportion of taxi drivers (often self-employed) who have foreign accents seems high from New York to Melbourne to Malmo, Sweden. And it is most noticeable where entry is easiest, e.g. in Washington, DC, where only small fees are required to put a cab on the road.

There does not seem to exist a reliable study of immigrants' business-opening for the US (though it is badly needed). In a 5 percent sample from the 1980 census, T. Sullivan found that immigrants "were slightly more likely than the US-born to be employed by their own corporation" (correspondence, 8 May 1985). But these data are not adjusted for age and other characteristics.

Borjas studied the extent of self-employment (a more general concept than small business) in a variety of immigrant cohorts, and among natives, in the 1970 and 1980 censuses. He finds that "Immigrants are more likely to be self-employed than similarly skilled native-born workers" (1985b, abstract). This result probably would be even stronger if physicians and dentists and similar professions were deleted from the sample. Borjas's analyses suggest to him that a "major reason for this differential is that geographical enclaves of immigrants increase self-employment opportunities, particularly for immigrants who share the same national background as the residents of the enclave".

Perhaps more important than the analyses with background held constant are the unconditional probabilities of self-employment found by Borjas: 0.165 for immigrant whites versus 0.117 for native-born whites, and 0.053 versus 0.037 for immigrant and native-born blacks. Immigrant Asians and Cubans also have higher propensities compared to native-born whites, as well as compared to native-born Asians and Cubans, respectively. Hispanics, both immigrant and native-born, have lower probabilities than do native-born whites. Overall, and most important, immigrants clearly have a higher propensity for self-employment than do the native-born. Unfortunately, however, Borjas does not provide unconditional data for immigrants who arrived in various periods so that they might be compared against the native-born stock.

In the 1890, 1900, and 1910 census data, Higgs found the number of male retail merchants per 1000 employed males in large cities to be greater for foreign-born whites than for natives (see table 4.14).

Light (1972, p. 13) found a similar pattern for six large cities in 1920, with additional interesting results for white natives with foreign-born parents, and for Orientals (see table 4.15). Fine-grained studies of Japanese and other Orientals in Los Angeles and California reveal startlingly large amounts of entrepreneurial behavior in both retail business and agriculture (Bonacich and Modell, 1980; Modell, 1977). The same is true of Cubans in Miami, and Koreans in Los Angeles and Washington (Light, 1984, p. 203).

Table 4.14 Retail merchants and dealers per 1,000 employed males, 1890, 1900, and 1910

	1890			1900			1910		
	Foreign-born whites	Native-born whites	Native-born blacks	Foreign-born whites	Native-born whites	Native-born blacks	Foreign-born whites	Native-born whites	Native-born blacks
13 cities	83	71	16	66	48	10	83	44	14
6 northern	80	70	16	64	46	11	80	41	13
7 southern	120	78	16	101	56	9	140	58	15

Source: Higgs, 1980, p. 92

Table 4.15   Retail merchants and dealers as a percentage of employed males 10 years of age or older, by nativity and race or color for six cities, 1900, 1910, and 1920

	1900	*1910*	*1920*
Foreign-born whites	6.86	7.46	7.36
Indians, Chinese, Japanese, etc.	9.73	9.4	7.8
Native-born whites, foreign or mixed parents	4.9	5.06	4.4
Native-born whites, native parents	5.03	3.53	3.46
Blacks	1.3	1.3	1.13

Source: Light, 1972, p. 13

A similar pattern is found in New Zealand:

The leading occupations of Chinese and Indians for nearly half a century have been market gardening and greengrocery in which they have served the national economy with an ever growing efficiency. Today, they own about 15 per cent of New Zealand's vegetable production. The large Asian gardens of the truck farming areas also provide both employment and accommodation for many Maori labourers and their families. In fruit and vegetable retailing also the Chinese and Indians have had an important role. In 1964 they owned 529 greengrocery shops, which comprised 56 per cent of the country's total. Since World War II the Chinese and Indian greengrocery shops have spread throughout the length and breadth of the country and they are now common in almost every town. (Taher, 1970, p. 62)

Canada

The Canadian Manpower and Immigration Department conducted a panel study of the first three years in Canada of a cohort of immigrants, entitled *Three Years in Canada*. Almost 5 percent − 91 of the 1746 males plus 291 single females in the panel sample on which there are data (Manpower and Immigration, 1974, p. 142) − had started their own businesses within the first three years in Canada. Not only did they employ themselves, but they also employed others, "creating" a total of 606 jobs. Based on the experience of the 2037 total immigrants, roughly 30 percent of the total jobs held by immigrants were created from scratch. Furthermore, these numbers surely were rising rapidly after the three-year study period; after one year there were 71 self-employed immigrants creating 264 jobs, compared with the 91 persons and 606 jobs after three years.[1]

From the 1971 Canadian census, Richmond determined the proportions of various immigrant and native groups that are employers of others, as seen in table 4.16 and table 4.17.[2] Among both male and female immigrants in Canada more than eleven years, a considerably higher proportion are employers compared to persons both of whose parents were born in Canada, but for Australia the evidence is mixed. Native-born persons with one or two parents born abroad have a considerably higher propensity to be employers than persons with both parents born in Canada: two immigrant parents are associated with an even higher propensity than one immigrant parent. The second-generation effect could be due, at least in part, to children of immigrant parents having parents who turn businesses over to them, but if so, it simply confirms that the first generation has a substantially higher propensity to start businesses than do natives. This indirect evidence of the first-generation propensity is particularly neat in that it avoids potentially confounding differences in date of immigration with respect to the census data, because the parents of the second generation probably have been in Canada a considerable length of time as of the census date. (These data are standardized by Richmond for age distribution; the effect appears much more strongly in the unstandardized data in the complete original table.) The fact that the propensity to start new businesses is higher even among immigrants only 15−24 years old than among comparable-age natives suggests that the experience of being an immigrant, as well as self-selection, may account for this propensity, because a considerable proportion of immigrants aged 15−24 must have come with their parents rather than having chosen to migrate of their own accord.

Some data on the capital that immigrants have available to start new businesses may be found in chapters 7 and 12.

Table 4.18 shows data for Asian and UK immigrants with various periods of residence, as well as for the Canadian-born. The high propensity of Asian immigrants, both male and female, to open businesses after ten years of residence is impressive. The low propensity for UK immigrants is also interesting. Together the two sets of data suggest that entrepreneurship is very much a function of "need"; immigrants who can easily find their way to a good living without starting a business are less likely to start one than are immigrants who face greater barriers to a well-salaried job, it would seem.

In Australia the picture is more mixed though the outlines are the same as for Canada. Harrison's data (table 4.19) show that even after five years, immigrants from English-speaking countries are less likely to be employers or self-employed than are Australian natives. On the other hand, immigrants from non-English-speaking countries have higher propensities to start new businesses than do native Australians, starting some time after five years in the country. (Unfortunately Harrison does not present more detailed data for longer residence in Australia.) These data are additional evidence that the more difficult the adjustment of the group to the wage

Table 4.16 Self-employment among males and females 15 years and over in the current experienced labor force, by birthplace of parents for native-born workers and period of immigration for foreign-born workers, in Australia and Canada (excluding Quebec, etc.), 1971 (percentage distribution)

Birthplace, period of immigration		Own account		Employer	
		Canada	Australia	Canada	Australia
Males					
Native-born					
Foreign-born Immigrated: Canada	Australia				
Before 1946	Before July 1947	8.2	9.7	5.1	6.7
1946–60	1947–61	6.1	7.2	5.2	4.9
		7.8	10.9	6.1	9.6
		5.7	7.7	5.9	5.5
1961–5		4.0		4.2	
	1961–71		3.9		2.2
1966–71[a]		2.9		2.3	
Females					
Native-born					
Foreign-born Immigrated: Canada	Australia				
Before 1946	Before July 1947	2.1	6.6	1.1	5.0
1946–60	1947–61	2.1	5.2	1.4	3.7
		2.4	7.9	1.5	6.6
		2.2	6.0	1.6	4.1
1961–5		1.7		1.4	
	1961–71		3.2		1.6
1966–71[a]		1.3		0.8	

Note: [a] Includes the first five months only of 1971.
Sources: Statistics Canada, 1971 Census of Canada, Special Tabulations; Australian Bureau of Statistics, Special Tabulation (A32)

Table 4.17 Canadian employers among the native population 15 years and over, by birthplace of parents, 1971 (standardized percentages)

Birthplace of parents	Percentage
Males	
Both born in Canada	4.6
One born in Canada	5.1
Both born outside Canada	6.3
Females	
Both born in Canada	1.0
One born in Canada	1.1
Both born outside Canada	1.3

Note: Percentages are standardized with the age composition of the population of Canada by sex, 1971.
Source: Richmond, 1980, pp. 291–2

Table 4.18 Employers among Asian- and UK-born Canadian immigrants, by period of immigration, and among natives aged 15 and over who worked in 1980 (percentages)

Class of worker	Native	Period of immigration					
		1960–9		1970–4		1975–9	
		Asian	UK	Asian	UK	Asian	UK
Males							
Employer	5.3	9.5	4.6	6.5	4.7	3.8	3.6
Self-employed	6.6	5.4	4.0	4.3	3.9	3.6	4.1
Wage earner and unpaid family worker	88.1	85.1	91.4	89.2	91.4	92.6	92.3
Females							
Employer	1.5	4.5	1.6	3.2	1.7	1.8	0.9
Self-employed	2.4	3.3	2.5	2.6	2.4	2.0	2.8
Wage earner and unpaid family worker	96.1	92.2	95.9	94.1	95.9	96.2	96.3

Source: Basavarajappa and Verma, 1985, table 5; originally from Statistics Canada, *1981 Census of Canada*, Special Tabulation

Table 4.19   Employers and self-employed by sex, birthplace, and period of residence in South Australia, 1981 (percentages)

Birthplace	Period of residence in Australia (years)	Employers		Self-employed	
		Males	Females	Males	Females
Foreign-born					
English-speaking	less than 1	1.1	0.3	3.2	3.0
countries	1–2	1.5	0.7	4.9	2.9
	3–4	3.1	1.7	5.6	2.7
	5+	3.1	2.5	6.9	4.7
Non-English-	less than 1	0.2	1.6	1.3	2.6
speaking	1–2	1.4	0.6	3.7	4.0
countries	3–4	4.9	4.6	4.8	5.8
	5+	6.6	4.9	13.4	10.6
Total foreign-born	less than 1	0.7	0.7	2.4	2.9
	1–2	1.4	0.6	4.4	3.5
	3–4	3.9	2.9	5.3	4.0
	5+	4.7	3.5	9.9	7.1
Australian-born		5.8	4.4	10.6	8.4

Source: Harrison, 1983, table 10, p. 35; originally from Australian Bureau of Statistics, *1981 Census*, table 27

economy – as seen in the data on unemployment rates among non-English-speaking persons above – the higher the propensity to start one's own business.[3]

Fertility

The fertility of immigrants is of interest for several reasons. First, though parents pay most of the costs of raising their children until the children grow up and become productive and creative members of society, children are something of a burden upon the society, mostly by way of public expenditures on education. Second, to the extent that having a large number of adults is either a burden or a boon for other persons in the society (and elsewhere I argue at length that, in a society such as the US in the late twentieth century, the benefits of more adults vastly outweigh the costs; Simon, 1977, 1981a) more children now represent more adults in the future. Third, and perhaps most important, nowadays having many children is viewed by some (though not by this writer) as a symptom of personal sloth and "primitivism." Fourth, a birthrate higher than that of natives leads some to worry about the effect on the US racial composition and cultural homogeneity.

United States

Table 4.20 shows that for women born in the twentieth century, fertility among immigrants has been about the same as among natives, except that as of 1970 fertility was considerably lower among immigrant than native women age 25–44. It is interesting to note that the fertility of native women of foreign or mixed parentage – who may be thought of as a result of recent immigration – show much lower fertility than do native women, except among women age 25–44 in 1970.

The oldest cohort of immigrant women shown in table 4.20 bore more children than did native women of the same age. Higher fertility for immigrants than for natives was apparently the rule in the more "advanced" societies in the past (Isaac, 1947, p. 185) which fits with the pattern that the countries from which the immigrants came had lower incomes and higher mortality on average than did the US. The more recent pattern reflects various crosscurrents in fertility which are affected by several variables and which are not yet fully understood. (For more discussion, see Simon, 1977, Part II, or Simon, 1974.)

Table 4.20b shows data from the 1980 census. Little fertility difference between native-born and foreign-born is seen.

The data in table 4.20b showing Cuban fertility much below all-US fertility, while all Spanish-origin (presumably including Cuban) fertility is

Table 4.20a   Children per 1,000 women in the United States, 1970

Woman's age (years)	Native women of native parentage	Foreign-born women	Native women of mixed or foreign parentage
15–24	364	413	306
25–44	2,565	2,141	2,522
45–64	2,530	2,534	2,177
65–74	2,479	2,518	2,064
75+	2,762	3,284	2,390

Source: US Department of Commerce, Bureau of the Census, *National Origin and Language*, publication PC2–18, appendix to *1970 Census of Population* (Washington, DC: Government Printing Office, 1973), tables 2, 11

Table 4.20b Children per 1,000 women in the United States, 1980

Woman's age	US total	Native	Foreign-born	Foreign-born, immigrated 1970–80	Foreign-born, immigrated before 1970	Cuban	Spanish origins
35–44	2639	2652	2509	2571	2478	2033	3202

Sources: US Department of Commerce, 1984, table 255; Perez, 1986; Bachu and O'Connell, forthcoming, table 5

much above all-US fertility, are a bracing corrective to the notion that fertility of immigrants is strongly a function of one or another culture.

Canada

Table 4.21 shows lower fertility for immigrants than for natives in almost every age group; and figure 4.3 portrays fertility rising with the number of generations in Canada up to at least the third generation, at all levels of education.

Table 4.21 Family size of Canadian immigrants and natives, by age of the family head, 1961 and 1971

Age of family head (years)	Average number of members			
	1946–60 immigrants		Native-born population	
	1961	1971	1961	1971
15–24	2.7	2.6	2.9	2.6
25–34	3.4	3.6	4.1	3.7
35–44	4.0	4.4	4.9	4.9
45–54	3.7	3.9	4.4	4.3
55–64	3.0	2.9	3.3	3.1
65–9	2.4	2.9	2.6	2.4
70+	2.3	–	2.4	–

Source: Richmond, 1980, p. 96

Australia

Table 4.22 shows that, except for a few small groups such as women born in Malta and the Netherlands, and Asian women ages 40–9, immigrant fertility is lower than native fertility, no matter which comparisons one makes. It is a bit surprising that the data show only slightly higher fertility for the newest-arrived cohorts, though in the younger cohorts the observations may be biased by differences in age distribution within the brackets.

Hugo and Wood (1983) find that Australian immigrant fertility in 1971 and 1976 (measured by the standardized fertility ratio) was 7 and 6 percent higher respectively among immigrants than among native women. But this difference is mostly accounted for by the higher propensity of immigrant women to be married; among married immigrant women, fertility is only 1

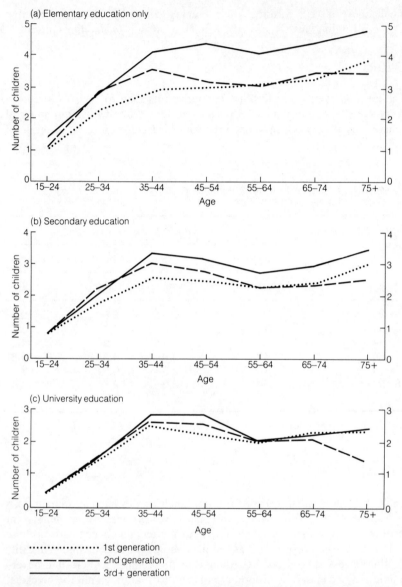

Figure 4.3 Number of children born to Canadian women ever married, by age, educational attainment, and generation, 1971

Source: Richmond, 1980

Table 4.22   Australian fertility differentials by labor-force status of wives, 1971

Labor-force status	Age of wives (years)		
	35−9	*40−4*	*45−9*
Australian-born wives			
In the labor force	2.82	2.79	2.65
Not in the labor force	3.26	3.25	2.99
Overseas-born wives			
In the labor force	2.40	2.47	2.38
Not in the labor force	2.88	3.02	3.91
Australian-born wives by birthplace of:			
Mother Father			
Australia Australia	3.12	3.10	2.89
Australia Overseas	3.01	3.00	2.80
Overseas Australia	2.98	2.96	2.77
Overseas Overseas	3.00	2.95	2.76
Overseas-born by period of residence (years)			
0−4	2.67	2.84	2.79
5−9	2.62	2.83	2.83
10−16	2.60	2.65	2.67
17−23	2.82	2.72	2.49
24+	2.66	2.76	2.68

Note: The fertility differentials were based on the average issue of existing marriages only.
Source: Hugo and Wood, 1983, tables 11.15−16

or 2 percent higher than among comparable natives. It also is interesting that fertility is lower among unmarried immigrant women than among unmarried native women, by 15 or 20 percent. Among immigrant groups there is considerable diversity in these respects, however, as table 4.23 shows.

Mortality

In Australia, mortality among immigrants is considerably lower than among natives (see table 4.24). This effect is most marked, and most interesting, in the 0−4-year-old category. There is some evidence that people in the countries of origin also have lower mortality rates than do people in Australia − which is a most unusual pattern in itself, given the usual

Table 4.23 Crude birth rates and standardized fertility ratios for Australian native and foreign-born women, 1971 and 1976

| Ethnicity or country of birth | Crude birth rate | | Standardized fertility ratio | | | | | | Proportions married among women aged 15–49 | |
| | | | All | | Married | | Unmarried | | | |
	1971	1976	1971	1976	1971	1976	1971	1976	1971	1976
Australia	20.1	15.8	100	100	100	100	100	100	0.65	0.67
All other countries	26.8	19.9	107	106	101	102	86	82	0.78	0.79
Individual countries										
United Kingdom and Ireland	20.3	15.4	95	95	90	92	103	96	0.76	0.79
Italy	32.3	19.5	117	115	108	104	28	34	0.85	0.85
Greece	49.8	29.0	127	127	113	108	40	50	0.86	0.87
Yugoslavia	36.3	26.0	120	123	100	100	115	121	0.84	0.85
Germany	33.3	21.4	94	90	88	89	99	106	0.77	0.80
Netherlands	35.1	25.1	113	113	106	107	92	107	0.77	0.79
New Zealand	30.3	23.4	95	91	94	99	165	128	0.64	0.67
Poland	8.1	5.7	75	78	77	81	68	48	0.82	0.84
Malta	45.8	33.1	127	127	117	120	51	69	0.79	0.80
Country groups*										
Other Eastern European	11.0	6.5	84	89	89	92	61	69	0.72	0.75
Other northwestern European	23.3	17.3	88	90	86	90	95	99	0.74	0.76
Arab	41.9	48.3	146	202	134	164	31	25	0.77	0.80
Chinese	24.5	23.5	80	94	112	122	19	35	0.59	0.60
Hispanic	32.9	23.7	110	97	107	90	43	51	0.78	0.79
Indian	25.3	20.4	97	98	110	105	42	31	0.71	0.72

Note: Specific birthplaces included in each group are as follows: Other Eastern European includes Albania, Bulgaria, Czechoslovakia, Estonia, Hungary, Latvia, Lithuania, Rumania, Ukraine, and the USSR; other northwestern European includes Austria, Belgium, Denmark, Finland, France, Norway, Sweden, and Switzerland; Arab includes Lebanon, Syria, and the United Arab Republic; Chinese includes China, Hong Kong, Malaysia, and Singapore; Hispanic includes Argentina, Brazil, Chile, Colombia, Ecuador, Mexico, Peru, Portugal, Spain, Uruguay, and Venezuela; Indian includes Bangladesh, India, Pakistan, and Sri Lanka.

Source: Hugo and Wood, 1983, p. 38; originally from F. Yusuf and I. Rockett, 'Immigrant Fertility Patterns and Differentials, 1971–1976', *Population Studies,* 35, pp. 413–24 (1981)

Table 4.24 A comparison of the death rates of the Australian-born and foreign-born in Victoria, Australia, 1969–73

Birthplace	Age groups (years)							
	0–4	5–14	15–24	25–34	35–44	45–54	55–64	65+
Males Foreign-born as a percentage of Australian-born	18	102	72	83	68	76	93	91
Females Foreign-born as a percentage of Australian-born	19	87	72	77	64	87	87	95

Note: Death rates are mean annual deaths from all causes, per 100,000 persons.
Source: Hugo and Wood, 1983, p. 20; originally in J. Powles and R. Birrell, *Mortality in Victoria, 1969–1973* (Melbourne: Monash University, Environmental Research Associates, 1977), p. viii

relationships among income and migration, and income and mortality — which might be a partial explanation of the observed phenomenon (Wood and Hugo, 1983). Another possible contributory explanation, particularly interesting from an economic point of view, is that immigrants are self-selected with respect to hygiene and general self-preservation.

For the US I could find no census data on mortality of immigrants. Schultz (1980) reports that immigrant children have lower rates of reported health problems than native children, though after the immigrants have been in the country for some time, the two rates converge. It seems reasonable to assume that the health of childen is correlated with the health and mortality rates of their parents, suggesting that mortality among immigrants is at least as low as, or lower than, that among natives.

Saving Rates

Saving obviously is important to any society. Hence it is worthwhile for us to learn what we can about the extent of saving by persons who might be added to the society as immigrants. In the past, financial saving which was transformed by investment into physical capital was preeminently important; nowadays, however, saving in the form of investment in human capital rivals physical capital in importance. It seems reasonable that saving for the two kinds of investment should be correlated (though they may be substitutes in some cases). If they are positively related, evidence about one activity provides information about both.

Two sorts of decisions affect saving: the allocation of the family's given income into current expenditure and savings, and the allocation of the family's time into leisure and the production of income. And there are several possible influences upon these decisions, and hence upon the amount of saving, including:

1 *Age distribution.* Immigrants tend to be younger than natives, and therefore they are likely to save more, according to the life-cycle theory of saving of Neisser (1944), Modigliani (1966) and Samuelson (1975). People save during the earlier work years so as to be able to consume when retired, as well as saving for special expenses during the later work years such as children going to college.
2 *Wealth.* It is reasonably obvious intuitively, and it can be shown simply with an adaptation of Patinkin's excess-demand-curve analysis (1965, chapter 1), or on more complex assumptions using Becker's time-allocation analysis (1966, reprinted in 1976; see also Simon, 1987, chapter 3), that greater wealth leads to the purchase of more leisure, *ceteris paribus*. It may be noted that this analysis directly contradicts Keynes's "psychological law" that the rich spend a smaller proportion of their income than do the

poor. And the evidence of Feldstein and others on the effects of Social Security entitlement upon saving supports this analysis and contradicts Keynes's position.

Greater wealth also implies less saving out of current income by way of the life-cycle saving-and-consumption mechanism.[4] (Some data on wealth brought by immigrants may be found in chapters 7 and 11.)

3 *Human capital*. Immigrants may differ from natives in amounts of education and in other background characteristics that affect saving.

The topic of saving as related to immigration deserves careful and detailed analysis in order to lay bare the partial influences as well as the overall effects. Regrettably, this research has not yet been done; therefore I will be able to do no more here than present some scraps of unrefined evidence culled from other countries' experiences.

Data on Saving Behavior

Home ownership data should be a meaningful indicator of saving behavior, though several apparently reasonable assumptions are necessary to link the two phenomena.

In Canada "the foreign-born were more likely to be home-owners except in the most affluent group" (Richmond, 1980, p. 408). Table 4.25 shows the evidence for Richmond's conclusion; it also shows that though cohorts in Canada ten years or less had lower rates of home ownership than the Canadian-born, those in Canada somewhat longer had much higher rates. The age of the respondents is a complicating factor, of course, but it seems unlikely that it explains all the observed differences. Furthermore, the fact that persons whose parents were born outside of Canada had much higher rates of home ownership than natives (interesting in itself) would seem to confirm the conclusion about immigrants, while being safe from the confounding influence of age (though it may be confounded by higher incomes of parents and higher education and incomes of immigrant respondents). (The underlying data, together with data on mortgages, could be productively studied in more detail to provide more data on this topic. The SIE survey, discussed in the Afternote to chapter 5, contains some similar data which might be used for this purpose.)

How Much do Immigrants Earn Compared to Natives?

Immigrants work and thereby produce goods and services. They themselves receive much of the benefit of this production through their own earnings, which they then utilize to pay for immediate consumption or for

Table 4.25 Homeowners by income, controlling for birthplace of parents for the Canadian-born and period of immigration for the foreign-born, Canada, 1971 (percentages)

Birthplace of parents/ period of immigration	Household income ($)						
	Less than 5,000[a]	5,000–9,999	10,000–14,999	15,000–19,999	20,000–35,999	36,000[b]	Total
Birthplace of parents for Canadian-born							
Both born in Canada	51.5	51.7	61.1	70.5	77.0	82.1	56.4
One born in Canada	50.0	54.4	66.9	75.0	80.5	86.0	60.7
Both born outside Canada	64.9	67.8	77.1	81.8	85.3	87.0	72.6
Period of immigration							
Before 1946	66.8	73.2	79.1	82.3	83.0	83.3	72.2
1946–60	51.3	65.8	75.2	79.7	84.1	87.5	69.6
1961–5	28.8	45.2	57.0	65.8	71.5	75.9	50.9
1966–71[b]	12.8	23.6	34.8	45.3	53.9	62.4	27.4

Notes: [a] Includes loss and zero income.
[b] Includes the first five months only of 1971.
Sources: Richmond, 1980, p. 404, table 12.1; 1971 Census of Canada, unpublished data

later consumption by way of savings. But through a variety of channels the rest of society also benefits from the immigrants' work. Chapter 5 will trace the effect of these earnings on natives through the taxes that immigrants pay. Chapter 7 will show how natives benefit through the return to the private capital that immigrants work with but that they do not own. Chapter 8 will discuss how productivity is improved as a by-product of immigrants' purchases out of their earnings, and as a result of the ideas that immigrants contribute to the production process. The higher the individual immigrant's earnings, the greater the likely contribution through all of those channels, as well as through other channels such as the immigrant's savings. High earnings are also likely to indicate that the immigrant has a store of skills that he or she may communicate to native workers with whom he or she works. For all these reasons, the amount an immigrant earns is a measure of the immigrant's contribution to natives' economic welfare.

The absolute amount largely determines the extent of tax contributions. Hence the level of average earnings by an immigrant cohort, relative to average native earnings, is the ultimate test, and chapter 5 summarizes the cost—benefit situation in that regard.

An immigrant's skills and productivity relative to those in the same occupation are also of interest, because individuals' human capital surely influences the productivity and the human capital of those with whom they work. Therefore, an immigrant's earnings relative to others of the same level of education and age (as proxies for occupation) are of interest to us. The *trend* in immigrants' earnings is also a matter of interest. If a person's income is increasing rapidly relative to others with similar background characteristics, it suggests desirable personal economic characteristics.

Chiswick did the first systematic work along this line, studying immigrants to the US (1978b); he has also studied other countries' immigrants (1982). This has blossomed into a large literature which will only be sampled here. Chiswick found that, holding relevant variables constant, earnings "cross over" − that is, they catch up with the pass − natives' earnings after 10 to 15 years in the US. The work of North (1979) and of Greeley (1982) points in the same general direction. Simon and Sullivan (forthcoming), using discrete rather than continuous functions for length of time in the US, find that the cross-over may be earlier than Chiswick suggested, depending on how you think about it. We also find that English-speaking ability has an important effect.

Blau (1980) applied Chiswick's technique to groups of immigrants, classified by industry and ethnicity, who were in the US as of the Immigration Commission's survey in 1909. While the data with which she worked were cruder than Chiswick's, the analogy is sufficiently close to make the comparison interesting. Blau found much the same as did Chiswick: Upon arrival, immigrants earned less than did native workers by somewhere between 12 and 18 percent for men, and between 10 and 14 percent for women. The time required for men to catch up with and then pass natives was 11−17 years for males, and 8−12 years for women. And native whites with foreign parents earned more than native whites with native parents, suggesting that there is a continuing positive effect of immigration by way of psychological−cultural factors.

There is also a fairly substantial body of research (e.g. Chiswick, 1982; Hirschman and Wong, 1980) comparing the earnings patterns of natives to particular ethnic groups, especially Asians and Hispanics: the Asians mostly do better, and the Hispanics mostly do worse. One could hypothesize that the longer the distance that immigrants have to come, and therefore the greater the difficulty of returning to the home country, the larger the likely element of self-selection on such characteristics as independence and confidence in one's capacities to adapt to a foreign land. One might also speculate that immigrants who cannot return home for political reasons should have a stronger motivation to invest effort in adapting to the new land, compared to those who can return home. But there are enough exceptions from the pattern, such as Filipinos (relatively less successful) and Caribbean blacks (relatively more successful), to call these speculations into question. More generally, there seems to be little solid scientific understanding of the underlying forces influencing the success or failure of particular racial or national or religious groups, as Greeley (1982) has argued persuasively. The social disorganization theory of W. I. Thomas, which Greeley discusses, is hardly more convincing than the genetic theories which it largely (but by no means completely) displaced; both are falsified by the speed of the rise by apparently handicapped immigrant groups toward average native economic attainment. (See Greeley's data as well as Chiswick's. And the economic successes of the Vietnamese in the few short years since they arrived, in a condition that was described by casual observers as socially shattered and demoralized, constitute dramatic though unsystematic additional evidence; see evidence below.) Greeley provides some empirical evidence that different immigrant groups follow different paths in adjusting themselves to the US, and in approaching or surpassing the mean level of native earnings in their economic accomplishments. But (as he is the first to assert) this evidence is not enough to support a comprehensive or compelling theory. For this reason, and also because it seems out of the question for US immigration policy to discriminate on the basis of national origin, I shall not further discuss this body of literature here.

The generality of the findings reported by Chiswick in his 1978 paper is enhanced not only by the historical evidence but also by evidence in other countries, as follows.

Canada

Tandon (1978) finds patterns in Canada quite similar to those in the US, which makes sense given that immigrants to the two countries come from somewhat similar backgrounds, and that the two countries' immigration policies have considerable similarity. Basavarajappa and Verma (1985) find that in 1980, immigrants (adjusted for age and educational attainment, though probably not adjusted in as detailed a fashion as in the work by Chiswick and by Tandon) from the UK earned more than the Canadian-born, but Asian immigrants earned less than the Canadian-born. The recent Asian immigrants do much worse than those who came earlier, though this is not so for those from the UK. It is not possible to know from these data the extent to which this is due to the time necessary for absorption, and how much it is due to lower economic capacity of immigrants in later periods (due to the increasing influence of family reconstitution immigration, and of the Vietnamese immigrants who arrived in substantial numbers in the later period) compared to those who came without relatives purely on the basis of their economic characteristics as measured by the point system.

Great Britain

Chiswick (1982) finds that the pattern for Great Britain is more complex in some respects. But the pattern is not inconsistent with the findings for the US, including the finding that an additional year of schooling abroad leads to less income in the new country than does an additional year of schooling by natives.

Australia

Stromback (1984) employed a model similar to that of Chiswick to study the earnings of immigrants from English-speaking and from non-English-speaking countries relative to the Australian-born. I rephrase his conclusions as follows: After adjustment for amount of education and for experience (closely related to age), migrants from English-speaking countries had earnings similar to those of the Australian-born: that is, the returns to their education and experience are similar to the situation for Australians. Among immigrants from non-English-speaking countries with more than average education, there are lower returns to education, both for those with no experience and for those with experience, and the returns to experience for these persons are relatively flat compared to Australians. The explanations for these patterns remain something of a puzzle.

Israel

The pattern for Israel seems different from that of the other countries, perhaps because immigration there was to a considerable extent affected by ideology and flows of refugees from Europe and Asia–Africa, which are outside the scope of interest here. Chiswick, however, argues that nothing in the Israeli results conflicts in principle with the results for the US and Canada, and I find his argument convincing.

Borjas (1985a) has argued that Chiswick's results for the US are due to changes in cohort "quality." The issue is still a matter of controversy. But the corroboration of the contemporary US pattern by turn-of-the-century data, and by the data for other countries, suggests to me that Chiswick's basic findings will hold up.

Mobility

Kuznets once remarked that it would be difficult to over-estimate the economic importance of domestic mobility and its enhancement of economic flexibility. It is logical that new immigrants should be particularly mobile, because (unlike natives) they do not already have a stock of knowledge of persons and institutions which make it cheaper to remain in a given place than to begin anew elsewhere. Indeed, in Australia it is found that "recent migrants are particularly *mobile*, although migrants who have been in Australia for many years tend to be no more mobile that the Australian-born population" (Norman and Meikle, 1983; italics in original). For example, among immigrants from the UK and Ireland (who may be considered representative in this regard of all immigrants) of those in Australia for various numbers of years, the proportions who moved their residence between 1976 and 1981 were as follows: 0–4 years: 91 percent; 5–9 years: 59 percent; 10–14 years: 48 percent; 15–21 years: 45 percent; 22+ years: 31 percent (Norman and Meikle, 1985, p. 80).

Data from the 1970 US Census tell a more complex story. Table 4.26 shows that, for those persons who resided in the US during the entire previous five years, the proportions who moved from one county (or state) to another are astonishingly similar among the foreign-born, natives of native parentage, and natives of at least one foreign-born parent. But if we include persons who were abroad five years earlier, a higher proportion of immigrants than of natives moved into the county in which they are now

Table 4.26   Percentage of US population moving to a different county or to a different state, 1965–70

Age	Natives of native parentage living in US 1965–70	Foreign-born living in US 1965–70	Native of foreign or mixed parentage living in US 1965–70	Foreign-born immigrating 1965–70
Different county, same or different state				
14–24	0.26	0.24	0.24	1.0
25–44	0.25	0.24	0.20	1.0
45–64	0.10	0.10	0.08	1.0
Different state				
14–24	0.13	0.12	0.13	1.0
25–44	0.13	0.13	0.10	1.0
45–64	0.05	0.05	0.04	1.0

Source: 1970 US Census, *National Origin and Language*, Table 2, 'Selected Social Characteristics of the Native Population of Native Parentage by Age and Race: 1970', and Table 11, 'Selected Social Characteristics of the Foreign Stock by Age, Nativity, and Country of Origin: 1970'

living during that five-year period. On the one hand, this latter observation suggests that more immigrants had moved to a new area, and therefore there was more new matching of job applicants to job openings (though this observation is diminished in importance by other data that show immigrants tend to move where there are countrymen rather than where unemployment is low; see chapter 12). On the other hand, the similar proportions moving of those *within* the country suggests similar propensities to move in the future. In other words, the mobility of immigrants may be a one-time thing, beneficial at that time but not indicating a continuing behavioral characteristic.

It is reasonable to expect more mobility among new immigrants than among the existing labor force simply because new immigrants are relatively young, and younger workers are more likely to change jobs than are older workers. Evidence for this is found in figure 4.4a, which shows the geo-graphical mobility of various age groups in the US, and in figure 4.4b, which shows the job mobility of various age groups in Australia. More direct evidence on the mobility of immigrants is shown in table 4.27, which shows that persons who arrived within the last two years changed jobs much more frequently than the average of the Australian-born, and much more frequently than persons who had been in Australia a longer time. This mobility is also attested to by the greater willingness of those who

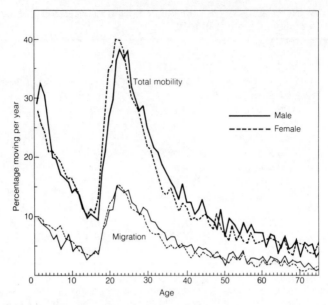

Figure 4.4a Age curve of mobility rates, by sex, 1981−2
Source: Bogue, 1985, p. 335

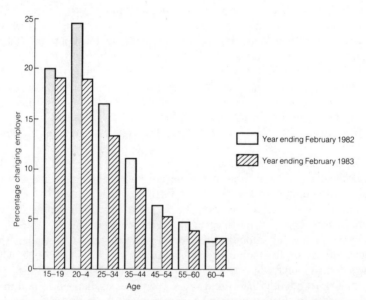

Figure 4.4b Australians, by age, who changed employers, 1982 and 1983
Source: Australian Bureau of Statistics, 1983, diagram 3

Table 4.27 Job mobility of employed persons who had a previous job in the year preceding February 1983, Australia

	Australian-born	Immigrants: period of arrival				
		Pre–1961	1961–70	1971–80	1981–3
Did not change job	85.7	91.0	85.5	83.3	59.2
Did change job	14.3	9.0	14.5	16.7	40.8
Same industry, same occupation	51.7	59.8	58.1	55.4	51.7
Different industry, same occupation	16.6	13.3	18.0	18.5	25.1
Same industry, different occupation	8.9	8.6	6.8	6.4	7.6
Different industry, different occupation	22.8	18.2	17.1	19.7	15.7
Total changed job	100.0	100.0	100.0	100.0	100.0

Source: Cooper and Constantinides, 1984, p. 72

arrived within the last two years, compared to the average Australian-born person, to move from the state of residence in order to find work − 51 percent to 38 percent (Cooper and Constantinides, 1984, p. 77). It is also interesting to note the greater propensity of immigrants from the main English-speaking countries of origin to change jobs than for other immigrants; this probably reflects their greater ease in communications within the job market. But there is only slightly greater willingness of persons in that group currently looking for work to move from the state than for other immigrants, or even for the Australian-born (who have more roots) − 40 percent compared to 35 percent and 38 percent (Cooper and Constantinides, 1984, p. 77).

Korean-educated physicians who come to the US are more likely to practise in small towns than are US-educated physicians (Shinn and Chang, 1988). This fact fits with greater mobility into the pattern of immigrants being particularly likely to be sensitive to market niches. Kindleberger (1967, p. 197) cites much higher labor turnover in Germany in earlier years after World War II for foreign than for domestic workers − 23 percent compared to less than 11 percent, and even this much domestic turnover was thought to be abnormally high because "substantial proportions of the expellees and refugees [from East Germany and elsewhere] have not decided on a permanent residence". Kindleberger views this high foreign-worker turnover as a business cost because of the expense of hiring and training. It may indeed be costly from the point of view of the firm, but the benefits to the economy as a whole should not be lost sight of. Kindleberger also suggests that the mobility of foreign workers may enable the domestic workforce to avoid the necessity of moving, thereby reducing the flexibility of the native workforce (p. 204), but this does not seem a weighty matter to me.

Vitality and the Propensity to Exert Work Effort

All of us recognize that people vary in the amounts of effort they exert in various tasks. Yet effort is not a variable in received economic theory. (On this general topic see Simon, 1987.) And there is very little evidence that bears directly upon the matter. Therefore, it is necessary to digress a bit to establish the reality of the phenomenon, as well as its importance.

Anyone who has exhorted herself or himself to "try harder" physically or mentally in a sporting match or in an examination, or who has "racked the brain" in trying to solve a problem, implicitly believes that the results are variable in response to inputs other than time and money. The same is true for cirumstances in which you have "driven yourself" − a telling term − to continue expending effort despite unpleasant sensations of pain from fatigue or injury or sickness. The same is true for the experience of exerting self-discipline, the essence of which seems to be a capacity to bear pain for a purpose. Studies of athletics show wide variation among persons in willingness to exert this sort of effort. Attention to the task at hand, and to the production of new ideas, seems to be related to this concept of effort. Change of any kind, including adjustment of one's ideas and institutions, seems to require effort. And given that migrating requires adjustment, it seems reasonable that immigrants are capable of exerting the unusual amounts of effort required to bring about change.

Not only do we observe that effort varies with the circumstances, but as consumers and employers we act upon that observation. We offer extra pay to a taxi driver to "try" to make the airport in time. We give bonuses for superior performance in business and in professional athletics. Sellers will literally pay prospective buyers to "try" new products.

There are several reasons to expect that immigrants will exert more effort than natives. One reason is that immigrants on average arrive with less material assets than natives possess, which follows from the fact that the immigrants are coming from countries where the level of income is lower on average (though see data on capital transfers in chapter 7). We may model the effort-exertion function as depending upon wealth (and opportunity) as follows:

$$\text{Effort} = f \left(\frac{\text{Wealth ex-post accepting the opportunity} - \text{wealth ex-ante accepting the opportunity}}{\text{wealth ex-ante}} \right)$$

This formulation is abbreviated and therefore cryptic: full explanation requires an entire book (Simon, 1987); hopefully, however, even this short statement is suggestive of the idea lying behind the notion that immigrants' lack of wealth is a spur to their achievement.

Another reason to expect greater effort from immigrants than from natives is that immigrants are likely to be self-selected on the basis of economically positive characteristics. It makes sense that those persons who believe that they have characteristics that will enable them to succeed in a new country will be the most likely persons to migrate: they are likely to earn a greater return on their investment of money and time in moving to and adjusting into a new country than are persons less likely to succeed in the new country. And the propensity to exert effort certainly is a characteristic that predisposes one to success in a new country.

I have found little direct systematic evidence on the extent of effort exerted by immigrants compared to natives. Therefore, we are thrust back on two sorts of evidence: anecdotal accounts from newspapers and elsewhere, and indirect evidence from various proxies for effort. Here is an example of the former:

Four owners of full-service gasoline stations in the Aspen Hill–Wheaton area have gone to court in Montgomery County to see if they can contain sales at "pump-your-own" stations that they say are driving them out of business.

The plaintiffs, who already enjoy more protection from self-service operations than their colleagues in most other states, are seeking monetary damages and a judge's order forbidding two owners of self-service stations from selling gasoline below a 7 percent markup that the plaintiffs say state law ordains ...

The defendants Boo Chung, a 42-year-old Korean immigrant with a station in Wheaton, and Abdhol Hussein Ejtemai, 35, an immigrant from Iran who runs a station in Aspen Hill, agree their prices are low. Ejtemai's charge of $1.119 for a gallon for self-service regular is in fact the lowest-priced gasoline in the metropolitan area, according to American Automobile Association figures.

The defendants say they are simply passing to their customers the savings of their no-frills operations and not selling gas for less than they paid for it. (*Washington Post*)

Returning to the observation that immigrants have a very high propensity to be taxi drivers, there would seem to be no other likely explanation than that immigrants are more willing to work hard, and more willing to work for earnings which depend upon their output, than are natives. It also seems that immigrants have a tendency to seek out jobs as domestics, which requires a certain amount of enterprise. For example, of the first thirteen newspaper advertisements our family called in the Washington area, twelve were placed by immigrants.

The data which indicate that immigrants have a greater propensity to save, to take second jobs, and to earn more than natives after some time on the job and after starting at lower salaries, are all consistent with the idea that immigrants exert more effort. The data showing that new immigrants work fewer weeks per year than do natives in the US, *ceteris paribus*, point in the other direction, but this latter result is more likely to be the result of the time it takes to enter the labor market than a shortfall of effort.

Shift work in France provides some direct evidence. Shifts other than daytime must require special motivation, and in fact the other shifts are usually paid somewhat more and are assigned to people with low seniority. A study of 54 French industrial firms that employed a high proportion of foreign workers found that while 54 percent of the first shift was composed of foreigners, the second shift had 64 percent foreigners, and the night shift 80 percent foreigners (Rerat et al., 1974).

Another direct piece of evidence comes from an Australian survey of employers. "Our surveys confirm that Australian employers find migrant workers generally more dedicated, hard-working ... than the Australian born. There is a clear positive preference for migrant labor" (Norman,

1984, p. 2). This observation is confirmed by the fact that, decade after decade, in country after country, the greatest opponents of immigration — the labor unions — pay immigrants the backhanded compliment of saying that native workers "cannot compete" with immigrants because the immigrants are willing to work harder than natives in dirty jobs that natives will not do. Embarrassing one would think, and therefore persuasive. As FAIR put it, "American workers are hurt by being forced into competition with illegal immigrants who work hard and scared and sometimes 'off the books,' who don't complain about unsafe conditions or low pay" (Conner, 1980). If those who are biased *against* immigrants, and who supposedly have first-hand knowledge of the workplaces, say immigrants work harder, should not the rest of us believe it true? (Additional discussion of this issue may be found in chapter 15.)

A factor influencing effort may be the perceived absoluteness of the break with the country of origin and hence the commitment to the country of destination. Indeed, Cubans have done much better in the US than have Mexicans.

"We had one major advantage," Mr. Suarez, the television cameraman, said. "We knew from the beginning that there was no way back to Cuba, and even more to pre-Castro Cuba." ("Cuban Refugees Adapt to Life in U.S.," *New York Times*, 29 September 1985)

Running against this theory, however, is that people from other Caribbean nations, who can return if they choose, do well in the US. But many of them do not have a language problem.

Intellectual vigor shows in the school results of immigrant children. *Item*: An astonishing number of new oriental immigrants have been winners of the high school Westinghouse Science Talent Search awards — 12 of 40 finalists in 1983, 9 of 40 in 1984, and 7 of 40 in 1985 (Bell, 1985, p. 26). *Item*: The Maryland Function Test results for Montgomery County show that Asian students, while they do considerably poorer (92 percent pass) than whites (99 percent pass) on Grade 9 reading, do considerably better in Grade 9 math — 85 percent pass versus 82 percent in 1983, and 88 percent versus 82 percent in 1984 (*Washington Post*, 9 January 1985, p. 84). *Item*: In a study of 1400 Southeast Asian refugee households, Caplan, Whitmore, Bui, and Trautmann

Investigated the academic achievement of approximately 350 school-aged children from the sample of refugee families. All of the children had arrived in the US after October 1978; most of them spoke *no* English upon arrival here. Yet, after an average of just three years in this country, these children were doing extremely well in school.

On national standardized tests of academic achievement, 27 percent of the refugee children scored in the 90th percentile on math achievement — almost three times better than the national average. And although they scored somewhat lower than the national average in English language proficiency, they outperformed their school-aged peers on general grade-point average, with 27 percent earning A or A-minus. (Caplan, 1985, pp. 5, 7)

Item: "The Berkeley student body is now 22 percent Asian−American, UCLA's is 21 percent, and MIT's 19 percent. The Julliard School of Music in New York is currently 30 percent Asian and Asian−American" (Bell, 1985, p. 26). *Item*: "35 of the 150 American Nobel laureates in the past 79 years were naturalized citizens of the United States" (Cafferty et al., 1983, p. 7).

How much of the vigor of immigrants is due to their being "hungry" rather than being settled and affluent, how much due to their being self-selected for vigor among the populations they come from, and how much due to the fructifying effects of living in the tension of two cultures is an open question; the success of Vietnamese refugee students in the American schools does not answer the question because those refugees were hardly a random sample of the Vietnamese population. An answer to the question would be interesting, but it is not crucial in a policy context; what matters is that the vigor exists. (A more difficult question, and one that probably has more implications, concerns the relatively poor performance of the Hispanics and blacks, as, for example, on that Maryland Functional Test in both reading and mathematics. Hypotheses there are aplenty, but a solid explanation is sorely lacking.)

The Children of Immigrants

The children they produce are an effect of immigrants. Earlier, this chapter presented evidence for higher labor-force participation for the children of immigrants than for other natives, and a higher propensity to start new businesses. Chiswick (1984) finds that in the 1970 Census data "men with a foreign-born parent have 15 percent higher earnings" than do natives (p. 29). A third of this difference is from higher earnings with the same background characteristics, whereas most of the rest of the difference is due to geographic concentration of the immigrant children in the North and urban areas. The children of immigrants do not, however, have a greater propensity to have substantially more years of education than other natives (Schultz, 1980).

Richmond and Zubrzycki (1984) show (see table 4.28) that the children of one or two immigrants earn much more than the children of two natives.

Table 4.28 Median earnings[a] of labor force, 15 years and over, in 1970, by sex, ethnic group, and birthplace of parents for the Canadian-born (excluding Quebec, etc.) (Standardized with age composition of Canadian population)

Birthplace of parents	British	French	Other Northern and Western Europe	Central and Eastern Europe	Southern Europe	Jewish	Asian	All other	Total ethnic groups
Males									
Both born in Canada	6,736	6,343	6,757	6,704	6,761	7,491	6,528	4,686	6,635
One born in Canada	7,486	6,997	7,137	7,022	7,310	10,039	6,896	6,926	7,391
Both born outside Canada	7,642	6,862	6,889	6,987	7,418	9,294	7,179	6,804	7,369
Females									
Both born in Canada	3,281	3,021	3,124	3,228	3,234	3,420	3,497	2,541	3,218
One born in Canada	3,506	3,178	3,247	3,310	3,319	3,658	3,973	3,255	3,444
Both born outside Canada	3,443	3,040	3,019	3,126	3,220	3,814	3,362	3,239	3,258

Note: [a] Excluding negative and zero earnings.
Source: Richmond and Zubrzycki, 1984, tables V-5 and V-7

These unconditional data (though age-adjusted) are the proper basis for policymaking, rather than data adjusted for education and other background characteristics; they properly show the effect of immigration (in the next generation).

The fact that having one rather than two immigrant parents generally leads to higher earnings is fascinating, but speculation about its causes is outside the scope of this volume.

Crime

Do immigrants have a greater propensity to commit crimes than do natives? I could find no study on the rates of crime among contemporary immigrants. But it seems reasonable that the records of crime among immigrants in other places and in earlier years should throw light on the matter.

Kindleberger (1967, p. 207) reviewed the evidence on guestworker crime in Europe since World War II. He concluded that the scare stories in the newspapers were mainly the product of overactive imaginations, and he found that there was no statistical evidence to suggest a higher age- and sex-adjusted rate of crime among immigrants than among natives; German data actually show less crime among immigrants. Many decades ago, Commons arrived at the same conclusion for the US (1924, pp. 168–9, reference from Kindleberger).

Steinberg studied the rates of crime among US immigrants up to the first quarter of the twentieth century for the Select Commission (appendix A). He notes that "Immigrants have been considered a source of crime and disorder in America since long before anyone ever thought of the US. Some of the claims about immigration which would evolve into the twentieth century were first heard early in the colonial period" (1981, p. 474). Steinberg found no evidence that criminality has been prevalent among immigrants. He concluded that, by any measure, the rate of serious crime has been less among immigrants than among natives, though the rate of petty crime (vagrancy, disorderly conduct, breach of the peace, drunkenness) has sometimes been greater among immigrants. When age and sex are controlled for, the rate of all crime has been less among immigrants than among natives. More specifically, two chief findings are:

1   "During both periods [1820–80 and 1890–1924], immigrants were more likely to commit minor offenses [vagrancy, disorderly conduct, breach of the peace, drunkenness] than were the native born. Natives tended to commit more property crimes and more crimes of personal violence than did immigrants" (p. 464).

2   "When immigrants and natives are compared using controls for age and

sex, immigrants are, at worst, equally prone to crime and, usually, less prone than natives" (p. 464).

Briefly discussed in chapter 15 is the finding by Muller (1984) that crime by Mexican illegals in California, standardized by age and sex, is lower than for natives.

Discussion

Various hypotheses have been advanced to explain the superior economic performance of immigrants. One such hypothesis has been that the least successful immigrants later depart the US; if a sample of persons arrive with average characteristics, such a phenomenon would leave behind a better-than-average sample. However, by comparing the time pattern of earnings of various ethnic groups that have greater and lesser ability to emigrate, Chiswick (1984) is able to arrive at a persuasive conclusion that selective emigration is not in general a crucial factor. However, in a comparison of schooling distributions by age in the 1960 and 1970 US censuses, he finds evidence that among Mexicans with less than five years of education, there was a greater propensity to return to Mexico than among Mexicans with more education, though this finding is not mirrored in the behavior of other ethnic groups (p. 24).

This evidence suggests by default that, at least to some extent, economic behavioral characteristics are a cultural phenomenon rather than being determined entirely by the economic conditions that the individual faces. This may seem perfectly obvious to most people, but in fact the empirical evidence concerning cultural factors is very limited, and is hard to develop rigorously because of the difficulty (or impossibility) of controlling all the relevant variables.

The tendency to assume that immigrants are different from natives in their general styles of life may often be off the mark, however. Morrison (1980) found that for immigrants living in New York City in 1907, holding income constant, "ethnicity is a poor predictor of spending habits," including the propensity to save.

Summary

Almost without exception the behavioral characteristics of immigrants are conducive to economic advancement for the community as well as for the immigrants themselves. Compared to natives of the same sex and age, immigrants work harder, save more, have a higher propensity to start new business, and are more likely to innovate. Two frequent negative allegations — that immigrants are more disposed to crime, and that they have large numbers of children which are a burden upon the native community — have no basis in fact.

With the demographic dimensions and behavior characteristics of immigration described in chapters 3 and 4 in hand, we may now proceed to the analysis of the various effects of immigration.

NOTES

1 There is little reason to believe that these results are due to a single isolated event. Aside from the single individual who employed more than 100 persons, and the 14 who did not answer about the number of employees, there were two employers with 20−44 employees, three with 11−19 employees, five with 6−10 employees, 15 with 3−5 employees, eight with 2 employees, 19 with one employee, and 24 with no employees.

2 Tables 4.16 and 4.17 are both included because they do not completely overlap. They cannot be combined because the samples are somewhat different geographically.

3 Evans has shown that, in addition to need, opportunity influences entrepreneurship. The larger a person's ethnic group in Australia, and therefore the larger the market for goods of that ethnicity, the larger is the propensity for being in business.

4 Consider a two-period work-and-retirement model. Initial endowment is $5000, income is $10,000. Consumption in each period will be $7500, with $2500 being saved from current income. Now assume initial endowment is $0, and income is $10,000. Consumption in each period will be $5000, with $5000 being saved. In general, for given income, higher wealth implies lower saving out of current income.

5 Effects of Immigrants upon the Public Coffers

Introduction
Conceptual Framework
Public Services used by Immigrants and Natives
Taxes Paid by Immigrants
Net Effect on the Public Coffers
Discussion
Summary
Afternote: About the SIE Sample

> Taxpayers are hurt by having to pay more for social services. (Roger Conner, Federation for American Immigration Reform (FAIR))

> We spend millions every month supporting people who are not supposed to be here. (Leonard Chapman, when Commissioner of the Immigration and Naturalization Service (INS))

Introduction

It is frequently said that immigrants to the US burden taxpayers by heavy use of welfare services. A 1986 poll showed that "47 percent of Americans felt that *most* immigrants wind up on welfare" (CBS/*New York Times*, 14 July 1986, p. 1). Often this charge is laid against illegal immigrants, as in the head quotations above, in which case the charge seems especially grave because the illegals are not "entitled" to the services they receive, unlike legal immigrants.

Both logic and compelling empirical evidence, shown in chapter 15, demonstrate irrefutably that this charge against the illegals is preposterous; even if they should wish to do so, the illegals could not take much advantage of welfare services because of fear of being apprehended. Therefore, the question to be dealt with here is whether *legal* immigrants impose a welfare burden upon natives.

This chapter first adduces excellent Census Bureau data to show that legal immigrants do not impose a burden upon natives by their use of welfare services such as medical care, unemployment pay, food programs, aid to dependent children, retirement payments, and schooling expenditures. Rather, immigrant families use less than their share of such services. This is due largely to the age composition of immigrant families, who typically are adults arriving in the US in the early prime of their working lives, with relatively few children. (Chapter 6 shows, however, that even compared to natives with the same ages and educational characteristics, immigrants do not use disproportionate amounts of such services.) The chapter then adduces other good data on the earnings and tax payments of immigrants which show that the average immigrant family pays more taxes than does the average native family.

The two sets of data, covering welfare use and taxes, are then combined in order to arrive at a combined estimate of the effect of immigrants upon natives through the public coffers. This combined welfare-and-tax result shows that immigrants yield a benefit to natives of sizable magnitude. Of course this effect is only part of the overall effect of immigrants, the other aspects of which are addressed in the rest of the book. But this part of the picture, showing that immigrants make a large net contribution to natives through the public coffers, is not only important, but also reinforces most of the other economic impacts of the immigrants.[1]

Conceptual Framework

Individuals and societies usually have assumed that the group benefits by adding unattached persons in the prime of life. The young and the strong produce more than they consume; they support and protect the aged and the dependent children. More recently this phenomenon was discussed by Neisser (1944), and then formalized by Modigliani (1966) and Samuelson (1975), who argue that a faster rate of population growth leads to a higher rate of saving because there is a higher proportion of young workers if population growth is faster, and young workers save in order to consume while in retirement. In an ongoing growth system the saving is in effect a system of transfers in each generation from the workers to the retired and the children; Samuelson (1975) compared this process to a chain-letter scheme, but unlike chain-letter schemes, there is no constraint that necessarily brings this process to a halt. Though the context of Modigliani's and Samuelson's discussions was the private financial system, much the same principle holds for the public tax-and-transfer system, which has obvious implications for the Social Security system.

If one adds to the analysis the transfers to children as well as to the retired, the analysis is less clearcut; Arthur and McNicoll (1976) made this criticism of Samuelson. Indeed, in some societies, such as Germany, the ratio of social transfer payments to children relative to the transfers to the retired is much larger than in the US; this could invalidate the above argument. Ultimately, it is an empirical question whether, given a particular society's transfer system, an additional baby implies on balance a lower or higher proportion of a worker's income transferred to dependents outside his/her family through taxes than if the baby is not born.

The Neisser-Modigliani-Samuelson reasoning applies with even greater force to immigrants than to new births, because the newcomers are typically young men and women who arrive without elderly dependents[2] and with a relatively small number of children already born.

The family rather than the household or the individual is the unit of analysis in this chapter, for reasons given in the afternote to the chapter concerning the SIE survey and sample used.

Public Services used by Immigrants and Natives

The aim of this section is to estimate the overall gross cost to US citizens of admitting immigrants to the US (gross benefits and net effects are discussed in subsequent sections). More specifically, we wish to estimate for the average immigrant in an entry cohort: (a) the amount of each type of service used in each year after entry, and (b) the yearly total. (Some interpolation is necessary because some cohorts contain more than one year's immigrants due to the SIE survey's classification system.)

The average of an entire immigrant entry cohort is the most important estimate for our purposes, because it is the relevant quantity for policy decisions about the total number of immigrants to allow in; it indicates the gross cost to natives of services to the average immigrant family.

Let us look at some scraps of data from other countries before turning to the US.

Canada

In the first three years, almost 50 percent of the immigrants attended part-time or short-duration educational courses financed by the Canada Manpower Training Program, an expensive service.

More important, though less direct, is the evidence on poverty among immigrant families, because it is families in poverty who especially need welfare services. With respect to the Canadian-defined "poverty line" income, a slightly higher proportion of immigrants than non-immigrants — 22 percent compared to 21 percent — were below the poverty line at the end of the immigrants' first year. But by the end of the second and third years, only 5 percent and 4 percent of the immigrants were below the poverty line — to be compared with the 21 percent among all Canadians (Manpower and Immigration, 1974, pp. 55–7). Also important is the very low proportion in or near the retirement age among the immigrants — 1 percent or less being 65 and over, and less than 5 percent are 50 and over (p. 142). This suggests very low present and future burden on retirement pension funds.

Great Britain

Because there are proportionally so many fewer immigrants than natives of retirement age (mainly "New Commonwealth," mainly Caribbean), immigrants receive much less in retirement pensions than do natives, and pensions are the largest item in the cost of national insurance and assistance benefits (Jones and Smith, 1970, p. 104). The latter are, in turn, the biggest share of social service expenses; the figures were £15.4 and £27.6 in 1961, and £16.2 and £28.3 in 1966 (p. 107). In other categories, expenditures per head for immigrants are much the same as for natives. In total, the expenditures per head for immigrants and total population were £47.5 and £61.0 in 1961, and £52.0 and £62.0 in 1966 (p. 107). Thus, immigrants are not relatively heavy users of welfare services; rather, they are relatively *light* users of welfare services.

Israel

Israel is quite atypical with respect to the supply of social services to immigrants, for several reasons. First, the immigrants from the USSR and elsewhere nowadays move largely for non-economic reasons, in contrast to most migrants elsewhere in the world. Second, the social services supplied — housing subsidies, special rights for the importation of autos and other goods, and acclimatization services — are quite large (though not as large as most Israelis believe) and they are hard to estimate because they vary considerably across immigrants. Third, foreign charity funds *more* than cover the costs of these social services, so they do not affect resident Israelis.

Australia

Using data on the relationship of demographic structure to government expenditure on education, social security, and welfare and health care, Tulpele (1984) calculated that migrants lower the necessary taxes paid by native Australians to finance such government expenditures.

United States

From the 1976 Census Bureau Survey of Income and Education (SIE, described in the afternote to the chapter), I constructed a picture of lifetime economic behavior by assuming that the information on immigrants who had been here, say, two years as of 1975 describes the representative immigrant family after two years, those in the US 10 years in 1975 stand for the tenth year of a representative family, and so on.

The services that most often catch the public eye are welfare and supplemental security payments, unemployment compensation, medical care, aid to dependent children, and food stamps. Table 5.1 shows the amounts of payments received by persons who have been in the US varying lengths of time. Columns 1−8 show the various transfer payments to natives and to immigrant entry cohorts, with the spotlight on the cohorts ranging backward from 1974 to 1950. The meaning of the results for families that arrived in 1976 and 1975 is exceedingly unclear, because the data supposedly refer to the calendar year 1975.[3] Data for the cohorts that arrived in 1949 or before are shown below for completeness, although they are not relevant to policy decisions concerning immigration because these older immigrants must now be seen as part of an equilibrium system to be described below, and because the effects happen so long after admission that their discounted present value is very low at admission. Their children, and the economic impacts of those children, are an important part of the total effects of this cohort, but data on their children are not available; for the same reason, the 1950−9 cohort should not be considered an important part of the sample.[4]

The mechanism of the above-mentioned equilibrium system is not immediately obvious, and requires amplification. We are concerned with the resource flows due to immigrants that affect the economic position of natives taken as a group. That is, we want to compare the consumption of natives (including consumption of services) in two hypothetical situations, one with and one without a group of immigrants. We are not concerned with legal obligations, entitlements, equity, or the consumption of immigrants.

A simplified model may help. Consider a community of subsistence farmers in which there is a surplus of land and each farm produces the same output. Each family consists of three generations: a married couple, two children, and two retired adults. Children do not work until age 20, at which time they marry, have two children, and work for 20 years. At age 40 the couple retire and live until age 60. On each farm, then, there are always one working couple, two dependent children, and two dependent elderly persons, a stationary demographic system. The farm is assumed to produce no surplus or saving; all production is consumed.

Consider, now, a newly married couple who move into the community. For 20 years the production of this immigrant family not only supports the couple and their children, but also leaves a surplus that the community can tax. During this period the family is an economic benefit to natives as a result of the taxes they pay. After 20 years, when the immigrant couple retire, the family has come to have the same characteristics as an "equilibrium" native family, and the retirement consumption of the immigrant couple is paid for by their children. This illustrates how there is a one-time benefit to natives during the first years that an immigrant couple is in the community, while there is no reverse flow after the couple retire. And the nature of the obligation between the immigrant couple and their children (which leads their children to support them) has no bearing upon the consumption of natives. The situation is analogous in a modern society except that the transfers do not take place within the family system but rather through the public coffers.

Column 9 in table 5.1 shows the totals for the five most important categories of welfare payment transfers aside from Social Security. The average family in each of the cohorts of immigrants since 1950−9 uses about the same or slightly more such services than do native families − ranging from $137 less to $148 more. But when Social Security[5] is included, we see in column 10 that immigrants receive much less such welfare payments in total than do natives − ranging from $294 less to $823 less. Given the consistency in composition from cohort to cohort, there is no question of the statistical significance of the smaller use of welfare transfers by immigrants than natives.

Expenditures on education must be considered, too. The SIE sample does not show the total number of children in the family, but it does show the number living at home. This latter number should be a satisfactory approximation for young families and for children aged 17 or less. Column 11 shows the average number of children per family aged 5 to 17. These numbers were multiplied by the 1975−6 average annual expenditure of $1,302 per student in public elementary and secondary schools;[6] the results are also shown in column 11. Immigrants use substantially more school services than do natives after a few years − $476 more per family for both the 1960−4 and 1950−9 cohorts.[7]

Table 5.1   Dollar values of transfer payments and services received in 1975 per person, by various entry cohorts and by natives[a]

Immigrant cohort by year of entry	(1) Unemployment/ workmen's compensation, veterans' benefits ($)	(2) Public welfare ($)	(3) Supplemental security ($)	(4) Aid to families with dependent children ($)	(5) Food stamps ($) (and %)[g]	(6) Social Security ($)
1974	204	131	91	91	15 (15)	3
1973	238	47	63	6	7 (5)	49
1972	237	85	38	164	12 (8)	127
1971	261	189	16	13	17 (12)	5
1970	341	100	50	11	16 (10)	34
1965–9	339	191	86	18	12 (12)	152
1960–4	385	91	69	18	12 (8)	326
1950–9	301	122	31	50	11 (9)	424
Natives	288	108	46	45	11 (9)	735
1976[e]	20	0	360	8	0 (0)	6
1975[f]	40	76	6	88	7 (9)	31
1920–49	239	32	73	11	3 (3)	2,229
Before 1920	164	30	116	56	3 (3)	3,090

Notes: The data for the 1975 and 1976 and pre-1950 cohorts, though they are not relevant, are included because some have expressed interest in them.
[a] Means weighted by sample probabilities to be unbiased estimates of the United States.
[b] At $592 per patient-year.

Next, we consider Medicare and Medicaid.[8] Columns 7 and 8 show the proportions of the various groups that use these services. The average cost per user of Medicare was $592 in 1975, and for Medicaid it was $126. (The average cost per person over 65 was $205 for Medicaid, and a considerably larger proportion of natives than of recent immigrant cohorts are over 65, but I shall not bother to make an adjustment for this.)

Special assistance to refugees — which in 1980 amounted to $1000 per

Table 5.1 Cont.

(7) Medicare[b] ($) (and %)[g]	(8) Medicaid[c] ($) (and %)[g]	(9) Total, cols. 1–5 ($)	(10) Total, cols. 1–6 ($)	(11) Schooling costs for children aged 5–17[d] ($) (and %)[g]	(12) Total, cols. 1–8 and 11 ($)	(13) Number of families
29 (4.9)	32 (25.6)	532	535	820 (63)	1,416	154
23 (3.9)	12 (9.7)	361	410	755 (58)	1,200	171
42 (7)	24 (19.1)	536	563	781 (60)	1,510	188
2 (0.3)	14 (11.1)	496	501	716 (55)	1,233	202
45 (7.6)	19 (15.7)	518	552	1,042 (80)	1,659	224
48 (8.1)	27 (21.2)	646	798	1,068 (82)	1,941	977
88 (14.7)	21 (16.9)	575	901	1,237 (95)	2,247	769
76 (16)	20 (15.6)	515	939	1,237 (95)	2,292	1762
167 (28)	20 (15.9)	498	1,233	859 (66)	2,279	11,212
0 (0)	(10.2)	–	–	(38)	–	50
(4.5)	(23.4)	–	–	(71)	–	204
(80.5)	(11.8)	–	–	–	–	3697
(12.9)	(18.6)	–	–	–	–	1075

(The last four rows are bracketed as "not relevant")

[c] *At $126 per patient-year.*
[d] *At $1,302 per child-year of schooling.*
[e] *Puerto Ricans not included with either immigrant or native.*
[f] *Data not reliable: see text in parentheses indicate proportions receiving the service.*
[g] *Percentages in parentheses indicate proportions receiving the service.*

person in cash plus some overhead to the assisting refugee organization, as well as some special programs – has also been excluded from the analysis, because there is no way of knowing which families in the sample were admitted as refugees. If one wishes to make a benefit-and-cost analysis specifically for refugees, it would therefore be appropriate to deduct this sum, multiplied by the average number of family members, from the present value calculated for the family, as discussed below. Refugees, however, are not considered as immigrants according to quotas and immigration law.

We are now in a position to estimate the average total cost of services used by the various cohorts, with results shown in column 12. There we see that the very recent cohorts use much less of services than do natives – for example, $971 less per family for the 1973−4 cohorts, considered together, than for natives. The amounts of services used by older cohorts are higher; they move upward and reach equality with natives some 10−15 years after arrival. Figure 5.1 plots the data on services used. A free-hand curve allows us to calculate the change in services with an additional year in the US.

Native families are used as a benchmark because if immigrants were to use services and pay taxes in amounts equal to natives, the immigrants would have no effect on natives through the public coffers; on average, taxes paid equal the cost of services provided. In the overall cost−benefit framework employed later, personal services used by immigrants cannot simply be compared to taxes paid by immigrants because the "overhead" of public goods must also be allowed for; the comparison to natives takes care of this.

Concerning illegal aliens now, the evidence is clear and strong that they do not use welfare services, both because they are young, mature, and strong, and also because they cannot use such services without fear of the law. Chapter 15 presents data on this.

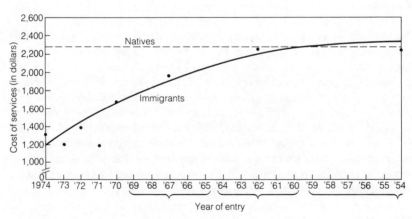

Figure 5.1 Cost of services used by various immigrant cohorts and by native Americans

Source: Table 5.1

Conclusion

The data from the "normal" cases — Britain, Canada, and the US — suggest that immigrants use a below-average quantity of services, largely because of the "favorable" age and sex composition of the immigrant groups.

Taxes Paid by Immigrants

Please notice the difference between the data on unconditional family earnings discussed in this section, and the studies of immigrants' earnings with as many factors as possible held constant in the large literature on that subject. Nothing is held constant in this cost–benefit analysis other than year of entry, because the aim of this chapter is to assess the unconditional impact of a cohort of immigrant *families* upon natives' standard of living. In contrast, the aim of the other studies is to understand the nature of the differences between *individual* immigrants and natives when such factors as education and age are allowed for. The broad patterns of the unconditional family earnings results, however, clearly are compatible with the results of the controlled individual comparisons.

Again, we shall first consider the fairly scanty but suggestive data for Canada, Great Britain, and Israel, before going on to a solid set of extensive data for the US.

Canada

No directly relevant tax data are available. We do know, however, that immigrants' average income was 12–14 percent below that of the native-born control group after three years, and hence the tax collections would be somewhat less for immigrants than for native-borns. It is reasonable to assume, however, that immigrants' incomes relative to non-immigrants rise after that, and wipe out differences in tax payments. Also some non-negligible segment of taxes goes for defense and other centralized activities in which there are major economies of scale. Hence, even immigrant tax payments somewhat lower than natives' might more than pay for an average person's use of services, let alone the lower use of services by immigrants, who include fewer retired persons and fewer in poverty.

Great Britain

The survey data available to Jones and Smith (1970) did not allow them to estimate immigrant income-tax payments. Their best guesses were as follows:

[T]here is some evidence that average income per employed New Commonwealth worker is lower than the national level, but we also know that the labour force participation rates are higher for the New Commonwealth than for the indigenous population, so total household income from earnings alone for New Commonwealth households may well not deviate much from the national average. If this were the only factor it would imply similar national insurance payments and income tax payments per head. But we also know that the dependency factor is higher for the New Commonwealth households and this would lead to greater income tax allowances and in consequence smaller payments. It is also known that there has been some tax evasion by immigrants and this has been estimated at 5 to 7 million [pounds] in 1966/7 by the Board of Inland Revenue; but now that this has been identified, an attempt will presumably be made to stop it. Whilst it is not practicable to estimate the relative contributions of immigrants in the form of national insurance contributions and income tax payments, it seems unlikely that, if New Commonwealth immigrants do pay less, the difference would more than outweigh their smaller share of the social services. (Jones and Smith, 1970, p. 95)

Israel

The tax situation of immigrants to Israel is quite atypical among countries because of (a) the non-economic motives for immigration, (b) the special subsidies and tax breaks for immigrants, and (c) the large defense burden. Of the taxes that *all* Israelis pay (perhaps 60−5 percent of GNP) a very large proportion (perhaps 40 percent) goes to defense. These contributions to the defense burden by immigrants − in taxes, and in time spent in the army − substantially lighten the portion of the communal burden borne by native Israelis.

The United States

The Census Bureau's 1976 SIE survey (mentioned earlier) allows us to estimate the taxes paid by immigrants. Though we lack direct information on taxes paid, we can make a fair estimate from data on family earnings.

Column 4 in table 5.2, and figure 5.2 based on it, show that the average immigrant family comes to earn about as much as the average native family somewhere between three and five years after entry, and after that earns more. (This finding uses an average for the 1970−3 cohorts.) This rapid approach to equality of earnings is heavily influenced, of course, by age and education composition, and especially by the absence of retired family heads among the immigrants.

Inferences from earnings data about taxes paid by various cohorts of immigrants, and by the representative native family, are tenuous but necessary. A key difficulty is that different proportions of overall taxes (not just income taxes) are paid by persons of different income levels (Browning and Johnson, 1979), which means that a proper calculation must be based upon the entire income distribution of a cohort, rather than just the mean.[9] A bit of light is thrown on the matter by the spread of the income distributions in our data, which show somewhat smaller standard deviations relative to mean income for immigrants than for natives, as seen in table 5.2 (in parentheses). This probably means that, for the same mean income, a group of immigrants pays somewhat less taxes than does a group of natives, due to fewer very high incomes. Nevertheless, we are not likely to go far wrong by assuming that taxes paid are proportional to mean income.

The total of taxes paid by immigrants – found in columns 10 and 11 of table 5.2 – are calculated as follows. The total receipts of state, local and federal governments were $771.9 billion in 1979, which we may approximate as 32.6 percent of gross national product ($2368.5 billion; *Economic Report of the President*, 1980, pp. 288, 203). The mean-taxes-paid taxpayer pays 29.1 percent of income; the taxes paid by the median-income taxpayer are 85 percent of that; that is, the rate at which taxes are paid by the person between the fifth and sixth deciles of income recipients – 24.8 percent of income paid in taxes – is 85 percent of the mean 29.1 percent for all taxable incomes (Browning and Johnson, 1979, p. 51). So even if immigrants are more concentrated near the mean than are natives, the effect on total taxes paid will not be large.

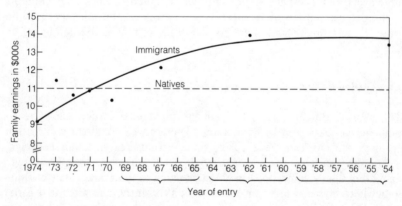

Figure 5.2   Family earnings by various immigrant cohorts and by native Americans
Source: Table 5.2

In brief, although the estimates of taxes paid by immigrants and natives are rough, the inaccuracy is unlikely to be important in this context because the incomes − and hence the amounts of taxes paid by the various cohorts and by natives − do not differ substantially.

Conclusions

Immigrants tend to pay quantities of taxes that exceed the costs of the public services they use.

Net Effect on the Public Coffers

If we know the amount of taxes paid by immigrants and the amount of welfare services used by them, we may then compute the net balance, positive or negative, for immigrants as a group. Additionally, we can then compute their impact upon the public coffers.

Table 5.3 consolidates the relevant data on services used and taxes paid. Columns 1 and 2 show the total transfer payments and services used by immigrants in various years after entry (actually, by various entry cohorts during 1975) and by natives. Column 3 shows the differences between columns 1 and 2. If we make the reasonable assumption that the average family just pays for the average family's services used − an assumption that says no more than that government receipts equal the sum of government expenditures for various purposes − then column 3 indicates the net balance of immigrants with respect to services alone. In other words, it indicates the amount by which services used by immigrants exceed or fall short of the amount an average taxpayer[10] pays for that.

Turning from services used to taxes paid, we first deal with government expenditures that are invariant to the number of people, or that at least are pure public goods in the sense that the services they render to any person are independent of the services others obtain from them. The government expenditures that seem clearly to fit into this category are national defense ($85,552 million in 1975), international affairs ($6922 million), and general science, space, and technology ($3989 million), out of total outlays of $326,185 million, or ($96,463/$326,185) = 29.6 percent (*Economic Report of the President*, 1980, p. 284). Federal government expenditures were ($356.8/$532.8) = 67 percent of total government expenditures (p. 288), so the public goods categories constitute (67 percent × 29.6 percent) = 20 percent of all taxes. Hence 20 percent of taxes paid by immigrants are shown in column 6.

Table 5.2 Family earnings and employment data for immigrants and natives, United States, 1975

Immigrant cohort by year of entry	(1) Head's wages and salaries ($)	(2) Spouse's wages and salaries (whether there is or is not a spouse) ($)	(3) Self-employment income ($)	(4) Total wages[a] and salaries ($)	(5) Total family earnings[b] ($)
1974	7,162 (8,107)	1,182	80	8,890 (8,773)	9,192 (10,688)
1973	8,351 (9,150)	1,774	497	10,880 (10,087)	11,387 (9,996)
1972	7,738 (5,901)	2,048	133	10,458 (8,218)	10,610 (8,383)
1971	7,603 (6,549)	1,574	1,409	9,416 (7,615)	10,826 (9,871)
1970	7,294 (5,876)	1,717	610	9,772 (7,502)	10,383 (7,295)
1965–9	8,313 (7,334)	2,070	635	11,543 (8,996)	12,247 (9,597)
1960–4	9,156 (8,782)	2,223	1,450	12,248 (9,925)	14,014 (11,310)
1950–9	9,592 (8,285)	1,874	1,090	12,343 (9,787)	13,542 (10,309)
Natives	7,503 (8,203)	1,614	722	10,164 (9,782)	11,037 (10,377)
1976	3,873 (6,880)	824	732	4,702 (8,359)	–
1975	5,520 (8,675)	659	149	6,531 (8,896)	–
1920–49	4,689 (8,308)	1,029	871	6,808 (10,219)	7,740 (11,248)
Before 1920	388 (2,997)	62 (729)	167 (1,517)	1,771 (5,707)	2,184 (7,254)

Notes: Means weighted by sample probabilities, standard deviations in parentheses. The data for the 1975 and 1976 and pre-1950 cohorts, though they are not relevant, are included because some have expressed interest in them.

[a] Total wages and salaries includes wages and salaries from other members of the household besides head and spouse, and hence column 4 should not equal the sum of columns 1–3.

[b] The figure for total family earnings may seem larger than warranted by the

Table 5.2 Cont.

(6)	(7)	(8)	(9)	(10)	(11)
Number of persons in labor force[c]	Number of earners	Number of persons employed	Number of persons unemployed	Estimated tax paid ($) on wages $0.29 \times (4)^d$	Estimated tax paid on earnings $0.29 \times (5)^d$ ($)
1.26	1.35	1.09	0.131	2,587	2,666
1.45	1.45	1.35	0.071	3,166	3,302
1.36	1.39	1.20	0.165	3,043	3,077
1.33	1.28	1.17	0.115	2,740	3,140
1.51	1.51	1.29	0.168	2,848	3,011
1.49	1.54	1.36	0.13	3,359	3,552
1.43	1.50	1.31	0.112	3,564	4,064
1.47	1.55	1.34	0.117	3,592	3,927
1.26	1.37	1.18	0.09	3,008	3,201
1.20	0.911	0.839	0.065	—	—
1.21	1.30	1.14	0.094	—	—
0.806	0.924	0.744	0.056	—	—
0.232	0.281	0.199	0.017	—	—

(column 9, last four rows braced: "not relevant")

individual columns for head's and spouse's wages and salaries, and for self-employment income. The data do add up in a sample of individual records. The likeliest explanation is that the family earnings are top-coded to $75,000, and are entered directly, but the other categories are top-coded to $50,000.
[c] In principle, columns 8 and 9 should add to column 6. The discrepancies probably arise from different perceptions of the different questions.
[d] See text for origin of 0.29 multiplier.

Table 5.3 Overall balance sheet of services used and taxes paid by immigrants, United States, 1975

(1)	(2)	(3)	(4)	(5)	(6)
Immigrant cohort by year of entry	Services used by cohort (table 5.1, col. 12) ($)	Services used by natives (table 5.1, col. 12) ($)	(3) − (2) ($)	Taxes paid by cohort, (table 5.2, col. 11) ($)	20% of taxes paid for pure public goods 0.2 × (5) ($)
1974	1,416	2,279	863	2,666	533
1973	1,200	2,279	1,079	3,302	660
1972	1,510	2,279	769	3,077	615
1971	1,233	2,279	1,046	3,140	628
1970	1,659	2,279	620	3,011	602
1965−9	1,941	2,279	338	3,552	710
1960−4	2,247	2,279	32	4,064	813
1950−9	2,292	2,279	13	3,927	785

Notes: [a] Per immigrant family
[b] Per immigrant family; no allowance for public goods contribution

Next we consider other taxes. The differences between the amounts of taxes paid by immigrants and by natives are shown in column 8 of table 5.3. To the extent that immigrants pay less or more than natives, immigrants are taking from, or giving to, natives through the public coffers, after allowing for the services they use.

We may summarize the logic of the tax calculation as follows:

Benefit to natives = (tax-paid services used by the average native family less tax-paid services used by the average immigrant family) + (20 percent of taxes paid by the immigrant family as a contribution to expenditures

Table 5.3   Cont.

(7)	(8)	(9)	(10)	(11)
				(4) + [(5) − (7)]
				Alternate
				calculation of
				net affect of
				immigrant cohort
Taxes			(4) + (6) + (9)	upon natives[b]
paid by			Net affect of	per immigrant
natives			immigrant	family, no
(table 5.2,			cohort upon	allowance for
col. 11)	(5) − (7)	(100%−20%)	natives[a]	public goods
($)	($)	× (8) ($)	($)	contribution ($)
3,201	−535	−428	968	328
3,201	101	81	1,820	1,180
3,201	−124	−99	1,285	645
3,201	−61	−49	1,625	985
3,201	−190	−152	1,070	430
3,201	351	281	1,329	689
3,201	863	690	1,535	895
3,201	726	581	1,353	713

on public goods) + (80 percent of the difference between taxes paid by the average native family and the average immigrant family, a negative quantity in some cases).

A calculation is also shown in column 11 of table 5.3 for the less realistic but more "conservative" assumption that there is no public-good element in immigrants' taxes that immediately lowers the tax burden of natives (or increases benefits from the tax-paid services).

We are now in position to sum the effects on a year-by-year basis. This summary is shown in column 10 of table 5.3. There we see that in every year following entry (until the immigrants themselves retire, at which time their own children are supporting them through the Social Security and

Medicare systems) immigrants benefit natives through the public coffers. And a calculation of the net present value of the stream of differences shows that immigrants are a remarkably good investment at any conceivable rate of discount, if we consider these partial effects only. At a 3 percent discount rate − roughly the long-run riskless rate adjusted for inflation in the Western World − each immigrant family was worth about $20,600 to natives around 1975, to be compared with the mean yearly native family earnings of $11,037; at 6 percent the present value would be about $15,800, while at 9 percent it would be about $12,400, in 1975 dollars.

When thinking about the totality of the economic effect of immigrants upon natives, one must take into account, in addition to the calculations discussed here, both capital dilution (negative effect on natives) and productivity (positive effect on natives). Estimation of these latter effects as well as the totality requires a model of the economy at large, plus some key parameter estimates such as the proportion of the returns to existing capital that are captured by immigrants. But based on the integrated model discussed in chapter 10, one may conclude that the average immigrant is an excellent investment for taxpayers on almost any reasonable set of parameter estimates.

For comparison, let us examine a set of data that comes from a smaller sample drawn in a less rigorous fashion, 1981 interviews of Jewish immigrants from the USSR (R. Simon and J. Simon, 1985). The separate amounts received in public aid, and paid in taxes, are not immediately comparable to the SIE data, and we did not draw a separate comparison sample of natives because this was only one part of a more general study of these immigrants. But the flows to and from the public coffers may be compared to see the overall effect on natives through the public coffers.

The flows to the immigrant families in public-aid transfer payments, educational services, and the "block grant" of assistance to refugees via the refugee organizations (the latter also spent for Vietnamese and other refugees), are shown in lines 1−3 of table 5.4, with the total shown in line 4 for the first six months and then for twelve-month periods after that. The average immigrant family's income is shown in line 5, the taxes calculated from that income are shown in line 6, and the net flows from and to the public coffers are shown in line 7. We see that in the first six months there is a substantial net flow from natives to immigrants, but the flow quickly reverses and by the end of the second full year the flows from immigrants to natives have become substantial. If one calculates the present value of these flows as one would other investments, at a 3 percent "real, riskless" rate as well as at 6 percent and 9 percent, one gets sums of $20,593, $17,692, and $15,262 (in 1981 dollars).

Table 5.4 Dollar flow between public coffers and a representative Soviet immigrant family

	Months in US							
	1–6	7–18	19–30	31–42	43–54	55–66	67–78	79–90 and subsequently
(1) Public aid	965	1,514	855	1,216	820	394	955	464
(2) Education	1,368	2,735	2,735	2,735	2,735	2,735	2,735	2,735
(3) Block grant	2,700	0	0	0	0	0	0	0
(4) Total public expenditures	5,033	1,514	855	1,216	820	394	955	464
(5) Income	4,306	13,814	20,548	18,197	23,976	24,643	28,299	26,844
(6) Taxes paid (22% of income)	947	3,039	4,521	4,003	5,275	5,421	6,226	5,906
(7) Taxes minus public expenditures (6)−(4)	(−4,086)	1,525	3,666	2,787	4,455	5,027	5,271	5,442

Discussion

1   A major limitation of the SIE data is that inferences about life-cycle behavior are drawn from a cross-section; the difficulty is widely understood. Furthermore, the sub-groups observed in the cross-section — cohorts that came to the US in different years — differ from each other in relevant characteristics. Yet the analysis assumes that all the cohorts are proxies for some portion of a single cohort's economic life — a cohort which has not yet arrived and whose composition is not yet known. The cohort-wide data shown here should provide fairly accurate general guidance, however; partly because average education has not changed greatly from cohort to cohort (though age and ethnic composition have changed). Also, the general logical consistency in the pattern of the various cohorts substantiates that the cohorts that have arrived in the past are reasonably similar, and offer a reasonable basis for prediction of the effects of future cohorts.

2   In principle it is possible to isolate the effects of various characteristics such as education, age, and perhaps ethnicity in past cohorts, and then to estimate the economic effects of a cohort expected to have a particular mix of these characteristics. But there is no basis on which to make such disaggregated estimates for a synthetic cohort until we know the composition of the future cohort — and it would not be worthwhile to do so unless we knew that it would be very different from past cohorts, of course. (Without further investigation, however, we can say that any policies leading to higher education and lower age of immigrants will be beneficial to natives.)

3   The contemporary public-coffers benefits to natives from immigrants derive overwhelmingly from the age composition of natives rather than from behavioral characteristics of immigrants; this may be seen in the importance of the Social Security effect.

4   Some opponents of immigration (and even some friends of immigration) have said, roughly, "Yes, the United States received much larger numbers of immigrants, relative to the number of natives, in the past than it does now, and absorbed them successfully. But the conditions were different then. There was no program of social welfare and public support that attracted immigrants and that was costly for natives to pay for." In fact, the argument actually points in exactly the opposite direction, because the contemporary structure of social services and taxes — which involves larger amounts of support to the needy, and therefore larger burdens upon the taxpayers, than in the past — implies that the public coffer is on balance a net beneficiary from immigrants rather than a net contributor to them. That is, more immigrants mean a lighter rather than a heavier burden upon natives because immigrants are, as we have seen, net contributors to the system due to their age and family composition. And this contribution is

greater than it was a century ago, say, because fewer services were then being provided that the immigrants helped to pay for.

So — perhaps ironically — the very phenomenon that causes many natives to object to immigration turns out, upon investigation, to be a strong argument for increased immigration.

5 About illegals: chapter 15 shows that illegals use practically no welfare services, while about three-quarters pay Social Security and income taxes. This means that illegals contribute heavily to natives in this regard; the native population is "exploiting" the illegals in this fashion, rather than the opposite.

6 Immigrants chosen for their economic characteristics rather than for their being relatives of families already in the US surely use far less welfare services than do relatives. Evidence for this comes from a survey of General Eligibility Migrants in Australia: "[T]his category of migrants is not a heavy user of, nor does it generally have unusual need for government services" (Northage & Associates, 1983, p. 63).

7 The question of different performance of different ethnic groups with respect to the public coffers is frequently raised. Chapter 6 shows that family structure overwhelmingly dominates all other variables in explaining welfare receipts aside from old-age programs; unmarried women with several children receive much more than do other types of families; and no group of immigrants is very different from others in this respect. In human-capital-adjusted regressions, Mexicans receive considerably less in services — $436 per year — than do other immigrant families on average. On the earnings-and-taxes side, Mexicans earn considerably less than do other ethnic groups, but the low amount of services used offsets this shortfall. Aside from this, there is not much noteworthy about the data for the various ethnic groups.

8 Refugees may be expected to take longer to establish themselves, and therefore to have higher rates of welfare usage for longer periods of time, than other immigrants. Therefore, it is of interest that as of mid-1983, the proportions of refugees (largely Southeast Asians) arriving from 1980 to 1983 and receiving cash assistance as of the survey date were: arrived fiscal year 1980: 7 percent; FY 1981: 13 percent; FY 1982: 26 percent; FY 1983: 24 percent (Church World Service, 1983, p. 38). The proportions with full-time employment, as reported by the sponsors and by the refugees, respectively, were: Fiscal year 1980: sponsors, 74 percent, refugees, 65 percent; FY 1981: 65 percent, 55 percent; FY 1982: 55 percent, 39 percent; FY 1983: 44 percent, 30 percent (Church World Service, 1983, p. 25).

9 The ongoing debate over Social Security is agonizing. Every proposed policy inflicts pain because it boils down either to a decrease in benefits to the elderly or an increase in taxes upon working persons. And so it must be, as long as the numbers of elderly and of workers remain unchanged.

It is unthinkable that the number of elderly be reduced by our health policies. There remains, then, only one condition that can lessen the tax burden upon working persons without reducing benefits — a larger number of young working persons. Having more children will help, but not until a couple of decades hence. Only immigration provides immediate help.

As soon as the average immigrant begins working — which generally is quite soon after arriving in this country — the immigrant begins to contribute to the Social Security coffers. The immigrant's own eventual receipt of Social Security benefits, decades in the future, does not offset these immediate benefits to natives, as we have seen.

The benefit to natives stems from the difference in age composition between the population of present residents of the US, and that of each cohort of immigrants. Immigrants tend to move when they are young and near the start of their working lives, as chapter 3 shows. For example, among immigrants who arrived in 1967–73, 4.3 percent were aged 60 or over, whereas 14.2 percent of the US population at that time were 60 or over, and the proportion is even higher now. And whereas 25.7 percent of the US population were in the early prime labor force ages 20–39, 46.4 percent of immigrants were in that age bracket. Moreover, even that small fraction of the immigrants who are elderly are not eligible to receive Social Security. Therefore each cohort of new immigrants contributes substantially to reduce the Social Security burden of natives, in proportion to its numbers.

The anti-immigration organizations attempt to talk away this benefit of immigrants by saying that the total dependency burden of the US population is not increasing because as the number of aged persons increases the number of dependent children decreases. For example, "Over the next generation, each member of the labor force will support fewer non-workers, even with less immigration than at present. There will be more older non-workers to support, but fewer young ones" (*The Data*, Environmental Fund, July 1982, p. 1). But dependent children have a very different impact upon the taxpayer than do the elderly. Parents pay most of the cost of raising their own children in this country, and do not receive the large child allowance payments some European countries give. Additionally, the living costs of a child for a year are far less than the living costs of an aged adult; this is obvious when one reflects on the comparative costs of housing, medical care, and transportation; children's public school education expenditures do not much alter the overall picture. So to lump together dependent children and dependent adults on a one-to-one basis obscures the matter.

As to whether US natives must pay the piper for this benefit from immigrants when the young immigrants get older and themselves receive Social Security — the answer is "no," for two reasons discussed earlier. First, the impact of this year's immigrants on Social Security say 30 years from now properly has little weight in the overall assessment, because a dollar to be received or paid out 30 years from now is worth much less now when discounted at even a modest rate. Second and more important is the mechanism analyzed above with a simple three-generation model. By the time the immigrant workers retire and collect Social Security, they typically have raised children who are then contributing taxes to Social Security and thereby balancing out the parents' receipts, just as is the case with native families. In this way there is a one-time benefit to natives because the immigrants arrive without a generation of elderly parents who might receive Social Security.

Immigrants are not a complete cure for the Social Security problem, simply because the numbers of immigrants that might conceivably be allowed by any likely US policy are limited. But the extent to which immigrants can be at least a partial remedy is easily underestimated. One reason that Social Security taxes per worker are as high as they now are is that − contrary to the impression that the anti-immigration lobby tries to leave − the country has admitted very few immigrants in recent decades, far less as a proportion of the population than in the decades around the turn of the century (see chapter 3). If additional immigrants to the extent of a quarter of our labor force had been admitted, say, the Social Security tax per worker would be almost a quarter lower than it now is.

The data showing immigrant fertility not to be high relative to native fertility may please some who worry (without cause) about a "population explosion." But in this context it should be noted that the fewer children immigrants have, the fewer persons there are in future decades to support their parents and others. This issue would be less pressing if the US were to move toward a self-financed retirement system and away from a pay-as-you-go Social Security system, but by the same token immigrants would thereby lose some of their attractiveness to natives because there would be less current welfare burden for them to help pay for.

Even if one favors replacing the Social Security program with private pension plans, immigration would still be of benefit, because the obligations to all those persons who are already covered by Social Security will surely be honored by the US government, and immigrants would be contributing to the liquidation of that body of obligation.

Summary

The effects in the years after arrival of an average immigrant family upon the income of an average native family, through the cost of welfare payments and schooling as well as through the benefits of the taxes paid by immigrants, are estimated from the 1976 Survey of Income and Education. From the time of entry until about 12 years later, immigrants use substantially less than do native families of such public services as welfare and unemployment compensation payments, food stamps, Medicare, Medicaid, and schooling for children, largely due to less use of Social Security because of the youthful age of immigrants. Later, immigrant use becomes roughly equal to that of natives. By the time the immigrant family retires and collects Social Security, it typically has raised children who are then contributing taxes to Social Security and thereby balancing out the parents' receipts, just as happens with native families. In this way there is a one-time benefit to natives because the immigrants arrive without a generation of elderly parents who might receive Social Security. After about three to five years, average immigrant families earn as much as average native families and thereby pay as much in taxes as do native families; subsequently they earn more and pay substantially greater taxes.

The net balance of the two forces − taxes paid and services received − has a positive effect on natives in every year. That is, immigrants contribute more to the public coffers than they take from them. When looked at by natives as an investment, similar to such social capital as dams and roads, an immigrant family is an excellent investment worth somewhere between $15,000 and $20,000 in 1975 dollars, even calculated with relatively high rates for the social cost of capital. (This is to be compared with mean yearly native family earnings of about $11,000 in that year.)

Data from Great Britain, Canada, and Israel confirm the key data concerning the US: Immigrants use little services, and pay substantial taxes, relative to natives.

Afternote: About the SIE Sample

The sample data used for the estimates made in this chapter also are the basis for estimates and analyses in other chapters. Therefore the data will be discussed in some detail.

The 1976 Survey of Income and Education (SIE), carried out by the US Bureau of the Census, gathered information on the 1975 incomes and use of social services by 158,500 households, stratified in such a manner as to include more-than-proportional numbers of households with children living in poverty, and is available on a set of tapes. The survey coverage is good, because only 7300 households refused interview. All households with foreign-born heads (about 15,000) constitute the main sample used in this work. A random subsample of about 11,000 native-American households drawn from the entire sample is used for comparison purposes.

The native sample was drawn with four systematic starts, so that the means of the subsamples may be compared as a quick check of sample variability.

Persons in private and public institutions such as nursing homes and hospitals were not included in the SIE survey.

Puerto Ricans are not included in the immigrant group because they are US citizens. As a separate group they may be of interest, but they are not relevant to the social decisions to which this book pertains.

It is not known how many illegals are in the sample of immigrants, because no question indicates such status. But given the relatively small numbers compared to the total of immigrants in the US, and given the relatively small number of persons of Mexican and Caribbean origin in the sample, it is doubtful that illegals could in any case have much of an effect in the overall results. Similarly, there is no question in the questionnaire that indicates whether a person is an "economic" immigrant, a "family completion" immigrant, or a refugee. But one may presume that many of the Cubans, and many of the Russians and Poles who entered subsequent to 1965 or 1970, are refugees.

Families with female immigrants married to male natives are excluded from the main analyses for the following reasons: Imagine a male immigrant who marries a female immigrant and has children. It is reasonable to view the effects of the couple plus their children as the full effects of the male's and female's immigration. Now imagine that the same male and female had instead married natives who would otherwise have married each other, and that both families are now counted in the immigrant sample. Though there is no more total effect on natives' income than before, on average, the results would show twice as much effect, which would be double-counting. We can get rid of most of the misleading double-counting by counting only male-immigrant-head and single-female-head families.[11] (Because the numbers of male and female immigrants are not the same − the number of female immigrants in the childbearing ages, all in all, is somewhat greater than the number of males − the procedure is not perfect. But the numbers are close enough for most practical purposes.)

The family rather than the household or the individual seems to be the appropriate unit of analysis, for several reasons. It is on the basis of family needs that public welfare, aid to families with dependent children, and similar transfers are received. Also, children are attached to both parents where present, rather than to just one of them. Furthermore, the earnings of the various members tend to be pooled by the family in consumption as well as for assessment of income taxes. The household (though in most cases it is identical to the family) is not such a long-lasting unit with respect to other nonrelated earners, nor is income so likely to be pooled within it, or transfers to be based upon it.

Associated with this reasoning is the decision to consider single immigrant women as a unit of analysis. A woman who immigrates single and then marries an immigrant disappears as an independent economic entity, and her impact is then through the family unit. For a single woman, the opposite is the case, and hence for unmarried adults, both males and females are included as separate families, without there being double-counting.

The status of persons born abroad who spend some or much of their pre-adult years in the US poses interesting questions. The most important issue concerns whether these persons and their families should be included in overall calculations for the immigrant family population. On the one hand, the presence of these persons is the direct consequence of social policies to admit immigrants; on the other hand, these persons are not likely to show the effects of the immigration experience. Luckily for the clarity of our analysis, however, practically none of these persons appear in the cohort samples for the first ten years or so after entry, because there is not sufficient time for them to become heads of families, and these newer cohorts dominate present-value calculations of the impact of immigrants.

NOTES

1 In a paper received too late to be thoroughly considered here, Jensen (1987) reported a careful study of 1960, 1970, and 1980 census data showing an increase in poverty among new immigrants, while poverty among natives fell. Poverty relates to both services used and taxes paid. It is not clear, however, what light that *trend* throws upon the *state* of transfers between immigrants and the public coffers, or what the explanation is.

2 If the aged do come, they do not qualify for public retirement funds.

3 George Gray of the Census Bureau, who was in charge of the SIE survey, said that there is no obvious explanation for the reporting of 1975 earnings and services used by the cohort who entered in 1976. The earnings could be earnings abroad, but the services could not be so explained. The likeliest explanation in his view is confusion on the part of the interviewers; the interviewers were not instructed specifically on this matter.

4 Additionally, discounting for a quarter century and more reduces the meaning of contemporary events attached to these persons.

5 Again, the fact that Social Security is "earned" is not relevant in this context. Whether a payment is "earned" or is "charity" refers to the legal and ethical obligations between persons. Our focus here is only on whether certain flows do or do not take place.

6 US Department of Health, Education, and Welfare, "Statistics of Public Elementary and Secondary Day Schools," Fall 1975, table 2.

7 Persons in the institutional population among natives and within the various immigrant cohorts are not included in the SIE sample. We can be sure, however, that such persons are found in larger proportions among natives because the elderly constitute a large part of that subpopulation. But given that less than 1 percent of the population is in institutions, implying an average annual expenditure of perhaps $60 per person in total (even less for public expenditures), the matter may safely be neglected.

8 US Department of Health, Education, and Welfare, "Medical Assistance (Medicaid) Finances Under Title XIX of the Social Security Act," Publication no. (SRS) 76-03150, NCSS Report B-1, December 1975.

9 The distribution can be partially estimated from these data (and it is done in chapter 13) but unfortunately the raw original data are coded to "$50,000 or more" for individuals and "$75,000 or more" for families despite the fact that the raw data included actual figures for the highest-income families. (Top-coding here is intended to avoid disclosure; top-coding was also done for data on assets such as value of home, and liquid assets.) Therefore, it is conceivable that two groups with the same calculated mean income from our data would actually pay different amounts of taxes (a) because distributions of families with the same mean income can pay different amounts of taxes; and (b) due to top-coding, the actual means can be different though the calculated means are the same.

10 The average immigrant may here be considered to be like the average taxpayer, subject to adjustments to come.

11 Comparisons have been made of married-couple families with (a) only the male an immigrant, and (b) only the female an immigrant, to see whether including only the males introduces bias. Direct comparisons holding entry-date and/or age of immigrants are inappropriate because the female immigrant's husband is, on average, several years older than the male immigrant. With this in mind, the comparisons do not indicate any major difference. Perhaps most convincing, adding the families with the female immigrant only to the general sample does not much affect the results.

6 How Much Welfare and Public Services do Immigrants (and Natives) Use?[1]

Conceptual Framework of Welfare Income Receipt
The Sample and Data
Results
Rule-of-Thumb Decision Analyses
Summary and Conclusions

The previous chapter disproves that immigrants are a burden upon natives because of the welfare services they use. The age distribution of immigrants implies less use of Social Security, by far the most expensive program among the various public services. This chapter studies whether, *aside from* Social Security, immigrants have a tendency to receive more welfare payments than do natives with the same general characteristics.

To put the matter more technically, the previous chapter discusses the *unconditional* amounts of payments and services that immigrants receive, relative to the amounts natives receive, as part of the cost−benefit analysis of taxes and transfers. This chapter analyzes the effect of various characteristics − especially the fact of being an immigrant, all else equal − upon the receipt of public welfare funds. That is, unlike the previous chapter, which was purely a cost−benefit assessment, this chapter seeks to understand the mechanism. The chapter also attempts to cast some light on how various background characteristics might be used as criteria for immigration policies so as to benefit the native residents of the country of immigration.

It is crucial to keep in mind that this chapter deals only with welfare payments *other than* retirement allowances such as Social Security and Medicare. In an analysis that includes Social Security, immigrant families are immediately seen to receive far less on average than do native families simply because immigrants tend to come when they are young, and the few aged immigrants are not entitled to Social Security. Retirement transfers are excluded from this chapter because they differ fundamentally from

Immigrants' and Natives' Use of Welfare and Services 133

welfare payments; the determinants of eligibility for and use of retirement programs are mainly age rather than indigency. For similar reasons, services such as schooling are also excluded from the analysis in this chapter.

Before beginning the main analysis for the US, let us take notice of some recent Canadian data. Table 6.1 shows that, except for Asians who arrived between 1975 and 1979, the proportions of Asian and UK immigrant families and singles who are below the poverty line − and presumably receiving some welfare assistance − are much lower than for the Canadian-born. The results for the recent Asian immigrants may partly reflect the

Table 6.1 Percentages of Asian- and UK-born immigrants and of Canadian-born population below low-income cut-off levels

	Period of immigration	Observation point	
		1971	1981
Economic families below low-income cut-off levels			
Asian-born	1975−9	n.a.	21
	1970−4	n.a.	11
	1966−71	27	9
	1961−5	13	9
UK-born	1975−9	n.a.	8
	1970−4	n.a.	7
	1966−71	12	7
	1961−5	7	7
Canadian-born	−	20	13
Unattached individuals low-income cut-off levels			
Asian-born	1975−9	n.a.	41
	1970−4	n.a.	28
	1966−71	42	28
	1961−5	26	33
UK-born	1975−9	n.a.	29
	1970−4	n.a.	27
	1966−71	28	27
	1961−5	19	29
Canadian-born	−	43	37

n.a. − not applicable
Source: Basavarajappa and Verma, 1985, pp. 35, 36

experience of Vietnamese refugees. But in any case, the data for Asian-born families who arrived earlier suggest that in time these more recent immigrants will also have relatively low proportions in poverty. That the Asian-born families do eventually suffer less poverty than Canadian-born families is shown by the results for the same families observed in 1971 and then in 1981. Of course the low proportions of immigrants needing welfare assistance derive directly from their age distribution as well as their educational distribution. But age composition is a fundamental fact about immigrants, and must be taken into account in all thinking about immigration policy.

For general interest, figure 6.1 shows the proportions of Southeast Asian refugees receiving cash assistance at various periods after entry into the US.

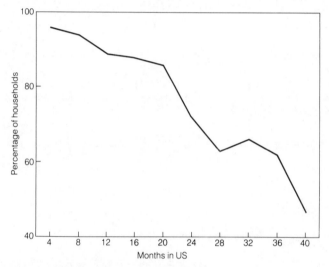

Figure 6.1   Southeast Asian refugee households receiving cash assistance by length of residence in the United States
Source: Caplan, 1985

Conceptual Framework of Welfare Income Receipt

Welfare transfer payments and other services may usefully be thought of as a kind of income, because they are "in-come" in nature, and also because there is likely to be substitution among earned income, unearned income, and transfer income. Therefore, the appropriate conceptual framework for thinking about transfer income is likely to be similar to that for other income receipts. The main lines of influence are set out in figure 6.2. The reasoning behind these lines of influence, which will be mirrored in the regression equations to come later, will probably be obvious to the reader, and therefore I shall not tax your attention with a discussion of them. One key supposition of the structure of assumptions may now be considered established theoretically: "There is substantial evidence that families decide whether to apply for or remain on welfare in an economically rational fashion" (Lyon, 1977).

The Sample and Data

The data come from the 1976 Survey of Income and Education (SIE), discussed in the afternote to chapter 5.

The dependent variable, TRANS, includes the following welfare payments: public welfare, aid to dependent children, unemployment compensation, supplemental security, and food stamps. Again, it should be noted that such retirement allowances as Social Security and Medicare are excluded from the analysis; inclusion of them in any cost−benefit framework immediately indicates that immigrant families receive much less than do native families. Schooling also is excluded, which goes in the other direction than Social Security though it is less sizable. The number of children associated with a given family structure is the number *at home aged 18 or under*. Data on total children in the family were not collected by the Survey of Income and Education.

Results[2]

The results for this study are unusually difficult to communicate because of the large number of family-structure subsamples that must be examined, and because it is not obvious which group(s) should be compared with which. I shall attempt to bring out the main results in a few short tables drawn from the most general analysis, the regression which is derived from the entire sample of natives and immigrants, male-headed and female-headed, with various numbers of children or none. That regression examines the effects of all the relevant variables, and includes family earnings on the assumption that the flow of reverse causation is not important. Its results, mainly that family structure has a dominant effect, are reproduced here as follows:

Basic regression results: Dollars received = $3189 (the amount received if the base case − female, single, 3+ children, low education, young,

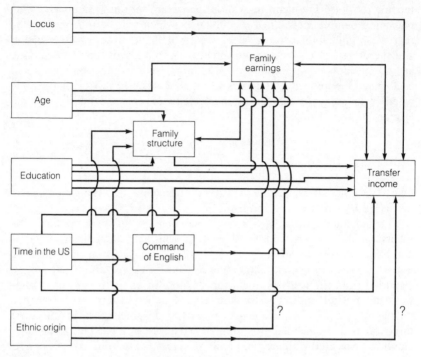

Figure 6.2   Conceptual framework of welfare income receipt
Source: Survey of Income and Education, 1976

native born): *less* $1566 if female, single, two children; *or less* $1885 if female, single, one child; *or less* $2403 if female, single, no children; *or less* $2057 if male, married, 3+ children; *or less* $2192 if male, married, 2 children; *or less* $2163 if male, married, 1 child; *or less* $2222 if male, married, no children; *or less* $2316 if male, single, no children; *or less* $166 (if immigrant, 1970−4); *and plus* $60 (if immigrant, 1965−9); *and plus* $54 (if immigrant, 1960−4); *and plus* $13 (if immigrant, 1950−9); *and less* $158 (if immigrant, 1920−49); *and plus* $23 (per year of family head's age); *and less* $31 (head's age squared); *and less* $43 (per year of family head's schooling); *and less* $0.02 (family earnings); *and plus* $133 (if English is poor).

The same information is presented in different form in table 6.2. Transfer payments received by families with various other structures are compared to the base-case family that includes a native young single female head and three or more children, the mother having minimum education and zero earnings. That base-case family collects much more welfare — on average $3169 — than do male-headed families and families with fewer children. An otherwise-similar female-headed family with only two children gets $1623, or $1566 less than the base-case family; and so on. The range among all families other than female-headed with two or more children is only $431. Regressions with other subsamples show that these amounts remain much the same no matter how the analysis is conducted. (The absolute amounts received by the various groups are also shown in table 6.2, but it should be remembered that these amounts are for families with the poorest earning-power characteristics and the lowest earnings.)

Turning to the central interest of this book, table 6.2 shows that the effect of being an immigrant is quite small and inconsistent, as long as English-language ability is held constant; this may also be seen in all the other regressions with the total sample and subsamples. Poor English increases welfare receipts by $133. The amounts received apparently are smaller for immigrants than for natives for the first five years, then rise to the native level after the first five years, and then are again smaller than for natives among those in the country the longest. However, the variation in results among the various runs suggests that the small observed variation is due to sampling error; from a practical point of view it does not matter much one way or the other, however.

Welfare receipts has an elasticity of −0.46 with respect to family earnings. And the elasticity with respect to schooling is −0.61.

Another way of looking at the results of the same regression with respect to the issue of immigrant effects is by comparison of various immigrant groups with the "average" native family. These results, shown in table 6.3, make clear that once other variables are held constant (especially family structure) the fact of being an immigrant rather than a native is of no consequence from the point of welfare receipts.

The overall picture, then, suggests that family structure is by far the most important factor, and the factors most directly related to being an immigrant — time in the US, and English ability — are not of great importance compared to family structure and perhaps earnings and schooling. The next step is to check further into this matter.

Because English ability is closely related to being an immigrant, a regression was run that is similar except for leaving out the variables for English ability. The average amounts received by each immigrant cohort (except for the oldest) are higher than when English ability is not held constant, but the pattern still does not indicate that immigrants receive more welfare transfers than natives, *ceteris paribus*.

The entry-cohort effects are not meaningfully different for the two sex subgroups. But the fact that in both groups the earliest and latest entrants

Table 6.2   Effect of family structure upon welfare receipts (excludes Social Security)

Family structure	Receives ($)	Amount less than base case ($)
Base case:		
Single mother, 3+ children, low education, young, low earnings, native-born.	3,189	n.a.
Instead:		
Native mother, 2 children	1,623	1,566
Native mother, 1 child	1,304	1,885
Native mother, 0 children	786	2,403
Married natives, 3+ children	1,132	2,057
Married natives, 2 children	997	2,192
Married natives, 1 child	1,026	2,163
Married natives, 0 children	967	2,222
Instead (otherwise same as base case):		
Immigrant arrived: 1970−4	3,023	166
1965−9	3,189	0
1960−4	3,243	−54
1950−9	3,202	−13
1920−49	3,189	0
Poor English	3,322	−133
Additional year of age	−	23

are relatively low in transfers received suggests that the observed effect is not due to sampling variation.

In the subsamples where English ability is held constant, being an immigrant has no observable effect. And even English ability does not have a strong enough effect to be consistent across the various categories, given the size of our samples.

Because family structure is so important a determinant of transfers, we want to know how immigrants and natives differ in this respect. Table 6.4 shows the distributions of families by family structure, for natives and for the various immigrant categories, in various age classes. (The variable for children indicates only the number of children *under 18 at home*.) By inspection of the data for those who came in 1970−4 and for natives, we see that in their early years in the US − which are the most important

Table 6.3   Effect of immigration upon welfare receipts (excludes Social Security)

Family situation	Receipts in transfers (excluding Social Security) each year ($)
Base case:	
Average family	514
Instead (otherwise same as base case):	
Immigrant head arrived: 1970−4	348
1965−9	574
1960−4	568
1950−9	528
1920−49	356

Table 6.4   Percentage of female-headed families with children in various subgroups

Immigration date	Two or three children Age of mother			One, two, or three children Age of mother		
	18−44	18−53	18+	18−44	18−53	18+
1970−4	6.4	5.9	5.6	8.3	7.7	7.3
1965−9	7.5	7.1	6.2	12.5	11.5	10.0
1960−4	7.0	7.2	6.0	9.9	9.6	8.0
1950−9	9.4	8.5	6.9	12.7	11.7	9.3
Natives	7.7	7.0	4.7	10.6	9.5	6.3

years with respect to policy decisions about admitting immigrants, because of the time preference for resources − among immigrants there are fewer female-headed families with several children, and for this reason (along with others) the welfare burden (even aside from Social Security and other transfers to the aged) is less for this group of immigrants than for natives. We also see that, among natives (by comparison of the 18−44 and 18+ columns) the category of single females without children is heavily dominated by older women who are likely to be relatively heavy users of welfare, rather than being young women who are relatively light users of welfare. (And of course in the background is the fact that the younger are more likely than are the older to be paying taxes for others' transfers.) After immigrants are longer in the US, family structure becomes more similar to natives of the same age.

Here it is important to recall that in any overall accounting of the effect of immigrants, age structure is all-important. Because immigrants come when young, they do not use much Social Security and Medicare, which are far and away the most important causes of welfare transfers in dollar terms. Therefore, immigrant families use much less total welfare services than do natives, on average, even including schooling; this is analyzed in detail in chapter 5.

Rule-of-Thumb Decision Analyses

The full analysis above, if done soundly, provides the basis for a guide to selection of immigrants with lowest predicted use of transfer payments and social services (to be combined with a similar analysis of highest predicted earnings), if the society decided that this were to be an appropriate policy. But decision-makers may decide that it is desirable to use some characteristics and not others as criteria for admission. That is, it could conceivably make sense to allow (among non-family-completion and other special-category immigrants) only male professionals below age 40 from Hong Kong, until all applicants have been taken, then only males with 16+ years of schooling below age 40 from Italy, and so on. But decision-makers are likely to decide that discrimination by sex or ethnicity is unacceptable, and they may therefore ask about the predictions for only "acceptable" criteria such as education and age,[3] though recognizing that this might result in implicit differentiation by ethnicity, sex, etc. We cannot know in advance what variables might be called for. Education, however, seems the likeliest, and therefore we shall make analyses for that variable by itself. And because the timing of transfer payments is very important − payments in the early years in the country must sensibly be weighted much more heavily than payments in the later years − the analysis must take account of entry date.

A flexible and informative format is to compare separate groups defined by amount of schooling and date of entry (or native status). Table 6.5 shows the transfers received by such groups. It is obvious that by admitting persons of the three highest education levels − or even more so, just the two highest education levels − the resulting immigrants would receive much less welfare services than the average for natives. In fact, by comparing the mean receipt of $554 per family for all families to the amounts received in 1975 by, for example, the two highest education groups in the 1970−4 cohort ($180 and $127, respectively) − which are $364 and $417 less than the average of natives − we see that the receipt of transfers by these

Table 6.5   Average dollar value of welfare transfers to immigrant groups by years of entry and schooling

Years of entry	Average welfare transfers ($) Years of schooling							
	0	1–4	5–8	9–11	12	13–15	16	17+
1970–4	632	933	955	868	650	337	154	95
1965–9	1,443	1,157	1,299	1,187	656	376	329	215
1960–4	819	1,659	885	1,019	637	456	77	144
1950–9	809	1,122	822	1,055	547	448	331	170
1920–49	601	413	349	470	306	411	228	199
Natives	1,273	852	613	747	455	431	237	166

Average value for total sample = $500.

immigrant groups is very low by any absolute as well as relative standards.

Rules based on family structure would not seem feasible because of the difficulty of predicting at entry what future family structure will be. Therefore, they will not be considered here.

Summary and Conclusions

Because of their size, transfer payments now have great influence on the US economy and on public budgets. Retirement allowances are most important. Because immigrants usually come when they are young, and because they are not entitled to benefits, they contribute to Social Security funding but do not draw benefits for many years (at which time their children are paying in to support them). Immigrants are obviously beneficial to natives from that point of view. But other welfare payments might be more heavily used by immigrants than by natives. The aim of this chapter is to analyze the determinants of welfare payment use, with special attention to the role that being an immigrant plays.

Family structure – and especially the presence of female-headed families with two or more children – is the most important determinant of the rate of use of transfer payments (aside from Social Security, Medicare, and other retirement transfers). Immigrant families are represented proportionally in the high-use categories.

Earnings and schooling also influence welfare receipt. Immigrants do not differ greatly from natives on average in these categories, so there is no important differential effect on welfare receipt.

The fact of being an immigrant has little or no effect on welfare receipt when the other relevant variables are held constant.

Differential admission rules based on occupation or education could result in immigrants receiving much less welfare than natives, and almost none in absolute amounts. Such rules could be effective agents of discrimination from the point of view of native income.

NOTES

1 Using my SIE data set, Blau (1984) estimated the *probabilities* of families receiving public assistance as well as the amounts. Her methods were quite different than mine, but the results were fundamentally the same, which suggests that the results are quite robust.
2 Additional detail may be found in my longer technical paper on this subject (Simon, 1982b).
3 The presentation of this material does not imply that the writer endorses any such plans; under most conditions he probably would not. Rules based on occupation, which would lead to similar results, would seem to have fewer objections.

7 The Effect on Natives' Incomes from Immigrants' Use of Capital Goods

Introduction

It is said: Immigrants are a bad deal for natives because they obtain benefits from capital they do not pay for, and thereby either reduce the amount of available capital per native or force natives to pay for capital to equip the immigrants. This is the standard Malthusian objection to additional persons applied to immigrants, and it has been developed at length by Usher (1977).[1]

By applying to the UK the theoretical apparatus discussed below developed by Yeager (1958), Borts and Stein (1966), and Berry and Soligo (1969), together with a complex set of assumptions about the "returns" to capital obtained by the immigrants, Usher calculated that capital dilution results in a large burden upon UK natives. The same conclusion would surely follow for the US and other developed countries if one followed

Usher's method, which I also proposed earlier (Simon, 1976). But that method seems to be fundamentally flawed.[2]

This chapter proposes a new approach; and the new approach implies much less diminution of natives' incomes in the US by way of the use of existing capital by immigrants than does the earlier approach.

The core of the present approach is separating the analysis of "production" capital used by immigrants on the job from the "demographic capital" used in such services as schooling and medical care. A key element in the production−capital analysis is a distinction between the effects in the private and public sectors. And a key element in the analysis of demographic capital is recognizing that the benefits which immigrants obtain from existing public capital are irrelevant to natives unless there is a congestion effect (i.e. unless the capital is not a true public good), because the existing public non-demographic capital's cost is sunk. This approach allows us to avoid several difficult issues, including the assessment of corporate taxes, which render Usher's and my own earlier approach unworkable.

The last section of the chapter prior to the summary discusses the effects of immigrants in their role simply as additional people upon the cost of private and social capital, and upon the likelihood that infrastructure such as roads will be created by the society.

Throughout most of this book I try to write in such a fashion that persons who are not professional economists can catch the drift of the discussion even if some or all the details are obscure. Regrettably, the argument in the present chapter is sufficiently technical that I have not found a way to render it into language that will be accessible to the non-economist, though I hope that the summary at the end conveys the gist of the argument.

Before beginning discussion of the effect of capital dilution, we should take note that in an industrial society capital *may not* be diluted by immigration, in which case the discussion of capital dilution's effect is nugatory. Economists have long speculated that immigration boosts capital investment (Kuznets and Rubin, 1954; Easterlin, 1968; Kmenta, 1966) and have observed a correlation between the two variables. But they did not identify the direction of causation. Baker (1987) effectively used the ARIMA method on Australian data from 1900 to 1975 to eliminate trend and reduce cyclical variation. The raw data are in figure 7.1. He finds "strong evidence that fluctuations in net migration cause subsequent fluctuations in per capita investment in the same direction" (p. 7). And Baker quantified the relationship: "a 1% increase in population leads to an 8% increase in investment ... the increase in private non-residential capital stock attributable to a 1% increase in population through migration is a little over 1%" (p. 13). That is, production capital is not diluted by immigration, and perhaps it is intensified.

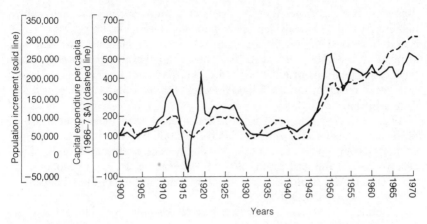

Figure 7.1   Capital expenditure and population growth, Australia, 1900–70
Source: Lyle Baker, 1987

The Effect of Immigrants through Dilution of Production Capital

A useful piece of theory which has been explained by Yeager (1958), Borts and Stein (1964), and Berry and Soligo (1969) – Y–B–S–B–S hereafter – has as its main thrust the distributional effect of immigration. But Y–B–S–B–S also teach this lesson about the aggregate effect: if immigrants do not own the physical capital with which they work, natives as a whole benefit from additional immigrant workers because of the additional returns earned by the capital[3] (though "workers" qua workers lose because their wages go down). If the immigrants share in the returns to the capital, however, this source of gain is partly forgone by natives, and may lead to a net loss to natives. Therefore, we must estimate how much of the returns to capital immigrants "capture" through various mechanisms which may give all residents (including immigrants) a share of those returns. ("Capture of capital returns" means simply the receipt of payments made to owners of private productive capital through dividends, interest, and rent.)

Before proceeding to the Y–B–S–B–S argument itself, let us note that the theory may be unnecessary because production capital may not be diluted much by immigration. Immigrants may bring with them, and then invest, sufficient capital to maintain the level of capital per worker. Some relevant evidence comes from Australia. In fiscal year 1983–4, principal applicants (excluding refugees) brought with them an average of 32,000 Australian dollars (Norman and Meikle, 1985, p. 122). If one excludes "spouses, fiancés, dependent children, etc.," the average is considerably higher. And if one considers only non-family-reunion immigration, the average is considerably higher still. "Business immigrants" brought an average of $383,600 Australian. In Canada, immigrant families *other than* business immigrants brought a mean of $17,841, and business immigrants brought a mean of almost $400,000 each (Samuel and Conyers, 1985). (For a bit more detail, see chapter 12.)

The mean capital imports into Australia and Canada would seem to be of the same magnitudes as the $30,000−$50,000 bandied about as the cost of the physical capital needed to equip the average worker in the US. (The relative cost of physical capital may be expected to fall as the economy is transformed away from heavy manufacturing and as human capital becomes relatively more important.)

A campaign by Canada to attract business people from Hong Kong as immigrants, in light of the future transfer of Hong Kong to China, is also relevant. Such persons can be expected to bring with them enough capital not just to maintain the level of production capital per worker in the economy but to considerably increase it. And Belize in 1986 announced that citizenship can be purchased with a $25,000 bond, half of it "non-refundable." This out-and-out payment of $12,500 to the government surely more than outweighs any government expenditures for social infra-structure on account of the immigrant family, as discussed in the latter part of this chapter. (In this connection one wonders: If it makes economic sense for the state of Kentucky, say, to advertise for businesses to move there from other states, why is it not at least as sensible to advertise for investors from abroad to move to Kentucky?) And while on the subject of capital importation by immigrants, fees as a means of allocating admission need mentioning, a subject discussed in chapter 16.

To return now to the Y−B−S−B−S argument: If immigrants do not share in the returns to capital and yet are paid their marginal product, the total returns to capital are increased by more than the sum by which natives' wages are lowered; hence immigrants increase the average income of natives under these conditions. This proposition is shown in figure 7.2, taken from Berry and Soligo, where the triangle X approximates the gain to natives as a whole,[4] on the assumption that immigrants do not share in the returns to the existing capital.

It is important to note that the Y−B−S−B−S effect is caused simply by there being in the economy more people of the same sort as already make up the labor force; it has nothing specifically to do with the additional people coming from outside the country. (The Y−B−S−B−S theory is discussed more lightheartedly in the concluding chapter.)

One wonders how the Y−B−S−B−S theory applies to human capital, along with its application to physical capital. That is, are there returns to

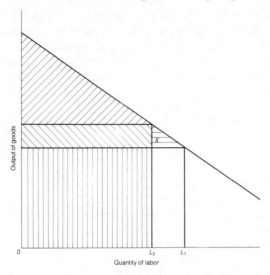

Figure 7.2 Total returns to capital from immigration labor
Source: Berry and Soligo, 1969

native human capital when immigrants arrive, in analogous fashion to the added returns to native-owned physical capital? The answer is not simple. On one hand, a native Nobel laureate can increase his/her productivity if there are more excellent immigrant graduate students to work with. On the other hand, a foreign Nobel laureate may immigrate and compete for excellent native graduate students, reducing the native Nobel laureate's productivity. Complication arises from the fact that an immigrant represents "labor" as a producer good that cooperates with native human capital, but also represents "capital" with which native "labor" may cooperate. A full answer would require more delicate analysis than is appropriate here.

Estimating satisfactorily the capture by immigrants of returns to the capital with which they work requires that we be very careful about our aim. We must agree that the main subject of inquiry is the creation of additional output by the immigrant, together with the effect of that output upon natives. It is crucial to recognize that the effect of this additional output upon the immigrant him/herself is not part of the inquiry; Usher (1977) implicitly did not see it that way, nor did I earlier (1976), and therefore those analyses simply estimated the proportion of the *total* capital in the society from which immigrants might receive returns either because the capital is owned privately or because of corporate and other taxes on the returns to capital. And of course the effect on the persons remaining in the land of emigration is not part of the subject here.

Let us (adopting Usher's notation, diagram and general approach for comparability) begin by noticing that the output with an immigrant present $(Q + \Delta Q)$ is divided among four types of recipients — the immigrant employee, the native employee, the owner of the industrial capital, and the "government," just as is output without the immigrant (Q).

$$Q = Q_p + Q_g = wL_p + rK_p + Q_g, \text{ where } Q_g = T$$
$$Q + \Delta Q = Q_p + \Delta Q_p + Q_g + \Delta Q_g = (w + \Delta w)(L_p + \Delta L_p) + (r + \Delta r)(K_p + \Delta K_p) + (T + \Delta T)$$

where: Q = native output

p = the private sector

g = the government sector

w = the wage level without immigrants

L = labor force without immigrants

r = after-tax rate of return to capital without immigrants

K = capital stock without immigrants

T = total taxes without immigrants

Δ = an incremental quantity, the difference between the situation with immigrants and the situation without immigrants.

Define private capital's "share" as the amount that owners of capital receive after taxes.[5] The only way that an immigrant working in the private sector can receive some part of the additional private product (ΔQ_p) other than his own marginal product is through corporate tax payments. Therefore, we must inquire into the nature of the additional corporate taxes paid due to the immigrant's arrival and consequent additional outputs (ΔT_p).

The total corporate plus personal additional taxes (ΔT) that are paid as a result of the immigrant's entry are as large as, or larger than, the additional expenditures (e.g. on schooling and transfer payments) that occur because of the immigrant. (Chapter 5 finds that immigrant families pay considerably *more in personal taxes alone* than they receive in services, largely because of their age composition.) There seems no reason not to think of the corporate taxes that go toward the extra services for immigrants being in the same proportion to total taxes as they are for all persons' services. That is,

$$\Delta T \geq \Delta G \text{ and } \frac{\Delta T_p}{\Delta T} = \frac{T_p}{T}$$

If so, there is certainly no loss to natives by way of corporate taxes, that is, ΔT_p is at least as large as the cost of any services to immigrants that it might be expected to cover.

Some of the additional corporate tax payments may be thought of as rent on publicly owned capital used by the corporation, e.g. roads and dams. And part of this rent may be obtained by immigrants, in similar proportion to other citizens. But what matters here is the effect on natives. And the amount of such "rent" obtained by natives is likely to be of a small order of magnitude, by any test, and hence we shall ignore it for convenience (though noting that excluding this factor reduces the apparent benefit of immigrants for natives, because we are ignoring a flow that benefits natives).

The argument so far adds up to the fact that because $\Delta T \geqslant \Delta Q_g$ – which allows us to say that $\Delta T = \Delta Q_g$ and $T = Q_g$ – we can rewrite

$$Q_p = wL_p + rK_p$$

$$Q_p + \Delta Q_p = (w + \Delta w) (L_p + \Delta L_p) + (r + \Delta r) (K_p + \Delta K_p).$$

If all immigrants worked in the private sector, and we could therefore treat the government sector simply as if it were a foreign company that sells inputs to the private sector, the $Y-B-S-B-S$ analysis would now follow without further ado; immigrants would benefit natives as a whole by the celebrated tiny "triangle" in figure 7.1.

(As noted earlier, however, this analysis may be nugatory because immigrants may bring enough capital with them so that private capital dilution may be small or even non-existent, and the damage to "workers" is thereby reduced.)

But some immigrants work for the government. In that sector there are no returns to capital that natives capture but that the immigrant in question does not capture. A key magnitude, then, is the proportion of immigrants who work for the government. The resulting loss to natives must be compared to the gain from the "triangle" in figure 7.1 in order to calculate an overall assessment of the impacts of immigrants through their involvement with the capital used in production.

Calculation of the Capture of Capital Returns

Let us begin by taking notice, as Usher demonstrated by expanding equation (7.1a) in a Taylor series, that the "triangle" of additional returns to the owners of private capital is small when the immigration is realistically small; in the context of Usher's Cobb-Douglas production function example the gain is about $1/219$ of the loss in labor income to natives. And in the simulation I made for Israel (Simon, 1976) I found that a flow to immigrants of less than a 2 percent share of the returns to private capital is enough to offset the triangle. Therefore we can ignore the $Y-B-S-B-S$ effect for practical purposes.

But we must still deal with the public sector, and to do that we must estimate the returns to public capital, by analogy with private capital. Let us make the simplifying assumption that the capital/labor ratio is the same in government as in industry. And for reasons of data availability let us estimate the ratios we need from the non-financial sector and project them to the entire private sector. Let

W_p = the amount paid for their labor to employees in wages and salaries in industry, \$1387 million in 1979

R_p = returns received after corporate taxes by owners for the use of their capital, \$390 million

Q_p = total of employee compensation and after-corporate-tax returns to capital = $W_p + R_p$ = \$1777

$\dfrac{R_p}{Q_p}$ = proportion of total returns that go to capital = 22 percent.

On standard neo-classical assumptions we may identify the share received by labor as labor's marginal product. That is, the marginal immigrant receives (100 percent $-$ 22 percent $=$) 78 percent of the total additional product due to him or her, and the owners of the capital receive 22 percent. One could also use Usher's stylized $25-75$ percent split without changing the result. If there are no returns to native capital owners, and the immigrant receives the returns to both his/her labor and to the capital he/she works with $-$ as is the case in the public sector $-$ there is a loss to natives due to the capital-dilution effect. If we assume the production function is Cobb$-$Douglas and the quantity of capital is temporarily fixed, returns to natives would fall by an amount roughly equal to the amount implied by the 22 percent gain to capital owners in the private sector.[6]

To allow for the immigrants working in the public sector we must know the proportion working in the public sector. From the cohort of persons who arrived between 1965 and 1970 there were, in 1970, 38,427 males and 24,256 females, out of 454,872 and 309,090 total males and females in the cohort employed of age 16 or over, who worked for the government $-$ that is, 8.22 percent among immigrants, which is much lower than the 16.5 percent among natives (US Department of Commerce, Bureau of the Census (1984, table 93). The proportion is not likely to change much from census to census). For those who arrived $1960-4$, $1955-9$ and $1950-4$, the percentages are 6.8, 7.8, and 9.0 respectively, say an average of 8 percent for all immigrants. (Immigrants arriving more than 20 years earlier are not very relevant to a policy analysis.)

If we now assume that the returns to the capital with which the government-worker cooperates are obtained by the worker, and assume also the same capital/labor ratio and average salary as in industry, then 8 percent of the total returns to private plus public capital due to immigrant production flow to the immigrant. This is a far cry from the 58 percent figure that emerged from Usher's method applied to the UK. And even this amount is dubious conceptually (see note 6).

A more meaningful comparison is the total amount that natives' income falls relative to the total income of the immigrants (or relative to the total additional product caused by the immigration). The effect on natives' incomes may be calculated as

> Effect on natives = total income of natives afterwards minus total income of natives before the immigration = total output after minus total output before minus amount going to immigrants in wages and capital capture
> $$= (Q + \Delta Q) - Q - [\Delta L(w + \Delta w)] - \phi[K(r + \Delta r)]$$
> $$= \Delta Q - \Delta L(w + \Delta w) - \phi[K(r + \Delta r)$$
> $$= L(\Delta w) + K(\Delta r) + \Delta Kr + \Delta K \Delta r$$
> $$- \phi[K(r + \Delta r)],$$

using

$$\Delta Q = [L + \Delta L)(w + \Delta w) + (K + \Delta K)(r + \Delta r)] - [Lw + Kr],$$

where ϕ is the proportion of the returns to capital captured by the immigrants.

Because $L(\Delta w)$ and $K(\Delta r)$ are, as discussed above, of similar size (and the positive difference between them from the point of view of natives just about offsets the negative differences to be calculated in this paragraph) and because $\Delta K = 0$ we can simplify

> Effect on natives = $-\phi[K(r + \Delta r)]$,

which is the total amount of the returns to capital that is captured by immigrants. In Usher's calculation $\phi = 0.58$, whereas in this calculation $\phi = 0.08$.[7] The ratio of the effect on natives to the total wages of immigrants, then, is $\phi[K(r + \Delta r)]/\Delta L(w + \Delta w)$. With Usher's ϕ this ratio is about 0.199, whereas with my ϕ the ratio is about 0.028 using Usher's 75 percent share to labor, or 0.025 using the above-calculated 78 percent share to labor.

The difference in implications of Usher's calculation and the present calculation is large no matter whether you look at it from the point of view of an average native or an average native worker, or from anyone else's pocketbook point of view. And a major policy implication of this difference appears in a more global analysis of the effects of immigrants. In the US the balance of taxes and welfare expenditures alone is such that natives gain considerably from the presence of the average immigrant family, on a present-value basis. On Usher's calculation, the loss to natives on the production-and-income side would be more than the tax-and-welfare gain. Using the present calculation this is not so; the average immigrant family's net contribution to the public coffers far outweighs the loss to natives through capture of the returns to capital by the immigrants.

Calculation of the Burden of Demographic Capital-Widening due to Immigrants

The above section discussed the dilution of public and private "production" capital as it affects the earnings of natives. We must now also consider that segment of public capital which immediately yields consumption benefits to natives and immigrants and whose use is subject to congestion. This category includes such "demographic capital" as schools and hospitals; more immigrants cause more of such capital to be needed if service standards are not to fall. On the other hand, such pieces of public capital as the Statue of Liberty, intercity highways, and space exploration installations rather clearly are public goods whose use by natives is unaffected by the number of immigrants. Some capital assets, such as new highway construction around cities, and new physics laboratories at universities, are difficult to classify, but luckily most public capital falls pretty clearly into one or another of these two categories.

A simple yet satisfactory rule of thumb[8] is that most chunks of federal capital are true public goods, while most chunks of local and state capital are demographic and are subject to congestion. The state-and-local category corresponds fairly closely to the sub-categories of education and hospitals and local roads. It would probably be possible to work with the latter functional sub-categories rather than with the federal-versus-state-and-local distinction, but the results would not likely be substantially different.

It may help to begin with this question: Why does any community allow additional US citizens to move into its tax district without assessing penalties to pay for the public capital the person will use? A church or synagogue or mosque that builds a new building free-and-clear from savings or current assessments is likely, for a number of years after the new building is built, to assess new members a special building fee over and above the dues that old and new members pay. Why does not a city or state do the same (assuming away legal impediments)? The answer would seem to be that new members of a community pay enough "rent" for the capital they use to cover a considerable part of the additional cost of any necessary capital-widening on their account. This is because — in contradistinction to a religious congregation that finances a new building without borrowing — a large part of public capital is built with borrowed money. And with the taxes they pay, new dwellers help cover the service of this debt to an extent that the new dweller is not a burden on old dwellers in this respect.

If all "demographic construction" (called just "construction" or "struc-ture" hereafter) schools and hospitals and other local facilities whose size must be affected by numbers of people served were financed by consol bonds, the immigrants would be paying more taxes than if they were to use only structures built for them and were to pay for the entire cost of that construction which they used. (Underlying the latter part of this sentence is a model of constant immigration under simple conditions. For now this is only to be a vague statement of self-financing as the benchmark.) This is simply because immigrants and their descendants would then be paying a full share for all new construction, and would also be paying for some structures that had obsolesced and were no longer in use; in the same way they would be paying more than their share for partly obsolesced structures.

On the other hand, if all construction were paid for on current account, immigrants would underpay for the structures they use, because they would then be paying only a part (on a per-person basis equal to natives) for the new construction necessary for them, whereas all of the cost of the new construction would be due only to them (causing increased expenditure by natives for the new construction) while not paying at all for existing structures they would be using. And if the number of immigrants were small and there were little or no physical depreciation, natives would pay almost the entire cost of structures for immigrants. This point comes out clearly if we notice that if all construction depreciated in, say, a year (which would be the same as the tax period), natives would not be paying extra for immigrants; all persons would then be on an equal footing. But because depreciation takes longer than the current period, and since natives have already built and paid for much of the construction they need, the additional construction for immigrants would be more than natives would otherwise need by a proportion greater than the proportion of new immigrants to natives. This last statement has not been stated rigorously, but perhaps it will be made to seem convincing by this third possibility: With respect to construction financed by debt, if the length of life of construction equals the length of time during which the debt is serviced, asssuming equal payments on the debt each year (that is, assuming that the building collapses the day it is paid off), and if the cost of construction and quality of buildings remain constant, then an immigrant would exactly pay for the cost of new construction built on his/her account. S/he would (a) pay a full share for new buildings built this year, just as does the average native; (b) pay nothing for buildings no longer in use; and (c) pay in proportion to the remaining length of life for older buildings still in service.

Therefore, we wish to combine the necessary elements – length of capital life, length of bond period, and proportion of capital financed by borrowing, together with the cost of equipping an average immigrant family – into an estimating equation, then develop estimates of the elements and calculate the burden on immigrants per immigrant family. We begin with notation:

C = cost of construction per unit of capital necessary for an additional family

c = proportion of construction cost financed by bonds

LL = length of life of a unit

b = bond period

$p_t = p_{t-1}$ = total number of native families

U = units of capital in existence, and $U/p = 1$

ΔU = units of capital built

$I = 1$ = number of immigrant families

E = expenditures

T = total taxes paid

0 = superscript indicating "without immigrants"

I = superscript indicating "with immigrants"

$$U_t = p_t$$

$$\Delta U_t^0 = \frac{1}{LL} (U_{t-1}^0) \tag{7.1}$$

in steady state, the number of units necessary to replace units worn out after LL years,

$$E_t^0 = \left(\frac{1}{LL}\right) U_{t-1}^0 \, C \tag{7.2}$$

expenditures each year in steady state without the immigrants

$$E_t^I = \left(\frac{1}{LL}\right) U_{t-1}^0 \, C + C \tag{7.3}$$

expenditures with the immigrants, because one additional unit is needed for I

$$T_0^t = \left(\frac{1}{b}\right) cE_{t-b} + \left(\frac{1}{b}\right) cE_{t-b+1}^0 \ldots \left(\frac{1}{b}\right) cE_t^0 + (1 - c)E_t^0 = E_t^0 \quad (7.4)$$

in steady state, that is, total taxes yearly without immigrants, which includes debt payments on capital financed in the past plus current payments on the portion of current expenditures not financed by debt[9]

$$\frac{T_t^0}{p_t} = \frac{\left(\frac{1}{LL}\right) U_{t-1}^0 C}{p_t} = \left(\frac{1}{LL}\right) C \text{ because } U^0 = p_t = p_{t-1},$$

taxes per person without immigrant in steady state

$$T_t^I = E_t^0 + \left(\frac{1}{b}\right) cC + (1 - c)C \quad (7.5)$$

because the first payment on the financial portion of an additional unit will be made in t, plus the non-financial portion's payment

$$T_t^I - T_t^0 = \left(\frac{1}{b}\right) cC + (1 - c)C \quad (7.6)$$

increase in total taxes in t due to immigrant

$$\left(\frac{1}{b}\right) cC + (1 - c)C - \left[\frac{\left(\frac{1}{LL}\right) pC}{p + 1}\right]\left[\left(\frac{c}{b}\right) + 1 - c - \left(\frac{1}{LL}\right)\right] \quad (7.7)$$

is the increase in burden of taxes to natives in first year because of an immigrant. The total burden over the years to natives is

$$b\left[\left(\frac{1}{b}\right) - \left(\frac{1}{LL}\right)\right]cC + (1 - c)C \quad (7.8)$$

because of the payment on the financed portion of the increment until the additional unit is paid for. Aside from that, an immigrant henceforth simply constitutes a proportional increase in the society and has no effect on natives.

The overall magnitude of the loss to natives (if there is one) depends, of course, upon (a) the proportion of capital investment that is funded with debt, (b) the cost of the units, and (c) heavily upon LL, the length of life of the structure. If *LL* is very short the immigrants pay for structures already destroyed, even if the bond period is also short. If the length of life is very long, then the cost to natives approaches the full cost of the structure. Therefore, to estimate the effect, we need to know C, b, LL. I/p may be assumed to be very small.

We may estimate C in several rough ways which, if they generally agree, should allow us to have some confidence in the composite estimate. (1) The current replacement value of government capital (structures, inventory and equipment) at the end of 1975 was estimated by Kendrick (1976) to be $981 billion. Dividing that total among units of government on the basis of capital outlay figures by the various units of government plus tentative depreciation yields an estimated $781.5 billion as the value of state and local capital at the end of 1975. Its ratio to GNP in the corresponding year was 38.1 percent. Therefore, one may assume that it costs an amount equal to that proportion times the representative family's income to equip an additional representative family.

A rough check for this magnitude uses the observation that employment in the state-and-local sector is 14.1 percent of all employment. If the capital–output ratio is 2 in that sector, as in the rest of the economy, and if average income is the same in that sector as in the rest of the economy, then a sum equal to 2×14.1 percent $= 28.2$ percent average income is the value of such capital for the average family. The value in 1979 for the median primary family (*US Statistical Abstract, 1980*, p. 451; the mean value for all families would be better, but will not be sufficiently different to make a difference here) was $(0.381 \times \$19,684) = \$7500$.

The average bond period b is 10.53 years. The estimate of this quantity as well as the quantities referred to in the next two paragraphs are described in the appendix to Simon and Heins (1985).

The average length of life of state-and-local capital is 14.76 years.

The value of c, the proportion of the capital that is financed with debt, is approximately 0.62.

Calculating now by inserting the necessary values into e.g. (7.8) the average cost to natives of equipping an immigrant family, assuming the family's income and use of services is average, is then $4172 or 21 percent of a year's income for a family, without discounting the future payments.

Leaving aside the relatively minor adjustments called for by a variety of factors working in both directions, let us now hit upon one-fifth of the average family's income as the cost of equipping the community for an additional average family's needs. For this to be an appropriate estimate for an average immigrant family requires that it be of the same size and composition as an average native family. This is probably not so far from the fact as to make inappropriate an estimate of 21 percent of family income.

Table 7.1 Public capital investment and financing in the United States, 1977

Authors' preferred magnitudes for 1977: $ billions at current dollar c. 1977

(1) Interest on debt, all governments, 1977 (*Stat. Abs. 1979*, p. 284)		46.3
(2) Education, total capital outlay, all governments (p. 288)	9.237	
(3) Highways, total capital outlay, all governments (p. 288)	12.565	
(4) Health and hospitals, total capital outlay, all governments (p. 288)	2.667	
(5) Sewerage, total capital outlay, state and local (p. 288)	4.208	
(6) Local parks, recreation, construction only, state and local (p. 288)	0.769	
(7) Housing, urban renewal, construction only, state and local (p. 288)	1.085	
(8) Air transport, construction only, state and local (p. 288)	0.513	
(9) Water transport, construction only, all governments (p. 288)	0.571	
(10) Local utilities, total capital outlay (p. 288)	6.107	
(11) Miscellaneous ('all other' is source, p. 288), state and local	6.124	
(12) Total, lines 2−10		43.876
(13) Increase in debt, 1976 to 1977, all governments (pp. 292 and 254)		73.8

Some other magnitudes for comparison

(14) City governments, capital outlay on construction and equipment (p. 307)	10.690	
(15) State government, capital outlay or construction (p. 300)	13.620	
(16) State governments, capital outlay on equipment (p. 300)	1.477	
(17) State and local governments, total construction put in place (p. 773)		30.855
(18) Private construction, total, put in place (p. 773)		135.826
(19) Gross private, fixed domestic investment, non-residential (p. 437)	190	
(20) Gross private fixed domestic investment, residential (p. 437)	92	
(21) Gross private fixed domestic investment, total (p. 437)		282

Note: The capital-outlay data are gross, whereas the appropriate data are smaller net data.
Source: Simon and Heins, 1985

This cost is certainly not negligible even when the returns to government capital from government immigrant workers are added in. However, it is considerably smaller than the present value of the stream of taxes paid and transfers received by immigrants − which is perhaps 1.5 or 2 times the average native family income (chapter 5) − and hence the capital effect does not dominate the overall impact of immigrants upon natives' standard of living, which is positive on balance even without considering the positive effect on natives through increased productivity. The latter element almost surely swamps all other effects in the long run (chapter 10).

Effects on the Cost of Capital and Provision of Infrastructure

So far this chapter has considered the effects of immigrants by way of "diluting" the quantity of capital available to natives, and also by burdening natives with the cost of increasing the stock of capital made necessary by the immigrants. Now we briefly consider an effect going mostly in the other direction, the effects of immigrants upon the cost of infrastructure capital, private and public.

There is a body of evidence indicating that capital is used more efficiently in larger communities. For example, less capital is needed for a given amount of productivity per person in larger cities (Alonso and Fajans, 1970, summarizing Mera, 1970, and Fuchs, 1967; Alonso, 1975). This jibes with the fact that wages are higher in bigger cities (although it is entirely possible that people are paid more in larger communities because they do more or better work, implying that the "efficiency wages" are the same in all communities; see chapter 2). Furthermore, interest rates are lower in bigger cities (see Riefler, 1930; and Stevens, 1978, for a review and a study of bank rates) which implies that capital is cheaper in bigger cities. In sum, the evidence suggests that one can get more output from a given capital investment where there are more people. And immigrants increase the population. (See also p. 177 below.)

The effect of immigrants on the cost and supply of capital shades into the effect on productivity through economies of scale, a subject which is discussed in the following chapter.

The effect of additional persons on the supply of capital is most marked with respect to social-overhead capital such as roads, which are crucial for the economic development of all countries; the effect of additional population is sharply positive, especially in less-developed countries. The connection between population density and the system of transporting goods, people, and information runs in both directions. On the one hand, a dense population makes a good transportation system both more necessary and more economical. Having twice as many people in a village implies that twice as many people will use a wagon path if it is built, and that twice as many hands can contribute to building the path. This is what happened in Europe and especially in England, where the increase of population density made it worthwhile to create and improve transport facilities.

On the other hand, a better transportation system brings an increased population, and probably leads at first to higher birth rates because of a higher standard of living, though later the birth rates drop. Furthermore, good transportation connections are likely to reduce a village's death rate, because the village is less vulnerable to famine.

The opposite condition, population sparsity, makes traveling slow and difficult. This is how it was near Springfield, Illinois, when Abraham Lincoln was a lawyer "riding the circuit" of courts.

Traveling was a real hardship − so real that the words of old lawyers, describing early days, become fresh and vivid when the circuit is the subject. "Between Fancy Creek and Postville, near Lincoln," wrote James C. Conkling, "there were only two or three houses. Beyond Postville, for thirteen miles was a stretch of unbroken prairie, flat and wet, covered with gopher hills, and apparently incapable of being cultivated for generations. For fifteen or eighteen miles this side of Carlinville, the country was of a similar character, without a house or improvement along the road. For about eighteen miles between South Fork and Shelbyville, there was only one clearing. I have traveled between Decatur and Shelbyville from nine o'clock in the morning until after dark over a country covered with water, from recent rains, without finding a house for shelter or refreshment." (Angle, 1954, pp. 102−3)

Indeed, the economics of transportation and communication systems, as well as those of public safety, have been the main reason why immigrants have been desired in places like the frontier country in the US, Canada, and Australia.

Glover and I (1975) made a cross-national study of the relationship between road density and population density, and we found that relationship to be very strong. Population growth clearly leads to an improved transportation system, which in turn stimulates economic development and further population growth.

Population density brings a similar increase in the efficiency of communications, easily seen in a comparison of cities of very different sizes. For the same price to the reader, the daily newspaper is much larger, and supplies much more information, in a big city like Chicago than in smaller Illinois cities like Champaign-Urbana. And the price charged an advertizer − whether a department store or an individual seeking employment − is lower per 1000 readers reached in a large city than in a small city, a clear benefit of a larger population.

Summary and Conclusions

There are three questions about capital and immigrants we must answer: (1) The effect through the private capital with which immigrants work, (2) the effect through the public capital with which immigrant workers work, and (3) the effect through public "demographic" capital used for consumer services by immigrants.

The first question, the issue of private capital dilution, can be dealt with swiftly. Yeager, Borts, and Stein, and Berry and Soligo, showed that while workers as workers lose through lower wages due to immigrant workers, owners of capital benefit by something more than the workers lose, and hence per-person native income goes up. The overall effect is small by Usher's and my reckonings, perhaps 1 or 2 percent, small enough to ignore safely.

If all immigrants worked in private industry, and if there were no corporate income taxes, we could now also forget about the entire subject of production capital dilution. Usher tackled jointly the second and third of these problems mentioned above by analyzing the properties of public and private capital for the UK. (I did much the same for Israel, independently.) Usher arrived at the conclusion that 58 percent of the returns to all the capital they work with are captured by immigrants even if they own no private capital, and therefore immigrants are a major burden upon natives. And of course in Usher's model there is no positive effect of immigrants upon productivity to counterbalance the effect Usher calculated. But I argue that this method used by Usher, and by me earlier, is not sound.

In contrast to Usher's large estimate, the method given here estimates that immigrants capture the returns from only 8 percent of the production capital they work with, which is the governmental production capital only; the result is a loss to natives of perhaps 2 percent of an immigrant family's income each year, about the same size as the gain to natives through the private capital with which immigrants work. The two factors trade off, and therefore both may safely be ignored.

The cost to natives of equipping the immigrant family with "demographic capital" – schools, hospitals, and local roads – depends upon the cost of such equipment, the proportion financed by bonds, the average length of life of the capital, and the average bond life. Heins and I (1985) developed an estimating equation, and calculated that the overall cost to natives in 1975 dollars is $4172, about a fifth of one year's income of an average family. This is not insignificant in magnitude. But this amount is considerably smaller than the benefits of immigrants to natives through their relatively low use of welfare services and their relatively high contribution of taxes, as discussed in chapter 5.

Afternote: The Effects of Immigrants' Remittances on Residents of the United States

Perhaps the least substantial objection to immigrants is that the remittances they send out of the country cause loss to natives. Yet a Commissioner of the INS has written: "There are other costs which are hidden and un-measurable. It is estimated that illegal aliens send about $3 billion each year out of the country" (Chapman, 1976, p. 7). And the Select Commission staff said: "[L]arge-scale removal of US dollars in the form of remittances constitutes a drain on the economy and adversely affects US balance of payments" (Staff Report, p. 518).

A remittance does no more harm to natives than does the same sum spent within the US, and may under some circumstances cost natives less; on this point I believe that there is general agreement among economists. Consider first the possibility that the remittance is not spent in the home country or elsewhere, but rather is simply hoarded in the form of dollar bills under a mattress. In that case, the US is a clear beneficiary because it has gotten the labor of the immigrant without having to trade any goods for it; if never spent, the dollar bills are simply cheap printed paper. The more likely possibility is that the foreign recipient spends the dollars on imported American goods: the result then is just the same as if the immigrant bought the goods in the US and carried them home. There are no other possibilities than these two. Converting the dollar into other currencies only lengthens the chain of events.

One may wonder about the political effect of another country holding a great many dollars. The mercantilist theorists before Adam Smith, and more recently Charles de Gaulle, thought that a stock of another country's money implied power over that country. Such a hoard (and a consequent payment "deficit" elsewhere) may create the basis for righteous jawboning of one country by another. But it constitutes no real power. Rather, the debtor tends to have power over the debtholder, as the world saw in the 1980s with respect to many debtor nations, because the creditor is dependent upon the goodwill of the debtor for repayment. Furthermore, the longer the dollars are held outside of the US, the more the benefit to the US from being able to have the use of the resources before they are claimed.

To dramatize the matter: If you will give me $1000 in cash now, I'll be delighted to give you a written promise to pay you back any time you like. I can deposit the $1000 in a money market fund and receive the interest. What will you gain? You have no power to force me to do your will in other ways, because the instant that you ask for your money I will draw the cash from the money market fund and pay you back, leaving me a gainer. And so it is with remittances. They do no harm to the US, while enabling less-well-off persons abroad to obtain some purchasing power and assets that they would not acquire otherwise.

One might wonder about the effect upon the balance of payments. The analysis must be given because the issue comes up frequently in discussion, but at the end I will conclude that the analysis is not very important because the forces it encompasses with respect to immigrants have little effect upon the balance of payments. Therefore, you may sensibly choose to proceed to other topics.

If many dollars are sent abroad, and foreign business people do not want to trade other currencies for the dollars because they do not find desirable US export goods at prices set at the current rate of exchange, the dollar will fall in value relative to other currencies. There are two possible ill effects of this fall. First is the psychological effect that the US may seem to be "slipping"; perhaps because a fall in a country's currency may also stem from a relative decline in productivity. If one is terribly concerned about his/her country's image in this way, then one may be willing to pay a price in forgone trade benefits to avoid the image, as de Gaulle apparently was. The other ill effect is that the dollar will not buy as much abroad as if it had greater value. But opposed to these ill effects is the benefit that it is easier to export if the dollar has a relatively low value, an effect sufficiently desirable that at various times countries have gone to extraordinary lengths to reduce the value of their currencies.

The simple fact is that some people will wring their hands when the dollar goes up, and some will wring their hands when it goes down. But the level of the dollar will not depend upon the presence of immigrants or their remittances; it will depend upon monetary and productivity variables in the US and in other countries. The balance of payments simply is not an important issue with respect to immigrants, nor are remittances generally.

NOTES

1 This chapter is an abridgement of an article written jointly with A. James Heins (1985). The criticism of Usher's work in this chapter is also a criticism of a very similar piece of work that I did independently (1976) with respect to Soviet Jewish immigrants into Israel.

2 Please keep in mind that the effects through capital use are only a small part of the overall impact of immigrants upon natives. Chapter 10 shows that the net balance of transfer payments and taxes is positive and outweighs the negative capital-effects calculated in this chapter. This implies a positive net effect of immigrants' effect on natives, even without including the positive effect of immigrants upon productivity.

3 This line of reasoning implicitly assumes that there is only one wage-earning occupation in the economy. If this assumption is relaxed, the analysis is more complex. If there are a variety of occupations in the economy and the immigrants come with the same distribution of skills as the natives, then the result is the same as if there is only one occupation. But if the immigrants come with a different distribution of skills, then the occupations that are disproportionally represented by the immigrants suffer worse wage declines than do the average. The Vietnamese immigrants of the late 1970s, and the Cuban immigrants of 1980, seem to have a broad spectrum of occupations, whereas Mexican immigrants seem to be largely semiskilled laborers. If the immigrant brings skills not found in the economy, there are the same sorts of overall gains to trade that occur in international trade of goods. An effect analogous to gains to trade was suggested in conversation by Mark Rosenzweig, and to my knowledge has not been analyzed. I have no feeling for how important it may be, but to the extent that it operates, it has a beneficial effect on the average native's income.

4 In response to a comment by Herbert Grubel, a note is necessary about how the quantity of human capital brought by the immigrants affects the logic and calculation. The key element is the proportion of the total returns that go to native owners of physical and organizational capital with which the immigrants work. This proportion is influenced by the amounts of human capital — and also non-human capital such as tools — that the immigrants bring with them. If human capital is relatively important, and physical and organizational capital are relatively unimportant in an industry — say, civil-engineering consulting — then natives are affected relatively little from the inflow of immigrants. Presumably the trend in this direction is indicated by the increase in "labor's" share over time. But it does not seem to me that the $Y-B-S-B-S$ model needs adjustment for the explicit introduction of human capital. Even the providers of unskilled labor supply that service out of a stock of human capital. And the organizational capital provided by native firms is really a form of human capital. All this is satisfactorily embodied in the $Y-B-S-B-S$ model.

Another point is relevant here: The reader may wonder how the representative immigrant's share of capital, and the returns to it, change with years of residence in the US and whether this is reflected in the model. With time, the immigrant's share rises to 100 percent, of course. But this is counterbalanced by purchase payments by immigrants that are necessarily financed by higher-than-average saving. Hence, the result should be the same whether this is explicitly shov n in the model, or implicitly, as in the present model.

5 As is shown by the long but fruitless controversy over the extent to which corporate taxes are passed on to the consumer, it would not seem sensible to discuss whether or not the taxes paid to government — corporate and "indirect" — come out of capital's "full" share; no definition of "capital's full share" would seem to make sense here, as these two considerations show: (1) No economist would like to argue that capital's "full" share is capital's "just" share. (2) The share of the output that capital would receive if government took no taxes is not obviously different (to a first approximation) from the share that capital receives after taxes, because one may assume that capital owners will bid up to the margin for the immigrant's services, and their marginal calculations will include the tax

effects of hiring the immigrant. So there is little reason to argue that the share which capital actually receives is different from an idealized "capital's share" or "capital's full share."

6 More generally, valuation of output in the public sector is necessarily a vague concept here, as elsewhere. It is hard to imagine how one would identify the marginal product. And the concept of returns to capital is hard to pin down here. Perhaps a more sensible approach would be to have the returns to capital flow to all citizens, in which case the loss from immigrant capital dilution would be far less than suggested in this analysis. Luckily, however, the subsequent analysis is so broad that it would not be affected by any conceivable way of construing valuations here. Distributional effects are not considered here. In thinking about that topic, it is important to keep in mind that the "worker" class actually obtains much of the returns to capital through capital ownership by pension funds.

7 Usher's calculation is for the UK, whereas this calculation is for the US, but that difference is a minor matter in this context.

8 Fred Giertz suggested this.

9 We shall assume that the bonds are amortized at a constant rate over their lives, that is, equal payments in each period until retirement, in the manner of a house mortgage. In reality, a given bond issue is floated with bonds of a variety of maturities, and the tax burden declines as more bonds are retired. But the constant-amortization assumption surely is a satisfactory approximation for our purposes here.

8 The Effects on Technology, Productivity, and Native Human Capital

Effects through Increased Market Size
The Statistical Evidence
Effects from More Creators
Human Capital Externalities
Immigration, Technology, and the Competitive Future of the United
    States
Conclusions

By far the most important determinant of society's standard of living is the productivity of the persons who make the goods and services. Productivity depends, of course, upon education, upon the amount of capital with which people cooperate, and upon the efficiency with which that capital is used. But productivity also depends upon the types of techniques, including the organizational practices, that are in use at any given time. And the types of techniques that are in use are heavily influenced by the state of technical knowledge ("technology").

Knowledge stems from human minds. Minds matter economically as much as, or more than, mouths or hands. In the long run, the most important economic effect of immigrants is their contribution to our stock of useful knowledge. And this contribution is large enough in the long run to dominate all the other benefits and costs of immigration.

Immigrants affect productivity and technology partly in their special role as immigrants by stimulating both natives and immigrants to create new ideas that are some combination of the transported ideas and the ideas that are already present in the country of immigration. They also carry ideas and practices from one society to another, thereby inducing natives to adopt the transported ideas.

The special role of immigrants as idea-transporters has been important throughout history. In earlier times the movement of people was crucial in transmitting ideas from one part of the world to another. As Childe tells us about ancient Greece, after it had learned some tolerance:

The foreigners in each city brought with them and celebrated there their own native cults. With these religions and their officiants spread new brands of magic and philosophy − a motley horde of quacks, astrologers, alchemists, and oracle-mongers − competing with traditional beliefs and legitimate sciences. (1942, p. 254)

In the Middle Ages, migrants carried new techniques such as advances in weaving looms from one part of Europe to another, thereby fructifying the countries where they settled. An American example is "the introduction of rice culture in South Carolina ... it was accelerated, if not determined, by the skills of the slaves brought into Carolina, many of whom had grown rice in Africa. Apparently the masters didn't know the first thing about rice culture" (Gallman, 1977, p. 29). And though modern communications greatly speed the transfer process, the movement of people is still very important in transmitting knowledge. For example, I learn much about Japanese and Indian ways of doing things from informal conversations with colleagues from those countries. Such is the stuff of advance in civilization and economy.

One of the nicer minor benefits of immigration is that it increases cultural variety − for example, Chinese and French restaurants. But the benefits of variety go beyond consumer and esthetic pleasures and spill over into economics. Variety is a key ingredient of invention. A minor illustration: as a result of eating in a Chinese or French restaurant and comparing the food with what he or she cooks, a homemaker or commercial chef or food processing executive may get new ideas for recipes combining the foreign and native cuisines. This minor example has often been writ large in major cultural advances produced by, or from contact with, immigrants. Because scientific and technical inventions occur inside the mind, and the process is not visible on the outside, it is difficult to find convincing examples of this process at work. But the process is quite obvious in artistic and religious meldings of many traditions.

Foreign graduate students raise the productivity of American university scientists as well as directly contributing their own new ideas and discoveries. Herbert Simon (along with Jean-Jacques Servan-Schreiber, 1987) recently wrote about the situation in his field of computer science, as well as engineering, the two most popular fields for foreign students. "As of 1986, more than 300,000 foreign students were enrolled in American universities, 60 percent of them in technical fields." They account for between 52 and 68 percent of the graduate students in the various engineering programs, and 40 percent in computer science.

In direct fiscal terms, these foreign graduate students are subsidized by American taxpayers to the tune of more than half their tuition. But, Servan-Schreiber and H. Simon say,

Foreign students give the United States as much as they get. They are paying for their long years of study with the most precious and expensive commodity, the one the United States most needs today: more knowledge, new knowledge, provided by their labor. By working in American laboratories for three to seven years of postgraduate study, thousands of young experts are by themselves the most efficient "subsidy" to scientific progress and economic development.

And as to whether the foreigners are displacing Americans, they quote Karl Willenbrock, director of the American Society for Engineering Education: "We don't have too many foreign students, we have too few Americans. We are not attracting enough of our students into graduate schools."

A second way in which immigrants affect productivity is in their roles as "regular people" who participate just like natives in the production process and then buy goods with their incomes. As consumers they increase the total volume of goods produced, which increases productivity through "learning by doing." As workers they increase productivity through their contributions to the development of improved production processes and better products. Both of these mechanisms will be discussed at length below, because of their great importance in a complete assessment of the overall economic effect of immigrants, even though the evidence concerning these mechanisms comes from observations on the society as a whole rather than from observations of immigrants alone.

Please keep in mind that this chapter (drawn mainly from Simon, 1981b) discusses *partial* effects of immigrants upon natives' standard of living, effects through changes in technology and productivity. This chapter does not take up the *overall* effect of more immigrants or more people generally; that topic is tackled in chapter 10, after this and the previous chapters have laid the groundwork for that overall assessment.

Effects through Increased Market Size

Immigrants constitute additional consumers who increase the size of the markets for the goods which they consume. Economists since William Petty and Adam Smith have understood the importance of market size in influencing productivity. As market size increases, greater efficiency results from the division of labor and other well-known economies of scale. In more recent years, economists have also noted the influence of the size of the market − the total output and income in a market − on the decision to invest. As Nurkse put it:

The inducement to invest is limited by the size of the market ... the level of productivity depends − not entirely by any means, but largely − on the use of capital in production. But the use of capital is inhibited, to start with, by the small size of the market. (Quoted by Agarwala and Singh, 1963)

Increased size of market also implies an increase in research development and in the adoption of new technology, with a consequent improvement in technique in practice. The modernization in technique occurs partly through the simplest route. New physical capital embodies newer technology. But additionally, as Schmookler (1962a, b, 1966) and Simon and Sullivan (1989) have shown, increased investment in an industry induces a higher level of invention in the industry, as indicated by patents and technical book publications.

Yet many economists − at least in this century − have refused to draw the most obvious conclusion from this line of reasoning: additional people lead to faster economic growth by increasing the size of the market, and hence boosting productivity and investment. That is, it is obvious that an increase in the labor force is overwhelmingly important in increasing total output and hence the size of the market. Nevertheless, very few writers have drawn the conclusion that in this way more people have a positive effect on overall economic well-being. Sometimes it is said that additional population growth no longer is beneficial through this mechanism because the market is *already* large enough. But no evidence in support of that qualification has been given. Thus, this qualification may be regarded simply as an unsupported opinion.

Let us now consider the matter in more sober detail.

The theory

The greater efficiency of larger-scale production stems from (1) the ability to use larger and more efficient machinery, (2) the greater division of labor in situations where the market is larger, (3) knowledge creation and technological change, and (4) improved transportation and communication. We shall take up each of these factors briefly, then in more detail. Please keep in mind as we proceed that there is no easy and neat distinction between increases in productivity due to increased knowledge, and increases in productivity due to economies of scale; they are interdependent, and both are accelerated by population growth and therefore by immigration.

(1)   A bigger population implies a bigger market, all else equal. A bigger market promotes bigger manufacturing plants that are likely to be more

efficient than smaller ones, as well as longer production runs and hence lower setup costs per unit of output.

(2)   A larger market also makes possible a greater division of labor and hence an increase in the skill with which goods and services are made. Adam Smith emphasized the importance of the division of labor and used the example of pinmaking; his predecessor Petty made the same point when talking of the advantages of a large city like London over a small city, and he used a more vivid example than did Smith:

[T]he Gain which is made by Manufactures, will be greater, as the Manufacture it self is greater and better . . . each Manufacture will be divided into as many parts as possible, whereby the Work of each Artisan will be simple and easie; As for Example. In the making of a Watch, If one Man shall make the Wheels, another the Spring, another shall Engrave the Dial-plate, and another shall make the Cases, then the Watch will be better and cheaper, than if the whole Work be put upon any one Man. And we also see that in Towns, and in the Streets of a great Town, where all the inhabitants are almost of one Trade, the Commodity peculiar to those places is made better and cheaper than elsewhere. (Petty, 1682/1899, p. 473)

Specialization can also occur with respect to machinery. If the market for its goods is small, a firm will buy multipurpose machines that can be used in the production of several kinds of products. If its market is larger, the firm can afford to buy more efficient specialized machines for each operation.

Larger markets also support a wider variety of services. If population is too small, there may be too few people to constitute a profitable market for a given product or service. In such a case there will be no seller, and people who need the product or service will suffer by not being able to obtain it.

(3)   Economies of scale also stem from learning. The more television sets or bridges or airplanes that a group of people produces, the more chances they have to improve their skills with "learning by doing" − a very important factor in increasing productivity, as many studies show. The bigger the population, the more of everything that is produced, which promotes learning by doing.

(4)   As discussed in chapter 7, a bigger population makes profitable many major social investments that would not otherwise be profitable − for example, railroads, irrigation systems, and ports. The amount of such construction often depends upon the population density per given land area. For example, if an Australian farmer were to clear a piece of land very far from the nearest neighboring farm, he/she might have no way to ship her/his produce to market and may have difficulty in obtaining labor and supplies. But when more farms are established nearby, roads will be built that will link him/her with markets and supplies. Such reasoning lay

behind Australia's desire for more immigrants and a larger population; this was also the case for the American West during the nineteenth century. Public services such as fire protection are other social activities that can often be carried on at lower cost per person when the population is larger.

There may also be diseconomies of increased scale, however, such as congestion. As the number of sellers and activity in, say, a city's wholesale fruit-and-vegetable market increases, transacting one's business may become more difficult because of crowding and confusion. Each additional person imposes some costs on other people by decreasing the space in which the other person can move around, and by inflicting her/his pollution (soot, noise) on other people. Therefore, the more people there are, the less space each person has and the more pollution each suffers from, all else equal. These effects would be felt both in a decreased ease and joy of living and in higher prices due to the higher costs of production caused by congestion. This sort of diseconomy is very much like the concept of diminishing returns from a given acre of land that is at the heart of Malthusian reasoning. Ultimately congestion must occur as long as there is some factor of production that remains fixed in size, be it land for the farmer or market area for the wholesaler. But if that factor can be increased rather than remaining fixed – by building a bigger market or by bringing new land into cultivation – then the diseconomies of scale, especially congestion, can be avoided or reduced.

An example of increasing congestion as population and economic activity increase is found in this news story:

NEW YORK – Lower Manhattan, the financial heart of the country, is suffering from massive hardening of its arteries.

The arteries are the subway tunnels and streets that lie at the base of the commercial center, which one planning organization describes as "the most densely populated square mile in the Western world." Though lower Manhattan probably has more transportation services than any site in the country, much of the time the decayed network is tied into a strangled knot of disruption and delay ...

The potential for total blockage is apparent in the cramped, twisted innards of many lower Manhattan subway stations, compared by one planner to a "rat maze." At the Whitehall Street–South Ferry station, for example, arriving passengers often take several minutes to clear the platform as they wait to mount four-foot-wide stairs to the street ...

Another problem is lower Manhattan's narrow, tangled streets. Laid out by Dutch colonists some 300 years ago, the roads are overburdened with cars, trucks, buses and pedestrians, who are squeezed off even narrower sidewalks. Passage is difficult; parking is almost impossible. One result: Wall Street Mail Pickup Service, a private mail carrier, recently added a second man to its trucks so that one employee can drive around the block while the other makes pickups. (*Wall Street Journal*, 15 October 1984, p. 35)

But such congestion is not a permanent condition. The news story goes on to quote New York's city planners about the situation: "There's nothing wrong with very high density as long as you take care of the transportation design." The subway system in lower Manhattan was built many years ago for a lower level of economic activity. When New York eventually deals with this situation, people on average will probably wind up better off than if the congestion had not for a while increased to the point of discomfort.

The Statistical Evidence

Let's begin our examination of the statistical evidence with an estimate of the overall effects of population size on productivity in less-developed countries (LDCs). Chenery (1960) compared the manufacturing sectors in a variety of countries and found that, all else being equal, if one country is twice as populous as another, output per worker is 20 percent larger. This is a very large positive effect of population size no matter how you look at it.

Now let us move from the national level down to the industry level, and let us shift from LDCs to more-developed countries (MDCs) because most of the available information pertains to MDCs.

In every industry there is some minimum size of factory that must be attained in order to reach a reasonable operating efficiency. But though this is the sort of economy of scale that has been most studied in the past (because of its industrial applications), it is not the economy of scale that is most relevant to population questions.

More relevant are studies of industries as wholes. As mentioned above, it is an important and well-established phenomenon that the faster an industry grows, the faster its efficiency increases – even compared with the same industry in other countries. The most recent and complete analysis is shown in figure 8.1a and b. There we see comparisons of the productivity of US industries in 1950 and 1963, and of UK industries in 1963, with UK industries in 1950 – and also comparisons of US industries in 1963 with those of Canada in the same year. The larger the industry relative to the U. K. or Canada base, the higher its productivity. This effect is very large: productivity goes up roughly with the square root of output. That is, if you quadruple the size of an industry, you may expect to double the output per worker and per unit of capital employed.[1]

The effect Chenery observed in economies as wholes, together with the effects seen in individual industries, constitutes strong evidence that a larger and faster-growing population produces a greater rate of increase in economic efficiency.

The phenomenon called "learning by doing" is surely a key factor in the improvement of productivity in particular industries and in the economy as a whole. The idea is a simple one: the more units produced in a plant or an industry, the more efficiently they are produced, as people learn and develop better methods. Industrial engineers have understood learning by doing for many decades, but economists first grasped its importance for the production of airplanes in World War II, when it was referred to as the "80 percent curve": a doubling in the cumulative production of a particular airplane led to a 20 percent reduction in labor per plane. That is, if the first airplane required 1000 units of labor, the second would require 80 percent of 1000 or 800 units, the fourth would require 80 percent of 800, or 640 units, and so on, though after some time the rate of learning probably slows up. Similar "progress ratios" have been found for lathes, machine tools, textile machines, and ships. The economic importance of learning by doing is very great.

The effect of learning by doing can also be seen in the progressive reduction in prices of new consumer devices in the years following their introduction to the market. The examples of room air conditioners and color television sets are shown in figure 8.2.

The studies discussed above automatically subtract any costs of congestion from the positive effects of scale. But it should be interesting to many readers to know how large the congestion costs are by themselves. If there really are important congestion problems in bigger cities, for example, one

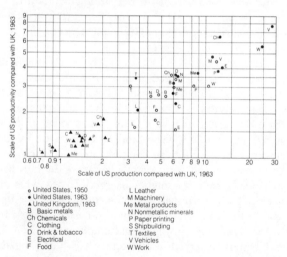

o   United States, 1950   L Leather
•   United States, 1963   M Machinery
▲   United Kingdom, 1963 Me Metal products
B   Basic metals   N Nonmetallic minerals
Ch Chemicals   P Paper printing
C   Clothing   S Shipbuilding
D   Drink & tobacco   T Textiles
E   Electrical   V Vehicles
F   Food   W Work

Figure 8.1a   The effect of industrial scale upon productivity, United States versus United Kingdom
Source: Colin Clark, 1967a, p. 265

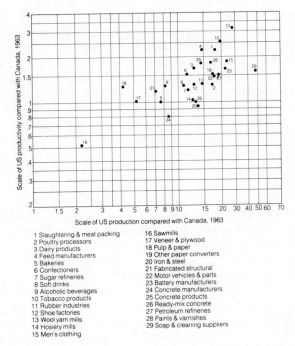

1 Slaughtering & meat packing
2 Poultry processors
3 Dairy products
4 Feed manufacturers
5 Bakeries
6 Confectioners
7 Sugar refineries
8 Soft drinks
9 Alcoholic beverages
10 Tobacco products
11 Rubber industries
12 Shoe factories
13 Wool yarn mills
14 Hosiery mills
15 Men's clothing

16 Sawmills
17 Veneer & plywood
18 Pulp & paper
19 Other paper converters
20 Iron & steel
21 Fabricated structural
22 Motor vehicles & parts
23 Battery manufacturers
24 Concrete manufacturers
25 Concrete products
26 Ready-mix concrete
27 Petroleum refineries
28 Paints & varnishes
29 Soap & cleaning suppliers

Figure 8.1b The effect of industrial scale upon productivity, Canada versus the United States

Source: West, 1963, pp. 18−22

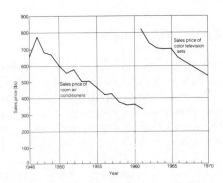

Figure 8.2 Sales prices of room air conditioners and color television sets, 1946−70

Sources: Simon, 1981; adapted from Bass, 1978, pp. 15 and 20

would expect them to be reflected in the cost-of-living data for cities of different sizes. But no strong relationship between size of city and cost of living is apparent. More detailed statistical studies of this evidence reveal that at most there is a tiny effect. The largest estimate is a 1 percent increase in the cost of living for each additional million people, for people living on a high budget; other estimates range downward to no effect at all.

A study by Love (1982) of the relationship of city size to the prices of over 200 individual goods and services found that although more prices go up with increasing city size than go down, for almost every good or service, workers are more productive in the larger cities after the higher wage in bigger cities is allowed for. And the higher incomes in larger cities more than make up for the higher prices, so that the overall purchasing power of a person's labor is greater in the bigger cities (Simon and Love, 1988). This suggests that the disadvantages of congestion are less than the positive effects of greater population (including better communications and more competition) upon the standard of living in larger cities.

In a general study of the costs of manufacturing production, Sveikauskas (1975) found an economically important advantage in efficiency in larger cities. There is also evidence that less capital is needed to produce a given amount of output in larger cities (see p. 162 above). And the cost of capital is lower in larger communities, as measured by bank rates. Another important element is the greater density of communications and transportation networks that accompanies denser population. This may be seen casually in the larger number of radio and television stations in larger cities. Also, Segal (1976) found that metropolitan areas (SMSAs) with populations of two million or more have 8 percent higher productivity than smaller SMSAs, because "economies exist in transport and communications in the very largest cities."

Effects from More Creators

It is a simple fact that the source of improvements in productivity is the human mind, and a human mind is seldom found apart from a human body. Because improvements — their invention and their adoption — come from people, it seems reasonable to assume that the amount of improvement depends on the number of people available to use their minds.

This is an old idea, going back at least as far as Petty in 1682.

As for the Arts of Delight and Ornament, they are best promoted by the greatest number of emulators. And it is more likely that one ingenious curious man may rather be found among 4 million than 400 persons. ... And for the propagation and improvement of useful learning, the same may be said concerning it as above-said concerning ... the Arts of Delight and Ornaments. (1682/1899, p. 473)

More recently, this benefit of population size has been urged upon us by Kuznets (1960).

In contrast, many of the doomsday writers completely omit from consideration the possibility that, all else equal, more people imply more knowledge and greater productivity. For example: "It is difficult to see how any further growth in world population could enhance the quality of human existence. On the other hand, one can readily envisage ways in which further population increments will diminish our well-being" (Brown, 1974, p. 149).

It cannot be emphasized too strongly that "technological advance" does not mean only "science," and scientific geniuses are just one part of the knowledge process. Many technological advances come from people who are neither well educated nor well paid: the dispatcher who develops a slightly better way of deploying the taxis in his ten-taxi fleet; the shipper who discovers that garbage cans make excellent cheap containers; the supermarket manager who finds a way to display more merchandise in a given space; the supermarket clerk who finds a quicker way to stamp prices on cans; the market researcher in the supermarket chain who experiments and finds more efficient and cheaper means of advertising the store's prices and sale items, and so on. The scarcity of additional producers of knowledge, and of their potential contribution to resources and the economy, also is manifest. Nobel prize winner Bethe tells us that the future cost and availability of nuclear power − and hence the cost and availability of energy generally − would be a rosier prospect if the population of scientific workers were larger. Talking specifically about nuclear fusion, Bethe said, "Money is not the limiting factor. ... Progress is limited rather by the availability of highly trained workers" (1976, p. 2).

Still another important element is the greater propensity to produce new ideas that accompanies living in larger cities (Higgs, 1971; Kelley, 1972), and the greater propensity for new ideas and trends to diffuse and be adopted in larger cities (Simon and Golembo, 1967). Just *why* people are more likely to create and pick up new ideas where population is denser is still the subject of sociological speculation, but the evidence for the phenomenon is rather solid.

Students of organizational behavior also tell us that, all else being equal, the larger an organization's resources in numbers of people and amounts of money, the more innovations it will come up with.

"If any one group of variables may be said to stand out among all others as empirically determined correlates of innovation, it is the group of inter-related factors indicating size, wealth, or the availability of resources." A variety of investigators "all conclude that organizational size and wealth are among the strongest predictors of innovation in the sense of readiness to adopt new patterns of behavior." (Mohr, 1969, p. 112)

Even a casual inspection of the historical record confirms this connection between population size and growth of knowledge. There have been many more discoveries and a faster rate of productivity growth in the past century than in previous centuries, when there were fewer people alive. True, 10,000 years ago there wasn't much knowledge upon which to build new ideas. But, seen differently, it should have been all the easier 10,000 years ago to find important improvements, because so much still lay undiscovered. Progress surely was agonizingly slow in prehistoric times. For example, whereas now we develop new materials (metals and plastics) almost every day, it took centuries between the discovery and use of, say, copper and iron. It makes sense that if there had been a larger population in earlier times, the pace of increase in technological practice would have been faster.

Population growth spurs the adoption of existing technology as well as the invention of new technology. This has been well documented in agriculture (Boserup, 1965) where people turn to successively more "advanced" but more laborious methods of getting food as population density increases – methods that were previously known but that were not used because they were not needed earlier. This scheme well describes the passage from hunting and gathering – which we now know requires extraordinarily few hours of work a week to provide a full diet – to migratory slash-and-burn agriculture, and thence to settled long-fallow agriculture, to short-fallow agriculture, and eventually to the use of fertilizer, irrigation, and multiple cropping. Though each stage initially requires more labor than the previous one, the endpoint is a more efficient and productive system that requires much less labor.

This phenomenon also throws light on why the advance of civilization is not a "race" between technology and population advancing independently of each other. Contrary to the Malthusian view, there is no immediate linkage between each food-increasing invention and increased production of food. Some inventions – the "invention-pull" type, such as a better calendar – may be adopted as soon as they are proven successful, because they will increase production with no more labor (or will enable less labor to produce the same amount of food). But other inventions – the "population push" type, such as settled agriculture or irrigated multicropping – require more labor, and hence will not be adopted until demand from additional population warrants the adoption (Simon, 1977, chapter 8; Simon, 1978). The Malthusian invention-pull innovation is indeed in a sort of race between population and technology. But the adoption of the population-push inventions is not in a race at all; rather, it is the sort of process discussed at length in the chapters on natural resources.

If a larger labor force causes a faster rate of productivity increase, one would expect to find that productivity has advanced faster and faster as population has grown. Ancient Greece and Rome have been offered as counter-examples to this line of reasoning. Therefore I plotted the numbers of great discoveries, as recorded by historians of science who have made such lists, against population size in various centuries. Figures 8.3a and b show that population growth or size, or both, were associated with an increase in scientific activity, and population decline with a decrease. (Of course other factors come to bear, too.)

As for the contemporary scene and better data, Solow concludes that the yearly rate of increase of productivity doubled, from 1 percent to 2 percent, between the 1909–29 and 1929–49 periods (Solow, 1957, p. 320); and the populations and labor forces of the US and of the developed world were larger in the latter period than in the earlier period. Fellner found the following rates of increase in productivity (using two methods of calculation): 1900–29, 1.8 (or 1.5) percent; 1929–48, 2.3 (or 2.0) percent; 1948–66, 2.8 percent (Fellner, 1970, pp. 11, 12). These results are consistent with the assumption that productivity indeed increases faster when population is larger – though of course other factors could explain part of the acceleration.

Here an important caution is needed: because of the economic interrelatedness of all modern countries, we should think about the population and productivity growth of the developed world – or indeed of the world as a whole – rather than think about any particular country. One country can, to some extent, ride on the coattails of the developed world as a whole, but this is less likely than is often thought, because local research and development are needed to adapt international knowledge to local conditions. For example, high-yielding seeds cannot simply be imported and planted successfully without extensive adaptation to the local sunlight angle, temperature, water and soil conditions, and so on. So, though our data refer to individual countries, or to cross-sections of countries, the unit to which our discussion applies best is the developed world as a whole.

But is it certain that the recent acceleration of productivity would not have occurred, even if population had been smaller? The connections between numbers of scientists, inventors and ideas, and the adoption and use of new discoveries, are difficult to delineate clearly. But the links needed to confirm this connection seem very obvious and strong. For example, the data show clearly that the bigger the population of a country, the greater the number of scientists and the larger the amount of scientific knowledge produced. More specifically, scientific output is proportional to population size in countries at the same level of income (Love and Pashute, 1978). The US, for example, is much larger than Sweden, and it produces much more scientific knowledge. Sweden benefits from the larger US population because it "imports" much more knowledge from the US than the US imports from Sweden; this can be seen in the references used in Swedish and US scientific writings, and in the number of patented processes licensed from each other.

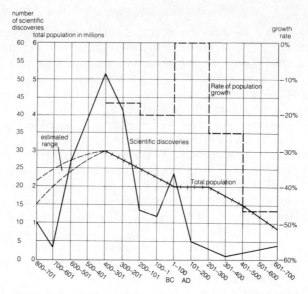

Figure 8.3a Population and scientific discoveries in Ancient Greece

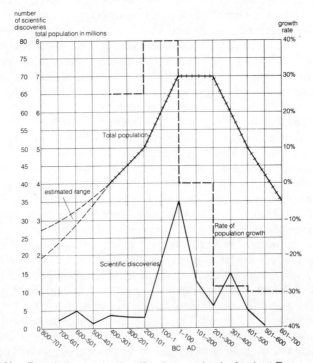

Figure 8.3b Population and scientific discoveries in Ancient Rome

Then why aren't populous China and India the most advanced countries of all, given that they have the largest populations? The obvious answer is that China and India do not produce as much new knowledge as the US or even the USSR, because China and India are relatively poor, and hence they are able to educate relatively fewer people. Yet it is instructive that, despite its poverty, India has one of the largest scientific communities in the world, just because it has such a large population. Put differently, would you bet on Sweden or Holland, against Great Britain and the USSR, to produce the great discoveries that will make nuclear fusion practical? (I have omitted the US from this bet because of its higher per-person income than Britain or the USSR.)

I am saying that, in the long run, the most important economic impact of population size and growth is the effect of additional people upon the stock of useful knowledge employed in the production of goods and services. And this positive effect is large enough (in the long run) to dominate all the negative effects of population growth. This is a strong statement, but the evidence for it seems strong, as I shall now try to show. (For a more detailed presentation of the evidence, see chapters 4 and 6 of Simon, 1977.)

Let's begin with a question: Why is the standard of living so much higher in the US or Sweden than in India or Mali? And why is the standard of living so much higher in the US or Sweden now than it was 200 years ago? The proximate cause is that the average worker in the US or Sweden now produces x times as much goods and services per day as does the average worker in India or Mali, or as did the average worker in the US or Sweden 200 years ago, where x is the ratio of the standard of living now in the US or Sweden, relative to that in India or Mali now or relative to the US or Sweden then.

Though the first answer is almost definitional, it points us to the important next question: Just *why* does the average worker in Sweden now produce so much more per day than does the average worker in Mali, or than did the average worker in Sweden 200 years ago? Part of the answer is that the average worker in Sweden today has available to him or her a much larger supply of capital equipment to work with − more buildings, tools, and transportation equipment. But that is only a minor factor; as proof, notice how fast West Germany and Japan were able to regain a high standard of living even after much of their capital was destroyed in World War II.

The all-important difference between the US or Sweden now, and those countries 200 years ago or India now, is that there is a much greater stock of technological know-how available now, and people are educated to learn and use that knowledge. The knowledge and the schooling are intertwined; in India now, unlike the US 200 years ago, the knowledge is available in books in the library, but without the schooling the knowledge cannot be adapted to local needs and then put to work. The stock of industrial capital is also intertwined with the stock of knowledge and with education; the value of much of our stock of capital, such as computers and jet airplanes, consists largely of the new knowledge that is built into them. And without educated workers, these chunks of capital cannot be operated and hence would be worthless.

The importance of the technical knowledge factor has clearly emerged in two famous studies, one by Solow (1957) and the other by Denison (1967). Using different methods, they calculated the extent to which the growth of physical capital and the labor force could account for economic growth in the US and Europe. Both found that, even after capital and labor are allowed for, much of economic growth cannot reasonably be explained by any factor other than an improvement in the level of technological practice (including improved organizational methods). Economies of scale due to larger factory size do not appear to be very important in this context, though in larger and faster-growing industries the level of technology improves more rapidly than in smaller and slower-growing economies. This improvement in productivity with technological practice did not come for free, of course; much of it was "bought" with investments in research and development (R&D). But that does not diminish the importance to us of the gains in technological knowledge.

How do immigration, population size, and population growth come into the picture? To repeat, the source of improvements in productivity is the human mind, and a human mind is seldom found unaccompanied by a human body. And because improvements – their invention and their adoption – come from people, it seems reasonable to assume that the amount of improvement depends on the number of people available to use their minds.

The reader may wonder whether a person need live in the US for the US to get the benefit of the person's impact on productivity. The answer differs somewhat depending on the person's origin – that is, whether the person is from a more-developed or a less-developed country. The answer may also depend on the person's education and occupation, but the effect of the former is clearer and probably much more important.

Recall, please, that a person may influence technical progress through both his/her demand for goods and her/his supply of knowledge. Let us consider demand and supply separately, looking first at the more problematic case, that of the person who already lives in a more-developed country such as Sweden or Japan, and then examining the case of a person who moves from a poor country to a rich country.

It is indeed true that there is international trade; a Swede's demand for goods may be satisfied by imports from the US. It is also true, and more relevant, that only a small proportion of US goods are sold abroad. It is more likely that an increment of US-made autos or newspapers or smoke detectors will be sold if a given person chooses to reside this year in the US rather than in Sweden. This should be enough evidence to make the point. An even stronger argument comes from a more general view of trade. If a Swede migrates to the US and still imports a Swedish auto, Sweden's imports (directly or indirectly) from the US will rise by the amount of other goods equal in trade value to the auto. Total production in the US, therefore, will rise by the amount of the immigrant's output and income, which will cause learning-by-doing and other demand-induced productivity-increasing mechanisms.

We must also consider, however, whether the flow of technology among developed countries is so free that it does not matter in which country the technical progress is first made. By now there seems to be consensus among students of the subject that it does matter. A first reason is that there is a time lag of, say, a minimum of three years. Second, much technical progress is a matter of local adaptation, such as new agricultural varieties and techniques that depend on particular soil and climatic conditions; this is why even individual states within the US can get a high return on research and development in agriculture (Griliches, 1958; Evenson, 1971).

If a person goes from a poor country, where little new technology is being created, to a rich country where much technology is being created, this argument is obviously even stronger. In this case the US benefits not merely by the person contributing to technology that will be differentially helpful to the US but also by the absolute increment of technology that the person creates. The more technically advanced (relative to the state of the art) is the industry in which a person works, the greater the opportunity for that person to advance the state of the art.

It is not a contradiction to this line of thought that the rate of economic growth per capita in the post-World War II period has been proportionately as high or higher in the poorer countries as in the US. The poorer countries can take advantage of the technological progress in the richer countries much more than the reverse can occur.

A reduction in the quality or amount of education that children receive is another possible negative effect of population growth or immigration upon the growth of knowledge. Human capital as well as physical capital is crucial in the productivity of an economy. And people might not wish to provide (or authorities might not demand) enough additional tax revenues to maintain an equivalent level of schooling in the face of population growth. If so, a larger population, with its larger proportion of children, might lead to less education on the average, and thus to less potential for individuals to increase the stock of knowledge, than a smaller population.

But this reduction is doubtful. The conventional theory underlying this idea is straightforward Malthus: a fixed educational budget of money and resources divided among more students implies less education per student. But we know from casual evidence that people and institutions often respond to population growth by altering the apparently fixed conditions. In agricultural countries, for example, having more children causes parents to increase their labor on the land. And in industrial countries, when there are additional profitable opportunities for investment, people will shift some resources from consumption to investment; additional children constitute such an opportunity. Therefore, we must allow for responses contrary to the simple Malthusian pie-sharing theory.

There is no way of knowing from theory alone which of the two effects – dilution of resources or increase of work – will dominate. Therefore we must turn to empirical analysis. A comparison of rates of population growth in LDCs with the amounts of education given to children shows that an increase in the birth rate reduces educational expenditures per child, and also secondary enrollment, but does not reduce primary or postsecondary enrollment (Simon and Pilarski, 1979). Perhaps the most important result of that study is that the negative effects are nowhere near as great as the simple Malthusian theory would suggest, and in general the effects do not seem to be large.

One may wonder whether the immigrants themselves obtain, through their earnings, all the benefits of the new knowledge that they create. This question can be answered confidently in the negative. A large body of excellent econometric studies have shown that the social rate of return to research and development tends to exceed the internal rate of return to investment at large. And given that firms are willing to pay their employees only for the benefits that the firm can obtain from their output, we can conclude that immigrant knowledge producers are not themselves able to extract all the economic benefit of the knowledge they produce, and hence the remainder is enjoyed by the rest of society.

Human Capital Externalities

A possible drawback to very large-scale immigration – which seems to have been overlooked in past technical discussions of immigration – is a force which we may call "human capital externalities." A person's output depends not only on the person's own skills and the quality of the machines one works with, but also on the quality of the skills of the people one works with. Immigrants from poor countries possess poorer productive skills than do people *with the same amount of formal education* in richer countries; this is almost definitionally true, and the effect can be seen in the lower incomes of those immigrants in the countries from which they have come than in the incomes they expect in the US (which is exactly why they come). So until they improve their *informally* learned skills — handling modern communications systems, for example, or getting used to doing things by telephone and computer rather than in person and with pencil and paper — they represent lower-quality human capital for American workers to cooperate with. And this will reduce the productivity (and growth of productivity) of American workers until the immigrants — in perhaps 2 or 5 years — pick up the informal learning (after which they forge ahead of natives).

Of course there is a linked positive effect, the beneficial impact of working with someone from a different culture. Immigrants cause new ideas to arise, even when higher-skilled persons are exposed to more "primitive" ways of doing a job. This effect is also likely to run out, however, as the immigrants become more Americanized. And there is no strong reason to believe that this positive effect outweighs the linked negative human-capital effect.

The size of the negative human-capital externality effect depends upon the proportion of immigrants that natives work with. If your work companions are 1 percent new immigrants, the negative effect may be small, and outweighed by the positive effect. But if you work with immigrants 50 percent of the time, the outcome might be quite different.

There is an analogy here to busing. The original notion of busing was that children from poor backgrounds could gain from the school environment (including the other children) that better-off children have, and the better-off children would not suffer thereby. Maybe this is true for 1 or 10 percent bused-in children. But what if it is 90 or 99 percent of the class? Quite obviously the result for the 90 or 99 percent would be no different than if they never left their neighborhood schools (aside from better teachers, if it is so), and for the better-off children representing 10 or 1 percent of the population, it would be as if they had been bused to the poor neighborhood school. If 1 million Russians or Indians or Chinese move to Champaign-Urbana, Illinois, the schools and workplaces would become like those in the countries of origin. And this is why towns on both sides of the US-Mexican border are somewhere between mainstream US and mainstream Mexican culture and productivity. This line of reasoning just spells out the person-in-the-street's thoughts about being "inundated" by a great many immigrants.

But — the average immigrant worker comes to have higher earnings than the average American worker after a few years in the US, due in large part to greater youth, and a high level of average education. This suggests that the human capital externality effect comes to be positive in a fairly short time. And it is probably positive on balance, as long as we weigh the future and the present normally.

Immigration, Technology, and the Competitive Future of the United States

As economics usually does, this book addresses the effects of immigration upon *individuals* — mainly US residents, as well as the immigrants themselves. Also following the usual practice of economics, the book mainly analyses immigration *incrementally* — that is, determining the effect of the "next" single immigrant — rather than asking about the effect of an entire large cohort of immigrants. At a very few points the question has been raised whether a large number of immigrants might have a different effect than a much smaller number of immigrants, or different than effects that are experienced with the current or historical volumes of immigration; for example, the effect on natives of working together with a relatively large number of immigrants was considered earlier in the chapter. But even in these exceptional cases only the possible special difficulties and not the possible benefits of a large cohort of immigrants were discussed.

In connection with consideration of a large cohort of immigrants, some readers might also wish to consider the *political* implications of the economic effect of immigration — and necessarily, the implications of a fairly large flow of special immigrants, rather than just the "next" ordinary immigrant. That is, the issue is the political standing of the US relative to other countries. It may reasonably be assumed that a nation's political standing is heavily influenced by its economic situation, both the standard of living of individuals and the total output of the residents taken together. And when we ask this question, we find that immigration represents perhaps the most amazing opportunity for the US that any country has ever had to get ahead of its political rival or rivals — the safest, cheapest, surest alternative ever available to a country. This statement is not made as a recommendation but rather simply as observation.

Nowadays the future of any country, and most especially the future of a major country that is in the vanguard with respect to production and living standards, hangs completely on its advance in knowledge and skill and productivity. This is more true at present than in the past because technology changes so rapidly nowadays. Even a single invention can radically alter a country's economic or military future — consider, for example, the atom bomb or the computer — with a speed that no invention could in the past, even the invention of the gun.

All that the US need do to sharply increase the rate of advance in its technology and its industrial productivity is relax its barriers against the immigration of skilled creators of knowledge. It could simply give permanent-resident visas to those foreign students who come to the US to study. Many foreign students already find ways to remain under the present rules — about half among the students of engineering and science (Servan-

Schreiber and Simon, 1987), a group that those writers argue persuasively is crucial to present progress. But even more foreign graduates would remain if allowed to, and they could push up the rate of progress even further.

Going even further, if young people abroad knew that they would be able to remain in the US after completing their education here, more would choose to come to the US to study. This would provide multiple benefits to the US. Given assurance that they could remain, these students could afford more realistic tuition rates than are now charged, which would benefit US universities. And these increased rates would enable the universities to expand their programs to serve both foreign and native students better. Most important of all, of course, would be the increased number of highly competent engineers and scientists of all kinds who would be part of the American workforce.

Going even further, a larger number of students requires a larger number of professors. And a larger number of openings for professors, especially in such fields as engineering and science, would attract from abroad more of the world's best scientists. This would reinforce the process which has brought to the US so many foreigners who have won Nobel prizes in the US to the advantage as well as honor of the US.

Just why knowledge workers produce so much more when they are located in the US than in poor countries is exceedingly hard to state clearly. It must be some combination of the reward structure, the resources available to work with, the colleagues (which is a self-reinforcing matter), closeness to the center of scientific activities, and so on. But the fact that the difference is great is indubitable.

Where would the physical capital come from for the additional scientists to work with, and to use for housing and schooling their families? Would this not mean a "dilution" of the capital supply in such fashion that there is less capital for natives to work with, and hence a diminution in the productivity of native workers? This bugaboo is discussed in chapter 7. The conclusion arrived at there, contrary to everyday common sense, is that — aside from the shortest-run considerations — physical capital does not pose a constraint. One matter not emphasized there that deserves special mention in the present context is that new investment opportunities are created by immigrant scientists and engineers, and capital must flow into the country from abroad to invest in these opportunities, which works to keep the supply of capital per worker from being diluted.

No other country has such opportunity. The USSR must even resort to compulsion to prevent its native scientists from leaving, and there obviously is little demand from foreigners to work there. Europe draws some, but is perhaps hampered by the fact that English is the international language of science, which makes it advantageous to live in an English-speaking country such as the US, Canada, Australia, or Great Britain.

Conclusions

Immigrants influence productivity both in their special roles as immigrants and in their general roles as additional persons. As immigrants, they bring new and different ideas from their old societies to their new society which may lead to useful improvements. As additional persons they increase productivity both directly as additional ingenious minds, and also indirectly by the impetus that their increased demand and consequent increased production volume gives to productivity by way of learning by doing.

NOTES

1 The US-UK comparisons in the same year are relatively free of the potential bias arising from the fact that those industries where world technology grew faster exogenously were also those whose scale of production therefore expanded faster, a bias which afflicts analogous time-series studies within a single country.

9 Impacts upon Natural Resources and the Environment

It is commonly thought that adding immigrants to the population reduces natural-resource availability for natives. As a popular writer on environmental issues puts it:

Until we accept the connection between world population control and migration, we shall be tilting at symptoms and flirting with destruction. And until we see the threat that faces the US from the increments of population represented by the great new waves of aliens pressing to come to America, we are doomed to experience environmental disasters that we cannot now even envisage.

Our resource base of raw materials is consistently shrinking. In the 1940s we were self-sufficient in all but five or six of the thirty-five most necessary minerals. Today we are dependent on other (and some less than friendly) nations for twenty-eight of those thirty-five elements. Just as we are prodigious consumers, so are we prodigious producers of wastes. Frantic state and national officials are alternately beseeching and threatening localities throughout the nation to surrender small sites for the burial of the noxious wastes constantly being added to our environment in increasing volume. There is no longer a single spot in the US where the air is wholly pure. As for the water we are forced to drink, it is universally polluted with germs and chemicals which we resolutely fail to itemize, and the disinfecting chemical universally employed − chlorine − has but recently been accused of inducing cancer. . . .

Sinkholes now mark the crisis points in our withdrawal of groundwater. Deserts are advancing. We annually lose two million acres of soil to erosion. We pave over another million acres of prime farm land. We cannot save vital species of plants and animals for want of human elbow room. The last thirty-eight cannot find living space, the grizzly bear is pressed for habitat, and the endangered species list now has the ominous total of 189 entries. We frantically seek space for our hazardous solid and liquid wastes. (Rienow, 1981, pp. 14, 15, 17)

The Senator most responsible for the Simpson—Rodino immigration legislation said about the bill:

The issue is whether we can or should give up benefits which stem from low population density – cleaner air, less traffic congestion, easy access to parks, and reduced anxiety levels. (Simpson, 1981, p. 9)

All this is part of a more general vision as expressed, for example, by Zero Population Growth's honorary president, Paul R. Ehrlich, who worries about the supposed danger of additional people to the "perilously shrinking water supply in this country. And to our food supply."

The United States in less than 50 years will be more crowded, more polluted, more ecologically unstable, more prone to political unrest, more burdened with social stress, and far, far more precarious than we can possibly imagine. (Ehrlich, 1982)

The impact of an immigrant upon the environment, and upon supplies of natural resources and energy, is similar to the impact of a native, thereby raising no special analytic problems stemming from being an immigrant. But the entire issue of population's effects is fraught with argument and confusion, because the effects of additional people upon natural resources and the environment are quite complex. A large portion of my (1981) book is devoted to showing that all the main resource fears voiced in the quotations above are without foundation in past trends. The conclusions may be summarized as follows:

1   The long-term trends for virtually every raw material (including energy) are toward *lower prices and increasing availabilities* (see figure 9.1). These positive trends have been concurrent with increasing population. That is, natural resources have been getting *less* scarce rather than *more* scarce, over the long run, as indicated by the fundamental economic measure of cost. This is quite contrary to popular belief.
2   An additional person necessarily causes increased cost, higher prices, and increased scarcity in the very short run. Critics of immigration focus upon this short-run effect as in this statement in an Environmental Fund article entitled "Immigration and the American Conscience" (Grant and Tanton, 1981): "Had the United States stabilized its population in 1970, we could have the same level of energy consumption and standard of living as we do today *without* any Iranian oil or a single nuclear plant."

The statement about short-run scarcity probably is true. But even more probably, and much more importantly, the statement also is terribly misleading – a snare and delusion that will have unfortunate long-run results if it is taken seriously by policy-makers and the public. This is why:

One important flaw in the statement just quoted is that the eleven years

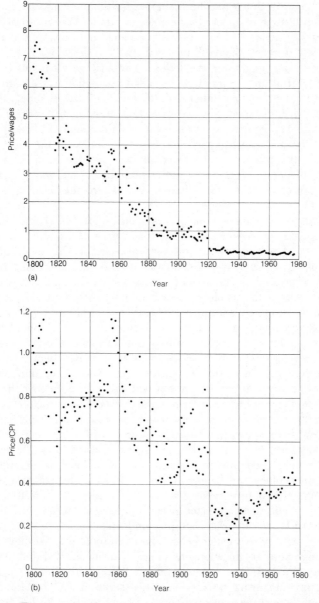

Figure 9.1 The scarcity of copper as measured by: (a) its price relative to wages (b) its price relative to the consumer price index

Source: US Department of Commerce, Bureau of the Census, *Historical Statistics, Colonial Times to 1970* (Washington, DC: Government Printing Office, 1975)

it encompasses is much too short a period for the most important effects of population change to appear. Babies take a quarter century to mature into producers of goods and ideas; even immigrants require several years in the new society to reach their full productivity.

It takes even longer for the following crucial development process to produce its fruit: (a) An immigrant-swelled population leads to greater use of natural resources than otherwise. (b) Prices of raw materials then rise. (c) The price rise and the resultant fear about actual and impending scarcity impel individuals to seek new lodes of raw materials, new production technologies, and, most importantly, new substitutes for the resources. (d) Eventually the price of the service of the resource in question − for example, the price of energy whether produced from wood, coal, oil, or nuclear power − falls lower than it was before the temporary scarcity began.

This resource-augmentation process takes quite some time, and is indirect. Yet this process has been the mainspring of economic advance for 5000 years. The process is, however, obscured in the above quotation, which makes it seem as if the main effect of the additional people is harmful, whereas the main effect (occurring some time after) is that we are better off than if the whole process beginning with more people had not taken place. If one substitutes the date 1900 or 1800 or 1700 for 1970 in the quotation above, the quotation is surely wrong: if population had stabilized earlier, we probably would not have the energy sources and prices as low as we now have them. In short, increased demand eventually leads in the long run to supplies greater than would exist otherwise.[1]

If all of history is any guide, we can now say with confidence that natural forces do not increasingly constrain our activities, though the physical world always must *somewhat* constrain what we can produce and consume. Much of my 1981 book shows that natural resources (including energy) are, with passing decades, less rather than more of a constraint to US and world growth. To cite such "limits" in discussions of national immigration policy is unsound geology and biology, incorrect history, and rotten economics. The progressive improvement that has occurred in the world's resource availability would not have taken place if population density had remained at the lower levels of earlier centuries and millennia.

3   Again contrary to popular belief, and contrary to the assertions by such anti-immigration organizations as The Environmental Fund and Zero Population Growth, the basic trends in US environmental quality are positive, accompanying (though not necessarily caused by) increases in population. The water and food supplies consumed in the US have been improving in past decades by every reasonable measure of quantity and purity. The air, too, has been getting purer rather than more polluted, according to the official Pollutant Standard Index and other measures

provided by the US Environmental Protection Agency (see Simon, 1981a; Simon and Kahn, 1984).

4 The weight of the evidence suggests that though additional people cause more pollution in the short run, in the longer run additional people lead to less pollution, strange as that may sound at first.

5 The fundamental building block of the anti-immigrant logic with respect to natural resources is that such resources are "finite." As we read in a publication of The Environmental Fund:

Can we take all who wish to come? Governor Richard Lamm of Colorado says no. In developing an immigration policy, Lamm states, "We must begin by recognizing that the resources of the United States are not infinite." (*TEF Data*, Environmental Fund, May 1981, No. 1, p. 3)

But it is *not meaningful* to assert that natural resources are finite and limited, because we can make more of them, though the explanation runs against all conventional thinking. The crucial issue is energy, the "master resource" that allows us to obtain more of all the other resources. And there will certainly be energy on earth as long as there is CO_2 and energy from the sun to grow plants, without even considering the possibility of nuclear fission or fusion or new sources of energy, or finding other suns before our sun runs out in seven billion years or so. (Extended explanation may be found in my 1981 book, chapter 3.) The supposed finiteness of resources is simply an uninformed prejudice.

It is not surprising that so many wrong economic ideas are held about the relationship of population growth to natural resources, because so much of the process is so contrary to everyday common sense. Take the case of population density and land availability. At first it seems almost ridiculous to assert that greater population density can lead to better economic results – that, for example, if all Americans moved east of the Mississippi, we would all be better off economically. Upon reflection, this proposition is not as unlikely as it sounds. The main loss to citizens involved in such a move would be massive amounts of farmland, and though the US is a massive producer and exporter of farm goods, agriculture is not crucial to the economy. Less than 3 percent of US income comes from agriculture, and less than 3 percent of US working population is engaged in that industry. The capitalized value of all US farm land is just a bit more than a tenth of one year's national income, so that even if the US were to lose all of it, the loss would equal only about one year's expenditures upon liquor, cigarettes, and the like. On the other hand, such a change would bring about major benefits in shortening transportation and communication distances, the "just in time" factor which has been important in Japan's ability to closely coordinate its industrial operations in such a fashion as to reduce costs of inventory and transportation. Additionally, greater population concentration eventually forces social changes in the direction of better articulated social organization, changes which may be costly in the short run but in the long run increase a society's ability to reach its economic and social objectives. If we were still living at the population density that people achieved (say) 10,000 years ago, we would not have the vital complex social and economic apparatuses that are the backbone of our contemporary society.

It is true that if all immigration were to stop tomorrow, any one of us would have somewhat greater opportunities than otherwise: a larger part of a national park to oneself, greater ability to draw from the waters of a river to the extent one chooses. This effect could be achieved even more completely if all the immigrants who had ever come to the US, or the descendants of immigrants who came in the last 300 years, were shipped out of the country immediately — all but the one person who would enjoy the solitude, of course. But this line of thinking does not take notice of several important facts: (1) If other persons — immigrants and descendants of immigrants — had not constructed such infrastructure as roads to the national parks, only a Daniel Boone or a native American could have enjoyed it. (2) As John Locke taught us, merely being born into a place does not necessarily or obviously confer a moral right to ownership of the asset that is primarily found rather than created by human efforts. (3) Without additional immigrants, there will be less future creation of new materials and less access to wilderness — without even mentioning resources created entirely by humankind such as art and music and the facilities to enjoy them, to which immigrants to the US have contributed so handsomely.

The anti-immigrationists' message boils down to this: they would like to draw to the full upon the resources made available by nature and developed by others who came before them, without any obligation to develop new resources to share with others who may come in the future. There is nothing logically incorrect with this viewpoint, but it may run counter to one's ethical sense.

In sum, for those who worry about increasing scarcity of raw materials, and about greater "pressure" upon the environment, immigrants represent additional persons in the society who use up more resources. But these apparently self-evident propositions about the relationship of population size and growth to natural resource availability, and to the quality of the environment, are not supported by the facts. In the very short run, additional people do push up prices, and cause crowding. But in the longer run, there occurs a process whereby the actual or impending shortage leads to the search for new resources, and after those new resources are discovered we are left better off than if the original scarcity problem had never arisen.

NOTES

1 An example: the discovery of plastics in the mid-nineteenth century derives from a shortage of elephant tusks to make billiard balls, due to increased demand. A maker of billiard balls offered a $10,000 prize for a synthetic replacement, and celluloid was the result.

   A theoretical framework for this process is offered (using the example of farmland) in Simon and Steinmann (1987).

10   The Overall Effect of Immigrants upon Natives' Standard of Living

The Empirical Relationship of Population to Economic Growth
An Integrated Simulation Model
Discussion
Summary and Conclusions

This chapter combines estimates of the partial influences discussed in previous chapters in order to arrive at an overall assessment of the effect of immigrants upon the standard of living of natives. As we proceed, it should be remembered that this chapter refers to the aggregate of all natives, employing the concept of the arithmetic average. Differential effects upon separate segments of the population through wages and unemployment, and as measured by income distribution, are discussed in chapters 11, 12 and 13.

We shall first examine the effect upon the economy, and upon natives, of immigrants simply as additional people, rather than by way of any special characteristics that immigrants have. That is, we first inquire about the observed effect of population growth historically and cross-nationally upon economic growth and level. The second section utilizes a simulation model to combine the effects of immigrants qua immigrants, as well as their effects as more people, to estimate the overall effect.

The Empirical Relationship of Population to Economic Growth

Empirical evidence bearing directly upon the overall relationship between the rates of immigration and of economic growth is hard to come by. Individual countries lack observation for time-series studies, and there are too few countries with comparable histories of substantial immigration to support systematic cross-national studies; nor has anyone yet produced a successful pooled analysis. The cases of massive immigration into West Germany, Japan, and Israel after World War II (see chapter 3 for data) would seem to show, however, that taking in large groups of people – even refugees who are ill-prepared for migration – is not a barrier to excellent national economic performance.

For some illumination, therefore, we turn to analyses of the effects of population growth in general.

The standard presumption is that additional people – children or immigrants – have a negative effect upon the incomes of the rest of the people. The usual reasoning is diminishing returns to fixed stocks of agricultural and industrial and social capital, together with the dependency burden of additional children and the consequent need for additional "demographic investment." (The special characteristics of immigrants in this regard are discussed in chapter 4.) Because this Malthusian theory is so firmly fixed in conventional thought, let us first confront the theory with the data, which flatly contradict the conventional Malthusian theory. Many of these data refer to countries when they were, or are, poorer and less industrialized than the US is now. But we lack a sufficiently large body of more comparable experience. And the data on less-developed stages and countries are still relevant because many of the same fundamental processes occur in economic development at all stages. Furthermore, the data on the less-developed stages of development are even more surprising to most people, and therefore the picture that they show may have greater power to make the basic point.

The concurrent explosion in Europe of *both* population and economic development from 1650 onwards is important case evidence. The failure of France to excel economically in the hundred years prior to World War II despite its low birth rate is an important vignette in this history. A fuller picture is given by the samples of countries for which long-run data on the growth of population and output per person are available. Figures 10.1 and 10.2 show that there is no strong relationship, which is confirmed by correlational analysis.

Concerning the experience since World War II, the overall pattern is revealing: contrary to common impression, per-person income in less-developed countries (LDCs) has been growing *faster* than in the more-developed countries (MDCs) (Morawetz, 1977) even though population growth in LDCs is much faster than in MDCs. No evidence here of a negative connection between population growth and economic growth.

Many systematic cross-country comparisons of recent rates of population growth and economic growth have been done. They have recently been reviewed and summarized by Lee as follows:

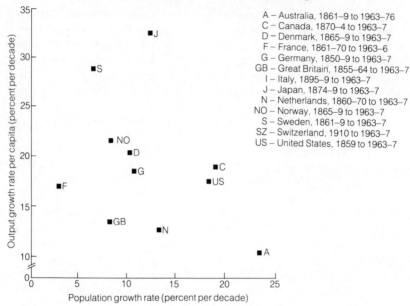

A – Australia, 1861–9 to 1963–76
C – Canada, 1870–4 to 1963–7
D – Denmark, 1865–9 to 1963–7
F – France, 1861–70 to 1963–6
G – Germany, 1850–9 to 1963–7
GB – Great Britain, 1855–64 to 1963–7
I – Italy, 1895–9 to 1963–7
J – Japan, 1874–9 to 1963–7
N – Netherlands, 1860–70 to 1963–7
NO – Norway, 1865–9 to 1963–7
S – Sweden, 1861–9 to 1963–7
SZ – Switzerland, 1910 to 1963–7
US – United States, 1859 to 1963–7

Figure 10.1   The non-relationship between population growth and growth of
living standards over a century
Source: Kuznets, 1971b, pp. 11–14

[D]ozens of studies, starting with Kuznets' (1967), have found no association
between the population growth rate and per capita income growth rate, despite the
obvious fact that at least since WWII, population growth rates have varied considerably. These studies control for other factors such as trade, aid and investment to
varying degrees. Two recent studies add historical depth to this analysis; even
within countries (and thus looking only at disequilibrium), over periods as long as a
century or as short as 25 years, there is no significant association of [the population
growth rate] and [the income growth rate], for either DCs or LDCs; put differently,
one can't reject the hypothesis that the regression coefficient of [the income growth
rate] on [the population growth rate] is unity. I know of just two exceptions to this
general picture . . . both dealing with cross-sections; both find negative effects of
population growth of magnitude roughly equal to the share of non-labor inputs in
production, as many theories would predict. However, data problems render these
results suspect. (Lee, 1983; notation and references omitted. See also my earlier
review, 1977, chapter 3.)

That is, population growth *does not* have a negative effect upon economic
growth. Elsewhere (Simon, 1986) I discuss in detail why these studies
constitute solid evidence of the absence of causal influence of population
growth upon economic development.[1]

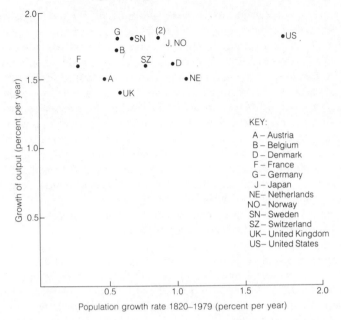

Figure 10.2 160-year growth rates of output and population
Source: Maddison, 1982, pp. 44 and 49

These overlapping empirical studies do *not* prove that fast population growth in the more-developed world as a whole *increases* per-person income. They do imply that population growth *does not decrease* economic growth. In the past I was not prepared to say more than that. Now I believe that we can proceed beyond this, however. Recall that the studies mentioned above do not refer to the *very* long run; rather, they cover only a quarter of a century or at most a century. The main negative effects of population growth occur during perhaps the first quarter or half of a century so that, if the negative effects are important, these studies will reveal them. These shorter-run effects upon the standard of living include the public costs of raising children — schools and hospitals are the main examples — and the costs of providing additional production capital for the additional persons in the workforce.[2]

The observations that immigrants (a) do not have a detrimental effect upon the supply of natural resources and a clean environment (chapter 9), and (b) have a net positive rather than negative effect upon the public coffers, far exceeding their negative effect through the use of public capital (chapters 5 and 7), combined with the absence of an observed negative effect on economic growth in the intermediate-run statistical measures, are enough to suggest that in the *very long* run more people have a *positive* net effect, because the most important positive effects of additional people – improvement of productivity through the contribution of new ideas as well as the learning-by-doing that accompanies increased production volume – occur in the long run, and are cumulative. To put it differently, the statistical measurements of the relationship of population growth to economic growth are biased in favor of showing the shorter-run negative effects. If such negative effects do not appear, one may assume that an unbiased measure of the total effect would reveal a positive effect of population growth upon economic growth. And of course the positive effect may be expected to occur much faster with immigrants than with additional births, and births rather than immigrants are the main constituent of the empirical studies under discussion.

The empirical studies mentioned above focus on the *process* of population *growth*. Examination of the relationship between the *attained level* of population – that is, the population density as measured by the number of persons per areal unit – shows an even more impressive effect. Studies of MDCs are lacking. But for LDCs, Hagen (1975) and Kindleberger (1965) show graphically, and Simon and Gobin (1980) show in multivariate regressions, that higher population density is associated with *higher* rates of economic growth (see figure 10.3). The effect seems strongest at low densities, but there is no evidence that the effect reverses at high densities. Stryker (1977) shows a similar effect for agricultural productivity. These data showing a positive effect of density upon economic growth also con-

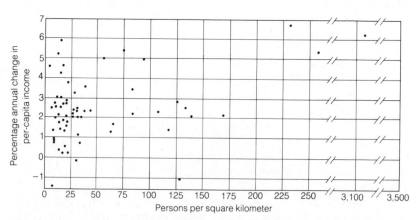

Figure 10.3   Economic growth rates related to population density in LDCs, 1960–5

Note: This figure shows only the existence of the relationship; for its size the reader should consult regression coefficients.
Source: Simon and Gobin, 1980

stitute indirect proof of a positive long-run effect of population *growth* upon economic growth, because density changes occur very slowly, and therefore, density picks up the very-long-run effects as well as the short-run effects.

Greater density can have a cost in congestion, as is seen in the news story about Lower Manhattan in chapter 9.

It may at first seem unbelievable that greater population density leads to better economic results. As noted in chapter 9, this is the equivalent of saying that if all Americans moved east of the Mississippi, our incomes would rise. But upon reflection, this proposition is seen not to be as implausible as it sounds at first hearing.

An Integrated Simulation Model

Now it is time to weave together the various influences of immigrants upon the standard of living of natives. An economist worth her/his keep must take into account the *size* and *importance* of the various effects and calculate the net effect. One can only obtain a satisfactory overall assessment of the effect of immigrants on the standard of living of citizens by constructing an integrated model of the economy and then comparing the incomes produced by the economy under various conditions of immigration and population growth.[3]

For simplicity and clarity, the model deals with a single cohort of immigrants; a continuous analysis yields similar results, however. Also for simplicity, I sometimes talk of a representative family instead of the cohort as a whole.

The question is whether the resident population − that is, the people living in the US *before* the immigrant family arrives − is better off or worse off economically if the immigrant family comes or does not. In more precise terms, we wish to know if the lifetime income of the (average member of the) resident population is higher or lower if immigrants come.[4] Therefore, we must estimate the natives' yearly gross incomes and taxes if there are, and if there are not, immigrants.

The structure of the simulation model

We start with the effect of the immigrant on natives' incomes through the two major lines of influence: the capital-dilution effect, and the economies-of-scale-and-productivity effect. The combined effect of these two forces will be estimated in a simple macro-economic simulation. The main conventional element is a Cobb−Douglas function, whose labor and capital coefficients add to unity, and where saving is a fixed steady-growth proportion of the prior year's output. A less conventional element is the effect of output and labor force on the technological-level coefficient (discussed in the following section).

In other recent work, I have explored a wide variety of technological progress functions and have found that, in a policy context such as this one, the result is rather insensitive to the choice of function. I have chosen Phelps's well-known and elegant function (though used by him for a different purpose), which is "conservative" in this sense: Phelps's function indicates that technical progress should have been progressively lower as population growth has declined in the twentieth century in the US and in the Western world generally. In fact, technical progress has apparently been higher in the more recent decades than in the early decades of this century, as discussed earlier. This implies that Phelps's function understates the contribution of population size and growth to the advance of economic welfare.[5]

In place of the size of the research force in Phelps's function, for simplicity I have used the size of the labor force. The function was written in Cobb–Douglas form to make its meaning obvious:

$$A_t - A_{t-1} = bA_{t-1}^{\gamma} L_{t-1}^{\Delta}, \text{ with } \gamma, \Delta = 0.5 \tag{10.1}$$

The exponents fit Phelps's requirement that the function be homogeneous of degree one, and his assumption that "if the technology level should double we would require exactly twice the amount of research to double the absolute time rate of increase of the technology." The assumption of the steady-state savings rate is also conservative in the sense that it is less advantageous to a larger population (and hence to immigrants) than would be a higher savings rate. This is reasonably clear upon inspection and is verified in other work by this writer. The coefficient b is that complement of the initial values chosen for A and L that starts the simulation smoothly into motion and that corresponds to the steady-state rate of change of A in the nonimmigrant case, which is equal to the rate of growth of the labor force. This, too, is a conservative assumption.

An iterative program is used to make investment a function of current-period income rather than prior-period income, so that the computer model would approximate the steady-state analytic model. The results are much the same with and without this refinement, however.

The other equations and parameters of the model are as follows:

$$Y_t = A_t^{\alpha} L_t^{\beta} \tag{10.2}$$

$$K_t, K_t = sY_{t-1} + K_{t-1} \tag{10.3}$$

$$L_t = L_{t-1} + 0.02 \, L_{t-1}. \tag{10.4}$$

The initial values are $A_t + 1.0$, $K_t = 1000$, $Y_t = 500$, $\alpha = 0.67$, $\beta = 0.33$, $\gamma = 0.5$, and $\Delta = 0.5$; b is chosen so that the initial rate of change of A equals 0.02 yearly. The initial L equals 1000 for the without-immigration case, and 1020 for the with-immigration case.[6]

For the income-effect calculations, the increment of immigrant workers in period $t=1$ must be large enough so that the effects are not obscured by rounding error. It was therefore set equal to the 2 percent increase in native labor force in year $t=1$ (10 percent in some runs to show that the size of the increment matters little). Then the difference in citizens' incomes in future years between the situations if the immigrants do come in $t=1$, and if they do not come, are calculated. The final calculation is in terms of the effect of one additional immigrant.

A key issue is the "returns" to the capital that the immigrant works with, and the payment for the additional demographic capital required to take care of the publicly supplied services such as schooling that the immigrant family needs, as discussed in chapter 7. Properly, each of these matters should be handled separately and in its full detail. The simulation, however, deals with capital in a much cruder fashion, by simply choosing two alternative levels of "returns to capital" and letting the level stand as the proxy for all the capital effects. One level chosen for experimentation is 20 percent; it seems at least as high as any plausible calculation would have it, on the following reasoning: Assume that (a) 8 percent of immigrants (those who work for government) get the full returns from the capital they work with, and the other 92 percent get none of the returns (see chapter 7); (b) no allowance need be made for private production capital, (reasons spelled out in chapter 7), and no allowance need be made for public capital such as roads and defense equipment which are essentially public goods; and (c) demographic capital, including schools and hospitals, is 24 percent of all capital,[7] and immigrants get a full share of that while paying for only $\left(1 - \frac{21}{38}\right) = 45$ percent of it through bonds and taxes (see chapter 7). The effects in (b) and (c) are not nearly substantial enough to raise the 8 percent in (a) to 20 percent, the figure in the main computation. Additionally, computations are shown for a level of returns to capital of 35 percent, far higher than is conceivable; the reason for including this level is to show that the conclusions drawn from the simulation are not sensitive to the level of capture of returns to capital that is assumed in a given run.

Results

Table 10.1 shows calculations with the two capture-of-capital-returns assumptions. Considering first the results without the effects of welfare transfers and taxes, and working with the 20 percent level, the pre-tax effects on citizens' incomes amount to the percentages of the immigrants' net income shown in column 1. Those figures may be interpreted as follows. In year 1, aside from taxes, citizens' incomes are (in the aggregate) lower by 7 percent of the income of the average immigrant (though the

Table 10.1   The effect of an immigrant on the incomes of natives at various
assumptions about the proportion of capital returns that go to
immigrants (expressed as a percentage of the immigrant's
earnings)

Year	20% Capital return			35% Capital return		
	(1) *Income effect (%)*	*(2)* *Social Security*	*(3)* *Total*	*(4)* *Income effect (%)*	*(5)* *Social Security*	*(6)* *Total*
1	−7	10	3	−14	10	−4
2	−7	10	3	−12	10	−2
3	−5	10	5	−11	10	−1
4	−4	10	6	−10	10	0
5	−2	10	8	−8	10	2
6	−1	10	9	−7	10	3
7	1	10	11	−5	10	5
8	2	10	12	−4	10	6
9	4	10	14	−3	10	7
10	5	10	15	−1	10	9
11	7	10	17	0	10	10
12	8	10	18	2	1C	12
13	10	10	20	3	10	13
14	11	10	21	4	10	14
15	13	10	23	6	10	16
16	14	10	24	7	10	17
17	16	10	26	8	10	18
18	17	10	27	10	10	20
19	18	10	28	11	10	21
20	20	10	30	12	10	22
21	21	10	31	14	10	24
22	23	10	33	15	10	25
23	24	10	34	16	10	26
24	25	10	35	18	10	28
25	27	10	37	19	10	29
26	28	10	38	20	10	30
27	30	10	40	21	10	31
28	31	10	41	23	10	33
29	32	10	42	24	10	34
30	34	10	44	25	10	35

effect on individual natives is small because of the small proportion of
immigrants relative to natives). By year 7, citizens' net incomes are higher
than they would otherwise be, because of the immigrants. By year 13,

citizens' incomes are higher by an amount equal to 10 percent of the income of each immigrant who arrives in year zero.

Next we take into account the immigrants' savings-and-transfer effect, as discussed earlier. Social Security is the main issue. Immigrants collect no Social Security, both because of age distribution and because they have no claims to benefits until they have worked for years. The immigrant family's contributions are assumed to be 10 percent of income (actually 12.8 percent of personal income in 1983; *Social Security Bulletin*, Annual Statistical Supplement, 1985. p. 66). This makes the account slightly positive in year 5 and thereafter, as seen in column 3.

Overall, the stream of negative and positive effects may be evaluated just as any other investment, with negative outgoings at the beginning and positive incomes later on. On a capital-returns assumption of 20 percent, the rate of return on the investment decision to bring in an immigrant is 18.4 percent per annum without the Social Security effect and 28.4 percent with it, an excellent investment by any standard.

The results of a variety of other specifications of the basic model with respect to savings rate, initial rate of technical progress, proportion of returns to capital captured by immigrants, and exponents of the technical progress function are shown in table 10.2.

Table 10.2 Rates of return on investment in immigrants for a variety of models (increment of immigrants equal to 2 percent of labor force in $t=1$)

| | | | | Rates of return per annum (percentage) | |
| | | | Capital capture (%) | Without Social Security | With Social Security |
b	s	γ, Δ			
0.02	0.04	0.5	0.20	18.4	28.4
0.02	0.04	0.5	0.35	9.3	19.3
0.02	0.07	0.5	0.35	12.2	22.2
0.02	0.10	0.5	0.35	14.8	24.8

Discussion

The model does not include a variety of other effects discussed elsewhere in the book. Hence a brief discussion of how they fit here seems appropriate.

1   Transfer welfare payments (*excluding* net retirement benefits) and taxes are likely to net out zero, as discussed in chapter 5.

2   There is no reason to think that illegal immigrants are different from legal residents with respect to the issues discussed in this chapter. With respect to welfare and taxes, they bestow a special boon upon natives, as discussed in chapter 15.

3   Case-by-case cross-national comparisons of the effect of total immigration upon aggregate economic performance can provide extreme examples in either direction. For example, Japan has shown extraordinary economic performance in the total absence of immigration (except for the movement of Japanese from overseas immediately after World War II). On the other hand, Germany showed extraordinary economic performance after World War II in the presence of very large numbers of immigrants from outside West Germany; in the 1970s, when immigration was low or negative, economic performance was less impressive. The worst economic performance of the US was during the 1930s, when immigration was negative. And so on. There are two reasons why one should not at present draw any conclusions from such examples: first, the number of examples is too small; and second, the causal relationship between economic performance and immigration runs in both directions, as in the US in the 1930s.

4   The model implies that a given immigrant increases the standard of living of natives. But nothing has been said about whether the immigrant being evaluated is number 1 or number 100,000 or number 1,000,000 or number 10,000,000 in a given year. The question then arises as to whether the impact varies with the number of immigrants.

In principle, immigrants at the rate of 1 per 100 natives should be much easier to absorb than at the rate of 1 to 10, or 1 to 1, or even 10 to 1. At the latter rate, it is the natives who would be absorbed into the immigrant culture if the immigrants are homogeneous.

The question may be schematized with figure 10.4. We wish for data to help us know which line in the diagram portraying the absorption process is most appropriate. We are interested both in the general shapes of the curves, and their absolute heights at each point.

Satisfactory data surely will be hard to find. We may try to consult history (the US at the turn of the twentieth century; the US at other periods; Germany and Japan after World War II; Israel in the 1950s). We may also look at a cross-section of US cities with varying amounts of immigration.

Please notice that the entire issue may well be one of time, however. That is, it may be that in a generation or so, with immigrants of equal education, adjustment will have taken place to the extent that income is no lower than if no immigrants had come.

The second issue is education. If many immigrants come with no skills, it is reasonable that the present high-level productive capacity of the US

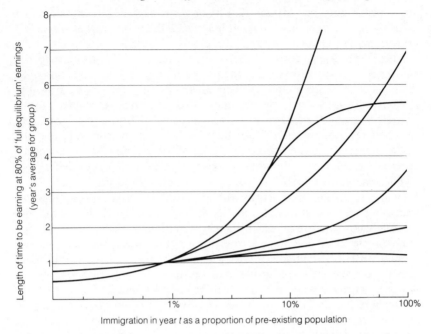

Figure 10.4   Possible absorption scenarios at various immigration levels

would be diluted so that the US income level would be like the poor countries that the immigrants came from, as discussed in chapter 8.

From a practical point of view, in my judgment it can safely be said that, at present levels of immigration, there is no difference in absorption between the first and the marginal immigrant. And judging by experience at the turn of the century, when immigration was relatively much higher, and judging also by experience in countries that have had much higher levels of immigration (see chapter 3), this could also be said at much higher levels of immigration than at present.

Summary and Conclusions

Almost two decades of well-done statistical analyses show that additional persons *qua* persons rather than just as immigrants (as measured by the rate of population growth) do not imply a slower rate of economic growth. These analyses compare the sample of nations for which data are available back into the nineteenth century, and also the larger sample for which data are available after World War II. The analyses have been conducted in a variety of ways. Yet almost every study agrees with the others that population growth does not have a negative effect.

These aggregate statistical studies are biased toward showing negative shorter-run effects if they exist; their time-span is too short to show fully the longer-run positive effects of added persons upon the rate of growth of technology and productivity, the most important effect of added people. Therefore, given the lack of negative effect in the short and intermediate run, and the positive effect after decades, it is fair to conclude that the longer-run effect on the standard of living of natives from adding people – especially immigrants – is positive, based on the empirical evidence.

The chapter describes a simulated macro-economic model which compares the incomes of natives with and without a hypothetical cohort of immigrants. This first model confirms the conclusion of chapter 7 that the possible gain to natives through increased returns to native capital, if the immigrants receive only their marginal product, is small relative to the loss to the natives if immigrants receive a realistic proportion of the returns to capital. And the life-cycle saving-and-transfer process works in a positive direction for natives, and is larger than the capital-dilution effect, according to chapters 5 and 7. The simulation shows that adding the saving-and-transfer process indeed more than offsets the capital-dilution effect.

The crucial effect of the immigrant upon productivity is also taken into account in the model, though this phenomenon has been omitted from previous work on the subject. This effect is the sum of learning-by-doing, creation of new knowledge, and economies of scale of various sorts. Within a few years the productivity effect comes to dominate the results and dwarfs the capital-dilution and saving-and-transfer effects, yielding a high rate of return to natives on investment in immigrants, on any reasonable parameters.

NOTES

1 Here are the points in brief:

First, two-variable correlation studies certainly do not indicate the forces that influence economic development. But a two-variable zero correlation can be very strong evidence, especially when buttressed by multivarious studies with a variety of specifications, that one variable (population growth) does *not* cause the other (economic development).

Second, many of the studies of population and economic development have indeed gone beyond simple two-variable correlations.

Third, not only does a correlation not "prove" causation, as the popular saw has it, but no other scientific procedure – not even a lengthy series of experiments – can "prove" causation, either.

Fourth, simple correlations of the rate of economic growth and the rate of population growth are biased toward a more negative (less positive) correlation, because the appropriate measure of economic development is the rate of change of output per worker while the usual variable is per person; substituting the former for the latter pushes the correlation coefficient in a positive direction.

2 This point is a bit complex. Only the additional capital needed for the public sector would reduce natives' wealth and income. The additional capital investment in the private sector would reduce natives' consumption but it would not reduce their wealth and income, because the expenditures on the new capital simply mean a substitution of investment for consumption.

3 After finishing this work, I discovered an interesting model by Ekburg (1977) that also makes technical progress endogenous in a migration context. Ekburg uses a Kaldor-like function, where the increment to technical progress depends upon the percentage change in the stock of capital. Elsewhere (Simon, 1986), I argue, however, that Kaldor's function is not appropriate for a study of this sort. My 1976 article on Russian immigration into Israel is the only other study of the sort that I know of.

4 That is, we want to know whether $Z_m > Z$ or $Z_n > Z$. Lifetime incomes with and without the immigration are, for our purposes here, functions of gross income less taxes

$$Z_m^v = (G_{m,t=1}^v - T_{m,t=1}^v) + d(G_{m,t=2}^v - T_{m,t=2}^v) + \ldots \text{ and}$$
$$Z_n^v = (G_{n,t=1}^v - T_{n,t=1}^v) + d(G_{n,t=2}^v - T_{n,t=2}^v) + \ldots$$

5 Phelps's function can be made more realistic with the addition of arguments representing the effect of educational level and national income on the production of technology, with the function still retaining its convenient mathematical properties. See Steinmann and Simon (1980) or Simon (1986).

6 There would appear to be no danger here that the choice of production function forces the outcome, as in the case in some studies of distributive shares. The cohort of immigrants whose effect is analyzed is small relative to the native population, and hence its effect upon the overall distribution between capital and labor is small.

Also, Ekburg (1977) experimented with a CES function and obtained the same results as with a Cobb–Douglas model.

7 Simon and Heins (1985) estimate that in 1975 the value of state and local capital was $781.5 billion, whereas the value of non-residential business capital in 1975 was $2470.6 billion (*US Statistical Abstract, 1981*, p. 545).

11 Job Displacement: Theory of Immigrants and Native Unemployment

Introduction
Conceptual Framework
Harrison's Theory Formalized
A Queue – Theoretic Analysis
Summary

Jacques Chirac, Prime Minister of France: ... for several years now, and particularly since 1981, large numbers of immigrants have been arriving in France. Given the economic situation, there are too many of them. Their numbers will thus have to decline.

Liberation [A Paris daily newspaper]: Can you assert that there is a link between the number of immigrants and the economic situation?

Chirac: Naturally. If there were fewer immigrants, there would be less unemployment, fewer tensions in certain towns and neighborhoods, a lower social cost.

Liberation: That has never been formally proven.

Chirac: It is easy to imagine, nevertheless. This means that we must not accept any new immigration and that we must severely curb illegal immigrants, rigorously apply the laws of the Republic, systematically expel those whose status is irregular ... (30 October 1984, taken from *Population and Development Review*, March 1985, p. 164)

Introduction

"Displacement" of natives by immigrants is the most emotional and politically-influential fear about immigration in the US and elsewhere. As the Committee for the Economic Development of Australia put it, "No issue fires the debate about immigration more than its alleged effects on unemployment in Australia" (Norman and Meikle, 1983). Concern about wages being driven down is a related issue, but wages seem to enter less into public rhetoric than does job displacement.

It is commonly asserted that immigrants "take jobs from citizens." Let us consider some typical statements.

A candidate for US Senate:

Sixty-five Americans lose their jobs for every 100 undocumented workers who are here. (Kent Hance, *The Washington Post*, 7 May 1984, pp. A1 and A4)

A low-skilled worker:

Belle Glade, Fla. (AP). [Headline] "Haitian Refugees Take Away Jobs" [text] "'Man, I can't find no work,' complains 20-year-old Mark Lane, a black American who once packed lettuce for $250 a week. 'Now the Haitians have got all the jobs. They're willing to do anything for $20 a day. Now, all I can do is stand on the corner.' Officials say more than 3,500 Haitians have flooded this city of 18,000 residents − 8,000 of them seasonal farm laborers − in the past year. They have ... crowded locals out of the hard-labor, low-pay farm jobs. ... Some observers say the Haitians have unwittingly created a 'slave trade' for farmers."[1] (*Champaign-Urbana News Gazette*, 29 November 1980, p. A−7)

Anti-immigration organizations:

[I]f 2 million immigrants settle in the United States every year, the unemployment rate could rise to 15.2% by 1990 and 19.1% by 2000. If immigration is within the range of 1.1 to 1.6 million annually, the unemployment rate could range from 12.2% to 13.9% by 1990, and from 12.8% to 16.4% by 2000. Such high levels of immigration will create unemployment rates that could seriously damage our economy and standard of living. (*The Data*, The Environmental Fund, November 1983, p. 2)

If illegal immigrants were not taking so many jobs in America, unemployment could be brought under 4% according to former Secretary of Labor, Ray Marshall − saving the American taxpayer millions that now go for unemployment compensation and other assistance programs. (Roger Conner, fundraising letter from FAIR, no date)

TEF [The Environment Fund] had ample opportunity in September to explain the effects of unchecked immigration on the U. S. labor force. In an unprecedented 15 sessions on Capitol Hill, TEF ran hourly briefings for congressional staffers on three successive days using our color-graphic computer presention, QUIC DATA.

With QUIC DATA projections, TEF was able to demonstrate that unemployment may rise to 14.7% by the year 1990, if present immigration and economic trends continue. Those that participated in these briefings were unanimous in their praise of TEF's comprehensive analysis of the effects of continuing massive immigration on the U. S. unemployment problem. (*The Other Side*, no. 34, October 1983, p. 1)[2]

The governor of Colorado:

[I]t is folly to import more labor. We are the only country in the world that imports a generation of poor people every year. The average American will earn less in real terms this year than a decade ago. Yet, we accept twice as many immigrants as the rest of the world combined. ... With 11 million citizens unemployed, this is demographic and economic insanity. (Richard Lamm, 1983)

In Germany:

About 50% of the West Germans surveyed worried that the East Germans are crowding the job market. (*Wall Street Journal*, 20 November 1985, p. 1)

Unions cite job loss when they argue for a policy of fewer immigrants.[3] The "official AFL−CIO spokesperson on matters concerning immigration and refugee policy" has written as follows:

The AFL-CIO opposes any program that would permit importation of foreign labor to undercut U. S. wages and working conditions ... abuses of our immigration laws and the lack of essential protections against displacement for American workers ... we do not favor the new [higher] levels of legal immigration which are part of the [Select] Commission's recommendations. (Otero, 1981)

And during 1982 Congressional discussion:

Ray Denison, chief lobbyist for the AFL−CIO, disclosed that the labor federation will oppose the bill unless it's assured that the Reagan administration and a majority of the House endorse proposed restrictions on U. S. hiring of foreigners as temporary workers ... the AFL−CIO long has been the prime backer of the bill's main element, which would make the hiring of illegal aliens by U. S. employers a federal offense. (*Wall Street Journal*, 2 December 1982, p. 7)

This comment comes from an Australian sociologist:

In present conditions migration will not lead to greatly increased spending (and thus job creation) because there is a limited pool of jobs in Australia, and migrants are winning jobs from the pool at the expense of Australian job-seekers (Birrell 1982a). ... I certainly think that the 25,000 New Zealanders who settle in Australia each year and come in virtually unchecked ought to be looked at. New Zealand is virtually exporting its unemployment problem to us. (Birrell, 1982b)

And the complaint of job displacement is an old one, probably as old as hired labor. John Toland wrote as follows in England in 1714 (p. 14):

The vulgar, I confess, are seldom pleas'd in an country with the coming in of Foreners among em ... from their grudging at more persons sharing the same trades or busines with them, which they call *taking the bread out of their mouths.*

As with popular accounts, the basis of professional discussion of the displacement issue frequently is simply that "everyone knows" displacement must occur. For example, Greenwood, one of the relatively few economists who has specialized in immigration, writes that:

[W]e can probably conclude with some assurance that New York, Los Angeles and Chicago [areas with high immigrant concentrations and highly developed industrial economies] experience labor market impacts due to immigration that are absolutely somewhat greater than those experienced elsewhere. The relative impacts are also likely to be fairly sizable compared to those on most other cities. (Select Commission Staff Report, 1981, p. 276)

But this "conclusion" is no more than supposition, and hardly a reasonable basis for important national decisions. Instead of supposition we need persuasive theory and/or reliable empirical evidence.

The displacement argument is often made with anecdotes about persons who formerly held jobs now being filled by immigrants. These anecdotes are undoubtedly painful. But when reading such anecdotes it would seem appropriate also to review in one's mind another sort of anecdote, that of the useful and productive immigrants one has known working in a variety of fields. In my own case, a quick survey turns up: C., a Cuban refugee and remarkable mathematician—physicist—computer expert whom I met when he was a 19-year-old student, just finishing a master's degree, who after two weeks as a hired research assistant turned into a full-fledged colleague and co-author; N., my older son's Tae Kwon Do (Korean karate) teacher, who had a remarkable effect upon my son's personality and confidence as he went from being a novice to a black belt; Dr C., our children's Irish pediatrician from first birth for the next 18 years. I find it hard to conceive that these persons "displaced" native Americans. And all of them became employers making jobs for natives.

Two more anecdotes illustrate the same point:

Item:
GEORGIA HIRES WEST GERMANS FOR SCIENCE AND MATH
Atlanta — Georgia education officials believe they may have found a way to ease the shortage of science and mathematics teachers that plagues high schools in this state and throughout the country: import West Germans. West Germany has a surplus of

such teachers. And the first ones who have come have been a considerable success. (*The New York Times*, 24 September 1984, p. A14)

Item:

Immigrants from Afghanistan seem to have opened fried-chicken restaurants in every corner of [New York].

There are already about 110 Afghan fast food shops in the New York area. They bear such popular all-American names as Boston Fried Chicken, Harlem Fried Chicken and Texas Fried Chicken.

Afghans have also opened restaurants in New Jersey, Pennsylvania, Washington, D.C., and most recently California, for a total of about 200 chicken places in the country.

Although many of the latest Afghan arrivals have entered the fried-chicken business, the man who started it all and some of the major chicken entrepeneurs [sic] from Afghanistan arrived before the Soviet invasion.

Taeb Zia, who is known in Afghan circles as the father of Kennedy Fried Chicken, studied engineering in Baku in the Soviet Union. "But I hated Russia and didn't like the factory work," he recalled the other day.

He came to the United States in 1972 and got a job with Kansas Fried Chicken through an employment agency. Three years later he had earned enough to buy the franchise. "Then I saw I could do chicken just as well and 15 to 20 percent cheaper with my own recipe and spices," Mr. Zia said.

Today he runs six Kennedy Fried Chicken Shops in Manhattan, Queens and Brooklyn, employing mainly Afghan refugees and providing technical assistance to many other aspiring Afghan entrepeneurs [sic]. His chain is named after the American President "just because Afghans like him a lot."

The Afghan incursion into chicken is a direct result of Mr. Zia's involvement. In a kind of pyramid effect, he hired Afghan refugees who worked in his shops and then went on to open their own. Although many Afghans arrived in the United States with language problems and little experience, they learned from him.

"We don't know what to do, and then we see Zia and learn how an Afghan can do business here," said Abdul Mosaver, who owns two successful New York Fried Chicken stores in Queens and one in Brooklyn, employing a total of 50 people, mostly Afghans. (*New York Times*, 7 October 1984, p. 47)

It would seem that at least some displacement and some reduction in wages *must* immediately occur when potential workers in a particular occupation are added to the labor force, whether those potential workers be laborers or physicians, unless the immigration has been expected and allowed for. Even if immigrants' occupations are in the same proportion as the distribution of occupations in the economy – and they are not too far from that, as chapter 3 shows – one might expect frictional increases in unemployment for at least some period of time. But expectations of the arrival of immigrants may generate new jobs in advance of the immigrants' arrival that offset the frictional competitive effect. Harrison's analysis of the imbalance between the demand for goods and the supply of job seekers also works against frictional effects, as discussed below.

In the years before World War I when the US did not restrict general immigration, and also in the 1930s, there was a natural check on job displacement. Immigrants already in the US often financed the transportation and settling expenses of their relatives in the "old country," as Isaac noted then (1947, p. 34). And when times were hard, relatives furnished less such support, hence reducing new entries to the labor force when there already was unemployment. But now that quotas are always filled, this check is absent.

This chapter presents some new theory that goes beyond the standard considerations. Empirical estimates of unemployment and wage effects are found in the following chapter.

Conceptual Framework

The idea underlying fear of job displacement is simple: If the number of jobs is fixed, and immigrants occupy some jobs, there are fewer available jobs for natives. This apparently obvious idea is found in several of the quotations adduced above.[4]

The opposite over-simplified view of the matter is that the supply of jobs expands instantly and without limit in response to market changes in wages, the way the supply of purchasers of vegetables seems to expand just before closing time in a farmers' market as prices are knocked down by sellers, so that no vegetables go unsold. In the 1930s, people concluded that this model does not describe the labor market; because it was discredited, its core insight was lost.

An adequate theory of the unemployment effect of immigration – or of school leavers or additional women entering the labor force, for that matter – must be more complex. It must treat both the wage response and the unemployment response, as well as the internal migration response that Manson, Espenshade, and Muller (1985) call to our attention and demonstrate in the case of Hispanic immigration into California. Manson et al. show that, unlike the western region of the US as a whole, net immigration to California declined between 1965–70 and 1975–80 (p. 17). Furthermore, they found that "the inflow between 1970 and 1983 was weighted toward more-skilled professional and nonprofessional workers, and that the outflow was largely comprised of less-skilled workers" (p. 21), the latter the type of worker the Hispanic immigrants most strongly compete with.

A satisfactorily complex theory is not at hand. But two pieces of theory may advance our understanding, and help us have narrower bounds for the effect than the poles of the two above-mentioned over-simplified notions. The first new piece of theory, that of Harrison (1983), ingeniously analyzes how exogenous increases in demand caused by immigrants' consumption affect the native and immigrant unemployment rates differently, and can *reduce* native unemployment even as immigrant unemployment rises. The second, newly presented here (though in brief) looks at the job market competition as a problem in queue theory, and some available parameters suggest upper bounds for the damage done to native unemployment.[5]

Harrison's Theory Formalized[6]

Harrison (1983) has contributed a quite new idea to the understanding of the effects of immigrants on native unemployment. He notes that an immigrant increases the demand for goods and services immediately upon arrival, and hence increases the demand for labor independently of starting work. If immigrant consumption is assumed (for now only) equal to the average native or family, the demand for labor goes up by one full job, and hence by the proportion $1/L$ that the immigrant bears to the labor force as a whole. The key point of the analysis is that the immigrant then has a *greater* than $1/L$ chance of being *unemployed* because most of the employed labor force does not change jobs each year. This would *decrease native unemployment* under conditions of wage fixity and an unchanged overall unemployment rate.

Harrison illustrates his argument with numerical examples. Simple formalization seems to bring out his point more clearly, and allows us (Kwang Ng and myself) to better analyze its implications with different sets of parameters. We assume that the ratio of workers to consumers is the same among natives and immigrants, and other conditions at large remain the same. Let:

U_n = the number of natives unemployed in the absence of the group of immigrants whose effect is being analyzed

U_n' = the number of natives unemployed in the presence of the group of immigrants

E_n = the number of natives employed pre-immigrants

E_n' = the number of natives employed post-immigrants

M = the number of immigrants in the cohorts whose effect is being analyzed

s = the proportion of natives who leave their jobs each year and seek new jobs, i.e. the job turnover rate

d = average immigrant's spending for consumption relative to average native spending for consumption, immediately upon arrival — a fraction likely to be unity or less, which may be thought of as the fraction of a new job created by an immigrant

a = the relative likelihoods of an immigrant and a native of being hired for a particular job opening, i.e. an indicator of the relative

job-getting success rates
aM = the "effective" number of job-seekers in the cohort immigrants.

We begin with the number of natives unemployed following upon the entry of the immigrants whose effect is being analyzed ("immigration" hereafter).

$$U'_{native} = U_n + sE_n - (sE_n + dM) \left(\frac{sE_n + U_n}{sE_n + U_n + aM} \right) \quad (11.1)$$

The first two terms on the right-hand side of (11.1) are, respectively, the numbers of natives originally unemployed, and job turnovers. From these are subtracted the sum of the jobs open due to turnover and to the increased demand due to the immigration $(sE_n + dM)$, multiplied by the ratio of the number of natives seeking work $(sE_n + U_n)$ to the sum of the natives seeking work plus the "effective" number of immigrants seeking work $(sE + U_n + aM)$.

Subtracting the "pre" native unemployment from the "post" native unemployment

$$U'_n - U_n = \frac{(a - d) \, sE_n M - dMU_n}{sE_n + U_n + aM} \quad (11.2)$$

For native immigration to fall, that is, for $U' - U$ to be negative, it is necessary and sufficient that

$$(a - d) \, sE_n - dU_n < 0, \quad \text{or} \quad (11.3)$$
$$d \, (sE_n + U_n) > asE_n$$

which is necessarily satisfied (but not only then) if $U_n > 0$ and $d \geqslant a$. That is, as long as there is any native unemployment it will fall due to immigration if an immigrant's consumption bears a higher proportion to native consumption than an immigrant's propensity to find a job bears to a native's propensity to find a job in the same market.

It is interesting to note that the job turnover does not enter into these conditions; it could even be zero. In fact, the situation is easiest to envisage with a zero turnover rate; if turnover is zero, in the absence of immigrants there are no jobs for unemployed natives to find. But the coming of immigrants creates some new openings due to increased demand, and hence some unemployed natives can find jobs.

Re-arranging we get

$$\frac{sE_n}{U_n + sE_n} < \frac{d}{a} \quad (11.4)$$

which shows that the conditions for native unemployment to fall are quite weak with realistic parameters. For example, if the native unemployment rate and the turnover rate are about the same (say 8 percent), then d need only be half as large as a for native unemployment to fall; if a is 0.8, d could be as low as 0.4.

The analysis has not referred to immigrant unemployment. It obviously will be higher than native unemployment at first even if $a = 1$, i.e. the job-finding propensity is the same for both, because some (most) natives have jobs whereas no immigants do, and more immigrants are hunting for jobs. The relationship of the immigrant and native rates obviously is heavily dependent upon the turnover rate. Estimates can easily be derived with various numerical assumptions.

When a higher rate among immigrants than among natives is indeed observed − as has been the case in Australia recently (see chapter 4) − it should *not* be viewed as a sign of added pressure upon natives, but rather the opposite; it may well be the sign of increased job opportunities and diminished unemployment for natives.

Harrison's analysis is not affected by whether the immigrants do or do not receive financial assistance from the government prior to finding employment. But the economic welfare implications are different if the financing comes from private immigrant funds or from government assistance.

Harrison models new immigrants like a Marxian "reserve army of the unemployed." This may or may not be an ethically desirable situation. But the immigrants clearly choose this period of unemployment as part of their long-term investment in migration, and native "workers" may be helped thereby. (In contrast, Marx's "reserve army" was for the benefit of the *capitalists*.)

Even if the actual parameters are such that Harrison's mechanism by itself does not produce an on-balance employment advantage for natives, the mechanism must work to substantially reduce the immigrant-caused increase in waiting period for natives seeking jobs that is modeled in the analysis in the next section. Together, the two lines of analysis suggest that the unemployment burden upon natives is small if it even exists at all.

A Queue − Theoretic Analysis

The aim of the theory newly offered in this section is to estimate the added time waiting for a job by natives who are unemployed, due to additional competition by immigrants. The analysis begins with two extreme hypotheses about the main forces which work in opposite directions, and then examines other influences which keep these forces from continuing to work to their extremes.

The first force is momentary job fixity and the associated queuing effect. To make the process concrete, I suggest that the main causes of delay in finding a job are, first, the time needed to search for job openings and to apply for them, and second, the time spent in waiting for several job candidates to be evaluated and one among them to be selected and hired. To some extent these waiting periods can be concurrent, but they will also be sequential to some extent. The more applicants there are for jobs, the more of a *given* person's applications will be unsuccessful, and the larger the total time waiting to be selected. (This phenomenon may be thought of as a congestion effect, though there is no reason to believe that the increase in waiting time is non-linear with the number of competitors for jobs.) If the number of jobs really were fixed and the persons in the queue are homogeneous and wait their turn the way taxis queue up at the airport, a single immigrant added to the queue would impose an infinitely large *total* added waiting time upon the aggregate of other people now living and to be born in the future. That is, if the person in the queue behind the immigrant has to wait an additional x hours for a job, the second person will also have to wait an additional x hours, as well as the third and nth person. If the number of persons who will eventually come is N, the total added waiting time is N multiplied by x, and if N is infinite, Nx is infinite.

For this not to be the case — that is, for a single immigrant not to impose a very large waiting-time burden upon natives — the number of jobs must expand as the queue grows larger. Of course this is what does happen. Therefore we must inquire what causes the number of jobs to increase, and how fast they increase in response to the queue size and to other possible influences.

The opposed force that expands jobs also has an infinitely great impact in abstract unmodified form. Imagine an immigrant who by persuasive skill induces a business which would not otherwise have hired anyone to hire the immigrant. This might be because the immigrant has skills that the employer wants but cannot find among natives now looking for work. Or the additional hire might be due to the immigrant offering to work at a wage lower than prevailing, thereby converting the employer's calculation into a positive reckoning for the hiring whereas it was negative at the prevailing wage. (That is, assume that the employer was just at the margin of decision before, and the lower wage tips the balance.) Or it might be that this immigrant is just a very good salesperson and talks the employer into the hiring. So the labor force is thereby increased by one person. But we must also trace the longer-run consequences of this occurrence.

After an immigrant finds such an "added" job, and after a period of adjustment to be discussed below, natives who are seeking employment are no worse off than if the immigrant had not taken that job. Almost as soon as the immigrant begins work, s/he spends his/her earnings either on consumption items or on portfolio investment which is then spent on producer goods.[7] This spending may be seen as complementary to the pre-earnings consumption that drives Harrison's analysis discussed above. We may expect that, in a short space of time, these added earnings will produce roughly one full job someplace else in the economy; this increase in employment must take place unless there are economies of scale working to reduce the effect[8]. And though this adjustment does not happen instantaneously, it should happen sufficiently quickly so that for many purposes we may safely ignore the time lag. (And we should keep in mind that if the entry of the immigrants into the economy is anticipated by managers, on the basis of normal flows, there need not be any lag at all.)

Toland well understood this process back in 1714:

We deny not that there will thus be more taylors and shoomakers; but there will also be more suits and shoos made than before. If there were more weavers, watchmakers, and other artificers, we can for this reason export more cloth, watches, and more of all other commodities than formerly: and not only have 'em better made by the emulation of so many workmen, of such different Nations; but likewise have 'em quicker sold off, for being cheapter wrought than thoise of others who come to the same market. (1714, p. 14)

At the bottom of popular thinking about immigration is a very different view of the aggregate production function, that no additional jobs are created when additional persons begin working and spend their earnings. The implicit assumption of such a view is that the economy somehow has the capacity to produce more goods without more labor, and therefore there will be no increase in jobs when the demand for goods increases. And we should not be surprised that people hold such a view; I confess to slipping into this sort of thinking myself when I am not careful. The intellectual difficulty is that the process is very indirect and very diffuse; though it is easy to imagine in one's mind's eye an immigrant sitting down before a machine and taking a place that a native might otherwise occupy, one cannot so easily picture in one's imagination the small effect on the labor force in the plant that manufactures the refrigerator that the immigrant buys, at the trucking firms that move the refrigerator along the channels of distribution, in the wholesaler's sales force or front office, in the number of sales clerks in retail stores, and so on. Each of these increases is far less than a single person, and in almost all of these places of work an additional person is *not* hired in response to the immigrant's earnings. But in *one* place the additional volume of business will be enough to cause a manager to move from a decision that previously was just marginally not to hire an additional person, to a decision to hire an additional person. And the next immigrant's spending will cause this sort of response someplace else. This process is very hard to visualize, and would be even harder to pin down if one should try to trace the linkage organizationally. Yet on average it must occur.

The process may become clearer by specifying more exactly what is meant by an "open job." A "job opening" is not a physical place, but rather a set of marks on a personnel recruiter's docket indicating that a worker is being sought. In contrast, an "existing job" may safely be thought of as a physical workplace and an accompanying paycheck regularly being issued. Given the state of economic activity at any given moment (as measured, perhaps by GNP), some firms will desire to hire additional people; and these desires are indicated on internal documents and perhaps by advertisements.

Now imagine that one person comes unexpectedly into the society, somehow causes there to be an additional "open job," and manages to get hired. When the person begins working, economic activity becomes greater than before the person began working. The signals emanating from this change in economic activity, between the situation before and the situation after the person begins working, induce a change in plans at some other firm elsewhere in the economy, based on the expectations of future sales and profits that have been revised in light of the change. This revision of business expectations results in a new set of marks on one personnel recruiter's papers somewhere in the economy, which constitutes another "open job" that did not exist before this train of events began.

This analysis in terms of signals and expectations, rather than in terms of workplaces connected with physical capital, should make clear that the process is not simply a case of an immigrant filling an "existing" job. Rather, when an immigrant manages to induce a new slot to be opened, there then occurs a series of changes in the demand for labor elsewhere in the economy as a result of the immigrant coming to work and collecting a paycheck. Admittedly, this is a rather slippery idea. At first thought it may seem as if the newly hired immigrant is only producing goods to exchange for the goods that s/he will then purchase and consume, without there being any other changes. But at a minimum, it should be obvious that there must be a change in the total production of some goods following upon the newly hired immigrant starting to work, and also a change in the mix of goods, because the immigrant produces only one kind of goods. Therefore, if the immigrant does not produce shoes but does wear them, makers of shoes will produce more shoes than before the immigrant goes to work. This change may result in a change in the hiring plans of a shoe manufacturer − or a hat manufacturer, or a violin academy. The only case in which the immigrant would not affect anyone else is if the immigrant becomes a subsistence farmer.

Contrast the above sequence of events with the sequence which begins with a native being laid off from an "existing job" which then is not refilled because of lack of demand for the product being produced, continuing with the event of the laid-off native or an immigrant finding what is then an "open job" elsewhere in the economy and going to work there, at which time that open job becomes an "existing job." There will be no change in total business activity in the economy (aside from any change flowing from the change in mix of output and a difference in salary), and no new demand for an additional worker elsewhere in the economy, following upon this sequence of events which is different from the case we are discussing.

The key element in the process under discussion is that the change in economic activity which occurs as soon as the immigrant begins working at the newly created job sends a signal out through the economy which then induces a change in expectations.

So, another employee is hired somewhere on account of this immigrant. But there is more to come. On account of the second person's spending, a third person is hired somewhere; and on and on indefinitely. This implies that a newly created job opening filled by an immigrant leads to an infinite number of other people also being hired as a consequence.

Just as we noted earlier that the waiting time for jobs caused to natives by the additional immigrant does not accumulate indefinitely, this process also cannot continue indefinitely, if only because at some point there are no more persons to hire (aside from the "frictional" unemployed); various influences must come into play so that the force of the immigrant's hiring eventually plays itself out.[9] Also, the process does not take place instantaneously; each hire takes time to generate another job.

One might wonder whether the same long chain of additional hirings takes place when a native replaces another native on a job, and if not, why not. The distinction between the "new" job which the immigrant (or anyone else) causes to be open, and an "old" job which was formerly filled by one person who leaves or is fired and then is filled by another person, is, of course, artificial. In both cases, employers make calculations about the profitability of making a new hire. But where a person was already working and spending money, it is reasonable to think that the adjustments in the rest of the system consequent on the start of that job have already occurred, and there is therefore no new impetus to additional economic activity when a replacement is hired. (Of course if there is a lengthy hiatus between the first person leaving the job and the second beginning on it, there would be a shrinking of economic activity and then a re-expansion, and the re-expansion would be analogous to the situation of the immigrant described above.)

It may be easier to visualize the process if one imagines the reverse process — the US after a random half of the working population were suddenly removed. For a while, workers would have larger incomes due to the larger supply of capital to work with, and due to the lack of necessity to build new capital for a while. But after the capital effect peters out after a few years, nothing would be different from what it would be if the halving of the workforce had not taken place, and incomes would be the same as otherwise (though lower because of productivity effects, as discussed in chapter 8). There would be no increase in employment. And so it is with immigration, except in reverse.

We can make concrete the two opposing effects with the device of a group of immigrants. Assume there are five in the cohort – Able, Baker, Charlie, Dog, and Easy. Able "opens up" a new job the first day, a job that previously did not exist and that Able brought about with a combination of persuasion and a low salary. This sets in motion the sequence that produces jobs for other persons, natives or immigrants, though we do not know how many additional persons or how long it takes for them to get hired, one after the other. The other four immigrants – Baker to Easy – do not find work immediately and stand in the queue searching and waiting for jobs, and thereby making it harder for natives to find jobs. Again, just how much extra waiting time they cause for natives is not known, nor do we have any way of estimating it.

An illustrative calculation may render the matter more understandable. For simplicity, assume that all hiring takes place discretely at ten-week intervals. At the moment when Baker or Easy get jobs after ten weeks, they cause four persons who would have gotten jobs then to wait an additional ten weeks for jobs. Now consider that Able generates another new job ten weeks after he begins work – a period equal to the average length of a spell of unemployment in the US. This removes one person from the queue. And at the twenty-week mark, three workers who would otherwise have gotten jobs now have to wait an extra ten weeks, having been pushed back by the sequence of the four immigrants but diminished by the one new job created. After another ten weeks the sequence begun by Able generates a second job, and now two workers who would otherwise have gotten jobs then have to wait an extra ten weeks. And at the thirty-week mark there is one worker who has to wait an extra ten weeks. So the combination of Baker to Easy standing in the queue, and Able starting a sequence of new job creation, results in $4 + 3 + 2 + 1 = 10$ periods of ten weeks, or 100 weeks in total, of additional unemployment, or twenty weeks per immigrant – *up to this point.*

The positive effects of the job-creation sequence continue, however, and at some time the continuing reductions in time unemployed will completely offset the 100 weeks in increased unemployment time for natives. This process theoretically would continue forever, or until prevented from further continuation by the economy running out of available workers or by leakages of one sort or another. And of course we must recognize that the bad effects of this sequence occur earlier than the good effects, and discounting would therefore make the overall assessment somewhat more negative than it appears in this scenario.

Wage decrease in response to the increased supply of labor in particular categories has, however, been omitted from the story until now, and it exerts a powerful force in mitigation of that increase. Though those persons steeped in the Keynesian analysis of unemployment are predisposed to assume that wages are rigid with respect to downward movement, an increase in immigrants (and in the size of an age cohort, which is quite comparable in this respect) results in significant wage change; the evidence is reviewed in chapter 12. (With respect to studies outside of the field of immigration, the review is selective rather than comprehensive, but this should be acceptable because the main aim is simply to communicate the main point of this literature rather than to critically assess the body of work.)

Perhaps the best estimate for our purposes is that of Morgan and Gardner (1982, pp. 398−9; see next chapter for details), even though it is short-run in nature and limited to agriculture in a few states. They find an elasticity of −3.2 between employment and wages (stated in this fashion because the causation must be mutual and simultaneous). And they find that while 210,000 additional persons were added to the work rolls as the wage declined by 9 percent, only 51,000 natives failed to find jobs who would otherwise have worked in the industry (and of course some portion of these persons moved on to jobs in other industries rather than remaining unemployed). And when considering a single industry, new jobs are not created by way of the income spent by newly hired workers, so the unemployment estimate is not biased downwards.

The Morgan−Gardner results imply that one immigrant may have to suffer spells of unemployment for each four immigrants who find work immediately. If this is so, the economy-wide job-creation effects following on their spending of their incomes should operate so strongly that the total unemployment caused to natives by the coming of the immigrants should be negligible.

It should be remembered that a reduction in wages in a particular sector due to immigration does not mean an overall loss of wage income to natives. Rather, most of what is lost to one sector is likely to be gained in wages by another sector, while not resulting in an increase in capital's share, simply because the wage share of total income is so large. It should be remembered, too, that the relative decline in wages is by no means always in the poorest sectors; in recent years, physicians have probably suffered a greater relative decline in income due to immigration than any other occupation.

Summary

The two analyses in this chapter – Harrison's, and the queue theory newly presented here – are complementary. Harrison focuses upon the exogenous consumption effect, and my analysis focuses upon the extent of additional labor-market "congestion" caused by additional competitors for jobs. Both analyses suggest that the effect upon natives' unemployment is much less than common belief has it, and native unemployment may even be lessened rather than increased due to immigrants. The next chapter describes empirical analyses that estimate the size of the unemployment effect, as well as the related wage effect.

NOTES

1 The importation of sugar workers nicely illustrates how we get ourselves into an unnecessary ethical difficulty in one market by attempting to manipulate another market for the gain of a few. The only reason that the sugar industry still exists in the US is the scheme of sugar quotas to protect the US growers at the expense of growers elsewhere; without quotas there would be no foreign workers whose entry one could oppose on grounds that we are "exploiting" them. On the other hand, abolishing the quotas would mean that those who now come to work in the US would earn less at home, either in sugar or in other industries. It seems to me that objecting to the importation of sugar cane workers is not a useful place to begin a reform campaign – unless one is only using it as a smokescreen for opposition to guest workers.

2 It should be noted that the QUIC DATA "model" is simply a single equation specifying a fixed number of jobs, which therefore produces apparent unemployment by simple arithmetic whenever the labor force is increased. More about this below.

3 The usual reaction is a call for restriction of immigration. An interesting example of a response to fear of displacement more subtle than quotas is the set of state restrictions on women's work, which, as Landes (1980) shows, tended to be enacted in states with heavy immigration.

4 It is of interest that many of these writers implicitly assume it is government which creates jobs. For example, The Environmental Fund writes: "high unemployment would trigger measures," (*TEF News*, Environmental Fund, 21 September 1983, p. 1) presumably government measures. This language implies lack of understanding that it is markets for goods and labor that lead to jobs, and that historically the process is roughly automatic, though not instantly responsive. From the TEF job-fixity way of thinking inevitably follows the belief that immigrants cause unemployment.

5 Warren (1982), following on Hughes (1975, referred to by Warren), discussed still another possible influence, an increase in job-matching efficiency caused by

a larger labor force swelled by immigrants. Warren does not find evidence for this hypothesis in the Australian data, and it does not seem to me of likely importance, because a large increase in the labor force would seem necessary to make a small improvement in matching efficiency.

6 The following formalization of Harrison's analysis was done jointly with Yew-Kwang Ng as an article entitled 'The effect of immigration upon native unemployment: A formalization of Harrison's analysis'.

While the book was being copy-edited, it was brought to my attention that Bruce J. Chapman, David Pope, and Glenn Withers, 'Immigration and the Labour Market,' (in Neville R. Norman and Kathryn F. Meikle, 1985, pp. 215–20), had earlier developed a model similar to ours, though with more complexity.

7 The notion that some of the earnings disappear in gold coins under the mattress has little reality these days. If the immigrant remits some of the earnings abroad, the effect is much the same as domestic purchases, because those dollars eventually buy imports from the US, though remittances sent abroad may slow the adjustment process a bit; see the final section of chapter 2 for more discussion.

8 The only fashion in which the economy could provide the additional goods and services bought with the immigrant's earnings without there being the equivalent of an additional person being hired throughout the economy is if there are economies of scale so that the cost in labor necessary for the creation of the incremental goods and services would be less than for the same amount of goods at lower levels of production. And even if there are some economies of scale, it is inconceivable that on average it might take less than, say, 90 percent of an additional person's labor – or 80 percent at the absolute outside – to provide the additional goods and services. There is nothing in the literature on industrial organization to suggest economies of scale of any such magnitude throughout the economy.

A side-benefit of the additional person joining the economy, as compared to not immigrating, is that the new job is likely to be in the most dynamic part of the economy; this is one of the advantages of any labor-force growth.

9 This description is related to the concept of the multiplier in regional analysis. But it is not clear whether there is anything worthwhile about that concept.

Some may worry that this analysis is faulty because it constitutes an infinite process. The Keynesian less-than-full-employment multiplier also raised such a question until the additional idea of "leakage" was introduced. (This analogy should not be interpreted as an endorsement of Keynesian analysis or policies, of course.)

12 Empirical Studies of Labor-Market Effects

Issues in Empirical Research Design
Discussion
Conclusions

Following on the theoretical material in the previous chapter, this chapter discusses the recently burgeoning body of empirical studies of the labor-market effect of immigration.

While this book was in production I received some of the papers from a January 1988 National Bureau of Economic Research conference on "Immigration, Trade, and the Labor Market." Several touch on the subject of this chapter, especially that by Topel (1988). All the findings reported there confirm the conclusions suggested by the studies described in this chapter.

Issues in Empirical Research Design

It is difficult to determine if immigrants cause unemployment among citizens at large because the job-creating process — which offsets the job-taking process — is so much more indirect and diffuse than is the job-taking process. It is even difficult to establish how many advertised jobs would stand open if immigrants do not come, because after a while employers make other arrangements, either by using machines instead of human labor or by reducing the scale of the enterprise. Assuredly, one learns nothing about the extent of "displacement" by simply observing either that immigrants are "occupying" jobs (see discussion below of Huddle's writing), or that immigrants are working at wages that do not attract sufficient natives to fill the jobs.

A cross-national study is not feasible, because few developed nations have experienced substantial quantities of immigration, though we may note that those countries which have had relatively high immigration in recent years – the US, West Germany, Israel, Hong Kong, Canada, and Australia, for example – certainly have not been marked by unusually high rates of unemployment by natives during the periods of high immigration. One might argue that this is not convincing evidence because the receiving country's unemployment rate influences the immigration rate (Jerome, 1926; Thomas, 1941; Kuznets and Rubin, 1954). But much of the post-World War II immigration into such countries as Hong Kong, West Germany, and the US has been pushed by politics and limited by quotas rather than just pulled by economic conditions, thereby reducing the importance of the pull factor and making the direction of causation from immigration to unemployment more clearcut. In the US in recent years the overall quota has always been filled, so the pull factor cannot operate differentially. Nevertheless, on balance, cross-national evidence is not likely to produce a satisfactory answer to the question at hand.

Time-series analysis of a single country's experience is not likely to produce a satisfactory answer either, because of the paucity of observations as well as because of the pull effect mentioned above. (But see the Withers–Pope study of Australia's experience discussed below.) Additionally, in the US in recent decades, the proportion of immigrants of working age to the total population of working age has been sufficiently small so that one would expect difficulty in detecting an effect in the overall unemployment rate even if the effect of an additional immigrant is relatively large.

Cross-sectional study of the experiences of American labor markets would seem to overcome some of the difficulties mentioned above. But another pull factor arises in such a study: immigrants may choose labor markets with low unemployment rather than choosing locations randomly (in the sense that the choice is unconnected to the unemployment level). Also, some natives move from areas of high unemployment to areas of low unemployment. Both of these forces may mask the effect of immigrants upon the unemployment level. Additionally, unemployment is measured in very different ways in different states.

With respect to the last-named difficulty, individual-level data permit better measurement of unemployment. But the main body of data available are censuses, and such data are available only every ten years. Current Population Survey data do not offer sufficiently large samples in smaller areas. Several studies of this type are useful, however, and will be described below.

Another way to mitigate the difficulties of a cross-section of labor markets is to work with *changes* in unemployment rather than with absolute levels, which may reduce much of the noise and bias caused by differences in state measurement methods. This device – used in the Simon–Moore study described below – also makes it possible in principle to detect an effect on unemployment of immigrants who move into low-unemployment areas. Another possible way to grapple with the latter problem is to independently assess the extent of the unemployment rate upon immigrants' choices of city, and then to adjust for it; others' research (e.g. Bartel, 1982; Rogers, 1969) as well as our own suggests that the effect may be very small, however, as we shall see.

The phenomenon of natives moving away from a labor market in response to additional competition for jobs caused by immigrants is more difficult to deal with. It might at first seem that if the pattern were one of immigrants moving to low-unemployment cities, this complication would not exist. But this need not be so; if a native were, for other reasons, just on the margin of moving from one city to another, even from a low-unemployment to a high-unemployment city, immigrants could slightly worsen the employment situation in the original city and thereby cause the move to take place. If this effect is important, it would vitiate an across-city analysis; aggregate (all-US) time-series analysis would then be the only conceivable way to assess the effect in which we are interested, and that method is not feasible for reasons given earlier.

Though there seems to be no feasible design that will avoid this latter difficulty, in principle it is possible to allow for the bias with the elasticity of domestic migration with respect to unemployment, as estimated by other studies, i.e. the total (unbiased) displacement effect would equal the observed (biased) displacement effect plus the domestic migration effect.

The special relationship between low-skill immigrants and the unemployment of low-skill natives is another problem, conceptually as well as empirically. Consider, for example, the following not-atypical news story about the difficulty that employers have in recruiting low-skill workers:

Help Wanted: Burger Flippers, Teens Preferred
Berlin, N.J. – Betty Hagen stands out among the employees at the Kentucky Fried Chicken restaurant here, not because her uniform is usually covered in biscuit flour, but because the hair tucked under her cap is gray. While nearly all her colleagues are teenagers, Mrs. Hagen is a 60-year-old grandmother.

About 3.5 million people work in fast-food outlets, and nearly three-fourths of the workers are between the ages of 16 and 20. But lately, youngsters have become more choosy about their jobs. Many don't like the fast-food product, pay, or image.

The result is giving fast-food managers headaches. More of them are closing the gap by recruiting people like Mrs. Hagen; McDonald's Corp. and Kentucky Fried Chicken Corp. look for help in churches and retirement homes.

But generally, fast-food managers are tackling the problem head-on, vigorously going after the nation's teen-agers. This summer, for instance, Wendy's International Inc. will recruit at a national Boy Scout Jamboree. In the Northeast, Marriott Corp.'s Roy Rogers division offers jobs on the spot to regular customers. To retain young workers, Pillsbury Co.'s Burger King offers its workers a bonus of up to $2,000, depending upon length of employment, that goes toward paying for college. (*Wall Street Journal*, 28 May 1985, p. 33)

If the flow of low-skill immigrants is sufficiently great that employers do not actively recruit young people and retired persons, should that be counted as employment harm to natives? In some sense, surely yes, even though harm would not appear in the unemployment rate. And some native workers' wages are higher than they would be if there were more immigrants applying for these jobs. On the other hand, some jobs that would be filled if there were more immigrants are instead standing open, with no harm to natives, and some are mechanized. It would contribute to an enlightened understanding if we knew the quantitative relationships among these phenomena – numbers of immigrants, wage rates, jobs filled by natives, open jobs, unemployed natives, and so on. But even then, to make real sense of the matter it would be necessary to go beyond one-industry short-run considerations, just as with tariffs and other trade barriers. And in a long-run perspective, these short-run effects wash out.

Several types of empirical evidence concerning the relationship between immigration and unemployment are discussed in this chapter: (1) Comparison of unemployment rates, and of labor-force participation rates, in areas with different levels of immigration. (2) Comparison of wages in places where there are more and less immigrants. (3) Comparison of wages and employment in industries when there have been more and less workers of the same labor class that characterizes a particular group of immigrants, such as factory workers. (4) Time-series analysis over business cycles. (5) Miscellaneous studies, including studies of the analogous phenomena of the effects of school leavers, and of increasing numbers of women entering the labor force. (6) Questionnaire studies of immigrants' experiences in the labor market. Experiments that remove illegal immigrants from jobs and then make the jobs available to legal residents are discussed in chapter 14. Because some studies fall into more than one of these categories, however, the order of studies to be described cannot neatly follow this classification.

Kuznets on Southern blacks

Kuznets greatly admired immigration's economic effects. Nevertheless, he was concerned about the effects upon subgroups of the population. He judged that rural Southern blacks benefited from the cessation of mass immigration.

It meant, once the worst of the depression of the 1930's was over, that the reduction in the inflow of immigrant labor opened up opportunities for more employment of native labor at similar skill levels, particularly of Negroes from the

South. It is hardly an accident that while the proportion of all Negroes in the country residing in the South hovered at about 90 percent from 1770 to 1910, it began to decline with World War I, and by 1970 dropped to 53 percent, with substantial shares of Negro population appearing in the other regions, particularly the North. Conversely, the proportion of foreign born in the total white population of the non-South, at a peak of about 21 percent in 1910, dropped to below 6 percent in 1970. (1977, p. 4)

Smith-Newman study of wages in Texas

Smith and Newman (1977) carried out the first convincing study of the effect of immigration upon wages, analyzing the effects of legal Mexican immigrants in various Texas cities with differing proportions of Mexicans in the population and at different distances from the border. They found that wages (actually, yearly incomes with adjustments for hours and weeks worked, as well as for age, education, occupation and migration history) are indeed much higher − a 20 percent lower wage near the border, where the Mexican population is proportionally greater than away from the border. But when they adjusted for the cost-of-living differences between these cities, the differential was reduced to 8 percent. And if they were to adjust for the well-known differentially higher wage in larger cities − Houston, in this case, compared to Corpus Christi, Brownsville and Laredo − the differential would be even less. On the other hand, the differential is higher than average for the lower-skilled occupational group.

Urban Institute study of Los Angeles County and elsewhere

Comparison of one area with the rest of the nation is fraught with the danger that special conditions of one sort or another, not connected with the relationship in question, may account for the phenomenon to be explained. And this difficulty must be kept in mind when considering the results of the comparison of labor-market conditions in Los Angeles County with the rest of the US by Muller (1984) and by Muller and Espenshade (1985). Yet these findings are of interest even if they are less conclusive than we would like (as all studies on this topic are less conclusive than some social-scientific studies).

This is Muller's description of his results concerning unemployment:

To what extent did the influx of immigrants entering Southern California in the 1970's reduce the jobs available to nonimmigrant workers? The answer for the 1970's is little if at all. Although Hispanic workers filled a large proportion of the jobs added during the decade, particularly in manufacturing, there is no indication that work opportunities for nonimmigrants lessened. Despite mass immigration to

Southern California, unemployment rates rose less rapidly there than in the remainder of the nation. Furthermore, the labor-force participation rate (the proportion of the population in the labor force) did not seem to be affected. In fact the participation rate for both blacks and whites was higher in Southern California than elsewhere in the state and nation. Moreover, the difference in the participation rate between Southern California and the rest of the country remains essentially unchanged since 1970, indicating that the influx of immigrants did not discourage people from seeking employment. (p. 13)

He continues:

Even the job prospects for black teenagers do not appear to be adversely affected by the influx of immigrants. Total teenage unemployment in Southern California is close to the national average, but unemployment among black teenagers is substantially lower than average. (p. 14)

Muller and Espenshade also conducted a cross-sectional study of black unemployment in 247 metropolitan areas in the US, and 51 metropolitan areas in California, New Mexico, and Arizona, states with large proportions of Mexican-origin persons. They regressed the rate of unemployment among blacks upon the percentage of Hispanics in the population, holding constant the percentage change in population between 1970 and 1980, the percentage of income from construction and durable goods industries, the percentage of blacks with a high school education, and the rate of unemployment for whites. They found as follows:

Black unemployment rates are not increased – if anything, they are lowered – by a rise in the proportion of Mexican immigrants in a local labor market. In the US sample regression, signs of the remaining coefficients are as one would expect. Thus, after accounting for general labor market conditions, most of the variation in black unemployment rates among metropolitan areas can be attributed to differences in black educational attainment, in the rate of population growth, and in the degree of durable goods manufacturing and construction. In the regression based on the Southwest sample, only the level of white unemployment stands out as statistically significant. (1985, pp. 99, 100)

The picture with respect to *wages* is different, however. From the evidence contained in table 12.1 Muller concludes:

There is little doubt that wages in several occupations and industries rose more slowly in Los Angeles than elsewhere as low-skilled immigrants, primarily Hispanics, entered the labor force . . . most notabl[y] in the manufacturing sector, particularly among production workers in industries where wages have been traditionally low such as in apparel and textile production and in relatively low-wage industries such as restaurants, personal services, and hotels where many Mexicans are employed.

Table 12.1   Muller's comparison of wages, Los Angeles County and the
United States, 1972—80

	Los Angeles wages, 1980 ($)	Increase in LA wages, 1972—80, as a percentage of US wage increase	Mexican immigrants as percentage of all workers, 1980
All workers	15,594	108.8	9.9
Low-wage manufacturing[a]	5.06[b]	76.7	47.1[c]
High-wage manufacturing[d]	7.97[b]	90.7	19.5[c]
All retail	9,469	108.3	9.5
Eating and drinking establishments (restaurants, bars)	5,591	89.1	16.8
All other retail	11,196	108.4	6.6
All services	14,099	115.8	5.5
Hotels, etc.	7,312[e]	95.1	15.0[e]
Personal services	8,069	92.2	15.2
All other services	14,659	117.2	3.9
Finance, insurance, and real estate	15,590	104.4	2.6

Notes: [a] Includes leather goods, apparel, textile mills, lumber and wood product, and furniture and fixture industries.
[b] Hourly wages include only production workers.
[c] Production workers only.
[d] Includes metals, machinery, stone, clay, and glass, food and transportation equipment industries.
[e] Estimated.
Source: Muller and Espenshade, 1985, p. 111

The relative declines in low-skill wages are especially noteworthy because wages in general rose 9 percent more rapidly in Los Angeles than in the rest of the country between 1972 and 1980.

Muller and Espenshade also made a special study of the effect of Hispanic immigration upon blacks, the group which they adjudged to be the Hispanics' closest competition in the labor market. They first examined the rates of labor-force participation and unemployment for the years 1970, 1980 and 1982, covering a period of heavy immigration with Los Angeles County, with these results:

Blacks generally, and black teenagers especially, do not appear to have been harmed by immigration in the period from 1970 to 1981. During the 1970s and into the 1980s, adult labor force participation rates increased in Los Angeles metropolitan area and in California, reflecting a national pattern of rising labor force participation. Throughout the period, participation rates in Los Angeles continue to exceed the national average, maintaining a fairly constant lead. Teenage labor force participation rates also increased over the period, and the rates for black teenagers in Los Angeles and in the state showed gains relative to the rate for black teenagers in the nation. By contrast, participation rates for all teenagers in Los Angeles declined relative to the national average, dropping below the national labor force participation rate for teenagers by 1982.

An examination of labor force participation data for Los Angeles by sex and race from the 1970 and 1980 censuses indicates that black women had gains that were above the average for them nationwide, while black men experienced a decline that was somewhat lower than the decline for them nationwide. And in 1982, when unemployment in California reached its highest rate in four decades, nonwhite labor force participation rates for both teenagers and adults in the Los Angeles area continued to exceed national rates.

Native workers who find their jobs jeopardized by immigrants may experience higher rates of unemployment, if they do not drop out of the labor force altogether. ... The period from 1970 to 1982 was marked by rising rates of unemployment, both nationwide and in California. For all groups in the United States, unemployment rates more than doubled. The smallest increases were for blacks in Los Angeles – 27 percent for adults and 35 percent for teenagers – followed by black teenagers in California. In sum, trends in unemployment rates do not provide evidence of sharp job competition between immigrants and blacks. (1985, pp. 96–7)

Table 12.2 (their table 16) shows a puzzling lack of effect upon blacks in three of the four lower-pay categories. And this finding seems not to be a statistical artifact; Muller and Espenshade ran cross-sectional regressions similar to those described above for unemployment, but now for wages of blacks, and found an effect that was statistically significant but very small in magnitude – $85 yearly, if the proportion of Hispanics were 7.5 percent rather than 5 percent in the given area, to be compared to average black family income of $15,818. Muller and Espenshade suggest that Hispanics and blacks are not close competitors in labor markets;[1] yet this finding needs more explanation.

Muller and Espenshade (1985) also tackled the difficult problem of estimating the number of new jobs created by Mexican immigrants. They compare the

average proportion of low-skill low-wage workers in the total labor force in the nation's twelve largest metropolitan areas – areas that, with the exception of Dallas, Houston, and Los Angeles, have relatively few Mexicans in the labor force – and

Table 12.2 Increases in median wages in Los Angeles County and California between 1969 and 1979 as a percentage of the national increase

Sex and selected occupation	Los Angeles	California[a]		
		Hispanics	Blacks	Others[b]
Men				
Engineers	95.3	99.5	98.3	97.4
Craftsmen	90.2	83.7	93.1	101.4
Operatives	62.2	71.4	94.7	90.4
Laborers (manufacturing)	62.0	85.3	103.1	87.7
Women				
Registered nurses	98.8	84.0	103.1	93.2
Administrative support	95.5	95.1	99.4	96.5
Operatives	71.5	80.8	101.5	90.1
Service workers, except private household	78.8	78.0	82.1	85.4

Notes: [a] Comparative growth rates based on Hispanics, blacks, and others in the United States.
[b] Estimated, based on median wage data.
Source: Muller and Espenshade, 1985, p. 118

use this average as a guide to what might be expected in Los Angeles in the absence of Mexican immigration. The actual number of operatives and laborers in Los Angeles in 1980 was 60,000 larger than the number predicted using this procedure. (p. 149)

This estimate jibes well with their estimate of the relevant number of Mexicans in various manufacturing jobs in Los Angeles. This "direct" effect may be compared with the estimate of 210,000 recent immigrants from Mexico.

Muller and Espenshade then go further to estimate the jobs *indirectly* caused by the Mexicans through complementary employment, consumer services to Mexicans, and so on, reaching a total that is not incomparable in size with the total Mexican migration. But this procedure is necessarily tenuous, so I will refer the reader to their book for further information.

McCarthy and Valdez study of California

Using methods similar to Muller and Espenshade − analysis of Census and Department of Labor data on employment, unemployment, wages, and population for Los Angeles and California compared to the US as a whole, in 1970 and 1980 – McCarthy and Valdez arrived at results similar to those of Muller and Espenshade.

Immigrants appear to have provided a net benefit to the California economy by supporting industrial and manufacturing growth.

Their negative labor market effects have been minor and concentrated among the native-born Latino population. (McCarthy and Valdez, 1986, p. 24)

This lack of effect is particularly striking because the growth in employment was large: While between 1970 and 1980 low-wage employment fell by 5.2 percent in the US as a whole, it grew by 46.1 percent in California and by 52.7 percent in Los Angeles; the corresponding figures for moderate wage industry were increases of 4.3, 20.6, and 6.9 percent, and in high-wage industry were 7.8, 27.6, and 11.4 percent. And the retardation in growth of wages relative to the US as a whole was less than seen in tables 12.1 and 12.2, though the data are not strictly comparable; the ratio of LA growth to US growth was 0.80, 0.86, and 0.96 for the three levels of industry, and the California-wide ratios were even closer to the US averages (1986, p. 40).

DeFreitas and Marshall

DeFreitas and Marshall related the percentage in 1980 of manual workers in SMSA manufacturing sectors who were born abroad to the average annual rate of change from 1970 to 1978 in the hourly earnings of manufacturing production workers in those SMSAs. They found that

higher concentrations of foreign-born manual workers have a statistically significant negative impact on wage growth rates. However, the magnitude of the estimated impact is relatively modest (less than one percentage point slower wage growth with every 10 percent increase in the immigrant share of manufacturing jobs), and it is significant only in SMSAs in which 20 percent or more of manual workers are immigrants. (1983 p. 155)

This effect is not easy to interpret, however. It may be partly caused by education or other characteristics of natives rather than by increased competition from immigrants (and indeed, productivity growth has a much larger coefficient in regressions including immigrants than without them) because the independent variable refers to the stock rather than to the flow of immigrants, and the recent flow must be a rather small proportion of the stock. But flows are related to stocks (see Bartel, 1982), providing some support for the analysis.

Grossman

In theory, immigrants will lower the wages of natives (a) to the extent that there is substitution between capital and labor; if the quantity of labor is relatively large with respect to the quantity of capital, the output per worker is relatively small, and hence wages are relatively lower; and (b) to the extent that there is substitution between immigrants and natives; if immigrants and natives can do the same job, in the presence of condition (a), the wages of natives will be depressed by immigrants. To the extent that the two kinds of labor do *not* substitute for each other, the effect of the capital constraint upon natives is mitigated.

Grossman (1982) estimated the effect of foreign-born workers upon second-generation workers, and upon native workers, in a sample of 19 SMSAs. In addition to the proportions of these groups in the labor force, she introduced a variable for quantity of capital. Her results implied a slight negative effect of immigration upon native wages. But her conclusions are weakened by the small number of observations, by the fact that the foreign-born represent all ages and lengths of time in the US and by the puzzling fact that the number of natives seems to have a strong negative effect upon their own wages – puzzling because larger cities are observed to have higher rather than lower wages.

DeFreitas

DeFreitas (1986), in a study noteworthy for its detail and depth, used a sample from the 1980 Census to investigate the effect of Hispanics – "the majority illegal," in his words – upon male and female groups of Anglos, Blacks, and Hispanics, separated into native and foreign-born, who immigrated between 1975 and 1980. He found no negative effect upon the wages of any group except black females.

For all low-skilled native men the results indicate that there are no significant negative effects on their wage levels from recent Hispanic immigration. In fact, such migration has a significantly positive influence on the Anglo-male earnings. ... The only persons whose wages appear to have been somewhat adversely affected by illegal migration since the mid-70's are black women,

and this effect is "relatively small" (p. 23). It must be noted, however, that the immigrants had been in the country up to five years; if the effect is mainly in the first year or so, rather than being more permanent, these data could not be expected to show it.

DeFreitas also examined the effect on the number of weeks worked per year, and on the amount of unemployment. He found that "For no racial/ ethnic group, male or female, is there a discernible negative effect of illegal immigration on employment. In fact, most of the estimated co-efficients are positive" (p. 24).

Borjas

Borjas (1983) studied the substitutability of black, Hispanic, and white workers in the 1976 Survey of Income and Education, and found Hispanics to be complements rather than substitutes for blacks, and perhaps for whites as well. No distinction was made between native and immigrant Hispanics, but the proportion of immigrants among the Hispanics certainly is large, and there is great similarity of labor-market characteristics between immigrants and natives among the 61 percent of the Hispanics who are of Mexican origin. Given the precision of the methods Borjas used, this evidence provides strong confirmation for deFreitas's finding.

Chiswick–Chiswick–Miller

B. Chiswick, C. Chiswick, and Miller (1985) estimated the elasticity of substitution by examining the ratio of skill-adjusted immigrant wages to native wages in five countries where the proportions of the two kinds of labor differ markedly[2] – the US, Britain, Canada, Australia, and Israel. The small number of observations causes doubt about the validity of the analysis, but experiments checking the sensitivity to the dropping of particular observations provides some confidence. "The estimated elasticity is high (about 28), but it is significantly less than infinity." That is, they found that immigrants and natives are close (though not perfect) substitutes. But this does not imply that immigrants increase native unemployment, for reasons given in the previous chapter, though it does indicate that absorption requires more adjustment than if immigrants were poor substitutes or complements to natives.

Bean–Lowell–Taylor

Bean, Lowell, and Taylor (1986) estimated the effect of the number of undocumented Mexican workers in the labor markets across the South-western part of the US upon annual earnings in 1979 of six labor force groups – (a) undocumented, (b) legal, and (c) native-born Mexican-origin males; (d) black males; (e) non-Mexican origin white males; and (f) females.

The (statistically significant) effects of illegal Mexican immigrants are negative upon white males' wages (substitution) and positive (complementarity) upon females' wages. The effects of legal Mexican immigrants are *positive* upon native-born Mexican males and black males. The magnitudes of the effects are hard to interpret, but the authors refer to them as "not very sizable. The concern that undocumented immigration may be depressing the earnings of native born workers does not appear to be borne out by these results" (p. 15).

Morgan–Gardner study of the bracero program's effects

Morgan and Gardner studied the bracero program of guestworkers from Mexico that operated from 1942 to 1964, in the broad context of the history of Mexican immigration and the economic–institutional context of Southwestern agriculture (figure 15.1 shows the year-by-year size of the program). Crucial for our purposes here, they estimated the number of native workers who lost jobs, and the extent of the fall in wages. Because they used data and techniques that seem as well-adapted to studying this particular topic as are available, I shall review the study in some detail.

Morgan and Gardner first develop a simple theoretical model to guide the econometric work and its interpretation. Then they discuss the kinds of variables that are necessary to fit the model to the situation at hand, as well as the kinds of data that are available to do the job, and the difficulties encountered in that quest. The resulting econometric model was as follows:

Our model of bracero labor supply is specified as

$$LB_{jt} = f(WMM_t, WH_{jt}, PL78_t, DA_t, SD_j) \tag{4}$$

where *LB* is thousands of bracero workers contracted; *WMM* is the minimum hired farm daily wage in Mexico in 1977 pesos converted to dollars; *PL78* is 1 if P.L. 78 was in effect, otherwise zero; *DA* (*Dona Ana*) is 1 if the year is later than 1961, otherwise, zero; *SD* is a state dummy variable for each state except California; *j* is 1, 2, ...; seventh state; and *t* is 1, 2, ..., twenty-sixth year (1 = 1953, 26 = 1978).

The structural equation for U.S. farm labor demand is

$$LH_{jt} = g(WH_{jt}, LS_{jt}, PR^*_{jt}, PP_t, HA_{jt}, AP_{jt}, SD_j) \tag{5}$$

where *LH* is thousands of hired farm workers; *WH* is the hourly hired farm wage rate in 1977 dollars; *LS* is hired labor's share of farm production expenses, *PR** is product price expectations, measured by the index of prices farmers receive, where 1977 = 100, lagged one year; *PP* is the index of prices paid by farmers for production items (excluding labor, land, interest, and taxes) where 1977 = 100; *HA* is millions of acres of cropland harvested, with linear interpolation between census

years; and AP is the index of agricultural productivity, where $1977 = 100$.
The equation for the U.S. farm labor supply is

$$LH_{jt} = h(WH_{ht}, \ WI_{jt}, \ U_{jt}, \ LB_{jt}, \ SD_j) \tag{6}$$

where WI is the hourly manufacturing wage rate in 1977 dollars; U is the percent of unemployment among the work force covered by unemployment insurance, and LB is the number of braceros, the dependent variable in the first structural equation above (Morgan and Gardner, 1982, pp. 385–6).

Morgan and Gardner then estimated the model using three geographic groupings to see how the results are affected thereby, and they tried both ordinary-least-squares and two-stage-least-squares regressions. In the light of their various results, as well as the results of other studies of the market for agricultural labor, they worked up an idealized summary as a way of presenting the gist of their results. Calculating on the basis of an effective 35 percent increase in the supply of labor (210,000 workers) due to the program (the approximate number between 1953 and 1964) they estimate a fall in wages of 9 percent, and a reduction of 51,000 jobs filled by natives. At the same time, they estimate a total increase of 120,000 jobs due to the decline in the wage rate. Morgan and Gardner are impressed at the relatively high responsiveness in the number of jobs (a labor–demand elasticity of -3.2) to the changes in wages, and they are also impressed at the relatively small decline in the wage rate induced by an increase in the supply of labor of the magnitude of 35 percent (pp. 398–9).

Despite the excellence of this study, it is not easy to think through its implications. Gardner and Morgan calculate that the aggregate economic benefits to natives are greater than the costs to native workers in forgone wages. The gains are obtained by the growers and by food consumers, but the authors are not able to compute the proportions of the gains between the two groups. From a perceived-pain point of view, we must notice that whereas the benefits are spread widely, the costs fall on one small group, the agricultural workers, which immediately raises questions about "fairness."

Going beyond these immediate calculations, there are several other important considerations. First, though our focus is the effect upon natives, there is also an important economic gain to the Mexican workers and Mexican society, constituting a large part of the workers' total wages. (Morgan and Gardner assume for the sake of argument that Mexican wages would be half the US wages, which leads to a *net* gain to the Mexican workers of more than the *gross* loss of wages to US workers.) And when we remember that many of the US workers who were "displaced" found jobs elsewhere, their net loss must have been even smaller.

Another consideration is that, without the bracero program, there would have been more substitution of mechanization than actually occurred, and hence some job loss anyway. As Morgan and Gardner put it:

This relatively high demand elasticity and job creation effect is consistent with the informal observation that braceros were a substitute for mechanization, notably in High Plains cotton, and that the end of the program substantially accelerated the mechanization of Texas cotton. This is also the period in which the tomato harvester came into widespread use in California. (p. 399)

To put the matter more generally, the appropriate analysis is not a comparative-statistics comparison between a given number of workers N employed in the industry at wages W if there are braceros or illegals, whereas there would be $N-X$ workers and $W-Y$ wages if there are no braceros or illegals, with the difference in wages as derived from static analysis. Rather, as Morgan and Gardner point out, one response to a regime that allows fewer Mexican temporary workers is a shift to more capital-intensive production, which might in the long run reduce employment more than would a regime which allows Mexican guestworkers. Also, some proportion of displaced workers find jobs in other industries, sometimes under conditions that they come to consider superior to the jobs from which they were "displaced." Hence the welfare loss is not that which is computed under comparative-statistics analysis, but rather something less.

Simon–Moore comparison of immigration and unemployment across cities in the US

Moore and I (1988) studied the relationship between the rates of immigration and of unemployment across cities in the US. Our samples cover the years 1960–77 for the various numbers of cities in the US for which Immigration and Naturalization Service data on immigration are available in various years. (This is the only period during which any data are available.)

We first investigate the relationship between the *level* of unemployment and the level of immigration. Here and elsewhere in the study we also experimented with other variables such as the rate of growth of population, the proportion of the labor force working in manufacturing and in durable-goods manufacturing, and the proportion of insured unemployment to total unemployment, but these control variables do not explain an important proportion of the variance.

At first glance there appears to be a positive relationship between the levels. But upon further inspection the correlation is seen to be almost as strong between unemployment in early years and immigration in later years – obviously not a causal relationship – as between years in which there might conceivably be a causal relationship. At the heart of the econometric problem is a very high similarity in immigration patterns across cities from year to year. Unraveling this pattern to determine the underlying relationship defied our efforts.

To avoid the serious difficulty of differences in measurement of unemployment among states, we also work with *changes* in unemployment from one year to another. Comparisons of samples of unemployment levels two years apart (surrounding the year of immigration) do not show any clear pattern of effect of immigration level; when the national unemployment level is rising the relationship seems positive, and when the unemployment level is falling the relationship usually seems negative. When we examine the differences between the farthest-distant years (1960 and 1977) the results seem at first to show a significant relationship, but when we allow for the secular rising national trend in unemployment by examining the farthest-distant pair of years having the same unemployment levels, the apparent relationship is no longer seen. It is not obvious which of these ways of looking at the data is the more appropriate.

We also carried out analyses with first differences on both sides of the equation, but these runs showed no relationships of any kinds.

Analyses of *levels* of unemployment and immigration in the 1970 Census of Population also show little or no effect, confirming our other analyses.

Ultimately, this sort of study ought to render the statistical findings into economic terms, that is, produce an estimate of the quantitative effect (if any) of an additional immigrant on native unemployment. There are many coefficients in the paper that might be the basis of such an estimate, many of them suggesting no effect at all. But for perspective, let us look at the largest of the coefficients, the one for the summed regression for 1960–75, and consider it an unlikely upper bound. It suggests that for each immigrant who entered during that period, 0.093 immigrants were unemployed during *each* of the fifteen years, or $15 \times 0.093 = 1.395$ years of native unemployment for each entering immigrant. That would certainly be a meaningful amount of unemployment to be caused by an immigrant on average. But even this most-unlikely upper bound is far distant from a displacement assessment of one job permanently lost to natives for each immigrant admitted; the coefficient would have to be 20 or 30 times that large for there to be any such suggestion.

The correlation in this and other regressions is strikingly low. It must be kept in mind, however, that immigration is small in volume relative to other population movements and components, and therefore it is almost impossible that immigration could explain a large proportion of the differences in unemployment, no matter how close the relationship. Furthermore, noise from errors in variables and other sources tends to depress the correlation. Still it is hard to find much policy importance in a variable that explains so little of the variance in the dependent variable, even assuming it to be statistically significant (which is probably an unwarranted assumption), no matter what the explanation of the lack of explanatory power.

Huddle

[Huddle and] 27 of his students in a labor seminar, juniors and seniors mostly, conducted several field studies during a two-year period, 1981–1982. Their objectives were to determine what industries hire illegal aliens and to what extent illegals displace U.S. workers or shut them out of the labor market in the booming Houston-Galveston metro politan area. (Huddle, Corwin, and MacDonald, 1985, introductory note)

Huddle concluded that

the social and economic implications of the penetration of the economy by undocumented workers is dramatic. If the sample proportion of illegal worker participation is projected onto city, state, and national construction programs alone, we find that all male youths and minority youths, aged 16–24, could, in principle, have been removed from the rolls of the unemployed as of the time of our study, and that adds up to more than one million U. S. workers who have been displaced. (no date a, p. 3)

Huddle asserts that

Some $18 billion per year are "being siphoned off into the pockets of greedy employers" of illegal aliens. (1984, p. 1)

And he recommends that

Arrest and deportation of illegal alien workers is currently the cheapest and fastest way of securing additional jobs for unemployed U. S. citizens. (no date b, p. 1)

I mention Huddle's reports here because they have been publicized heavily by the INS and discussed extensively in the press. But upon several inquiries to Professor Huddle, I have not been able to obtain any material other than the above-quoted press releases and a general article by Huddle, Corwin and MacDonald (1985) containing no scientifically detailed description of what he did. Until the research methods and data are made public, it would seem prudent to completely disregard this work. And it is obvious from the press releases alone that Huddle did not make any study at all of displacement — that is, the effect of illegals upon native workers — but rather simply made an unsubstantiated extrapolation from his estimate of the proportion of illegals working in the construction industry.

The only detailed description of Huddle's work that I know of was given by Huddle in testimony before the US District Court for Colorado in August, 1982, as excerpted by Flores (1983). The method bears no resemblance to reliable scientific technique. Yet the INS and the ex-Secretary of Labor continued to rely on that work for such estimates as that "overall displacement was about 0.7 for urban nonagricultural jobs: i.e., for every 10 undocumented illegals working in urban jobs about 7 U.S. workers were displaced" (Marshall, 1984).

It should also be noted that the latest piece (Huddle et al. 1985) asserts that a "modal estimate for 1983 would be 8 to 9 million" illegals in the US, a statement made wholly contrary to (and without mentioning) the Census Bureau's 1981 and subsequent much lower estimates (the NAS's 1986 estimate is even lower; see chapter 15 on these estimates).

Easterlin's study of cyclical unemployment in the United States

In earlier decades of this century, when immigration to the US was quite free, and much larger relative to the size of the US labor force than now, the waves of immigration coincided with the waves of business activity in the US. Immigration increased when the demand for labor was great, and decreased (or even became net out-migration, as in the 1930s) when demand for labor fell and unemployment rose. About immigration in the free-entry period before World War I, based on his own work and that of previous investigations, Easterlin concluded:

[T]he swings in immigration were a response to corresponding swings in the demand for labor in the United States. The evidence is as follows:
   In the United States, turning points of long swings in output growth typically preceded those in the rate of immigration, suggesting that immigration was responding to changed conditions in the United States rather than abroad [figure 12.1] . . .
   During long swings in the U.S., a rising immigration rate was typically preceded by a rising rate of growth in hourly wages and, as far as the limited evidence goes, a declining unemployment rate; a falling immigration rate tended to follow a decline in the growth rate of hourly wages and a rising unemployment rate [figure 12.1]. Since the growth of the U.S. labor force from domestic sources, whether from demographic factors or participation-rate change, showed but slight evidence of long swings before World War I [figure 12.1], the implication is that immigration waves were one of several symptoms of common origin, namely, alternating tightness and slack in the labor market associated with swings in the growth of labor demand. The immediate stimulus to migration was probably changes in unemployment conditions.
   There is a substantial similarity in the timing of out-migration waves from diverse areas of origin − different parts of Europe, Canada, Latin America, Asia, and even the rural sector within the United States. This observation is consistent with the view that these areas were responding to a common external stimulus such as swings in labor demand at destination. (1968, pp. 30−1)

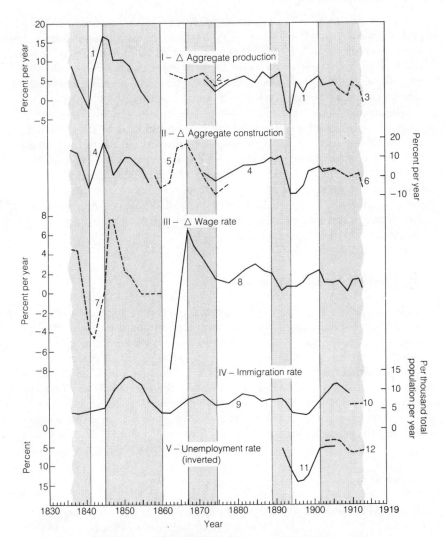

Figure 12.1 Average annual rate of change in aggregate production, aggregate construction, and wage rate; and average level of immigration rate and unemployment rate, NBER reference cycles, 1834–1914

Source: Easterlin, 1968, p. 32

The linkage between employment conditions and immigration had the beneficial effect upon the native labor force of reducing competition for jobs in bad times, while increasing the demand for labor in both good times and bad. There is no reason to doubt that future immigration would also respond to employment conditions in the US, and thereby reduce the severity of unemployment cycles, if it were unconstrained by quotas.

Withers and Pope (1985) applied the technique of Granger causality to quarterly Australian unemployment and immigration data from 1948 to 1982, enabling them to distinguish the direction of causation. They found no increase in the rate of unemployment due to immigration. They did find that unemployment influences later immigration, which accounts for the correlation between the series. Summarizing this study as well as several earlier studies of the topic, Chapman, Pope and Withers (1985) concluded that "immigration has not increased unemployment within the range of Australian post-war experience."

Jones and Smith on Great Britain

During the 1961−6 period studied, general unemployment was sufficiently low that Jones and Smith did not even attempt to determine whether immigrants caused natives to be unemployed. Though the unemployment among immigrants was also very low, it tended to rise relatively faster than general unemployment during the business cycle. Jones and Smith therefore concluded that the immigrants have the positive effect on natives of buffering the changes in their unemployment rates: "coloured immigrants bear, in these instances (a rise in general unemployment) an above average amount of the economy's real burden of unemployment" (1970, p. 45).

Bahral on Israel

Bahral (1965) studied the effect on wages of the mass immigration of unskilled North African Jews into Israel from 1948 to 1958. He found that the differential between skilled and unskilled workers widened, as standard theory suggests, even though wage determination in Israel takes place mainly through collective bargaining rather than individual employer− worker agreement. That is, even institutional barriers to the operation of supply and demand did not prevent the wages of the category of workers that became more abundant from falling relative to other workers. It should be noted, however, that the quantity of immigration into Israel was extremely high compared to other countries' experiences; the labor force more than doubled between 1948 and 1984, for example.

School leavers

The phenomenon in which we are interested here is analogous to the large surge of new-labor-force-entrant school leavers in the summer time, entrants not offset by a surge of retirements at the same time. This increment to the labor force from school leavers is much larger than the yearly increment from immigrants, and it all occurs in a single month or so. Figure 12.2 shows seasonal patterns of unemployment and employment for persons of ages 16–19 and 20+. There is no discernible effect of the school leavers upon older persons. Unemployment among persons older than 16–19 is not higher in the months after the school leavers hit the job market than in the months before – indeed it is lower in the second half of the year than in the first half. And the unemployment rate of the youths shows very little impact of school-leaving after the summer. These data call for systematic analysis, however (analysis which might also improve methods of seasonal adjustment of unemployment and employment statistics).

Effects of cohort size

The post-war "baby-boom" cohort of entrants into the labor force in the US and elsewhere is much larger than previous cohorts. The "additional" persons may be considered analogous to a cohort of immigrants. The large body of research on the labor-market effects has been reviewed and summarized by Bloom and Freeman (1986b).

There is strong consensus that – at least for a while – baby-boomers' unemployment is higher, and wages lower, than they would be if their cohort were smaller. This squares with the higher unemployment for immigrants than for natives seen in Australia (though Harrison's analysis [chapter 11] does not apply so well in this situation, because the baby-boomers were consuming even before entering the labor force). There is less agreement about how long the effect lasts and the extent to which the adjustment to the increased "pressure" on the labor market is through lower wages and how much through higher unemployment; the trade-off apparently differs from country to country.

If one's main interest is the effect of immigrants upon the *native* population, however, one wants to know the effects on *native* unemployment and wages. And the baby-boom studies do not throw light upon those questions. Furthermore, the fact that the baby-boomers' wages are *relatively* lower than they otherwise would be suggests that others' wages are relatively *higher*. Theoretical support for such a conclusion follows from the complementarity of age groups. The only ways that the baby-boomers could lower

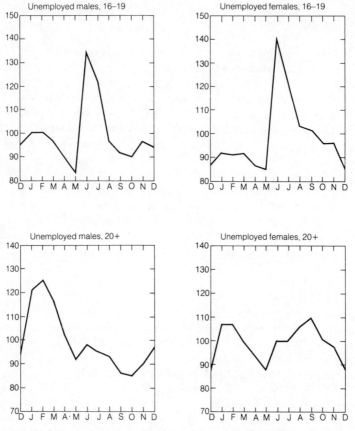

Figure 12.2   Seasonal patterns in unemployment and employment series by
sex, age brackets 16–19 and 20+ (1967–77 average seasonal
factors)

Source: National Commission on Employment and Unemployment Statistics, *Data
Collection, Processing and Presentation*, National and Local Government Printing
Office, Washington, DC, 1980, p. 329

the wages of others are if (a) total output per person falls due to capital
dilution, or (b) a greater proportion of total output flows to the owners of
physical capital. Possibility (b) seems unlikely, given the data on labor's
share in recent years. And I know of no data showing that possibility (a) is
an actuality. So we must consider as not implausible that, to the extent that
the baby-boom studies throw light on immigration, they show that natives
on average receive *higher* wages due to the immigrants.

Baby boom plus increased female labor-force participation: Grant–Hamermesh

Grant and Hamermesh examined the interrelated effects of the entry of the unusually large baby-boom cohort of youth into the labor force between 1960 and 1980, and the concurrent increase in the labor-force participation of women. They found that the wages of both groups were lower than if the other group's entry rate had been lower. But the "competition from adult women did not itself increase the rate of unemployment of youths" (Hamermesh and Rees, 1984, pp. 104–5).

Creation of new businesses

Chapter 4 presents evidence that immigrants have a higher propensity to start new businesses than do natives. Usually these are small businesses, because most businesses start in a small way. But one should not therefore underestimate the job-creation capacity of such small businesses. A study of the new jobs created by firms in different size categories indicates that an astonishing 66 percent arose in firms with 20 or fewer employees; see table 12.3, taken from Birch (1981).

Samuel and Conyers considered several of the avenues through which new immigrants into Canada create new jobs. They state (though without further citation) that in 1983–4 the 3940 business immigrants – entrepreneurs and self-employed persons who have funds to invest in Canadian

Table 12.3 Percentage of jobs created by size of firm and region

Number of employees in firm	Percentage of jobs created				
	Northeast	*North Central*	*South*	*West*	*US average*
0–20	177.1	67.2	53.5	59.5	66.0
21–50	6.5	12.0	11.2	11.6	11.2
51–100	−17.4	5.2	5.5	6.3	4.3
101–500	−33.3	3.1	9.4	9.3	5.2
501+	−32.9	12.4	20.4	13.3	13.3
Total	100.0	100.0	100.0	100.0	100.0

Source: Birch, 1981, p. 8

enterprises – brought "a total of $1544 million to Canada" with them, a mean of almost $400,000 each (1985, p. 7). And Norman and Meikle report the mean amount "available" for transfer in 1983–4 to Australia by "business immigrants" of Australia was $383,600 (1985, p. 123). There is little or no solid information about the relationship between additional capital injected into an economy as investment and the number of jobs created, though numbers such as $30,000 and $50,000 have been talked about in the US in past years; and of course the relationship must vary among industries; the small businesses that immigrants tend to start should require lesser amounts of such capital than industry on average. There is little doubt that this amount is more than enough to be consistent with the estimate of six jobs per business-starting immigrant found by the *Three Years in Canada study* (Manpower and Immigration, 1974).

Additionally, Samuel and Conyers state that immigrants other than business immigrants brought with them a mean of $17,841 per immigrant family. How much of this goes into investment, how much into consumption, and how much remains in idle savings is anybody's guess. But at least *some* of it must go to investment, providing additional jobs in that way. And of course, sums spent on producer capital also have all the effects of sums spent on consumption.

As to the relationship between consumption (and also investment spending) while immigrants are still unemployed, Samuel and Conyers cite Vanderkamp's estimate that for inter-regional migration within Canada, for each five unemployed persons who leave, two more persons become unemployed by way of the drop in consumption. They suggest that it is reasonable to turn this around with respect to immigrants – that each five immigrants who come, even while they are unemployed, cause two more additional jobs for others. (This may be a reasonable basis for estimating the consumption effect that Harrison uses in his model, discussed in chapter 11.) Samuel and Conyers then make calculations based on the adult-equivalent values of the children and non-working adults in the 1983–4 immigrant cohort and, using the Vanderkamp job ratio, they estimated that "the presence of 1983–4 immigrants should have resulted in at least 58,560 new jobs in Canada (16,400 more jobs than required for 1983–4 immigrants)" (1985, p. 10).

Experiments removing illegals from jobs

Two experimental forcible removals by the authorities of illegal immigrants from hundreds of jobs in California were followed by checkups on what happened to the jobs that the illegals held. In both cases there was a relatively low rate of substitution of natives for the illegals. This evidence is discussed in chapter 15 in connection with illegal immigration.

Discussion

1   As with trade policy, a large difficulty with immigration policy is that −
inevitably − any labor-force change causes some groups to suffer some
harm in the short run. This expected harm causes opposition to the
change. But preventing the change forgoes benefits to other groups, and in
the long run usually harms even the groups that fear and oppose the short-
run effect.

The capacity to cry "unfair" is seemingly unlimited. As of 1986, the
physicians in the US assert that there is a surplus of doctors, though their
net incomes average over $100,000 yearly. Hence they are currently at-
tempting to limit the admission to practice of those who were trained
abroad (*Washington Post*, 19 June 1986, p. A25).

In 1981 a newspaper article stated that "1,250 Kirghiz have applied for
visas to start a new life in Alaska because that climate is the best fit for
their temperaments and traditions" (*Wall Street Journal*, 16 December
1981, p. 21). Were this possibility to become a live one, chances are that
the Eskimos would object to additional competition for economic resources
(Really.)

It would seem prudent, then, to discount the urgings of particular
occupational groups when making immigration policy.

2   Perhaps it would be a useful exercise for the reader to reflect on the
issue of displacement from the perspective of someone else observing *you*
and asking, with tongue somewhat in cheek: What would be the effect
upon the labor market if you the reader − assumed to be employed by a
private or public enterprise − were to suddenly stop working?

There would immediately be an additional job opening. After some
shorter or longer period of time a person who might otherwise not be
working might be hired for your old job, thereby decreasing the unemployment rolls. Or some person now working might take the job, and either the
second person's job or else the job of someone else down the line might be
filled by an unemployed person. So from the point of view of unemployment as a welfare measure, your ceasing to work might be seen as socially
beneficial in the very short run. (Of course it is understood that the
valuable output that you produce in your job would be lost to the public
that buys it, and material welfare would thereby be decreased unless the
unemployed person who finds a job because of your leaving your job
produces output as valuable as yours. But this effect is not germane to the
immediate discussion.)

Does this conclusion leave you feeling satisfied? Do you consider that it
tells enough of the story when it says that social welfare, as measured by
unemployment, is increased by your leaving your job, implying that it would

be a socially desirable act for you to quit tomorrow? Upon reflection, most of us would probably think the matter through a bit more, to counter this threat to our self-respect as well as to make this conclusion jibe with the belief held by most of us that our working is a good thing for other people. And indeed there are several possibilities that immediately mitigate or controvert this conclusion. One such possibility is that you own and run a private enterprise that employs other persons. If you stop working, some or all of your employees will become unemployed, temporarily or permanently. And though some of those persons might later become employed in firms that take over some of your business, there would almost surely be some slippage and loss of output and employment as a result. That outcome certainly would represent a loss of welfare on balance. And indeed, many immigrants and their children *do* start new businesses that employ other people, and they almost surely have a higher propensity to do so than natives (see chapter 4), both because of the otherwise limited opportunities available to them when they arrive and because of immigrants' putative greater drive to succeed and build for their children. (After all, was not every one of the businesses in the United States begun by immigrants or their descendants?)

Another thought that might occur to you is that your successor might not be as competent as you — or why else does your employer continue to keep you on the payroll? And indeed, it seems to be true that one of the main reasons that employers hire immigrants is that they are more competent than available natives at the same wage. (It is a rather embarrassing lament on the part of the labor unions that immigrants — legal and illegal — should be kept from competing in the labor force on the grounds that they will work harder, and work longer hours, than will natives.)

It also is likely to occur to you — and this is probably the most important line of thought, though the hardest to perceive in its fullness — that when you cease working you cease earning, and when you cease earning you cease spending. When you cease spending, the demand for labor falls in the industries that produce and sell the products that you might otherwise buy. Thus, some people who would otherwise work will be unemployed, and wages will fall somewhat in those industries. Such is the fundamental nature of an exchange economy; we all take in each other's washing, and if you can't recompense me, there will be no work for me to do. This explains why we can have an economy with as many jobs as there now are, growing at the rapid rate at which the economy has been growing, despite the large numbers of people newly entering the labor force.

This process is difficult to comprehend because there always is a period of adjustment between the additional new competitor for a job entering the labor force, and the process playing itself out to its final benign conclusion. One's understanding is also hindered by the process being indirect and hidden from view. But to ignore the process because it is difficult to perceive, and to focus on the immediate effect on the implicit assumption of a fixity in the number of jobs, and to assume that that immediate effect also will be the final outcome, is either to have a too short a time horizon or a defective view of the economy or both.

The simple truth is that you, dear reader, probably are not so expendable from your job as the simplest arguments suggest you to be. And if you stopped working for a while and then returned, your coming back to work would not be an imposition and a burden upon other people but rather (aside from the shortest-run adjustment difficulties) would likely be a blessing to the rest of us, even without considering the taxes you pay, the productivity increases you cause, and your other positive effects described elsewhere in this book. And so it is with immigrants; the complaint of taking jobs from natives, and thereby causing damage to them, is a fore-shortened and misleading view. But it is the point of view which underlies the public policy of excluding immigrants, and of preventing foreign students and tourists from working, not only in the US but also in many or most countries.

Conclusions

Taken together, the empirical studies reviewed in this chapter suggest that general immigration causes little or no unemployment at large, even in the first year or two; the same is true of low-income Hispanic immigration even among the groups most likely to be "displaced" by them. This finding emerges from studies using a variety of methods, studying various periods, and in a variety of geographical areas.

Hispanic immigration into Texas and Los Angeles results in lower relative wages in particular occupations where Hispanics are a large presence. But some (even all) of this gap may be due to a real increase in wages among higher-skill groups rather than a real decrease in low-income groups.

The extent to which the immediate effect of immigrants is distributed among unemployment of natives, unemployment of immigrants, wage declines, or even advance expectations of immigrants leading to expansion of business, cannot be sorted out at this time. The pattern probably varies considerably from place to place and time to time, depending upon the nature of the economy and of the economic conditions.

When there is no constraint upon immigration, immigrants improve the situation of native workers by smoothing out employment over the business cycle. This is especially true of temporary (including illegal) immigrants, because they go and come in response to the job situation.

Immigrants not only take jobs, they make jobs. They open new businesses that employ natives as well as other immigrants and themselves. And they do so in important numbers. The businesses immigrants start are at first small, of course. But surprisingly, small businesses are now the most important source of new jobs.

Concerning policy: where the society responds with restrictive action to the request of every group − even every relatively poor group − which is threatened by imports or immigrants or technological change or change in public tastes, there will be no end to the claimants, and the economy will suffer from drag. Not only will the overall size of the pie be smaller than otherwise, but as a result of the jockeying of the claimant groups, few or none of the groups do much better even relatively than if the society adopts a more open policy. Almost everyone would be better off in the long run if *no* group is protected. But this is cold comfort for a particular group that worries about injury, and few of us are willing to take the broader and longer view when it is our ox being gored. It is my view that we do best by trying to help people move and adjust to new occupations, rather than trying to shelter them from competition in their existing occupations.

NOTES

1 Between 1970 and 1980, for example, net black employment in Los Angeles increased by 107,000 persons, with 98,000 of this total in white-collar occupations. Conversely, Mexican immigrants in Los Angeles who arrived during the 1970s held 210,000 jobs in 1980, but fewer than 25,000 of these were in white-collar employment. Even though the total number of jobs in the low-skill occupational categories of operative and laborer declined during the decade, the number of Mexican immigrants holding jobs in these occupations soared by 108,000.

> The rising job status of black women is especially noteworthy. In 1980, seven out of ten black women working in Los Angeles held white-collar jobs, a ratio higher than elsewhere in California or in the nation. There was only one black woman textile machine operator for every fifteen Hispanic women in such jobs in Los Angeles in 1980, and almost all the net additional jobs taken by black women since 1970 were in white-collar occupations. By contrast, only one out of every ten Mexican women who came to California during the 1970s was employed in a white-collar occupation. (Muller and Espenshade, 1985, p. 101)

2 This follows from their equation 3 on standard assumptions about profit maximization and the implication that relative marginal products are equal to relative factor prices.

13 The Effects of Immigrants upon Income Distribution and Prices

Effects upon the Computed Income Distribution
Effects upon Particular Occupations and Income Groups
Summary

These three effects of immigration fall under the rubric "income distribution": (1) Immigrants affect the width and shape of the computed distribution of income; this may have a psychological effect upon the other members of society even if it does not affect their incomes. (2) Immigrants may also affect the receipt of income by persons in particular occupations and income brackets; chapter 12 contains additional data on this topic. (3) Immigration may affect relative prices. These topics will be considered in that order.

Effects upon the Computed Income Distribution

We may separate the effects of immigrants on the computed income distribution of natives into short-run and long-run effects, first discussing the former and then the latter.

Short-run effects

If a very rich person enters the society, the computed income distribution widens in the short run even if the person does not work and even if s/he does not consume but rather simply reinvests the income from his/her investments, and therefore has only very indirect effects upon the other members of society. There may be psychological effects by way of people's perceived sense of well-being, but aside from that, the change in the income distribution may not signal any material effects for other persons in the society. It is therefore necessary to inquire why we might be interested in the computed income distribution, in the context of a study of the effects of immigration upon natives.

A measure of income distribution is most useful as a supplement to a measure of average income. Two countries with the same average income but with different distributions are likely to differ both in their productive capacities and in the material welfare of the different groups within their populations. This does not imply, however, that a change in measured income distribution necessarily indicates a change in such conditions, any more than the change in computed average income the instant a baby is born indicates a change in welfare or productivity. An additional rich (or poor) person living in a country by himself/herself does not affect the production or consumption situations of the rest of the population. The effect of immigration upon the income distribution may therefore not be of economic interest with respect to natives.

One might suggest, nevertheless, that the presence of additional poor or rich people in one's society can be unpleasant to natives for reasons of the pain of pity or of envy. At present such effects are beyond the scientific scope of conventional economics. Nevertheless, let us adduce some theory and data that operate in the reasonably short run, on the assumption that pity and envy may matter.

In theory, immigration of persons without capital, or with lower than average amounts of capital, should increase the disparities in income distribution in a society (as long as the immigrants' earnings are not above average). The theoretical process is that the additional supply of labor increases the earnings of the "capitalists" who are assumed to represent the upper-income group, while it decreases the earnings of the "workers" who are assumed to represent the lower-income group. Hence the income distribution would be wider.

Operating in the opposite direction, immigrants often bring substantial amounts of capital with them, which mitigates the capital-induced widening in the income distribution.

The educational and skill distributions of the immigrants influence the effect of the immigration upon the income distribution in the short run and in the long run. In recent years, the average education of immigrants has been roughly the same as for natives, with a relatively large concentration at the high-education end of the spectrum, and some relative concentration at the low-education end. And as we saw in chapter 3 − surprisingly, in light of the view of immigration expressed by Emma Lazarus' "tired ... poor ... huddled masses ... wretched refuse" and by Handlin (1951) in his famous *The Uprooted* − immigrants have always come reasonably well-equipped with education and skills relative to natives, even back into the previous century (Hill, 1976). This is prima facie evidence that the most likely cause of a widening income distribution due to immigration is not present.

Choosing the appropriate methods of measuring income distribution is a thorny problem; theory provides little guidance. The family rather than the individual seems the appropriate choice of unit, because family size is endogenous, influenced by income of the earner(s). On the other hand, the economic possibilities for individuals are affected by the number of children in the family, and by whether there is an adult couple or not.

Immigrants' initial low positions in the distribution may understate their lifetime situations. A more satisfactory inquiry into the subject would look at a wide variety of measures, but that is beyond the scope of this chapter.

One piece of evidence relevant to the question at hand is the amount of dispersion in the *family* earning distributions of natives and immigrants. The SIE data displayed in table 5.2 (and discussed in the afternote to chapter 5) show that the dispersion of incomes (as measured by the standard deviation) was in 1975 considerably less for each cohort that arrived since 1965 than it was for natives, even though average income was as high or higher for immigrants than for natives (except for the 1974 recently arrived cohort). The dispersion is slightly higher for the cohorts who came before 1965, but this is overbalanced by their relatively higher earnings compared to natives. Of course, a low income distribution for immigrants could widen the overall distribution even if it is narrow, but this does not appear to be the case.

A more explicit and intuitive approach is to examine the proportions of families in the various age brackets. Table 13.1 shows such data from the 1970 Census. The 1965–70 cohort shows a larger proportion of immigrants than natives in the lowest age brackets, but this figure is confused by the fact that the income data were for 1969, before the 1969 and 1970 portions of the 1965–70 cohort were in the US for a full year of work. The 1960–4 cohort already has a substantially lower proportion of families with the lowest incomes than do natives. In the SIE sample, too, we see in table 13.2 that starting with the second year after entry (the 1974 cohort in 1975), there are fewer immigrant families in the lowest income categories than among natives, and this continues to be the case up to the oldest immigrants. And for the first eleven years after entry the proportion of immigrants in the highest income brackets is lower than for natives. Including income from assets for both natives and immigrants would surely intensify this pattern. We can therefore say that for at least the first decade after entry, immigrants reduce the family income distribution at both the high and low ends. (These measures are likely to be quite misleading from a welfare-judgment point of view, of course, because of the very different age and size compositions of the native sample and the various immigrant cohorts. One could attempt to control for such variables, but that will constitute a major investigation in itself.)

Table 13.1 Total and immigrant US families by income bracket (percentage), 1969 (data from 1970 Census)

	Under $1,999	$2,000–$3,999	$4,000–$5,999	$6,000–$7,999	$8,000–$9,999	$10,000–$14,999	$15,000–$24,999	$25,000 or more
Total US	5.9	9.3	10.8	12.9	13.9	26.6	16.0	4.6
Immigrants entered								
1965–70	9.0	10.2	13.5	14.9	13.6	24.0	12.6	2.1
1960–4	4.5	6.5	10.9	13.5	14.7	29.2	16.9	3.7
1955–9	4.3	5.5	9.1	12.1	14.6	30.5	19.4	4.5
1950–4	4.1	6.0	10.0	12.1	14.2	30.1	19.4	5.6

Source: US Bureau of the Census, Census of Population: 1970 Subject Reports, Final Report PC(2)–1A, National Origin and Language (Washington: Government Printing Office, 1973), p. 466

Table 13.2 1975 Earnings distributions of families for immigrants and natives in percentage of each group (weighted for stratification)

Year entered US	<$2,500	$2,500–4,999	$5,000–9,999	$10,000–14,999	$15,000–19,999	$20,000–29,999	$30,000–39,999	$40,000–49,999	$50,000–74,999
1974	12.0	22.9	26.6	22.6	4.5	8.4	0.2	2.0	0.4
1973	16.5	10.8	30.4	20.2	10.7	13.5	0.8	0.9	2.2
1972	1.5	15.4	33.7	21.7	12.3	9.5	5.2	0.7	0.1
1971	5.7	15.1	37.0	18.9	8.7	8.3	2.6	1.9	1.7
1970	7.5	9.8	29.4	27.9	16.1	6.4	2.3	0.4	0
1965–9	4.5	9.5	28.6	24.0	14.2	14.8	2.7	1.0	0.6
1960–4	6.6	7.1	19.2	24.7	14.6	19.1	4.1	3.2	1.5
1950–9	6.5	7.2	22.3	21.2	18.9	16.3	5.4	1.2	1.1
Natives	10.7	8.7	21.5	22.3	15.8	15.5	3.3	1.2	1.0

Source: SIE

In order to estimate the effects of immigrants on the various earnings classes in the labor market we must consider not the entire group of immigrant families in each cohort compared to all native families, but rather participants in the same general labor market. Therefore we examine the distribution of earnings by the male heads of families, aged 24−64, in the various immigrant cohorts and among natives,[1] as seen in table 13.3. There we see that immigrants come to have a smaller proportion of men in the lowest earnings bracket than do natives after 10−15 years. Until that time immigrants may have a negative effect upon the lowest-earning groups. It may also be, however, that the observed effect is due to the youthful composition of new immigrant cohorts, and that if we were to hold age composition constant, the effect would disappear. Unfortunately, the numbers of persons of various ages in the various immigrant cohorts are sufficiently small that a refined analysis would be necessary to answer the question.

In assessing the findings in this section, the reader may wish to keep in mind that the ethnic composition of immigrants has been changing over the years, especially since 1965 (see table 3.12). The earlier-entering cohorts were much more heavily European than were the latest-entering cohorts, and there probably were changes in mean education levels as well (perhaps increases in the proportion of both low and high educational levels, with a decrease in the middle, as North (1979) suggests). This limits our capacity to extrapolate from past experience to the future. For any specified distribution of characteristics of an entry cohort, however, the data for the past cohorts could be made to yield more comparable estimates. The next section bears tangentially on this matter.

Interesting corroboration comes from the Australian and Canadian data in tables 13.4 and 13.5. The differences between mean and median incomes were smaller for immigrant families than for families with Australian-born heads, suggesting that there are fewer very large and/or very small incomes among the immigrants than among natives. This in turn implies a narrower income distribution among immigrants than among natives, and a narrower income distribution of the society as a whole due to immigration.

Longer-run effects

Now let us consider the effects of immigrants upon the overall income distribution once they have had a chance to be absorbed into the society − either just themselves, or themselves plus their children later on. In principle, one would like to compare income distributions with and without the immigrants. An empirical proxy would be to examine the income distributions of a sample of countries that have had varying amounts of immi-

Table 13.3 Earnings distributions of male heads of families age 24–64, in male-headed families, for immigrants and natives, in percentage of each group (weighted for stratification)

Year entered US	<$2,500	$2,500–4,999	$5,000–9,999	$10,000–14,999	$15,000–19,999	$20,000–29,999	$30,000–39,999	$40,000–49,999	$50,000+
1974	13.8	22.9	34.5	18.6	2.6	3.9	0.2	2.6	0.9
1973	11.2	12.7	35.1	21.7	7.8	6.7	0.5	1.3	3.0
1972	2.3	12.9	47.1	22.4	7.1	8.2	0	0	0
1971	9.8	15.0	41.5	20.2	6.1	5.1	1.5	0.8	0
1970	7.3	8.7	44.2	23.5	12.6	2.5	0.6	0.4	0
1970–4	5.4	11.0	35.4	26.6	12.2	6.9	1.3	0.5	0.8
1965–9	2.2	9.1	28.8	29.8	11.5	13.1	2.7	1.0	1.3
1960–4	4.2	4.2	24.5	29.0	22.3	11.8	2.7	0.4	0.9
1950–9	4.1	5.2	18.5	29.6	21.0	16.3	2.6	1.5	1.4
Natives	4.3	5.3	24.1	33.5	18.1	10.9	2.3	0.6	0.8

Table 13.4 Family income by birthplace of head of family, Australia

	Median income ($)		Mean income ($)	
	Australian-born head	Overseas-born head	Australian-born head	Overseas-born head
Number of income earners				
0	2,410	2,250	2,990	2,320
1	6,360	6,240	7,140	6,780
2	9,320	9,330	10,250	9,790
3 or more	13,410	12,750	14,310	13,400
Number in family				
2	6,300	6,430	7,190	6,980
3	7,860	8,670	9,100	8,870
4	8,360	8,480	9,730	9,370
5	9,060	8,410	10,230	9,050
6	9,931	9,170	11,260	10,160
7	9,870	8,490	11,030	9,250
8 or more	9,860	11,550	10,770	12,060
Total	7,820	8,030	8,890	8,520

Source: Australian Bureau of Statistics, 1978, cat. no. 4101.0, 1978, table 9.21

Table 13.5 Average and median incomes for all persons with income, Canadian- and foreign-born, by age and sex (excluding Quebec, etc.)

Age group (years)	Males				Females			
	Canadian-born		Foreign-born		Canadian-born		Foreign-born	
	Average	Median	Average	Median	Average	Median	Average	Median
15–19	1,229	n.a.	1,526	n.a.	968	n.a.	1,312	n.a.
20–4	4,167	3,979	4,311	4,206	2,891	2,792	2,983	2,971
25–34	7,449	7,333	7,516	7,406	3,337	2,988	3,482	3,283
35–44	8,888	8,165	9,211	8,380	3,216	2,614	3,414	3,116
45–54	8,593	7,634	9,189	8,129	3,380	2,747	3,500	3,118
55–64	7,359	6,259	7,375	6,469	3,285	2,371	3,050	2,255
65+	4,204	2,538	3,924	2,526	2,406	1,665	2,062	1,571
Total	6,535	5,829	6,903	6,251	2,854	1,996	2,850	1,993

n.a. – not applicable
Source: Richmond and Zubrzycki, 1984

gration. But such a study would be a demanding task, and I cannot undertake it at this time. Therefore, the evidence will be more casual.

One relevant fact is that though the US has, over the past two centuries, swelled greatly by immigration, the income distribution in the US is not particularly wide. A second relevant fact is that some groups with the highest earnings in the US – people of Italian, Chinese, Irish, Japanese, and Eastern-European–Jewish extraction – are of rather recent vintage in the US (Greeley, 1982). This second fact suggests that even if the short-run effect of immigrants is to increase the disparities, the longer run does not reveal such an effect; if anything, this fact of earnings *higher* than average suggests that immigration will narrow the disparities in income. A third relevant fact is that immigrants apparently cause little aggregate unemployment, as seen in chapter 12; the creation of aggregate unemployment would tend to widen the distribution, *ceteris paribus*.

It should be noted that even unskilled immigrants need not have a *long-run* worsening effect upon the income distribution. Many of the Chinese and Irish arrived as unskilled railroad laborers, and many of the Italians and Jews began work without saleable skills at the unskilled bottom occupations in the big cities. But by now both groups have long ceased to drag down the bottom of the income distribution. In short, unskilled immigrants temporarily widen the income distribution in the US. But in the long run, this effect tends to disappear or reverse so that the distribution narrows because of them.

Effects upon Particular Occupations and Income Groups

Before beginning this section, a word needs to be said about its importance. Focusing on the effect of change upon particular groups, rather than upon all of the society, often produces a zero-sum mentality rather than a growth mentality, and increases conflict at the expense of creative work. As George Will put it, in an essay aptly entitled "The F Word":

Sooner or later every parent must rise up and lay down the law to the children about the use of the word that parents often refer to delicately as "the F word." It is a four-letter word. It comes tripping off even very young tongues. It is a disturber of the peace. The word is "fair."

Unless that word is banned from children's vocabularies the evening meal becomes even more stressful than it inevitably is. Arguments erupt when Billy says he has been given an unfair (slightly larger than Suzy's) stalk of broccoli and Suzy says her scoop of sherbet is unfair (slightly smaller than Bill's). Bedtime becomes bedlam as Suzy, five, says it is unfair that Billy, 15, gets to stay up later than the age difference warrants. And breakfast brings an especially virulent outbreak of fairness-mongering when Billy and Suzy, in harmony for once, say it is unfair that they have to eat oatmeal while the kids next door are tucking into bowls of fudge-coated sugar-munchies.

Recently American society and the government that both shapes and reflects it have come to resemble a quarrelsome, elbow-throwing family that needs a vacation from itself and its fussing about fairness. (*Newsweek*, 26 May 1986, p. 80)

Let us take the point. Nevertheless, differential effects certainly are of *some* concern to us.

Additional competitors for jobs and customers can have a direct effect upon the workers in a given occupation, or upon the members of a particular income stratum. More immigrant dentists surely have a depressing effect upon the earnings of native dentists, *ceteris paribus*. And additional unskilled workers must cause some damage to native unskilled workers, *ceteris paribus*. Before we go any further, however, the importance of the *ceteris paribus* clause must be emphasized. If more of *all* occupations enter the country in the same proportions as they are found among natives − if, for example, the proportions of dentists and laborers among immigrants are the same as among natives − then native dentists and native unskilled workers will not suffer from depressed earnings. Therefore, it is necessary to inquire into the proportions of various types of persons entering as immigrants.

Of great interest to many is the proportion of persons with low education and low skill, because of the threat they represent to the poorest segment of the native population. But the data shown in tables 13.1 to 13.3 do not give much evidence of such a danger.

With respect to particular occupations, such as physicians and college professors and plumbers, *some* occupations must be hurt in the short run, because the occupational mix of immigrants is never perfectly neutral. But this does not imply that governmental actions should be taken to prevent such damage. Here there is sound analogy to international trade in goods. Imports hurt the particular domestic industries with which they compete. But a policy to prevent the threatened immediate damage in each threatened industry condemns most of us to being worse off in the long run, because it prevents the re-allocation of labor that is required in a changing world if a leading country is to maintain its lead.

There is an important difference between the movement of goods and of people, however, in that the import of goods benefits natives as consumers whereas there is no such "trade" benefit to natives from the entrance of immigrants; this is the main point of chapter 2. On the other hand, an immigrant immediately benefits workers in all the industries in which he/she does *not* work by spending his/her income, and thereby increasing the demand for labor in the wide range of other industries. That is, if *goods* are imported in all categories of goods, there is immediate harm to workers in all industries, which is only remedied when exports are later increased to pay for the imports (which must happen eventually). But if *immigrants* arrive and go to work in all industries, the compensating benefit of increased sales in all industries is likely to occur almost immediately.

If immigrants did not also bestow benefits of various sorts upon natives, the damage to workers in particular industries where they enter disproportionately might be reasonable grounds to bar them even though workers in other industries benefit from the immigrants, just as the damage to workers in particular industries might be reason enough to bar imports if the import did not bestow benefits on the rest of us. But the fact is that natives as a whole *do* benefit from immigrants taken altogether, as much of this book shows. Therefore, it makes sense not to pay heed to the requests by injured workers in particular occupations that immigrants be barred, but rather to make attempts to smooth the adjustment of workers in those industries who wish to move to other occupations. The reduction in wages of those who remain in that industry is regrettable, but the hurt must be seen as part of the pattern of gains and losses to particular groups that is the inevitable result of economic change.

Evidence about the extent of damage to workers in particular broad groups may help to keep in perspective the harm that immigrants actually cause. The people that elicit most concern, to others as well as to members of the group itself, are those with low skills and low incomes. The opponents of immigration argue that natives would fill the jobs that unskilled (and especially illegal) immigrants push them out of. But the proponents of immigration argue that because natives have access to the welfare system, whereas new immigrants do not, the "reservation price" of natives (the wage at which they will choose not to work) is high enough that few of them will fill these jobs at the same wages that immigrants will. Chapter 15 describes some experiments that bear upon this matter, tending to indicate that the substitution between natives and immigrants is relatively low; if immigrants are prevented from taking jobs in the restaurant and hotel and textile industries, for example, relatively few natives will take and keep the jobs. But the experiments do not throw much light on the more fundamental questions: If immigrants were not available, how many of the employers would raise wages enough to attract natives? How many would simply forgo having the work done? And how many would replace labor with machinery?

Morgan and Gardner (1982) answer the forgoing questions reasonably well for the case of farm workers, as described in chapter 12. But one further question remains unanswered there: How many of the native workers who do not find jobs in the industry in question find jobs elsewhere? And, how much lower are their wages there? Without some answers to these questions, it is not possible to estimate the damage to the groups in question.

Effects on Prices

Effects of immigration upon prices affect groups differentially, because the mix of purchases differs, which is why the subject is treated in this chapter. The effect of immigration upon prices is very diffused, and should be even harder to detect than the effects upon wages of a subgroup such as black teenagers. Yet to ignore the diffused and indirect effects because they are not obvious is to violate one of the major elements of wisdom of economics. It is a great merit of Muller and Espenshade (1985) that they made a bold attempt to estimate the effects of Hispanics upon price levels in Los Angeles County.

Muller and Espenshade found a slower increase in the Consumer Price Index than in comparison cities San Francisco and San Diego, and a lower increase in the BLS computed cost of living than for the US as a whole. However, this might be simply a chance variation, or due to a variety of other factors; Muller and Espenshade perform no tests of significance. They do examine the finer structure of prices, however, as follows:

Specific items for which relative price increases in Los Angeles were lower than the U.S. average included personal care, homeownership, apparel, entertainment, food away from home, and household goods and operations. Price increases for apparel and for entertainment were sharply lower than the average increase for the United States. Prices for medical care, rental housing, private transportation, and fuel rose faster than prices nationwide, and the price of rental housing was noticeably higher.

These price changes follow the pattern one would more or less expect to accompany a growth in the immigrant population. Professional services such as medical care would not be affected by the availability of low-wage labor, but personal care would be. Apparel prices would be expected to be somewhat lower because large quantities produced in Los Angeles are for the local and regional markets. Because most immigrants live in rental units, the rental housing market would experience substantial pressure from the rising immigrant-induced demand. (1985, pp. 152–3)

Summary

In theory, immigration of persons without capital, or with lower-than-average amounts of capital, should increase the disparities in income distribution in the society (as long as the immigrant's earnings also are not above average). The theoretical process is that the additional supply of labor increases the earnings of the capitalists who are assumed to represent the upper-income group, hence widening the income distribution.

We have no direct evidence to test this proposition. But several facts adduced in the chapter cast doubt on this theoretical outcome. Even if the short-run effect of immigrants is to increase the disparities, the longer run does not reveal such an effect; if anything, immigration will narrow the disparities in income.

Also, immigrants often bring substantial amounts of financial capital with them, which mitigates the capital-induced widening in the income distribution.

There is no doubt that workers in some industries suffer immediate injury from the addition of workers in the same category. But exactly the same may be said about those workers if more of the goods that they make are imported from abroad. And in many cases immigration is a substitute for production abroad because of restrictions on imports, as in the case of vegetables grown in the US near the Mexican border. Therefore, it would seem reasonable that the two sorts of complaints for the same special interests should receive the same sort of sympathy – or lack of it. And it might seem appropriate to suggest that one source of melioration of the position of low-skill workers who suffer from increased competition would be an increase in the number of high-skill immigrants which would increase the complementary demand for low-skill workers. Therefore those writers who oppose immigration in general on the ground that it injures low-skill workers (which is not generally true of legal immigration) call their credibility into question if they are not prepared to urge an increase in high-skill or general immigration.

Even if some group of persons in the economy suffer loss because of a disproportionate flow of immigrants into their sector, it might be short-sighted even for them as a group to conclude that they would be better off without the immigration. The immediate static "classical" effects are likely to be small relative to the dynamic effects, and are likely to be small even relative to the immediate welfare-and-tax effect. It is this orientation away from the shortest run and toward the longer run which is crucial in getting a balanced view of the welfare effects of immigrants upon natives.

NOTES

1. The 24–64 break, rather than the more common 25–64 break, was simply for convenience.

14 The Sending Countries, the Immigrants Themselves, and the World as a Whole

Abandonment of Social Capital
Reduction in Returns to Capital
Externalities of Population Size and Density
Remittances
Reduction in 'Surplus' Labor Force
Brain Drain
Population Density and Size
Effects through the Public Coffers
Effects upon Immigrants
Migration and the World Standard of Living
Conclusions

This book focuses on the effect of immigrants upon the country which receives them, the US in particular. Fierce policy debates focus upon that subject. And in the course of such debates, the effect upon the *sending* countries sometimes arises; those who oppose immigration argue that the immigrants' countries of origin, and the immigrants themselves, are harmed. The matter also bears upon such US policies as requiring Fulbright scholars to leave the US after their scholarship period. Furthermore, the subject is of intrinsic interest. It is for those reasons that a brief chapter about the effect upon the sending countries, and upon the world in general, is included here.

It must be said that much of the apparent concern about the ill effects of emigration upon the sending countries and the immigrants is pious hypocrisy on the part of those persons who are against immigration and are willing to use any plausible-sounding argument to advance their cause. But there certainly also is sincere concern on the part of some persons, and particularly those within the sending countries themselves. The matter therefore deserves to be taken seriously.

These are the main mechanisms by which out-migration might affect the sending country: (1) abandonment of social capital by emigrants; (2) reduction in returns to capital; (3) brain drain; (4) reduction in "surplus" labor force which receives more than its marginal product from private and public sources; (5) remittances; and (6) externalities of population density and size. We shall consider them in that order. To a considerable extent, these mechanisms with respect to sending countries are the same mechanisms at work in the receiving countries but in reverse, and therefore the discussion given in the other chapters need not be repeated at any length.

Abandonment of Social Capital

In the grand tradition of classical economics, formal economic theory pertaining to emigration has focused on physical capital. And indeed, an economic motive throughout history when countries have expelled a minority group — examples in the twentieth century are the expulsion of the Indians from Africa and from Ceylon, and the Jews from Germany — has been the intention of the natives to gain the benefits of the expelled emigrants' real and business property, either by forced sale below market value or by expropriation. The same logic holds with respect to voluntary emigrants and public capital such as roads and irrigation systems. It is this logic which Usher (1977) formalized, as discussed in chapter 8. (His calculated example, however, is not sound, for reasons given in chapter 8.)

The gains to remaining natives from the capital abandoned by refugees are not likely to be of great importance, even in the short run. True, some people will wind up with much nicer houses than they could otherwise have acquired, as was the case with some Israelis in Jerusalem after Arabs fled in the 1948 war. Abandoned businesses, however, usually lose most of their value after the owners depart. And the gains to those remaining from diminished congestion in the use of public goods such as roads and harbors are not likely to be of any importance. Those who hope for big capital gains to the society as a whole from emigration are likely to be disappointed. Tobin renders a pungent and surely wise verdict on that activity in the context of East Africa:

> Sometimes official economic rationales of policies of Africanization, implicit and explicit, seem to be based on an image of the economic process quite different from the models discussed above. The image is an economy whose aggregate wealth and income are naturally and exogenously determined, independently of the effort, skill and saving of the inhabitants. Jobs and shops and businesses are just tickets that allow the holders to claim shares of these exogenously fixed, though it is hoped growing, amounts of wealth and output. The tickets can be reassigned without danger to the total, so obviously the lot of citizens can be improved by giving them

tickets formerly held by aliens. Maybe such an economy is approximated by an oil-rich sheikdom or by a country whose land effortlessly yields crops for export or home consumption or displays scenic beauties greatly prized by foreigners. But it is a dangerous model for almost all real countries, and a possibly serious consequence of expulsion policies may be that these rationales will be believed by the governments that espouse them and the people the policies are supposed to benefit. (1974, p. 18)

There will be some gain to the sending society from the lessened need to build new demographic capital such as schools and hospitals, especially if the population of the sending country is growing even in the face of emigration. Chapter 8 estimated this factor in reverse for receiving countries to be a cost of about $4172 per migrant family in 1975 dollars. The amount of saving might be somewhat less in a poorer sending country, because of lesser costs of construction, but this might still be the correct order of magnitude, and is not insignificant. There are, however, important but intangible costs that accompany an aging stock of real and physical capital, because stationary technology and inadequate or deteriorating systems (such as electrical systems) are built into that capital.

Reduction in Returns to Capital

If there are fewer native workers, the owners of capital will make less money from the operation of their plant and equipment, because wages will be higher and therefore the capital will be used less intensively. This is the Yeager–Borts–Stein–Berry–Soligo line of thinking which was discussed in chapter 7 with respect to the effect of immigration upon receiving countries, and therefore it needs no further explication here. Except in the case of massive emigration, this mechanism is not likely to be important in the contemporary world, however.

Externalities of Population Size and Density

Fewer people may mean less congestion in public facilities for a while. But in the longer run, when there is time for new construction, congestion need not be a function of the population density per square mile, as Hong Kong and Singapore demonstrate sharply. And in the longer run, greater density is likely to be advantageous because of shorter distances over which goods and messages must travel; such shortness of distances is the key to Japan's "just in time" factory supply and inventory system, as discussed in chapter 10. Therefore diminution of population density due to emigration is likely to have unfavorable results.

Greater population size also implies faster growth in productivity due to larger industry volume as well as a larger supply of inventive minds, as discussed in chapter 9. Emigration is likely to have negative effects for this reason, also.

Remittances

Remittance of funds from emigrant workers to family members remaining in the sending countries is one of the few aspects of international migration that is not symmetrical in sending and receiving countries. Remittances sent out of the immigrant-receiving country do not harm the rest of society, for reasons explained in chapter 7. But remittances constitute a distinct social benefit in sending countries. The effects are asymmetrical because the person sending the remittance is the only person whose consumption is affected in the immigrant-receiving country, and that person is (by definition) made better off in an overall way by sending the remittance, or else he/she would not send it.

Remittances are an important part of the economy of many immigrant-sending countries, as is immediately obvious when traveling through such places as towns in the West Bank of Jordan where there clearly is no industry and the agriculture is marginal, yet there are many new homes that are financed with funds from abroad. The remittances are large in magnitude relative to public and private budgets in many countries, though their aggregate size is not great relative to world trade. Moreover, the payments go directly to the final recipient, in contrast to government-to-government foreign aid which often is so diluted by bureaucratic costs and plain corruption that much of it fails to do much good. And the sender of the remittances has personal knowledge of the capacity of the recipient to make use of the funds for consumption or investment, which must lessen the likelihood that the funds will be squandered.

Taylor (1987), in a study distinguished from other work on this topic by the care taken in the method used, estimated not only the amount of remittances per illegal Mexican working in the US, but the amount of earnings in Mexico forgone by being in the US, and the difference between the two quantities for the average illegal Mexico-to-US migrant from a sample of households in rural Mexico. He found that expected remittances for the average migrant were US$974.96. (Expected earnings forgone by being in the US for this group were estimated at $411.25.) He also found that the migrants from rural areas are not the best-qualified earners in terms of education and other variables, which diminishes concern about the effects of a brain drain.

As long as remittances do not imply savings rates for immigrants lower than for natives (or lower than some other standard), they have the same macro implications for the country of immigration as does any other pattern of consumption expenditure.

Remittances will be put into a wider perspective below when they are considered together with the brain drain in the simulation model of Gold-farb et al. (1984).

Reduction in "Surplus" Labor Force

To avoid misunderstanding, let us be clear that "surplus" labor, as the concept was first used concerning Eastern Europe at the end of World War II by Rosenstein-Rodan (1943), and as it was discussed by Lewis (1955), simply does not exist. Marginal productivity never reaches the zero point, as T. Schultz taught us (1964). But it may well be the case, especially in poor-country agriculture, that marginal productivity falls relatively fast with additional labor. If so, and if workers receive their average product, then reduction in the labor force will substantially increase average income. On the other hand, chances are that people in the sending country will over-estimate the benefit to those who remain, because they may assume that the total product will remain fixed rather than decline when the emigration takes place.

A related benefit is that the reduction in the labor force may induce the adoption of more advanced labor-saving methods, thereby speeding up economic development.

Brain Drain

The flow of highly trained persons from poor countries to rich countries has aroused more interest and concern than has any other aspect of international migration with respect to the sending countries. For example, *The World Population Plan of Action* adopted by the United Nations Fund for Population Activity and its supporting nations says,

[T]here is an urgent need to formulate national and international policies to avoid the "brain drain" and to obviate its adverse effects. ... Developing countries suffering from heavy emigration of skilled workers and professionals should under-take extensive educational programmes, manpower planning, and investment in scientific and technical programmes. (1979, p. 47)

Some time ago the brain drain was the subject of two symposia which convened the most thoughtful and prestigious groups of economists who have written in connection with international migration. And there have been other capable studies (e.g. Grubel and Scott, 1977; various articles in Adams, 1968), and thorough investigation of a proposal by Bhagwati (1976) for compensation to the poor countries for brain drain. Yet there still is almost no solid evidence on the economic importance of the phenomenon, which is not surprising in view of its elusive nature. And of course there is great controversy about what ought to be done if the facts eventually show that the emigration of skilled professionals does indeed cause remaining natives of the sending countries to be worse off than if the emigration does not take place.

The influence of highly skilled persons upon the productivity of other persons in the society because of complementarity of skills is the focus of most discussion. That is, a topnotch engineer, through the high quality of her/his designs, is thought to increase the value of the product of construction workers. And it is implicitly assumed that the engineer is not able to capture in earnings all the value of his/her skill; if instead the worker is paid all of his/her marginal product, as the neo-classical theory has it, then there is no externality to be discussed as brain drain. It would seem very difficult to determine the extent to which this assumption fits the facts. And for purposes of an assessment of brain drain, the validity of the assumptions clearly is important, even if assumptions have a different status in the kind of positive-economics situation that Friedman (1953) addressed.

The influence of highly trained persons in increasing the productivity of fellow workers by their learning on the job is another phenomenon that may be important. Examples are a skilled physician who imparts some of his/her know-how to younger physicians while on the job, and a world-famous physicist who passes on knowledge in a university classroom. It is not likely that the highly skilled person will be able to obtain the full benefit of this effect in his or her own earnings, for reasons given in the discussion of the comparable effect in the context of the richer country in chapter 2. Therefore, within any grade class within an occupation — that is, among those earning the same salary — it is the best of them who will choose to emigrate, because they stand to benefit most in increased income. This necessarily implies a loss to the sending society.

Analysis of the likely importance of the brain drain, in conjunction with the remittance effect, is found below in the context of Goldfarb, Havrylyshyn, and Mangum's model (1984). A discussion of policies for compensating poor countries may be found in chapter 16.

Goldfarb et al. assume reasonably that the brain drain and remittances are the two most important aspects of emigration. They work with the case of physicians from the Philippines, and they evaluate the matter with respect to several criteria, the most relevant being the welfare of all persons in the sending society other than the persons who emigrate. These are the parameters of their model: lifetime physician's incomes in the Philippines and in the US (treating the social externality of a physician in the Philippines as a multiplier of physician income) the proportion of physician income in the US that will be remitted to the Philippines, and the marginal propensity to consume. They find that on most reasonable sets of assumptions about these parameters, those who remain behind will benefit from having physicians emigrate (as compared to the case of those physicians not migrating). Or to put it differently, it pays the Philippines to train physicians for export.

The issue of unemployment among the educated persons in LDCs complicates the issue. If the number of persons that will be educated and the number of them that would otherwise be unemployed are taken to be fixed independent of migration opportunities, then out-migration of representative members of that group has no opportunity cost. If the migrants are the most productive persons in the group, however, the conclusion is less clear-cut. And Blomqvist (1985, 1986) points out the additional complication that the possibility of out-migration might increase the number of persons who would choose to become educated, which on some assumptions might impose a loss on the sending society. To the extent that education is paid for privately, however, the possibility of such a loss is reduced. A numerically specified model with realistic parameters, including allowance for remittances, would be necessary to establish the likelihood of damage to the sending society.

Whatever the facts about brain drain, however, the implications for national and international policies are by no means obvious, because there are important disagreements about relevant values. For example, if a nation has subsidized an individual's education, does that nation have the ethical right to demand repayment of the subsidy before the individual may leave, as the USSR did with respect to Jews and others for some years? And how is this ethical judgment influenced by the fact that the potential migrant's parents, on average, paid for that subsidy through taxes? Would the individual's parents' consent be relevant? And if one believes that a nation has this right, is it implied that nations should move to a system where an individual's cohort on average pays for its own education later on, as in Yale University's system for financing loans to students?

Another example: Bhagwati (e.g. 1976) advocates a tax on emigrants to be paid by their earnings in their new country because of the loss of the individual's externalities to the individual's country of origin, even if there has been no national subsidy in raising the individual. (This suggestion is also implicit in the cost—benefit calculations concerning emigration of professionals from Colombia by Berry and Mendez, 1976, p. 259.) But what justifies the nation's claim to obtain any of the benefits of an individual's productive life? Bhagwati apparently believes that a loss in "welfare" to the inhabitants of the country of origin is a self-evident justification, but the justification is not self-evident to me. The issue here must be at least as deep philosophically as the issue of whether a nation is entitled not to keep its border open to immigrants, discussed in appendix 1.

The following is offered as an appropriate intellectual framework for thinking about the brain drain: (1) Does the emigration of professionals cause injury to the particular LDC, and if yes, what kinds of injury occur? (e.g. externalities, export of subsidized education, etc.). (2) If there is injury, what options are there to prevent an injury with market mechanisms that would not restrict movement or impose taxes? (e.g. require payment for education when rendered). (3) If market mechanisms do not suffice, does the LDC have a "right" to prevent some kinds of injury? (e.g. loss of externalities arising from private investment). The fundamental question here is the extent to which the state "owns" a person's output.

Population Density and Size

The effects of emigration through changes in population density and size are the opposite side of the coin from the effects of immigration through the same mechanisms. Aside from the shortest-run impacts, the effects are likely to be negative. The arguments need not be reviewed again here.

Effects through the Public Coffers

Emigrants are generally young, just at the beginning of their period of maximum net contribution to the public coffers by paying taxes but not using welfare services. Therefore, emigrants constitute a major loss to the sending country to the extent that the sending country collects taxes, just as the migrants are a major gain to the US through the same mechanism. The persons who would otherwise support aged and child dependents withdraw their support when they leave. In the short and intermediate run, this is likely to be the greatest negative effect upon the sending country.

Effects upon Immigrants

Immigrants mainly come to the US because they expect to improve their economic situations, and most of them do better themselves; among those who do not succeed, many emigrate. There is little more to say on the topic without proceeding to the issues of how fast the immigrants succeed, or which groups do better than which, which I leave to the extensive literature on the subject that has developed since Chiswick (1978b); for a recent list of references, see the bibliography in Borjas (1985a).

Occasionally one hears the argument (though mostly with respect to illegals) that we ought not to let immigrants in because we exploit them economically when they get here, by paying them low wages. At the base of this argument is the notion that the speaker knows better than the potential immigrant what is good for the potential immigrant, that even if the potential immigrant prefers to work in the US for whatever he or she will earn, it would be better to stay home and earn even less. This strikes me as nothing but arrogance and selfishness parading as analysis and idealism — and the selfishness is even without foundation!

The anti-immigration groups have recently taken this line of thought one step further by comparing the entry of low-skill immigrants to the institution of pre-Civil-War slavery (see discussion on p. 284). It would seem that the key element of slavery is legally-sanctioned compulsion and involuntary servitude, which is clearly not present in the case of immigrants, even (or especially) with respect to illegals.

Migration and the World Standard of Living

The general level of living

If we consider both the sending and the receiving countries as part of the same world, then — and on this every economist agrees — the overall effect of the migration on the average standard of living of the world's people is positive. The reason for this is that the migrant goes from a place where he or she is less productive to a place where he or she is more productive. This increased production benefits the standard of living of the community as a whole, as well as that of the migrating individual. In addition to the private benefits, it would seem that the positive external results of the "brain gain" must be at least as great as the loss from the brain *drain*.

Migration and economic development

The paragraph above suggests that migration can improve the overall standard of living by putting a given individual in a context where the cooperating elements — capital and infrastructure — enable the person's skills to be more productive. But there is also a mechanism which leads a person to be more productive by *changing the person* — by "educating" him in the broadest sense. This may well be a more powerful force affecting the standard of living in the poorer countries and in the world as a whole than the change in circumstances alone.

Economic development requires learning new ways of working and living; and migrants are likely to learn these new ways faster if they migrate than if they stay at home. The learning referred to here is neither schooling nor on-the-job training. It is, rather, the learning acquired outside of school and outside the family, if the family is poor. Examples are knowledge of sanitation, understanding the importance of punctuality, belief that ambition can result in benefits, knowledge of educational opportunities, ability to ride a bicycle, and styles of behavior such as driving a car carefully. This sort of learning includes a change in much of what is called "culture" by the anthropologists. It is the process of "modernization," and constitutes the difference between less-developed and more-developed economies. This learning takes place by association with others on the street and in community life.

Consider Patinkin's observation about the first decade of Israel, a country which has had a proportionately large number of poor immigrants:

Interestingly enough, formal education does not seem to have played too great a role in the development of Israel's efficiency over the period of [mass immigration, 1950−8].

On the other hand the role of informal education has possibly been more significant. This may have expressed itself at the simplest level in the acquisition by the new immigrants of both the language of the country and its ways of life and work. (Patinkin, 1959)

Urbanization is a crucial part of the migration process. Hawley (1969) states: "The city is a school. It inculcates habits of mind and behavior that can be learned nowhere else. There the person learns adaptability to the challenge and flux of new experience. He gains a cosmopolitan outlook . . ."

Migration tends to equalize incomes among different geographic areas. This is shown by the lesser dispersion among per-person incomes in different parts of the same country than among per-person incomes in different countries. For example, the range of the highest and lowest state incomes in the US, Mississippi and Alaska, was from $6580 to $12,790 for 1980, whereas the spread in incomes in 1982 between Chad and Switzerland was from $80 to $17,010 (*US Statistical Abstract, 1982*).[1]

The smaller areas and the greater homogeneity in underlying conditions within countries, as compared to the differences between countries, do not account for this phenomenon; the difference in per-person income between Coahuila and Texas across the river from each other, for instance, is probably not very different from the difference between the per-person incomes of Mexico and the US, $1612 and $10,742 respectively, in 1979 (1982 *US Statistical Abstract, 1982*, p. 865). Nor is the relatively small intra-country dispersion of incomes explained by the mobility of capital flowing from place to place within a country, population remaining fixed; capital also moves relatively freely across international borders.

The equalization due to migration likely is accompanied by a raising of the general level of income. And much of the increase in level likely is due to the changes in the individuals and their work habits, as well as changes in their circumstances.

Conclusions

In the short run, the major loss to the sending country is from the drain of young people who otherwise would be paying taxes to help support the aged and children, while consuming only small amounts of such services. In the longer run, the productivity effect of reduced population density and size is likely to be most important. The brain drain's effect is mixed, and may well be positive on balance because remittances may outweigh the positive externalities of the skilled emigrants. Capital effects are not likely to be important in the short or long run. In general, the effects of emigration are the opposite of the effects of immigration described elsewhere in this book.

This book is mainly about the effects of immigration upon the incomes of natives of the US. But virtually all of the recommendations that will benefit the natives of the US can also be seen as benefiting the average standard of living in the world as a whole. Where there are losses — as there are losses to owners of capital in the countries of origin — the losses tend to be less than the corresponding gains in the country of destination, simply because the output per person is greater in the richer country of destination. Therefore, there is no disjunction between the point of view argued here, and a more universalistic point of view. Those who argue that the US has a moral obligation to prevent migrants from leaving their country of origin cannot justify their arguments in terms of the overall welfare.

NOTES

1 In my judgment, based on prices in the various countries as well as on the quantities of household durables owned, US per-person income is considerably above that in any other country, including Switzerland and Sweden. And US *productivity* is even higher, relatively, once labor-force participation and hours worked per year are allowed for.

15 The "Question" of Illegal Immigrants and Guestworkers

Estimates of the Total and Mexican Illegal Populations
Demographic Profile of the Illegals
Welfare Services Used and Taxes Paid
Labor-Market Effects of Illegals
Remittances
Lawlessness, and the Guestworker Alternative
Illegal Immigration and Dangers to the Public
Conclusions

> Illegal immigration is reaching alarming dimensions ... the United States is probably undergoing now the greatest surge of immigration in its history ... totally out of control. ... They often hold good paying jobs at the expense of a citizen ... displacing citizens and legal resident aliens by working at less than standard wages. ... Immigration fraud is rampant ... illegals cost our taxpayers over $13 billion a year in services, welfare, unemployment and costs of citizens displaced from jobs ... illegal aliens send about $3 billion each year out of the country ... hundreds of millions of dollars each year are lost to our nation's treasury through earnings paid to illegal aliens, on which little, if any, income tax is paid. (Leonard Chapman, then-Commissioner, Immigration and Naturalization Service, 1976)

The subject of illegal immigration raises emotions and − aside from studies of the volume of illegal immigration − is of little theoretical interest. But the subject must be dealt with because it distracts attention from legal immigration; one can hardly mention legal immigration without the conversation immediately shifting to illegals.

There is less solid data about illegals than we would like.[1] But it should be noted that we are not *entirely* without data. There is far more information on the subject than is often supposed, enough to put to rest many of the prevailing myths about illegals.

Even when they apparently are addressing themselves to the more general question of legal immigration, the most active anti-immigration organizations – Federation for Immigration Reform (FAIR), Zero Population Growth (ZPG), and The Environmental Fund (TEF) – constantly harp on the theme that we are being "overwhelmed" by a "horde" of illegal Mexican entrants. They dwell on the "loss of control of our borders."

The frightening assertions in the press feed upon each other as one newspaper simply refers to a story in another paper as its "evidence." For example, in the *Christian Science Monitor* (reprinted in the *Champaign-Urbana News Gazette*, 28 March 1983, p. A4), Richard Strout, called by some of his colleagues the "most respected" reporter in Washington, quotes the *New York Times* as saying: "The stream of illegal aliens pouring into the United States has become a torrent ... the Border Patrol is inundated." And an Associate Attorney General says, without supporting evidence, that: "In the next 20 years the Caribbean world may attempt to empty out much of its population on our shores as political and economic pressure throughout the area continues to build," and then is so quoted by Strout.

This image of the situation as being – in ex-Commissioner Chapman's words quoted above – "totally out of control" inspires fear of chaos and social breakdown, as well as concern about large-scale loss of jobs by natives. Illegal immigration allegedly hurts everyone except business and agriculture. And for good measure, everyone is supposedly hurt in more than one role – as American workers, property owners, taxpayers, teenagers, users of government services, and so on. Even scarier is the plight of future Americans who will face supposed shortages of food and resources, caused by a multitude of alien mouths to feed and bodies to house. Moreover, the illegal immigrants themselves, by being induced to break the law, are said to be – in the words of FAIR's executive director (Conner, 1980), "exploited and mistreated, denied ... rights and privileges." And Conner continues with the dark allegation that "powerful economic forces are benefiting" from the illegal immigration, and presumably are the cause of its continuation.

Senator Alan Simpson, driving force behind the 1986 congressional legislation, said "we had something like that [illegal immigration] about 125 years ago; it was called slavery" (*Cato Policy Report*, September–October 1986, p. 8).

It is outside an economist's professional competence to speculate about why the organizations which are generally against population growth and immigration constantly shift the discussion to illegals. There is no doubt, though, that this focus on illegals and their alleged ill effects colors people's views about the subject of legal immigration (see appendix B).

The stock and flow of illegal persons working and living in the US in any given period, thorny and vexing questions, will be discussed first. Presented next are the data on the extent of use by immigrants of welfare services, and the incidence of payment of taxes by them. Next comes a brief discussion of the labor-market effects of illegals. Then follows analysis of the effect of a guestworker program on the flow of illegals and upon the economy. Last is a discussion of the issue of illegality and its social effects.

Estimates of the Total and Mexican Illegal Populations

Stocks of immigrants

The number of aliens illegally residing and working in the US is an issue that enters into the discussion in many ways. It is the focus of the writings of those who oppose immigration, and it is used to generate strong feelings on the grounds that it causes a breakdown in law and order in the country, and corrupts attitudes toward the law. Huge numbers are thrown around to suggest that the US is vulnerable to invasion or other unnamed dangers because Americans have "lost control of our borders."

Let us, then, examine the available research on the number of aliens illegally in the US, beginning with a brief history of such estimates. We shall see that the evidence for the largest and most frightening estimates that have been given is shockingly flimsy or even non-existent. There seems to be a strong inverse relationship between the quality of the research and the size of the estimate.

The Immigration and Naturalization Service (INS) has given a variety of high estimates, starting as high as 12 million. But as noted by a study made by the Bureau of the Census staff at the request of the Select Commission on Immigration and Refugee Policy: "A description of the 'methodology' underlying Commissioner Chapman's [later] estimate of 4–12 million for 1975 has never been made available by the INS" (Siegel, Passel and Robinson, 1981, p. 16). Apparently this estimate was based on nothing more than a wild guess based on the number of illegals apprehended either crossing the border or on the job. The INS gave no reference to evidence in support of this estimate. And apprehension records are obviously a fallacious basis on which to make any such estimate; the same person may be apprehended several times during a single week.

The INS later shifted its estimate to 8.2 million persons as of mid-1975, deriving the figure from a Lesko Associates study (1975) it had commissioned. The basis for the estimate was the "Delphi technique," a fancy name for asking a small panel of people for a series of opinions. The technique may be quite appropriate for such tasks as forecasting technological developments. But for a subject such as the number of illegals, the technique fits Samuel Johnson's stricture that a compendium of gossip is still gossip. Even Lesko called the estimate "not analytically defensible." Yet for a long time this estimate was the basis for much of the political debate on the subject.

The INS then offered an estimate of 6 million illegals as of 1976. This was derived by asking INS District Directors to estimate the number of illegals residing in their districts. According to the Bureau of the Census description:

The district offices were asked to provide, in addition to estimates of illegals for their districts, a description of the methodology used to generate the estimates. None gave specific procedures. Rather, all but one referred to the 'experience' of officials as the basis for the estimate; the other claimed no 'scientific' basis at all for his estimate. Thus, the overall estimate may be characterized as 'synthetic specu- lation'. (Siegel et al., 1981, p. 17)

Ingenious statisticians have tackled the question in a variety of interesting ways, including: analysis of alien deaths in the US (Robinson, 1979); changes in Mexico's population (Goldberg, 1974); comparisons of data such as Social Security and income-tax records in which illegal aliens are fairly sure to be counted (Lancaster and Scheuren, 1978; Korns, 1979); analysis of changes in the Mexican-origin population reported by the Current Population Survey (Heer, 1979); and surveys of persons returning to Mexico, and of Mexican families, concerning their migration histories (Zazueta and Corona, 1979).

This is a summary of information on the *stock* of illegals:

1   The admirably careful and thoughtful survey of literature by Siegel et al. concluded that "The total number of illegal residents in the United States for some recent year, such as 1978, is almost certainly below 6.0 million, and may be substantially less, possibly only 3.5 to 5.0 million" (1981, p. 19).

2   Siegel et al. also concluded from the variety of studies they surveyed that a considerable proportion of the illegals are not Mexican. "The avail- able evidence indicates that the size of the Mexican population living illegally in the United States is smaller than popular estimates suggest. The Mexican component of the illegally resident population is almost certainly less than 3.0 million, and may be substantially less, possibly only 1.5 to 2.5 million."

3   Of the Mexicans illegally in the US at any given time, a very large proportion are here for a matter of months and will return voluntarily. "The gross movement into the US of Mexican illegals is considerable, as is reflected in the large numbers of apprehensions made by INS, but this

'immigration' is largely offset by a considerable movement in the opposite direction. . . . Apparently, most of the Mexican nationals who enter the US illegally in any year return to Mexico . . ." (pp. 33–4).

The quotation marks that Siegel et al. put around "immigration" in the citation just above are worth noting. Their aim is to distinguish the number of persons presently living in the US at any given moment – "possibly only 3.5 to 5.0 million" – from the number of permanent illegal immigrants, which is a considerably smaller number. But the INS blurs the distinction which leads to higher numbers rather than lower numbers.

4   Korn's study (1979) of illegal-alien employment suggested that there was no increase in the total number of illegals after an expansion period that occurred between 1964 and 1969. And the Census Bureau's Associate Director for Demographic Fields, George E. Hall, commented that "To date, the Census Bureau has not been able to detect explosive growth in the illegal population in any of its data collection systems" (1981, p. 8). It is because most immigrants who enter illegally leave when their jobs end, or when they have earned what they came to earn, usually after a half-year or less, that there can be a constant inflow and yet little or no increase in the total number of immigrant residents.

5   In contrast to the Mexicans, the non-Mexican illegals – who typically either overstay their visa periods or enter with fraudulent documents, rather than by crossing the border clandestinely without documents – are much less likely to return to the home countries. "Hence, non-Mexican illegal immigration may add to the permanent resident population to a far greater extent than the Mexican migration flows," conclude Siegel et al., on the basis of the studies surveyed. This last point suggests that expensive efforts to reduce clandestine border crossing may be a waste.

Some valuable studies done since the Siegel et al. review in 1980 must be described in some detail because, whereas the earlier studies summarized above were reviewed by Siegel et al., the reader cannot rely upon Siegel et al.'s assurance that the procedures render these newer studies worthy of attention.

6   Warren and Passel compared the 1980 census count of aliens "with estimates of the legally resident alien population based on data collected by the Immigration and Naturalization Service in January 1980" (1983, abstract). This comparison yielded estimates of the *minimum* total number of all illegals (about 2 million) and of Mexican illegals (over 900,000) living in the US as of 1980. On the basis of what the Census Bureau has learned about the rate of undercounting of various other groups, however, the authors are able to make some reasonable suppositions beyond the observed magnitudes. For example, they note (p. 12) that if there were to be six million illegals in the country, a 60 percent undercount rate by the Census would be implied, and they add that "undercount rates of this magnitude

seem improbable in light of the characteristics of the illegals counted [large proportions of women and children, and almost 30 percent of the counted having been in the US more than 10 years] and of persons usually missed in the census." They note that (a) "the highest undercount rates measured recently for any group in the US are roughly 20 percent for adult black males in their 30s," (b) very few housing units were missed, and (c) the undercount was about 1 percent for the legal population. They conclude that "the assumption of extreme undercount rates for the illegal population would require substantial evidential support." In other words, estimates far above the minimum levels they estimated would run counter to their evidence.[2]

Muller (1984) corroborates part of the Warren–Passel assumptions about the rates of undercount, finding that "School enrollment data for all children and for children of Hispanic origin correspond closely with the Census estimates in both Los Angeles County and California [as a whole] suggesting that the Census did enumerate most Mexican immigrant families with children, whatever their legal status" (p. 5). This implies that it is only the more recent immigrants, many of whom do not themselves know how long they intend to stay, who are substantially undercounted. Among those more recent immigrants, who tend to be single young males, Muller believes the undercount is "considerable," based on a sex-ratio comparison. (In total, he estimates that "between 200,000 and 300,000 undocumented persons were not enumerated in Southern California, with Mexicans probably accounting for somewhat over one-half of the total" p. 5).

Another implication of Muller's estimates of undercounts is that there is little underenumeration among those illegal immigrants who use schools, which are the most expensive public services for immigrants. "Most of the immigrants not counted by the Census will have no effect on such public services as school and social services relevant for families. In fact those immigrants probably pay more in taxes and compulsory public program contributions than they receive" even though their incomes and tax payments are considerably lower than the average for natives (p. 5).

Muller's overall estimate is a total of 1,086,000 illegal net immigrants entering into California in the 1970–80 period, of whom he estimates 589,000 to be from Mexico and 497,000 from elsewhere. What this implies for all-US estimates was not worked out by Muller.

7   Bean, King, and Passel (1983) calculated the number of illegal Mexicans in the US in 1980 from the Mexican census, from assumptions about sex ratio at birth, the proportion of males among emigrants age 15–39, and the proportion of all emigrants that are age 15–39, together with US data on the number of legal immigrants (subtracted from the total of all emigrants). Their estimates range from 1.5 million to 3.9 million, depending upon the assumptions. The lower end of the range — rather than their midpoint of

2.7 million — would seem the most likely in view of the undercount analysis of Warren and Passel. Even 2.7 million Mexicans would imply an undercount of 2.7 million−0.93 million = (1.77/2.7) = 62 percent, which is higher than seems plausible.

If we assume that half of the Mexicans illegally in the US stay for only a short time and are not therefore immigrants, an assumption backed by various surveys reviewed by Siegel et al., then the *maximum* number of Mexican illegal *immigrants* as of 1980 was less than 2 million. Even that number, together with the Warren−Passel findings above, would imply an undercount in the census of about 50 percent, which does not seem plausible in light of undercount experience, Warren and Passel suggest. If we take the midpoint of the Bean et al. estimates, 2.7 million, and consider that half — 1.35 million — are permanent immigrants, then this would imply an undercount of 31 percent, which is still high but perhaps plausible.

The implication of these findings about the number of permanent illegal Mexican immigrants in the country is surprising. If, say, half of 5 million illegals in the country at any one time are Mexican, this implies 2.5 million illegal Mexican residents. And if more than half of them intend not to remain permanently, then something less than 1.25 million Mexicans are true illegal immigrants — less than a million if the lower estimate of the Census Bureau study is correct. This certainly is not a large number by any economic test, and it certainly is far less than the frightening figures promulgated widely in the past decade.

In reflecting on these stocks of illegals in the country at any time, one should keep in mind that the number of *workers* is less than the total number of *persons*.

8   The most recent study of immigration statistics, by the National Academy of Sciences, concluded as follows about the stock of illegals:

As a result of this review of empirical estimates of the size of the illegal population of the United States, what can we conclude? First, the procedures that have been used, though often imaginative and sometimes elaborate, all invoke numerous assumptions that often cannot be adequately justified and to which the estimates ɔbtained are sensitive. Second, even the commonly quoted range of 3−6 million illegals may be too high, though none of the procedures reviewed produces compelling upper or lower limits. The study by Warren and Passel suggests that it is unlikely that less than 1.5 million or more than 2.5 million illegal aliens were included in the 1980 census; locations data suggest that a figure under half a million is unlikely; Mexican census data fail to confirm the permanent absence in 1980 of more than half a million Mexicans who might be illegally resident in the United States, and the figure could be substantially lower. Though no range can be soundly defended, a population of 1.5 to 3.5 million illegal aliens in 1980 appears reasonably consistent with most of the studies. (Levine, Hill, and Warren, 1985, p. 243)

The most recent, and probably the best estimate, then, is 1.5 to 3.5 million illegal aliens resident in the US as of 1980.

Rate of entry in various periods

Information about the rate of entry of illegals in various periods in the past is of interest for several reasons, perhaps chiefly that it may help to estimate the stock of illegal alien residents in the past and present. Here follows some relevant material:

1   Between the expansion that occurred in the period 1964–9 and the end of his study period, Korns' study (1979) of illegal alien employment (of sufficiently high quality that Siegel et al. include it in their review), implied a zero rate of entry, suggesting that there has been no increase in the total number of illegals. This estimate provides a lower limit to the range of estimates in other studies, which suggest that there has been an increase. (Compare FAIR's Conner (1980) about the same date: "Any estimate of the number of illegal immigrants living in the US is only a guess, but we know that the trend is upward.")

2   As noted above, the Census Bureau's then-Associate Director for Demographic Fields, George E. Hall, commented that "the Census Bureau has not been able to detect explosive growth in the illegal population" (1981 p. 8), implying a low rate of net entry.

3   Warren and Passel's study (1983) offers some insight into the rate at which illegals who have remained in the US have entered in various periods. They counted 570,000 as having entered 1960–9, 551,000 as having entered 1970–4 (roughly double the rate in the earlier period), and 890,000 as having entered 1975–80. The comparable numbers for Mexico alone are 138,000, 280,000, and 476,000 (see their table 3). Two offsetting forces must be noted when we consider the latest period's data: On the one hand, the undercount is likely to be more severe among those here a shorter time and therefore less well-established; on the other hand, a substantial number counted as being here in the most recent group are not permanent but rather will be returning home, especially Mexicans. Taken altogether, these data suggest some rise in the rate of entry, but not an explosive rise.

On the basis of the Current Population Survey, Woodrow, Passel and Warren (1987) summarize the situation since 1980 as follows:

Comparing the November 1979 and June 1986 estimates, the estimated annual change is 218,000, with 115,000 for Mexico as country of birth. The annual changes estimated for other regions of birth are low, but positive. The estimated average annual change in the undocumented population between the 1980 census and June 1986 was 176,000. The estimated annual change in the Mexico-born undocumented population was 170,000

The annual average change in the undocumented population is likely to be in the range of 100,000 to 300,000. More than half of the growth is likely to be of Mexican birth. (p. 3)

Passage of the 1986 immigration legislation may have altered the situation significantly, but information on the matter has not yet come to light.

4   It has been common among both laymen and demographers to infer rates of gross and net illegal immigration from the rates of apprehensions by the INS. And frequently, authors show the data starting, say, 1965 as proving a rising rate of entry (e.g. Fogel, 1977). Perhaps so. But a longer time series puts the recent data in perspective, as seen in figure 15.1. The very high rates of gross and net illegal immigration from the rates of apprehensions by the INS. And frequently, authors show the data starting, say, 1965 as proving a enter them in the official program" (Keely, 1982, p. 44), and hence one cannot infer rates of entry from these observations. Nevertheless, the rates of apprehension prior to 1960 stand as a warning about the use of apprehensions data as the basis for inference about rates of gross and net entry.

Figure 15.1 also suggests a strong relationship between illegal entry and a legal guestworker program, corroborating that the two kinds of labor are close substitutes for each other. And all else being equal, employers would prefer to hire legal workers rather than illegals because the wages paid may be the same (for data on illegal female workers in Los Angeles, see R. Simon and DeLey, 1984; but see Kossoudji and Ranney, 1986, discussed below, p. 293) and there is less uncertainty about how long legal workers will remain on the job because they are not in danger of being apprehended.

Care must be taken in extrapolating the relationship seen in figure 15.1, however, because the nature of illegal immigration changes over the years as networks between the US and places of origin build up, as learning takes place, and as attachments form within the US. This complex process is well described by Massey (1986).

Demographic Profile of the Illegals

The staff of the Select Commission on Immigration and Refugee Policy surveyed the available studies of illegals and compiled the following generalizations about their age and sex:

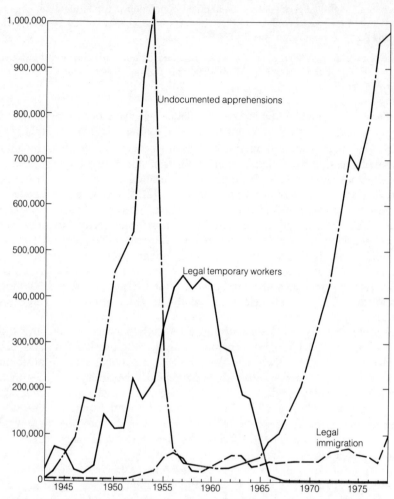

Figure 15.1   Mexican migration to the United States and apprehensions
of illegal entrants, 1943–78
Source: Select Commission on Immigration and Refugee Policy, *Staff Report*, 1981,
p. 471

1   The illegals are "predominantly male" (1981, Staff Report, p. 485).
The proportion varies from study to study. A survey of the most recent
literature found that "Estimates of the percentage of males among Mexican
migrant workers range from 67 percent to 91 percent" (Taylor, 1985, p. 7).

Among Mexicans the male proportion is higher than among non-Mexicans.
2 The illegals are "young (between the ages of 15 and 45)" (Select
Commission, 1981, p. 485). The median age is in the middle to late
twenties (Taylor, 1985, p. 7). Extremely few children are apprehended by
the Border Patrol after illegal crossings.
3 The illegals are "as likely to be married as unmarried" (Select Commission, 1981, p. 485).
4 Mexico-US migrants in general do not originate from households at
the very top nor at the very bottom of the rural income distribution (Cross
and Sandos, 1981, p. 76). Households at the top of their village income
distribution, in general, have fewer motives for sending illegal migrants to
the US than households at the bottom and middle of the income distribution. The former typically enjoy both income-earning opportunities and
social status without having to make the material and psychological sacrifices
associated with sending family members clandestinely into an unfamiliar
foreign labor market. At the other income extreme, although the poorest
rural households might stand to benefit significantly from Mexico–US
migration, they often lack the financial resources and economic security to
risk sending members illegally across international frontiers. Members of
these households are more likely to supplement their family's income
through seasonal migration within Mexico, often returning home to assist
in critical agricultural tasks on the family farm (Taylor, 1985, pp. 10–11).
5 Length of average stay depends upon the distance to the border. "Of
undocumented Mexican male migrants apprehended within 25 miles of the
southern border in 1979, only seven percent had been in this country for
more than six months" (Select Commission, 1981, p. 503). But further
from the border in California, the proportions who had been in the country
for several years were much larger.
6 Unlike legal immigrants, illegals have on average less education and
skills than the native labor force. Part of the explanation is that lower-
income Mexico shares a border with the US. But Canada does, too, and
sends fewer illegals. Chiswick offers another explanatory element:

A creditable threat of apprehension and deportation will influence investment
decisions. Deportation means the loss of human capital investments made in the
destination that are specific to the employer or to the destination labor market in
general. Meanwhile, skills specific to the country of origin that were acquired prior
to the illegal immigration depreciate during the time spent in the destination. The
potential depreciation of skills associated with immigration and apprehension/de-
portation is of course least for workers without skills or with skills that have perfect
international transferability. The absolute magnitude of human capital investments
specific to a country (including firm-specific skills) tends to rise with a worker's skill
level. It is, therefore, not surprising that apprehended illegal aliens tend to have a

lower level of skill than legal immigrants, other things the same, and that the difference in the relative skill levels between illegal and legal immigrants is greater for immigrants from countries with higher levels of skill. (Chiswick, 1985b, p. 15)

7   Mexicans illegally in the US earn less than do Mexicans in the US legally, according to Kossoudji and Ranney (1986) who studied a 1978−9 survey carried out by the Mexican government of return migrants (see Garcia y Griego, 1983a) in which the average daily wage differential was 27 percent.

Of the 27% observed wage differential in daily wage rates in the U.S. for legal and illegal temporary migrants from Mexico, roughly 9% can be attributed to differences in observed characteristics and the different returns to those character-istics in the legal and illegal migrant labor markets. The remainder of the wage differential appears to be associated with unobserved variables that affect both illegal wage rates and legal status. (Kossoudji and Ranney 1986, p. 21)

That is, some of the 18 percent differential associated with illegal status after observed background characteristics are allowed for may be due to unobserved characteristics that affect both legal status and earning capacity. But R. Simon and DeLey (1984) find no difference.

Welfare Services Used and Taxes Paid

I apologize for this section being as argumentative as it is. The tone is not pleasant or appropriate to a scholarly book; and controversy dates as fast as today's newspaper. But because of the wide public interest in the topic, and because it is necessary to meet attacks on the position presented here lest that position be impugned, some argumentative material seems necessary.

The headnote quote of former INS director Chapman typifies the view of many Americans that illegals are a drain upon the taxpayer by way of the use of welfare services. Or as FAIR's Conner puts it, "Taxpayers are hurt by having to pay more for social services" (1980). Nothing could be further from the truth. By now a considerable number of studies have been done, using a variety of unrelated techniques such as interviewing illegals who are being sent back home, and studying persons in their home villages who had at one time been in the US illegally. These studies may be discussed in two groups: those that provide data on whether immigrants do or do not use services and pay taxes − that is, yes-or-no data − and studies that calculate the net dollar effect of what immigrants take from, and give to, the public coffers. I shall discuss the two groups of studies in that order.

Studies of rates of use of services

There is general agreement among studies of the proportions of illegals using services and paying taxes, as conveniently summarized by the Select Commission (1981, Staff Report, pp. 549–51): very small proportions of illegals receive free public services. The data collected by North and Houstoun may be considered as representative (see table 15.1).

There are two persuasive explanations of the observed low use of public facilities. First, the immigrants typically are young adults who need relatively little health care. Second, illegals are afraid of being apprehended if they apply at government offices. The other studies cited by the Select Commission also corroborate the previous findings of North and Houstoun about the proportions of illegals that pay taxes: 77 percent of illegal workers in their sample paid Social Security taxes, and 73 percent had federal income tax withheld. The proportions are likely to have risen since then as a smaller proportion of illegals have worked in agriculture. Table 15.2 is the Select Commission's summary.

Table 15.1 Use of welfare services by illegal immigrants

Service	Percentage using service
Used free public hospital or clinic service	5.0
Collected 1 or more weeks of unemployment insurance	3.9
Have children in US schools	3.7
Participated in US-funded job training programs	1.4
Secured food stamps	1.3
Secured welfare payments	0.5

Source: North and Houstoun, 1976, p. 142

Cost-benefit analyses

Before beginning to consider the balance of illegals' taxes and costs, I refer again to the analysis of (mostly legal) immigrants using Census Bureau data discussed in chapters 5 and 6. In brief, those data show that, *aside from* Social Security and Medicare, immigrant families average about the same level of welfare services as do citizens. When programs for the elderly are included, immigrant families use far *less* public services than do natives. Immigrants also pay more than their share of taxes. Within three to five years, immigrant-family earnings reach and pass those of the average

Table 15.2 Impact on services of undocumented/illegal aliens
(a) Public services

	Bustamente (1977)	North and Houstoun (1976)[a]	Keely et al. (1977)[b] H	Keely et al. (1977)[b] DR	Van Arsdol et al. (1979)[c]	Poitras (1980) ES	Poitras (1980) CR
Hospital use							
Average	7.8	27.4 MEX: 22.0 WH: 37.8 EH: 29.7 VA: 41.0 EWI: 22.1	44.5	76.5	37.3 Male: 38.3 Female: 35.7 PA: 44.4	7.3	24.5
Hospital insurance							
Average		44.0 MEX: 45.1 WH: 44.2 EH: 37.3	24.0	58.8	n.a.	25.1	40.4
Children in US schools							
Average	0.9	3.7 MEX: 2.7 WH: 5.5 EH: 4.0 VA: 7.1 EWI: 2.2	12.9	29.4	21.1 Male: 19.6 Female: 23.7 PA: 25.0	23.9	41.1

Table 15.2 Cont.
(b) Government transfer payments

	Bustamente (1977)	North and Houstoun (1976)	Keely et al. (1977)		Maram (1980)		Van Arsdol et al. (1979)	Poitras (1980)	
			H	DR	G	R		ES	CR
Welfare Average	3.2	0.5	0.0	5.9	n.a.		Male: 7.8 / 5.8 Female: 11.3 MEX: 8.1	1.2	2.2
Unemployment insurance Average	n.a.	3.9 MEX: 3.6 WH: 5.6 EH: 1.4	12.9	29.4	6.5 MEX: 6.4 PRA: 38.3	2.9 2.7 35.5	n.a.	1.2	7.3
Food stamps Average	n.a.	1.3	3.7	5.9	n.a		n.a.	n.a.	

Key to abbreviations:
CR: Costa Rica
DR: Dominican Republic
EH: Eastern hemisphere
ES: El Salvador
EWI: Entered without inspection
G: Garment workers
H: Haiti

MEX: Mexico
n.a.: Data not available
PA: Previously apprehended
PRA: US citizen, permanent resident alien
R: Restaurant workers
WH: Western hemisphere, except Mexico

Notes: [a] Percentage of those who reported one or more visits to US medical facilities and those who reported having one or more children in US schools. Hospital insurance was only that deducted from paychecks.
[b] Percentage of those who have children in US schools and those who personally used a clinic or a hospital.
[c] Percentage of those owing bills to county hospitals and those who have one or more children in US schools.

Source: Select Commission, *Staff Report*, 1981, pp. 550–1

American family. The tax and welfare data together indicate that, on balance, immigrants contribute to the public coffers an average of $1300 or more per year *each year*. And what is true for legal immigrants necessarily is even more true for illegals, who are not in a position to use most welfare services and who are more likely to be in the US without wives and children who are heavier users of welfare services. That is, the main reason that immigrants make net contributions to the public coffers is that they tend to come when they are young and strong, and this is even more true of illegals as a group than of legals.

It is regrettable that research which has not the slightest claim to scientific reliability is often presented in public discussion of these issues, and muddies the waters; it therefore must be discussed here. For example, a memo by the Western Regional Office of the INS ("Illegal Immigration Costs to US Taxpayers," 1983) is cited by FAIR as a "study" done by "The Immigration Service" which supposedly indicates a "net cost to the taxpayers for every million illegals in the country in excess of $900 million." However, this estimate is mainly driven not by the costs of welfare services used by illegal aliens, but by an estimated cost of supposed "job displacement"; of the $2.2 billion gross cost estimated for a million illegals, $1.5 billion is attributed to displacement, and only $700 million to welfare services, which is less than the $995 million that the same document estimates the illegals pay in taxes.

Let us begin our quantitative assessment by clearing up a frequent confusion. Though with respect to all the public coffers *taken together* the balance of illegal immigrants is positive, the picture may well be different with respect to a *particular local or state jurisdiction*. For example, the Urban Institute's study of families that the Census managed to interview in California found that the costs to the State of California are greater than the state's tax revenues. Mexican immigrants (both legal and illegal) "contribute less to the state [of California] than is spent on public services for their use" (Muller, 1984, p. 28). This is due partly to their average income being lower than the average of all households, and partly to their larger-than-average number of children in public schools (1.09, somewhat more than twice the household average for Los Angeles County). However, the Urban Institute's sample excluded immigrants not counted by the Census, and about that group Muller says, "those immigrants probably pay more in taxes and compulsory public program contributions than they receive in benefits." It is reasonable to speculate that the immigrants who were easy for the Census to find, and hence were overrepresented in the sample, were those immigrants with families, whereas those without families use much less services but may pay almost as much in taxes.

Muller and Espenshade (1985, chapter 5) also estimated state and local revenues from, and expenditures for, Mexican immigrant families by carefully pulling together a wide variety of pertinent data, though the authors

are candid about the difficulties of the method and the consequent uncertainty of the estimates. Their estimates generally confirm the afore-
mentioned findings, and indicate a state-and-local shortfall of $2245 per
Mexican immigrant household, in comparison to a state-and-local shortfall
of $139 for all households in Los Angeles County. The immigrants'
relatively large number of children in school, and relatively low earnings,
mainly account for the shortfall.

Though illegal and legal immigrants may cost a state or city more than
they pay in taxes, the same is *not* true for the community at large when
federal taxes and Social Security contributions (as well as federal services)
are included; federal levies dwarf state and local levies. These results may
be interpreted as suggesting that states and cities with heavy immigration
should receive additional aid from the federal government to spread the
burden more evenly. But this is not grounds for concluding that illegals are
a net cost to the US *as a whole*; just the opposite is true.

Weintraub and Cardenas (1984) deal explicitly with these two issues.
They provide reliable evidence that the taxes paid by the immigrants
considerably exceed the cost of the services they use. "Despite our biasing
the costs upward and the revenues downward, tax revenues from undocumented aliens clearly exceed costs to provide public services to them"
(p. xxxi). For the sum of the impacts upon the *state-and-local* coffers, their
estimates are as follows: *cost* − high estimate: $132 million dollars, low
estimate: $63 million; *revenue* − high estimate: $286 million, low estimate:
$162 (p. xxx). But even these figures greatly understate the overall positive
effect of these illegal immigrants upon natives because they completely
omit the Social Security taxes paid to the federal government by them, and
omit 32 percent of the federal income tax paid by them. (The authors
assume that 68 percent of federal income tax returns to the state; p. 79.)
And these omitted quantities are large relative to the quantities included in
their calculation; including them makes the low and high estimates of
revenues $359 million and $580 million, that is, more than twice the state
revenues alone. And the federal costs left out of their state calculations
cannot be large; food stamps is the only major federal program used by
individuals as individuals. So the overall excess of government revenues
over government cost caused by the illegal aliens is very great, absolutely as
well as relatively; the magnitude of the effect in dollars may be roughly
assessed by observing that the average undocumented worker has more
than $1000 withheld each year in income and Social Security taxes (p. 51;
this is after allowing for the roughly one-third of workers who do not pay
such taxes); all other taxes are about the same amount as the cost of all
state services; hence the federal taxes are pure gain to natives, figuring
roughly. On a household basis the contributions to the public coffers are
even greater, because there are two workers in a large proportion of
households.[3]

It may also be relevant that Weintraub and Cardenas find that an overwhelmingly large proportion of the costs for services used by the illegals — somewhere between 85 percent and 93 percent — goes for education. This should effectively demolish the myth that illegals come to the US and immediately become leeches on the public by living on welfare and unemployment compensation. Even more direct evidence on this point is the low rate of unemployment among the illegals (1.5 percent); the high rate of labor-force participation among all adults, male and female (76 percent; p. 47); and the high rate (over 6 percent; p. 27) of all respondents holding two or more jobs.

The Congressional Budget Office was asked the cost of services used by illegals, and the widely publicized response seemed to suggest that illegals are a net cost. In fact, all that the CBO study did (because of the way the question from Congress to CBO was framed) was to estimate how much *more* services the illegals would use if their status were made legal. As Rudolph Penner, CBO's director wrote (correspondence, 11 May 1984):

CBO's estimated cost for the [Simpson—Mazzoli] bill in no way implies that aliens use more in services than than pay in taxes. Nor does it account for secondary effects on the economy, but only on direct effects on federal and state and local government budgets. Precisely because *unauthorized aliens contribute to the US economy on balance*, [italics added] the bill's costs might be even higher if secondary effects were considered; the employer sanction provisions of the bill, if effective, would reduce numbers of unauthorized aliens in the US, possibly reducing GNP and government revenues ... the immigration estimate in no way implies that aliens do not make a net contribution to the economy.

The anti-immigration organization FAIR (see e.g. Conner, 1984) has tried to negate the findings of the various studies of the use of welfare and payment of taxes by illegals in two ways. First, it has adduced a study by North (1981) of the receipt of unemployment compensation by a group of illegals who gave Social Security numbers when they were apprehended. Indeed, that group shows a raw figure for unemployment insurance use far higher than the previous studies, though probably lower than native Americans. There are two key points about that study that FAIR does not mention, however. First, when one considers dollars — which are the "bottom line" — rather than proportions of users, even in this group the illegals are seen to be net contributors to the public coffers on a staggering scale. North's own calculations suggest that the estimated tax contributions on their account *for unemployment insurance alone* exceed the cost of that program (p. 57). And contributions to the state for unemployment insurance are only a drop in the bucket compared to the contributions for Social Security and income tax, which are not counterbalanced by any use of services. North estimates that the contributions for Social Security alone were twelve times the unemployment benefits obtained, and this group of people "drew no [other] benefits" (p. 71).

Even if North's study had shown that this group was on a balance a net cost to the public coffers — which it certainly does not show — these data would not be relevant evidence, however, because they are startlingly unrepresentative. Recall that the group was selected by choosing *only those who gave Social Security numbers at apprehension*. It is reasonable that on average these are persons far more integrated into American society over a long period of time than most illegals, especially those from Mexico. Indeed, North's data show that more than 40 percent of this group were paying Social Security for at least six years at the time the study was conducted. Just how unrepresentive they are is shown by one of North's footnotes: "a recent review of more than 500 I−213s of illegal immigrants apprehended by the Livermore (CA) detachment of the INS Border Patrol hundreds of miles north of the border during 1977 turned up exactly two SSNs" (p. 5). And North does not indicate how many forms he searched through to obtain his sample of 580.

A second way that FAIR has tried to argue away the body of evidence on the low use of welfare services by illegals has been to say that recent studies show a higher rate of use than did the earlier studies. "In this monograph, FAIR reports upon recent studies of welfare use by illegals. These force a blunt conclusion: later and sounder examination reveals high and increasing levels of welfare utilization by illegal immigrants" (Graham, 1982, p. 7). This line of argument is seen to be wrong oı several grounds. First, the recent studies by Weintraub and Cardenas, and by Muller, which are better methodologically than are most of the earlier studies, show *low* levels of usage. Second, the earlier studies are not, as FAIR tries to say, less representative than are the studies that FAIR relies on — North (1981), Van Arsdol et al. (1979) and Heer and Falasco (1982). Rather, it seems to me that these latter three studies deal with far less representative populations — North's as discussed above, Van Arsdol's with a group of "covered aliens who sought to regularize their civil status in the US at the offices of One-Stop Immigration, a legal assistance agency in Los Angeles" (Conner, 1982, p. 14) and Heer−Falasco's with a group of "women of Mexican descent who had live births in Los Angeles County hospitals" (Conner, 1982, p. 15). Third, and the most compelling reason why FAIR's argument that new studies show a new picture is not persuasive: the percentage rates of use are only imperfect proxies for the total dollar effect upon the public coffers. And every study that provides dollar estimates shows that when the sum of the tax contributions to city, state and federal government are allowed for, those tax payments vastly exceed the cost of the services used, by a factor of perhaps five, ten, or more. This is the true "bottom line," and it is found in the studies that FAIR relies on such as North's (1981) as well as Weintraub and Cardenas' (1984), and Muller's (1984). This argument takes precedence over all the others, and should end the discussion — though it surely will not.

On balance, then, the conclusion is quite the opposite of what is commonly supposed: natives exploit illegal immigrants through the public coffers by taking much more from the illegals in taxes than is spent on them in public expenditures.

Labor-Market Effects of Illegals

Loss of jobs by natives, and reduction in natives' wages, constitute the most emotional economic charges against immigrants in general and illegals in particular. This news item is representative:

Teamsters union President Jackie Presser met Wednesday with presidential counselor Edwin Meese III and several other White House aides .... Presser's main concern, the source said, was the negative impact of deregulation, not only in trucking but in the airline industry, and of foreign imports and illegal aliens on the jobs of American workers. (*Washington Post*, 14 October 1983, p. A11)

As FAIR puts it: "American workers are hurt by being forced into competition with illegal immigrants who work hard and scared and sometimes 'off the books', who don't complain about unsafe conditions or low pay" (Conner, 1980). Extraordinary claims are made about the benefits of ending illegal immigration, such as "If illegal immigrants were not taking so many jobs in America, unemployment could be brought under 4%" (FAIR letter, no date), and "If the 4 million illegal aliens estimated to be working in the country were replaced by U.S. citizens, the unemployment rate would drop by almost four percentage points" (*Business Week*, 23 June 1980, p. 80). And the harm supposedly is not just to the poor, but rather "They often hold good paying jobs at the expense of a citizen" (Chapman, 1976, p. 6).

Many of the assertions about the labor-market effect of illegals are incredible, in the original sense of that word, such as the *Business Week* hypothesis that each illegal could be replaced on the job by an unemployed US citizen. Some of the assertions are simply uninformed, such as Chapman's statement about the "foreign student program." Often the evidence is anecdotal, without supporting logic or statistics, such as this story related by the then-commissioner of the INS:

One such example is an East Indian national located in Houston, Texas. He held a masters degree in engineering obtained from Stanford University and when he came to our attention was earning $17,000 per year as a product development engineer with an electronics firm.

His employment was a loss in two ways. His own country was denied the use of his needed skills — the original intent of the foreign student program was to help developing countries gain these skills — and he was displacing an American on a job. (Chapman, 1976, p. 6)

Another story was related by the "official AFL—CIO spokesperson on matters concerning immigration and refugee policy" who served on the Select Commission:

an example of the terrible exploitation that takes place . . . a raid, led personally by Secretary of Labor Donovan, on sweatshops in New York City's Chinatown. The secretary and his Sweatshop Strike Force found more than sixty illegal aliens, many from Hong Kong, including a young girl in the sixth grade and a ninety-year-old woman, both working for only one dollar an hour. In all, they found twenty-two children illegally employed, including ten-year-olds who used sharp trimming shears and twelve-to-fifteen-year-olds who operated sewing machines. (Otero, 1981, p. 40)

A different impression is left by another news story:

IN THE SILICON VALLEY, L'ENFANT TERRIBLE IS ALSO L'ENFANT RICHE

SCOTTS VALLEY, Calif. — The spotlight shivers on a fuming wall of dry ice. A drum roll sounds, the crowded ballroom falls silent. Even the guests ripping slabs of meat from the whole roast pig on the buffet turn to watch.

Eventually, the night's host glides into center stage, his considerable girth draped in a purple and gold tent — er, toga — and a wreath of grape leaves on his head. "All hail Bacchus," someone bellows. He hoists his saxophone in salute and begins to play.

The saxophonist and host is Philippe Kahn, the founder and owner of Borland International and the self-appointed court jester of Silicon Valley. Even here, where extravagant indulgence and eccentricity are commonplace, the expansive software publisher has become a legend within two years of his arrival from his native France.

An illegal alien here until he received his "green card" recently, the 33-year-old Mr. Kahn has made a fortune in millions almost overnight by publishing some of the biggest hits on the software charts. (*Wall Street Journal*, 4 June 1985, p. 1)

The INS Western Regional Office memo mentioned earlier in this chapter provides an opportunity to assess the quality of the evidence that is offered concerning job displacement by illegals. The INS document says that:

This cost was developed from a weighted average of the displacement rates estimated by the U.S. Department of Labor and the San Diego County Report of 1980. The Department of Labor postulates a displacement rate of 20%; the San Diego County report postulates low and high rates of 32% and 41% respectively.

No source is given for these estimates, and empirical studies of the topic described in chapter 12 are wholly inconsistent with such estimates. The term "postulates" suggests that these numbers were picked out of the air on the basis of who-knows-what logic. But having been disseminated by those sources, they have become a reputable basis for further calculations by INS. And then INS's "estimates" become the basis for statements by FAIR, which are then disseminated by other organizations and media, and on and on. And that is how the public "learns" of the damage supposedly done to natives by illegal aliens, and by immigrants in general (see appendix B for poll data).

The labor market effects of illegals are similar to, and an inextricable part of, the effects of all immigrants. Therefore the main treatment of the subject is with the discussion of unemployment ("displacement") effects in chapters 11 and 12, and with the discussion of wage effects in chapter 12. But particularly appropriate for this chapter on illegal immigrants are DeFreitas's work and the experiments sending illegals home.

DeFreitas's study of 1980 Census data

As noted before (see p. 240), DeFreitas investigated the effects of Hispanic immigrants who arrived 1975–80, "the majority [of whom] appear to be illegal" (1986, p. 16), using micro-data from the 1980 Census. To repeat, he found that:

For all low-skilled native men the results indicate that there are no significant negative effects on their wage levels from recent Hispanic immigration. In fact, such migration has a significantly positive influence on the Anglo-male earnings .... The only persons whose wages appear to have been somewhat adversely affected by illegal migration since the mid-70's are black women, [but this effect is] relatively small (p. 23).

He also found that "For no racial/ethnic group, male or female, is there a discernible negative effect of illegal immigration on employment. In fact, most of the estimated co-efficients are positive" (p. 24).

Experiments removing illegals from jobs

Consider this news story:

Foreign accents prevail among dishwashers at many restaurants.

Increasingly, immigrants − some of them illegal aliens − take over the low-paying jobs that many natives shun. "It's hard to find somebody who is dependable and good and speaks any English at all," says an executive of Restaurant Associates

Inc., which operates 70 East Coast eateries. Even "high school kids" don't want dishwashing jobs any more, complains an International House of Pancakes official – "they want to be president of the company." (*Wall Street Journal*, 10 October 1978, p. 1)

The implication of the news story – that natives do not want and will not take many or most of the jobs that illegals fill – is a matter of hot dispute. Some light is shed by two experimental programs designed to fill with unemployed citizens or legal aliens those jobs formerly held by illegal aliens. In one case, 2154 illegal aliens were removed from jobs, and the California State Human Resources Agency tried to fill the jobs with US citizens, but without success. This is the explanation given in a report of the County of San Diego Human Resources Agency:

Some of the reasons for the failure were: (1) most employers paid less than the minimum wage rate, (2) the job categories were not appealing to the local resident (a matter of prestige), and (3) applicants were discouraged by not only the low wages but also the difficulty of some jobs, and the long hours demanded by the employers. (Villalpando, 1977, p. 59)

A different but complementary explanation is given by the California Employment Development Department:

Almost all employers who have lost illegals to the immigration authorities say they don't want to use our services, or give us substandard job orders to which we cannot refer American citizens because they pay less than the minimum wage laws allow or pay less than the wage rates prevailing in their industries. (*Los Angeles Times*, 3 July 1975, pp. 1ff.)

The second experiment was as follows:

On November 16, 1975, the Immigration and Naturalization Service in San Diego initiated the "Employer Cooperation Program." This program was to assist employers to identity illegal aliens on the job, remove them from the payroll, and fill the job slots with local unemployed residents. Since the inception of the special project in November, 1975, through the termination of the program in April, 1976, 340 illegal aliens were identified and terminated from their places of employment. . . .

The major jobs being performed by the 340 illegal aliens were in the area of hotel maintenance, food handling, food processing, laundryman and operative. The highest number of illegal aliens (160) were found working in hotel related situations. One hundred-nineteen aliens were located in light manufacturing businesses, 41 in food processing locations, and 20 in general service situations. The largest percent (81%) of the illegal alien workers were earning $2.00 or less an hour. The hourly wages of the vacated job slots ranged from $1.75 to $7.05.

The results were as follows:

The San Diego "Employment Cooperation Program" was successful in getting all the 340 vacancies filled. The newly created 340 job opportunities, however, were not occupied by unemployed San Diegans. Instead 90 percent of the positions were occupied by "commuter workers" from Baja California, Mexico. (Villalpando, 1977, pp. 61–2)

Though these two experiments are far from conclusive, they support the view that many, if not most, of the jobs that illegals hold would not be filled by natives in the absence of illegals, and therefore the illegals do not much harm natives by working at them. Furthermore, the experiments imply that many of those jobs would simply disappear – some would be automated, and still others would not be filled if employers had to pay higher wages – if illegals were not available. The result would be a deleterious effect upon total output and industrial activity.

Remittances

The headnote quote from ex-Commissioner Chapman castigates illegals for sending remittances abroad. His suggestion that this is somehow a drain upon the native public is simply without foundation. Sending remittances abroad is hardly more troublesome to natives than is expenditure of immigrant income for consumption within the country. This topic is explored in the afternote to chapter 2; illegals are no different from legals in this respect.

Lawlessness, and the Guestworker Alternative

An argument given for enacting strong sanctions to prevent Mexican immigrants from entering the US illegally is that the presence of illegals promotes lawlessness and disregard ("flouting") of society's rules. This raises the spectre of a breakdown of order and a loss of social control. As the final report (1981) of the Select Commission on Immigration and Refugee Policy put it, "Most serious is the fact that illegality breeds illegality .... As long as undocumented migration flouts U.S. immigration law, its most devastating impact may be the disregard it breeds for other U.S. laws" (p. 42). And again, "It is this undermining of national values that poses the greatest threat to U.S. society, not the displacement of U.S. workers or use of social services by undocumented workers" (Staff Report, p. 560).

The lawlessness issue makes a persuasive argument, and I myself agreed with it until recently. But upon reflection, I now think that for many who raise it, it is a smokescreen, a convenient way of avoiding having to deal with the attitudes many Americans have toward Mexicans and other immigrants.

Disregard of the law certainly is bad. But any fair-minded person must agree that the speed limit of 55 miles per hour, and even more so, the present structure of income tax laws, breed incomparably more lawlessness than does illegal immigration. So do laws against marijuana and betting. The existence of a worse problem is not a reason for ignoring a lesser problem, but attending to the lesser problem may reveal something about the motives of those who attend to it.

Also, illegal immigration must be the most victimless of crimes. Neither natives nor illegals are injured, even in their pocketbooks, by the illegal immigration. And one cannot make the argument that preventing illegal immigration reduces moral corruption, as one might (or might not) with prohibition and vice laws; nor can one argue that it saves people from injuring themselves, as is the case with laws against high speeds or suicide.

Let us agree nevertheless that it is not good for people to knowingly break the law. If so, and if the persons who now enter illegally do not place burdens upon natives but rather mostly confer benefits, why not let them in legally?

The standard answer to this question is that unless there are barriers to immigration, vast numbers of Mexicans and others will flood into the US. Letters to the newspaper make such statements as: "We cannot make it easy for the millions of potential immigrants to come to this country. We would be overwhelmed," and "Lifeboat U.S. would quickly sink." The demand for immigration is discussed in chapter 3, which concludes that it is much less of an open-and-shut question than it might seem. But no matter what the actual overall demand for immigration by persons all over the world, there is good reason to doubt that large numbers of Mexicans would come to the US as permanent residents even if there were no barriers at all. As the estimates concerning illegal immigration discussed earlier in this chapter show: (a) there are many fewer Mexican illegals at any one time than is popularly believed; (b) the number of illegals in the country at any time overstates the number who intend to remain permanently, especially among Mexicans; and (c) a large proportion of the illegal aliens residing permanently in the US are from countries other than Mexico. These findings imply that we could do away with the lawlessness involved in the present situation, and not increase the number of Mexicans in the US very much, if we were to allow potential immigrants to enter legally.

A legal guestworker program would not resolve the entire problem, however, because if all who wished to were allowed to enter legally, there might (though by no means surely) be a much larger number of persons who would come permanently from countries *other than* Mexico. Whether or not that would be a good thing for the US is not easy to know − even though we can be pretty sure that somewhat larger numbers of immigrants than now arrive would be beneficial − because we have had no experience with immigration on a very large scale since before World War I. So let us take the more cautious course and assume that we are not willing to simply throw open the doors to the US. That seems to leave us on the horns of a dilemma, being ready to let Mexicans come freely, but not being ready to freely admit persons from all countries.

There is, however, a path between the horns of the dilemma: Legalize temporary stays for the purpose of working in the US, that is, create a guestworker program similar to the bracero program that operated from 1942 to 1964. Experience with the bracero program[4] provides solid evidence that a legal temporary worker program will indeed reduce illegal immigration, as seen in figure 15.1.

A temporary worker program for Mexicans meets with two objections. First, it is said that, once in the US, they will not go home. Though as we have seen, most Mexicans who come to the US do return to Mexico, European countries have been troubled by this phenomenon. But if temporary workers are brought in for specified reasonably short[5] periods of time, various arrangements can provide considerable incentive to return. One possibility is making the receipt of their Social Security benefits from their US work dependent on leaving at the appointed time. (See Neal, 1981, for a review of several such plans.) Or an arrangement might be made with Mexico concerning Mexican pension payments. Yet again, some sort of deposit scheme for part of the earnings could be established. Certainly, some will stay, just as some illegals do not go home even now. But there is little reason to think that the number of stayers will increase relative to the present situation (the appropriate comparison) because after their period of temporary work expires, the temporary workers would not have any more secure status than illegals do now. (The number of stayers may well *decrease* because of the financial incentives to go home under the proposed program.)

The unions have fought the bracero and proposed guestworker programs by saying that temporary workers damage the work prospects of US citizens. But there seems little reason to believe that *legal* guestworkers would more heavily damage natives than do illegals, who have reasons to work even cheaper than legal temporary workers. Perhaps − just perhaps − the labor unions will some day finally put aside this hobgoblin in the name of generosity, even if it is really no sacrifice for them at all.

Another reason given for opposing temporary workers is that such a program wrongs and exploits the temporary workers themselves. Here we must ask the fundamental practical and moral question: Compared to what? Participating in the program must be better for at least some persons than not participating, or else there would be no participants in the program. The program must be better than being an illegal; if this is not obvious, then the fact that many Mexicans chose the bracero program rather than entering illegally should be evidence enough. Being a temporary worker may well be inferior, and may even seem "unfair," compared to full admission as a legal immigrant, but this simply is not a realistic alternative; to compare a temporary worker program unfavorably against a non-existent alternative is either thoughtless or dishonest.

Illegal Immigration and Dangers to the Public

Related to the issue of lawlessness is the implied threat of street crime, riot, and other disturbance of the peace due to illegals. Terrorism and disease threats are joined to these.

In Texas:

[U]nsuccessful gubernatorial candidate Kent Hance appealed to voters' fears that illegal immigration would increase the crime rate as well as the unemployment rate. And last month in Brownsville, the City Commission sent a resolution to the president seeking more federal immigration officers to help fight "an alarming and ever-increasing number of robberies, rapes, physical assaults and thefts." (*Wall Street Journal*, 14 May 1986, p. 1)

And the legislator mainly responsible for the 1986 immigration legislation, Alan Simpson, said "The word 'security' is entering the debate" (*Wall Street Journal*, 14 May 1986, p. 1). FAIR plays up the Cuban boatlift where, they say, "we were forced to take a large number of Castro's 'undesirables.' He emptied his prisons, his mental hospitals, and we took them .... As a result, serious crime in the Little Havana section of Miami jumped 138% in August 1980 over the same month in 1979" (FAIR letter, no date). And using terms like "invasion" and "swarm," Mumford writes, for instance, that "Maintenance of U.S. security and global peace is at stake. The Roman Catholic Church, whatever its original humane interest, through its activities concerning illegal migration, seriously threatens the security of the United States (1981, p. 30).

Congressman Dan Lungren, using the rhetorical device of taking no responsibility for the assertion that he was putting forth, said:

While I do not believe that the United States faces a genuinely imminent threat from a terrorist march across our border, one cannot ignore the empirical roots that give rise to worry among border area residents. (*Spotlight*, 4 August 1986, p. 17)

A recent pamphlet puts in this way:

Although immigration into the United States from Mexico, Central America, and the Caribbean has led to serious problems of law enforcement and crime in some areas, there has as yet been little politically motivated terrorism as a result. Given the extreme left orientation of the Sanctuary movement, however, its sympathy for Marxist insurgencies in Latin America, and its development of cadres skilled in clandestine techniques and willing to violate the law for political purposes, it cannot be excluded that Sanctuary will evolve or splinter into a support movement for Central American terrorists who seek to operate in the United States or even into a violent movement itself. (Francis, 1986, p. 49)

A former governor of New Hampshire warns of danger to public health if amnesty is extended to illegals:

[T]he fatal AIDS virus has been linked back to Haiti. Yet an estimated 30,000 Haitians illegally came into the U.S. last year. If we grant amnesty to all Haitians, how many will bring the AIDS virus into the U.S.? (Thomson, undated)

The only study I could find on the rates of crime among contemporary illegals is Muller's (1984), and his summary does not indicate much about the methods used. Muller found that "In the city of Los Angeles, crime rates in the two police districts with the highest Hispanic population were somewhat below the city average in 1982." And he goes on to speculate that "Undocumented immigrants in particular are understandably reluctant to be involved in criminal activities that attract the attention of the authorities" (p. 12).

It seems reasonable that the record of crime among all immigrants, as reviewed in chapter 4, should throw light on the matter. To repeat: For the period around the turn of the century, Steinberg concluded that, by any measure, the rate of serious crime has been less among immigrants than among natives, though the rate of petty crime (vagrancy, disorderly conduct, breach of the peace, drunkenness) has sometimes been greater among immigrants. When age and sex are controlled for, the rate of all crime has been less among immigrants than among natives. And one would expect petty crime among illegals to be even less than among legal immigrants because of their fear of being sent out of the country. For the 1930s, Taft (1936) found that crime among both immigrants and among children of immigrants was lower than among natives. All this would suggest a relatively low rather than a relatively high rate of crime among illegals.

Conclusions

The Federation for American Immigration Reform (FAIR) and The Environmental Fund (TEF), the two organizations most active in fighting against immigration, focus on illegal immigrants and dwell upon the word "control." In its newsletter TEF uses headlines such as "Uncontrolled Borders Cost the U.S. $12 Billion," and phrases such as "If the current situation of uncontrolled immigration were to continue ..." (TEF *The Data*, Environmental Fund, May 1982). We read "We are losing control of our future because of uncontrolled illegal immigration," and "'Uncontrolled' is indeed the word to describe the results of current U.S. immigration policy," and "Do we truly want 'open borders'?" (Conner in FAIR letter, no date). This rhetoric plays to a fear of chaos and social breakdown, a fear found especially among those who believe that unless social and economic activities are governmentally planned they will not function well. And the supposed large-scale loss of jobs by natives due to illegals is a major objection to immigration generally, and especially by labor unions; discussions of illegals and of immigration often blur the two topics, whether unintentionally or disingenuously.

The analysis of the economic effects of illegal immigrants is quite similar to the analysis for legal immigrants, and leads to the same mainly-positive judgments with respect to native economic welfare. There are two important differences. First, the illegals, and especiallly those from Mexico, tend to have less education and less skill relative to legal immigrants. This means that they have a disproportionate negative effect on natives with low skills and education. This might seem to call for reduction in the number of illegals. But this should be seen in the broad context of protection of all lower-skill groups threatened by imports and immigration and technological change; if such protection were afforded to all, all persons in the society would be damaged.

The second major difference between legals and illegals — especially among those from Mexico — is that illegals are thought to cause a sense of lawlessness. This can be avoided rather effectively by a guestworker program.

NOTES

1 Please forgive this unattractive shorthand, but no other term is nearly as accurate. Interesting journalistic accounts of many aspects of illegal immigration are given by Crewdson (1983).
2 For a summary of the recent work by Passel and associates see Passel (1986).
3 An example of how the all-important federal taxes are systematically omitted

from popular discussion comes from Richard Lamm, a governor of Colorado who is one of the leading anti-immigration campaigners:

> Almost all public services provided to illegal aliens are the responsibility of local city and county governments. Researchers Sidney Weintraub and Gilberto Cardenas directed the Undocumented Workers Policy Research Project at the University of Texas at Austin. In their 1984 study of illegal aliens' use of public services in Texas, they concluded that the state of Texas received more money in tax revenues from illegal aliens than it paid to provide direct services to them. The state received tax revenues that were 1.75 to 2 times its cost for services. But they also found that Texas cities and counties paid 1.8 to 2.7 times more to provide services to illegals than they received in tax revenues from them.

4 For an excellent short survey of the bracero program, see Garcia y Griego (1983a) and references therein.

5 Massey (1984, following on the hypothesis of Bohning, 1972, and Piore, 1979) has shown in a survey of four Mexican sending communities that the propensity to return to Mexico decreases with the length of time in the US.

16 Evaluation of Immigration Policies

This chapter discusses a variety of possible US immigration policies, and evaluates them.

The visa allocation system at present is roughly as follows: In the class of "numerically exempt immigrants" who are admitted immediately are spouses, children, and parents of US citizens at least 21 years of age. The total of "numerically-limited immigrants" is 270,000 per year. The "preferences" and sizes are shown in table 16.1. Each country is limited to 20,000 persons born there. Refugees and some other special categories of persons are not covered by this system.

Total Number of Immigrants to be Admitted

The total number of immigrants to be admitted legally is the key *economic* element of immigration policy. If *no* applicants will be admitted legally, the only remaining immigration decisions concern illegal immigrants. If *all*

Table 16.1 Visa allocation system as of 1988

Preference	Groups include	Percentage and number of visas	
1st	Unmarried sons and daughters of US citizens and their children	20	54,000
2nd	Spouses and unmarried sons and daughters of permanent resident aliens	26	70,000*
3rd	Members of the professions of exceptional ability and their spouses and children	10	27,000
4th	Married sons and daughters of US citizens, their spouses and children	10	27,000*
5th	Brothers and sisters of US citizens (at least 21 years of age) and their spouses and children	24	64,800*
6th	Workers in skilled or unskilled occupations in which laborers are in short supply in the US, their spouses and children	10	27,000
Non-preference	Other qualified applicants	Any numbers not used above*	

* Numbers not used in higher preferences may be used in these categories.

applicants will be admitted, there are no further decisions to be made.

The alternatives that I think realistic are: (a) substantially more immigrants than now, (b) substantially less immigrants than now, and (c) about the same number as now. By "substantially" I mean a change up to a doubling (and perhaps subsequent doublings) or halving of the immigration rate. Furthermore, it would seem likely that, given the nature of politics and social decision-making in the US, changes in the amount of immigration would be made in several steps — a sequential process of "muddling through" as we learn by trial and error. Recommending only "substantially more" or "substantially less" would seem to be consistent with this prevailing political process. A recommendation of either zero immigrants or an open door would have no chance of being adopted by American society now or in the foreseeable future, and therefore it would hardly be useful to make either recommendation even if it were warranted on strictly economic grounds.

Please remember, however, that immigration presently is *not* high relative to historic levels. In proportion to population size, immigration was five or six times greater at the turn of the century than in the 1970s and 1980s. The practical question is whether the US is better off with, say, one million or even two million rather than 500,000 immigrants yearly.

Another reason for not considering an open-door policy is that it might – though there is no evidence that it would – result in a flow of immigrants larger than the US or other nations have experienced in the past, relative to population size, and hence with results that are not predictable. As Kuznets noted in a discussion of related issues, "long-term projections into ranges well beyond those covered by the observed past are subject to wide errors; and the variables and parameters ... are too diverse and too crude to permit adequate analysis" (1977, p. 14).

The most important economic considerations with respect to the total number of immigrants would seem to be the effects upon (a) total national product, and (b) natives' per-person income. The model analyzed in chapter 10, which embodies influences through the supply of capital, productivity change, and transfers of taxes and welfare services, concludes that natives benefit by additional immigrants almost immediately, even without balancing the greater advantages in the longer run versus the less positive effects in the shorter run. This result suggests admitting more immigrants than at present.

More specific considerations also seem favorable to admitting more immigrants. The balance of transfers and taxes is positive with respect to natives' welfare, as chapter 5 shows. Because immigrants are self-selected with respect to their drive and energy, and/or because they do not begin their lives in the US with the material and social advantages enjoyed by natives and therefore are "hungry," they apparently make a greater effort in economic endeavors than do natives. As discussed in chapter 4, this effort level results in innovation, increased productivity, and especially a high level of entrepreneurial activity which produces new jobs, along with other benefits to natives. The most potent objection to immigration heard in political discussions of immigration volume – the purported increase in native unemployment due to "displacement" by immigrants – seems to be a small or even non-existent problem, as chapters 11 and 12 discuss.

Given that, at the present level of admissions, immigrants are economically beneficial rather than a drain on the taxpayer, a policy of *more* immigrants than allowed by present or proposed laws would benefit American citizens. I will not recommend a total number of admissions into the US, however. One reason for not doing so is that our knowledge at present is far too thin, especially — and inevitably — with respect to immigration levels that have never been experienced in the US or elsewhere, or that have not been experienced in recent years.

Some persons may also be interested in the effect of the total number of immigrants because of the contribution to total population, and thence its effect upon international political position. This factor, along with the political effect of admitting more students and graduates in scientific and engineering discussed briefly in chapter 8 and below, will not be mentioned further here because political considerations are outside the purview of this book.

Recommendation: Increase the volume of total immigration in substantial steps unless there appear negative effects that are unknown at present.

Guestworkers or No Guestworkers?

A difficulty in assessing a guestworker policy is that it is not clear against which alternative a guestworker policy should be compared. Comparing guestworkers against the same state of affairs except with no guestworkers is quite different from comparing a policy of guestworkers against an increased number of illegals doing the same work that the guestworkers would do.

Another difficulty in discussing a guestworker policy is that there is a tendency to consider guestworkers as second-class citizens, and to argue against a guestworker policy because it creates an ethically unacceptable division of classes. Compared to a beautiful world of no borders and perfect freedom to live with full rights wherever one likes, having both citizens and non-citizens within a country may seem undesirable. But compared to a world in which every country controls who may enter (some even control who may leave, who may become a citizen, and which rights non-citizens have), the comparison may seem quite different. And making a distinction between citizens and aliens need not be invidious; American engineers, Peace Corps members, and servicemen/women who work in countries where they do not have the same rights as citizens apparently do not feel demeaned or otherwise injured by such a status. It seems to me, therefore, that a guestworker policy should not be rejected out of hand for non-economic reasons of human dignity. (And indeed, giving people the choice of whether they do or do not wish to serve as guestworkers seems to be more dignified than deciding for them that serving as guestworkers would not be good for them.)

The analysis may best be conducted in several steps. Let us first consider the aggregate effects of having foreigners do the work that *either* guest-workers or illegals would do, as against no such workers. The Yeager—Borts—Stein—Berry—Soligo production—capital analysis discussed in chapter 7 implies that, from an aggregate point of view, having guest-workers is clearly (though only slightly) beneficial through that channel. Transfer-and-tax considerations strengthen this conclusion considerably. Demographic-capital effect that goes in the other direction is not very relevant for guestworkers. Additionally, none of the complications that enter into the analysis of permanent immigrants apply to temporary immi-grants. Hence we may say with confidence that temporary immigrants increase average per-person income among natives as long as there is demand for their services.

The distributional effect of guestworkers (or illegals) is another matter, however. Unlike "normal" permanent immigrants, guestworkers are likely to be concentrated in low-skill and low-paying jobs, and in a few industries such as agriculture, restaurants and hotels, and textiles. Hence, those natives who work in the industries that would employ the guestworkers would suffer some damage. As discussed at greater length in chapter 13, in this respect (though not in others) the situation is exactly analogous to that in which a country permits the import of a foreign-made good: the workers in the domestic industry producing the same product are injured, and it is cold comfort to them that economic welfare on balance is increased.

There is, however, a difference between the import of goods and the import of workers which makes the latter relatively less painful: the import of workers is likely to cause a reduction of wages but not a loss of jobs (chapter 12), whereas the import of goods is likely to reduce jobs in the short run. And loss of jobs seems to many to be more painful than reduction in wages. Furthermore, the empirical studies suggest that the wage effect is small even among the worst-affected groups.

A drawback attributed to guestworker plans is that the guestworkers will not leave when their contractual period is over, but rather bring their families and settle permanently; European countries have complained of this recently. But such an outcome can be avoided or minimized by various financial incentive arrangements; examples include deposits of Social Security payments in the person's home country that are forfeited if the worker does not live up to the agreement, or deposits in escrow upon entry (see Neal, 1981, for further discussion of such schemes). Various pairs of countries such as Italy and Australia already have reciprocal social security agreements.

Recommendation: A guestworker policy should be adopted, along with a device that ensures the guestworkers' return to their home countries after their contract period is complete.

Policy toward Illegals

Reducing illegal activity is worthwhile in itself, because illegality is hardly beneficial to a society. From a more specific economic point of view, commerce is hampered unless people habitually play by the legal rules of the game. Furthermore, allowing some people to enter illegally while others who seek legal entrance wait their turn is not fair to the latter, and induces the latter group to take the law into their own hands.

This said, it does not follow that an all-out effort should be made to curb illegal immigration. One drawback of such an effort is that such a campaign may have high material and non-material costs, and the efficiency may be low. Another drawback is that valuable immigrants may thereby be lost to the economy.

Again, the key difficulty in making sound decisions about illegal immigration is in choosing a reasonable comparison state of affairs. For example, if one compares the existing state of affairs against a state of affairs that is identical in all ways except that the immigrants do not have illegal status, then obviously the latter is preferable on non-economic grounds. But the latter state of affairs is not a realistic alternative. Also, it should be noted in passing — because it helps keep this issue in perspective — that natives are better off if a given immigrant worker is currently working in the US illegally rather than legally, because the illegal pays about the same taxes but receives less social services and transfer payments because of his illegal status, as discussed in chapter 15. But I doubt that many would justify maintaining the persons in illegal status for that reason.

A guestworker program would seem preferable on all grounds to having the same persons work as illegals (unless one considers it a benefit that illegals cannot use social services they would be entitled to if legal). (It is noteworthy that the much-cited estimate by the Congressional Budget Office of the "cost" of the Simpson–Rodino bill finally enacted by Congress in 1986 referred only to the *difference* in welfare services used by an immigrant when legal rather than illegal. See chapter 15 for the details.)

The more difficult question is whether having illegals is preferable to having no illegals or guestworkers, that is, whether it makes sense to try to reduce the flow and stock of illegals. Again, the only drawback is distributional, and the meaning of a distributional change cannot easily be valued economically.

Another relevant comparison is a guestworker program, or a de facto program of illegal immigration, versus different policies of the Mexican government toward US investment in Mexico. Mexico has a "maquiladora" program which allows US firms to operate wholly-US-owned plants in such border cities as Ciudad Juarez, subject to certain requirements about shipping the output back to the US rather than selling in Mexico. The basic $1.30 per hour wage (as of 1986) is attractive to US firms, and is considerably higher than most other comparable opportunities in Mexico. The program surely affects the flow of illegals and guestworkers. Ciudad Juarez "suffers from a labor shortage," indicating that the supply of labor is not inexhaustible. This suggests that a policy which widens opportunities for US and other investors within Mexico could have a substantial effect on the flow of migrants northward, as well as having other desirable effects.[1]

An editorial in the *Wall Street Journal* in the late 1970s summarized the recent history of US policy toward illegal immigration as alternating episodes of tightening and loosening control of the borders, somewhat in response to public concern and to changes in general regional conditions. The editorial then arrived at the surprising conclusion that this messy implicit resolution to the problem of illegal immigration from Mexico is probably preferable to any possible solution that would be neater, and suggested that the US simply decide to continue with the present system which is at least livable even if not esthetic. This proposal, unpalatable though it is, has much to recommend it.

Recommendation: In the absence of a guestworker policy, muddle through as has been done in the recent past with respect to illegals.

Refugees

One might think that refugees are less desirable immigrants than are immigrants who choose to come for economic reasons alone, because refugees are less self-selected according to economic motivation and belief in their own capacity to get ahead economically in a strange and perhaps hostile environment than are economic immigrants. Indeed, Chiswick (1982) interprets his results for various ethnic groups, including Cubans and Soviet Jewish immigrants, whom he believes are largely political refugees, as showing that refugees do not get ahead as fast as non-refugees, holding constant such characteristics as education and age. One might further argue that the age and family composition of refugees is not quite so favorable as is the composition of non-refugee economic-immigrant families; the refugee heads of families are likely to be older and already have children. (See chapter 3, figure 3.10.)

On the other hand, several communities of refugees have arrived with exceptionally favorable educational and occupational characteristics, for example, the Jews driven from Europe by World War II, the Cubans fleeing Castro, and perhaps the Vietnamese War refugees. Some of the refugee communities who came to the US as a result of the Vietnam War, however, have little education. For example the Hmong are often said to be unusual among refugees in that respect. (But see Baker and North, 1984.)

Often it is difficult to distinguish between "economic" immigrants and refugees. Fleeing oppression is a more reasonable decision when you are anxious to improve your economic status, and when you believe that you will succeed in the country of refuge.

Refugees are likely to have the characteristic of not expecting to return to the country of origin. This would seem to be favorable to making an especially diligent effort to adapt to the new economy and society. Indeed, the (to me) most persuasive explanation for Mexican immigrants not advancing as rapidly as other immigrant communities with the same educational characteristics — including other Hispanic communities — is that many Mexicans do not cut their ties so sharply with their home communities because geography allows them to go back and forth so readily (see the data in chapter 4 on naturalization rates). On the other hand, this characteristic means that those who do not succeed in the US cannot leave, and hence may turn out to be a burden upon the community.

On balance, I do not find any major difference between refugees and economic immigrants with regard to their economic prospects, and therefore I believe that no distinction need be made in the analysis for this characteristic.

Even if one assumes that the US has a responsibility to assist victims of political repression, however, there may be desirable methods other than admitting them as immigrants. One possibility is to influence other countries to assist them, as the US has done to some extent with Vietnamese refugees. If there should be a choice between refugees and "economic" immigrants within a fixed quota, it would make sense for the US to provide funds to other nations to take in some or all of the refugees, and thereby to increase the welfare of a larger number of persons, to a greater degree, than it could by displacing economic immigrants with refugees. Of course it would be unseemly to carry out such a program explicitly even though it is done implicitly, but to cluck about it is simply hypocrisy.

Recommendation: Consider refugees as indistinguishable from ordinary economic immigrants in all economic policy-making. If refugees are to be handled differently, the grounds should be non-economic rather than economic. If refugees would not be as desirable economically as other potential immigrants, pay other countries to take in some of the refugees.

Family Reconstitution

Jasso and Rosenzweig (1986) have estimated the extent to which an immigrant leads to additional immigrants in the future by way of the preference system. Their method is too complex to describe here, but seems reasonable. They conclude that the system does not "explode" in the sense that family reunification would not drive out all "independent" immigration. But they do not calculate the "equilibrium" proportion of family-unification persons that would result from a constant admission process. (They note that any "temporary" increase of immigrants boosts the backlog of requests.) The data for Philippine immigration (figure 16.1) are relevant and interesting, however.

Arnold et al. (1987) tackled the same problem by interviewing samples of Filipino and Korean families about to immigrate to the US. While the number of potential relatives who *conceivably* might also immigrate is very large — about 25 and 17 per immigrant in the Philippines and Korea respectively — the number newly added to eligibility by a given immigrant's change in status is much smaller — between 1.0 and 1.8, and between 0.5 and 0.7 for the two countries respectively, depending upon the assumptions one makes. And many of these persons cannot come immediately because of quota limitations, so that these numbers apply, not immediately, but during the course of the new immigrant's lifetime. These findings reinforce the findings of Jasso and Rosenzweig.

Allowing persons to enter as immigrants on the basis of family ties rather than on other — and especially economic — characteristics is by definition a non-economic decision. But once a decision has been made to give preference in admission to various classes of relatives, those relatives who come must be taken into account in any assessment of an admission policy. Independent persons selected on economic grounds would be preferable to relatives, were there to be no humanitarian considerations. This change is unlikely, however, so no further consideration will be given to the matter.

Permanent Residence for Foreign Students in the United States

Students who come to study and then choose to stay are not given preference under present policies, and may even be discriminated against. The contributions of foreign graduate students even before they graduate were mentioned in chapter 8. And valuable as they are while students, they are even more valuable to the US after they receive their degrees, having particularly favorable characteristics as potential immigrants. By the time they have finished most courses of study, the graduates have mastered English. They are at the perfect age, being just ready to enter the labor force with their entire earning lives ahead of them. Usually they have already well assimilated themselves within the US society. They have seen enough of the US to have formed a well-founded judgment about whether

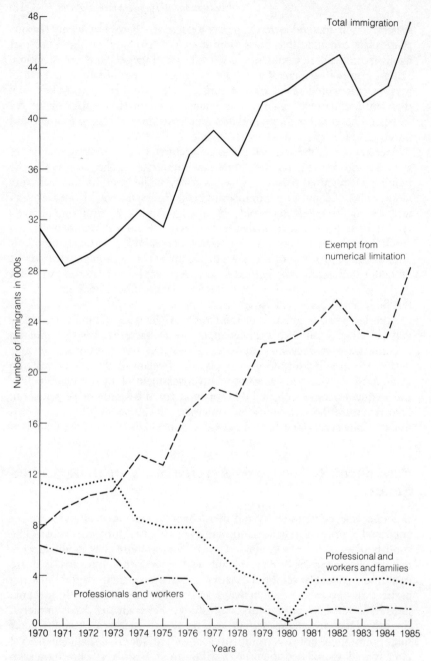

Figure 16.1 Philippine immigration to the United States, 1970−85
Source: DeJong, Root, and Abad, 1986

it is a country in which they would like to remain. They usually have investigated the markets for their skills, and therefore are likely to find employment relatively rapidly. And of course they are, on average, an extremely well-educated group.

On balance, then, it would seem that foreign students have extraordinary promise as valuable contributors to the US economy. And foreign graduate students studying engineering and science have even greater benefits for the US than foreign students at large, as discussed in chapter 8.

An objection is that admitting foreign students as immigrants will result in damage to the countries of origin because of the "brain drain." Whether on balance countries of origin really suffer much from such emigration is discussed in chapter 14. For now let us assume that whether or not there is real damage, many in the countries of origin think that there is. Let us therefore ask how the US might admit the students as immigrants and at the same time prevent the feeling of damage by the origin countries.

One possibility is that the students make reparations payments to the countries of origin during the course of their productive earning lives; this is the essence of Bhagwati's scheme (1976; or in Chiswick, 1982). The US could then require as a condition of admission that the student commit him/herself to such a contractual arrangement.

There would seem to be no ethical obligation for the US to place qualifications upon admission with respect to the potential immigrant's relationship to the country of origin. To suggest that there is such an obligation is to suggest that countries own their subjects and have a right to prevent their emigration, which seems counter to existing international law as embodied in the Helsinki accord. In fact one might argue that for the US to place such an obligation of reparations upon immigrants is itself unethical. Yet the US obviously would like to prevent other countries from feeling damaged by US policies that seem to be undertaken for the US economic interest. So there is a complex political/ethical issue to be dealt with here.

If the US were to adopt a policy of sale of admission, as discussed below, and were also to decide to remit some part of the fees to the countries of origin, this would immediately resolve this problem.

Some may wonder whether it is "fair" for the US to take advantage of the rest of the world's supply of brains. From the point of fairness alone, can it be less than fair to give to any individual the opportunity to better himself or herself? Persons who believe in the sanctity of the state may answer in the affirmative, but US public philosophy clearly answers in the negative. Furthermore, nations from which these persons come are likely to benefit from the movement of such persons, as discussed in chapter 14. And I there see no reason not to believe that the supply of excellent brains to be educated is quite elastic. As more openings and opportunities arise in LDCs due to movements to the US, more students are drawn into the educational process who otherwise would not have the chance to develop their excellent brains and contribute their fruit to their communities and to the world.

Others may wonder whether the world might not have its cake and eat it too — have the benefit of these scientists and engineers without them leaving their home countries. In principle this makes perfect sense. In practise, there is some set of conditions in advanced countries, and even more so in the US, which makes them much more productive places for advanced knowledge workers to study and work. Perhaps the best evidence for this comes from the people who are in the best position to judge with respect to their particular contributions — the individuals involved. One might say that it is only a herd instinct that leads so many students to want to study in the US rather than in Europe or Japan or the USSR. But these same persons, many of whom have had the opportunity to know the professional and personal life of knowledge workers in Europe as well in the US, choose the US in large numbers. Who is prepared to contradict them about where they can best live their lives, for their own profit and the profit of the rest of the world?

Recommendation: Give special preference to foreign students who have completed their courses of study in the US.

Admitting Undergraduate and Graduate Students for Study

Study in US institutions of higher learning is a best-selling "invisible" export. And as long as foreign students pay the true cost of their education, having them come is of extraordinary value to the US, for several reasons. First, education is an excellent product for the US to sell. Second, it enables the US to maintain larger universities than would be possible otherwise, which is a boon to research programs. Third, the students tend to have attitudes favorable to the US when they leave. Fourth, it serves as a feeder for immigration, as discussed in the above section. This recommendation seems the least arguable of all the recommendations.

Recommendation: Promote the coming of students from abroad who will pay the costs of their education.

Welfare Programs for Immigrants

Probably from the first days of the human species, our charitable feelings have been at odds with our desire to improve character. (Seen another way, the conflict is between altruism in the short and long runs.) For example, on one side there is the desire to assist immigrants who need help in a new land, while on the other side there is the aim of not making the new land attractive to persons who do not intend to, or cannot, take care of themselves.

This conflict seems quite easy to resolve. An unworthy immigrant takes the place of a more-worthy potential immigrant who would otherwise be able to enter and take advantage of what the US has to offer, while at the same time being able to give to the society more than s/he takes from it in transfers. Therefore, there seems to be a compelling argument for stringent requirements that immigrants (perhaps with the help of a sponsor) take care of themselves economically, with effective sanctions for those who do not do so. Two present provisions of the Immigration and Nationalization Act try to prevent immigrants from becoming a welfare burden. One states that aliens are ineligible to receive visas if they are "likely to become public charges" (8 USC 1182, quoted in *Report to the Congress by the Comptroller General*, "Number of Newly Arrived Aliens Who Receive Supplemental Security Income Needs to be Reduced", 22 February 1972, p. 5). And another provision orders deportation if the immigrant "has within five years after entry become a public charge from causes not affirmatively shown to have arisen after entry" (ibid., p. 1251). Still, more might be done.

Requiring immigrants to be self-supporting has at least three advantages. First and most immediate is that it benefits natives through the public coffers. Second, in the longer run it improves selection of immigrants for the economy and society. And a third benefit: by reducing the number of egregious cases of welfare abuse by immigrants, it defuses an objection to immigration which is really founded upon unrepresentative anecdotes about gross abuse drawn from newspapers and gossip.

Recommendation: Tighten up procedures preventing immigrants from taking illegal advantage of welfare services, to prevent hostility to immigration as well as to reduce costs.

Bringing Poor Persons from Poor Countries

Earlier (1971, 1982a) I described an improbable-seeming plan for speeding the economic development of poor persons in poor countries: an international organization would pay countries that bid successfully for the opportunity of admitting groups of such persons, for the purpose of transmitting to them the economic culture of advanced countries. This scheme would require an international taxing body, which would somewhat reduce the sovereignty of nations. The scheme seemed infeasible at the time I proposed it, though I thought that it might be feasible several decades in the future, just as the liquidation of empires seemed most improbable before World War II but happened speedily. As it has turned out, there has been some increase in related international activities since then. On the other hand, the United Nations seems to have come into poorer odor since then. On balance, the prospect of such a scheme being practical seems even less than when proposed, rather than more likely. Nevertheless, a word or two about the scheme may be relevant here, for completeness only.

Were such a plan to be inaugurated, it would behoove the US to bid low enough to win (though according to the scheme, the fee per person to the US would be greater than for less wealthy countries, because its potential to raise the productive capacity of immigrants is greater). Submitting a winning bid is recommended because the cost to the US would not be much greater than in other countries, though it might seem so at first; most goods are cheaper in the US than in poorer countries, and many services could be contracted for with foreign professionals. And the social difficulties are less in the US than in many other more homogeneous countries. In the long run, too, these persons and their offspring would make an economic contribution rather than be an economic drag, as this book argues.

Recommendation: None called for now.

Discrimination by Country of Origin

It might be that there are differences in productive "quality" among immigrants from various countries of origin even after the obvious control variables such as amount of education have been allowed for. Some persons would see in this a potential device to increase natives' welfare by discriminating according to country of origin. I shall not, however, discuss this possibility for two reasons: First, such a policy seems contrary to the spirit of US democracy, which asks us not to consider an individual's racial or religious background in any decisions other than personal relationships. Second, there does not seem to be massive conclusive evidence of major differences. And third, there is a strong possibility that studies finding differences among persons of different ethnic origin are confounded by the fact that prejudice in the US affects the earnings of persons of some ethnicities, though I do not suggest that prejudice accounts for all the observed differences.

Recommendation: None

Selective Admission by Education

A country generally benefits from having a greater supply of material capital. By analogy it would seem desirable for a country to have additional human capital. But adding human capital is more complex than adding material capital. One reason is that material capital arrives complete in its package, and has no important effects other than its productive capacities, whereas human capital arrives accompanied by a person who has a variety of effects upon others in addition to the increase in production effected by the capital. Also, the "owner" of the additional human capital is not a native, as discussed in chapter 2, and therefore the returns to that capital are not appropriated by natives, unlike the case with physical capital acquired by natives. Additionally, along with the human capital come claims upon the society for various services, as well as various social effects such as intermarriage. And though additional physical capital analogously lowers the return to existing physical capital, the negative effect of additional human capital upon existing native human capital is likely to produce much more concern than the negative effect of additional physical capital. So additional human capital in the form of immigrants is not an unmixed blessing.

This section discusses policies to increase the amount of human capital for *a given quota* of immigrants, by choosing for admission people with a relatively large amount of human capital. This policy is in contrast to simply admitting immigrants willy-nilly without regard to their education. Of course there already are in force various policies that discriminate among potential admittees on the basis of special skills with respect to special needs of the country. But these policies are mainly arbitrary, in that decisions about which categories are to be admitted are made bureaucratically on the basis of "expert" assessment of the nation's needs. The policy discussed in this section would be more automatic − setting up rules that favor people with high education without reference to specific contemporary national needs.

There are several obvious large benefits of admitting people with more rather than less education. Most measurable is the effect upon the flow of welfare services and taxes. Chapter 6 shows that persons with low education receive much more welfare assistance of various kinds than do people with high education. And people with high education pay more taxes because they earn more income, on average. Additionally, people with high education would seem more likely to improve the skills of the natives they work with, thereby increasing those natives' human capital and earning power.

There are other likely benefits from having immigrants with relatively large amounts of human capital. They are more likely to be mobile, moving to locations where their skills are needed, when they are needed; such domestic mobility is very important in economic development. People with high education are more capable of retraining themselves when such retraining is needed. They are more able to make voluntary contributions of skill to the community through various organizational activities. They raise native children who acquire a relatively large stock of human capital. They are more likely to contribute valuable innovations. Many more such advantages of education could be added.

The long list of advantages from having people with more human capital makes it seem as if a decision to discriminate in favor of people with more education necessarily makes sense. But there are two sets of reservations, one economic and the other ethical. They will be discussed in turn.

Discriminatory admission by education is intended to be rule-governed rather than arbitrary. But constructing rules for gauging a person's education would not be easy. The difficulties that universities in the US face in appraising the amount and quality of high school and college education of applicants, even from within the US let alone from abroad, are small compared to the difficulties that the US would face in deciding whether or not to count, say, years of education studying barbering or theology in foreign and perhaps little-known languages. The sort of policy envisioned here would not discriminate among disciplines studied. But is semi-formal education in a religious institution to be counted? What about sports education? Certification of institutions could be very different in different countries. And certification fraud would certainly follow on the onset of such a policy; the frauds with respect to religious education during periods of military draft are notorious, and stories of foreign medical school frauds were in the newspapers in 1985. One might argue that the worst that could happen as a result of such subversion of the policy is that it reduces its effectiveness and leaves matters closer to where they would be with no such policy, but no worse off than with no such policy at all. Perhaps so. But promoting fraud is seldom wise in the long run.

It is relevant that Canada, which has a point system having much in common with discrimination by education, has not found the system easy to implement (Staff Report, US Commission on Immigration and Refugee Policy, 1981, ch. 8), and its effectiveness is subject to question (Ornstein and Sharma, 1983). A problem with a point system is deciding on the system. Even among the professional staff of the Select Commission on Immigration and Refugee Policy there was large disagreement on the matter, including much disagreement about how to weight particular continents of origin (see Jasso, 1986).

Another possible drawback of such a policy is that it would lead to too much competition among educated persons, with consequent "academic unemployment." But educated persons are less likely to immigrate when their job prospects are poor; witness the very low rates of immigration of foreign lawyers, whose skills are not easily transferable, compared to the high rates for physicians, whose skills move readily. (The displacement issue is dealt with more thoroughly in chapters 11 and 12.)

Another potential drawback of such a policy is that key skills which do not require much formal education would be shut out, e.g. machinists and electricians. Special provision might be made for such skills, but that leads back toward the bureaucratic process of selection that the policy under discussion is intended to avoid, or toward a complex point system.

The appropriate data for analysis of the effect of admitting various educational groups are simply the earnings of various educational categories in various periods after entry. This analysis may be seen in figure 16.2, which compares each immigrant cohort to natives. The large possible gains to natives from such discrimination are obvious even without a full taxes-and-transfers cost–benefit analysis.

One might also consider selection by age at entry as well as schooling. Table 16.2 shows that young persons with much schooling immediately

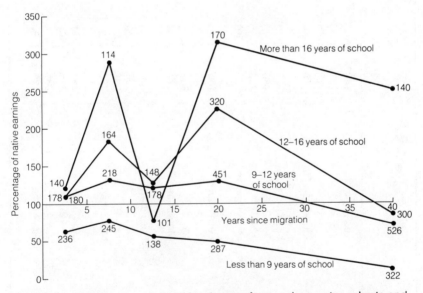

Figure 16.2 Average earnings of immigrants from various entry cohorts and educational levels as a percentage of average earnings of natives

Note: Numbers shown at each observation point are cell observation sizes.
Source: Simon and Sullivan, forthcoming

Table 16.2 Earnings patterns of immigrants by age, schooling, and period of entry

Entry cohort	Schooling (years)	Age (Years)							
		25–34		35–44		45–54		55–64	
1970–4	Less than 9	140%	(94)	91%	(69)	8%	(54)	[51%]	(19)
	9–12	131	(104)	92	(42)	107	(21)	[40]	(12)
	13–16	115	(109)	74	(46)	[273]	(19)	(214)	(4)
	More than 16	76	(93)	200	(34)	[860]	(11)	(2009)	(2)
1965–9	Less than 9	127%	(82)	77%	(64)	49%	(62)	43%	(34)
	9–12	140	(98)	91	(76)	209	(29)	[305]	(14)
	13–16	232	(77)	210	(57)	126	(23)	(18)	(8)
	More than 16	277	(50)	345	(50)	[339]	(10)	(2)	(4)
1960–4	Less than 9	109%	(32)	49%	(52)	39%	(34)	[60%]	(19)
	9–12	160	(72)	98	(57)	92	(30)	[139]	(19)
	13–16	263	(57)	231	(53)	65	(28)	[9]	(10)
	More than 16	177	(21)	82	(40)	52	(23)	(52)	(8)
1950–9	Less than 9	[40%]	(17)	89%	(92)	55%	(101)	20%	(77)
	9–12	137	(116)	163	(132)	175	(131)	47	(72)
	13–16	239	(134)	164	(82)	329	(72)	177	(32)
	More than 16	496	(52)	537	(43)	165	(57)	[248]	(18)
1920–49	Less than 9	(241%)	(4)	53%	(22)	31%	(93)	7%	(203)
	9–12	215	(44)	233	(52)	91	(162)	38	(267)
	13–16	236	(46);	112	(40)	127	(91)	40	(123)
	More than 16	190	(28)	657	(21)	210	(41)	234	(50)

begin to earn at high rates relative to comparable natives, whereas older immigrants do not do so well. This reinforces the powerful Social Security funding argument for bringing in younger rather than older immigrants.

Canadian data enable us to assess the effect of selecting by age alone. Table 16.3 shows that foreign-born immigrants aged 25–54 earn considerably more than does the *average* Canadian with income, aged 15 and over, both among males and females. (Note that it is the *total* Canadian figure which is relevant, and not age-group earnings.) Keeping in mind that admitting immigrants does not impose costs on the native population, because the immigrants' own children will pay for their parents' public retirement program later, and also because of discounting those payments an average of 25 years into the future when persons 24–34 are admitted (both matters are discussed in chapter 5) – a public policy that would admit immigrants aged 25–34 would have large economic benefits for natives. Such a policy would be heavily reinforced by selecting according to education as well.

Though selection by ethnicity is another obvious possibility, it will not be considered here, because of its analytic complexities as well as because such a policy is not likely to be considered consistent with other national goals.

Table 16.3   1975 Earnings of immigrants as a percentage of natives: entry-by-schooling analysis

Schooling (years)	Entry cohort				
	1970–4	*1965–9*	*1960–4*	*1950–9*	*1920–49*
Less than 9	63 (236)	78 (245)	56 (138)	50 (287)	14 (322)
9–12	110 (180)	132 (218)	122 (178)	130 (451)	73 (526)
13–16	110 (178)	183 (164)	126 (148)	227 (320)	87 (300)
More than 16	119 (140)	287 (114)	76 (101)	312 (170)	250 (140)

Notes: Results based on weighted regression.

Dependent variable: log of wage and salary income.

Entries for the table give the immigrant groups' average earnings as a percentage of natives. Calculations are based on a regression with school-by entry date dummy variables and converted to percentages based on the formula 100 $\exp(b_i)$ where b_i is the estimated regression coefficient.

Number of observations for the immigrant group is given in parentheses.

Source: Simon and Sullivan, forthcoming

A command of English would seem particularly beneficial as a criterion for admission. Skill with English is helpful no matter what one's occupation. And having gone to the trouble of acquiring a sound knowledge of English probably indicates a strong desire to succeed in the new country, which certainly is a desirable characteristic. Furthermore, it is relatively easy to devise a test that would be reliable and fair to all.

One might argue that it is unfair to discriminate in favor of better-educated persons and therefore against the poor. I think that this ethical issue can best be dealt with in two steps. First, if we feel that uneducated persons should be admitted for humanitarian reasons, even if their economic effect will be negative (though this is not likely), then the first step is to make that decision explicitly. The next step is to decide about admitting better-educated persons purely on their merit. (There is a parallel here to various domestic issues where it may be preferable to give money to the poor directly, rather than to frame other policies that will indirectly benefit the poor.)

Recommendation: Give weight to the amount of formal education in the admissions procedure, subject to an ethical veto. And discriminate among potential immigrants on the basis of their tested skill in English. This recommendation would improve the present policy, but may well be inferior to other potential policies to be discussed below.

Selective Admission by Amount of Investment Capital

Adding financial capital to a country may be presumed beneficial. Though financial capital may at first be simply portfolio investment rather than direct investment in US plant and equipment, in all likelihood such portfolio investment eventually flows into US plant and equipment rather than into investment abroad or into such non-productive investment as collectibles (which probably cannot simply be a sink for investment, either).

The most important role for capital brought with an immigrant, however, is as start-up money for a new business, or as purchase money for an existing small business. The act of an immigrant going into business for him/herself produces two important benefits to natives. It increases the total stock of entrepreneurial capacity in the country; more and more it is recognized that the stock of such entrepreneurial capacity is a crucial element for an economy, there never being too much of it. And entrepreneurial activity increases the number of jobs for natives and immigrants. By "making" jobs entrepreneurs offset immigrants "taking" existing jobs; this is one of the mechanisms which work to reduce unemployment for natives.

Surprisingly large amounts of capital are brought to Canada and Australia by "business" immigrants (and also by other immigrants); data are given in chapters 7 and 12.

Does discriminating by investment capital have indirect economic ill effects by displacing some otherwise desirable immigrants? It is hard to imagine any other group of persons who embody a more valuable amount of human capital on average than those who go into business for themselves, and therefore I think that this question may be answered straightforwardly in the negative.

There is an ethical question about whether it is acceptable to discriminate on the basis of wealth. The question is at base identical to the question about the ethics of discrimination on the basis of human capital, except that financial wealth seems a less attractive and less "meritorious" characteristic. The issue reduces to whether a nation may use its immigration policy to do well by itself or whether it is unethical to use such a policy for national ends even if the policy thereby maximizes the welfare of the world as a whole. (And it does not take very many or very strong assumptions to make an argument that a wealth-discrimination policy really does maximize world economic welfare.) If the answer is "yes," then it makes sense to separate the decision about this discriminatory policy from the decision about whether a certain number of poor or uneducated people should also be admitted as charity (though keeping in mind that such people also are likely to have a positive effect upon natives on balance, though less so than people with more capital or education).

When one questions whether an asset-discrimination policy is ethically acceptable, other general questions arise: Is it unethical for a merchant to sell a piece of merchandise to a rich person when a poor person would buy the merchandise at the same price or for slightly less? Would a decision to sell to the poorer person constitute an ethical act vis-à-vis the richer person? In what respects is a state like or unlike an individual or a business firm in its "business" actions? (Here we must keep in mind that "economic" immigrants and not refugees are the subject of discussion here.)

I am well aware that if quoted out of context the discussion in this section, as well as in neighboring sections, would produce the impression that the author is hardhearted and/or nationalistic. But I believe that dispassionate analysis shows these policies to increase welfare for disadvantaged as well as advantaged persons, in the long run.

Recommendation: Give preference to applicants with financial assets, subject to ethical veto. If direct investment can be made a criterion, that would be an improvement.

Selling Foreigners the Right to Immigrate[2]

To suggest selling the right of immigration into the US to the high bidders inevitably is to label oneself an inhumane brute, or an "ivory tower" theorist, or both. Selling admission smacks of trafficking in human flesh. And of course such a scheme will not be politically feasible in the foreseeable future. But perhaps even those who will immediately reject the idea out of hand may agree that there is pedagogical value in studying a radical plan for the light it may throw upon more conventional schemes.

Please notice that it is reasonable to compare this scheme against other quota systems; comparison to an open-border system is outside the present frame of discussion, in part because an open border is vastly less likely than even an auction scheme.

An auction plan clearly promises economic benefits to Americans. Additionally, one can see (if one gets past the instinctive revulsion) that this plan also is less arbitrary, and thus fairer, than the existing policy as well as most alternative policies, and it can also improve the lot of the residents of the countries of origin more than other policies.

The right to immigrate has been sold before, but (so far as I know) only in the form of bribes to officials rather than as a publicly stated explicit policy. (A white market rather than a black market is under consideration here, of course.) And some countries already have policies tantamount to selling admission when they offer low taxes to induce persons to reside there, as do Monaco and Caribbean countries, though perhaps the lesser demand for immigration into those countries compared to the US makes the situation different there. Belize had a plan to sell citizenship for a $12,500 payment and a $12,500 government bond purchase (*New York Times*, 25 March 1986, p. 2). And Canada has been waging an ardent campaign to lure Chinese businessmen fleeing Hong Kong – especially those willing to invest a quarter of a million Canadian dollars or more in a job-creating business (*Washington Post*, 8 March 1986, p. A11).

I hope to show that this plan is better than other quota plans with three key tests: (1) US natives' incomes, (2) fairness, and (3) welfare of people in sending countries.

It should be noted that though the use of a market to allocate immigrant admissions seems peculiar to non-economists, this approach is almost second nature to economists, and they are quick to promote it. Indeed, the general scheme I suggest was invented independently by at least two other writers (Becker, 1987; Chiswick, 1982), and surely would be re-invented again and again if more economists were to address the problem.

Benefit to natives

An auction policy would have a better effect upon the incomes of US natives than does any other policy because it will efficiently identify those potential immigrants who have an especially large capacity to produce goods of high economic value while working in the US. A point system also discriminates among potential immigrants by their economic worth. But a system of rationing by auction has all the best features of a point system and more, because it *self-selects* persons who have the best chance to make an economic success. Those persons can and will take into account not only their occupations and the demand for them, but also their talents in their occupations, their willingness to work hard for success, and other characteristics that cannot be easily established objectively.

Charging a fee for admission would also accentuate the tendency for immigrants to move when they are young and strong, because admission has higher (discounted) future lifetime value for young persons than for older persons, *ceteris paribus*.

The analysis of age and sex distribution in various admission categories in Australia in chapter 3 (figure 3.10) reinforces the recommendation that, from the point of view of the economic welfare of natives, self-selected immigrants — in comparison to family-reconstitution immigrants — are particularly desirable, because they arrive just at the beginning of their work lives, with the maximum number of years before them during which they will be paying taxes and not receiving old-age assistance from the public coffers.

For the above reasons, an auction puts additional purchasing power into the hands of natives. The amounts of money would not be insignificant relative to other aspects of the governmental budget. Becker (1987) calculated that at $20,000 per immigrant — the discounted present value of a $2000 "profit" by an immigrant each year, compounded at 10 percent — half a million immigrants would bring in ten billion dollars each year.

Persons who are willing to pay a lot to enter the country must believe that the opportunity to do so will be valuable to them. For a few, this may just be an opportunity to live a pleasant and free life. But for the many it would represent an opportunity to make a lot of money in the large and rich market that is the US. And an immigrant who makes a lot of money for herself or himself will accordingly be a large benefactor of the community by providing jobs and contributing taxes (putting aside unusual cases such as Mafiosi). To such a person, a large payment to purchase a ticket of immigration would simply represent an investment, which would often be accompanied by further investment in business assets. This further investment would generally be an additional benefit to natives.[3]

Furthermore, by benefiting natives an auction plan should make additional immigration more popular among natives. It might even increase the number of unwealthy immigrants, too, by improving public attitudes toward immigration and thereby leading to larger total quotas.

Evidence that emphasis on economic factors is the high road to successful immigrant adjustment comes from a recent study in Australia of what are known as General Eligibility Migrants, those who are admitted on the basis of personal characteristics rather than being refugees or relatives of families residing in Australia. Their "high incidence of employment success leading to economic viability, and acceptance in the workplace, justifies the emphasis placed on economic factors in the migrant selection process" (Northage & Associates, 1983, p. 57). And Canadian data show that Asian immigrants who arrived between 1960 and 1969 have done much better economically relative to immigrants from the UK and Canadian-born persons than have Asian immigrants who arrived between 1970 and 1979; a larger proportion of Asian immigrants in the latter period were admitted on the basis of family reconstitution than in the former period, whereas for immigrants from the UK (and of course for the Canadian-born) this was not the case, showing that family reconstitution is significantly less good a policy as selection on economic characteristics (see table 4.18).

Another virtue of an auction plan: selling admission avoids "chain" migration whereby an entrant later obtains admission for relatives through the preference system. If it were known in advance that relatives would only be allowed if the admission fee were paid for them, too, then a potential immigrant could take that possibility into account when deciding whether to immigrate, and there would no longer be "humanitarian" grounds for a preference system except for spouse and children, neither of which have the same degree of uncertainty and multiplicability as other relatives.

Fairness

The present scheme is in no way "fair." It does not give to all potential immigrants the same opportunity to be admitted to the US. Only a worldwide lottery would be fair in that sense (though perhaps a lottery might only need to include those people who indicate a desire to immigrate, which might not be many times greater than the present number of immigrants). Nor is the present scheme fair in the sense of giving all persons with the same qualifications the same opportunity. Persons in some countries (say, Canada or Great Britain) have a much better chance of admission than do similar persons in other countries (say, Malaysia or India). And an even more serious departure from fairness is that the relatives of persons in the US have a vastly greater chance of being admitted than do similar persons without relatives; this is a case of "connections" on the broadest scale imaginable, a departure from fairness which is not mitigated by the fact that we may have good social reasons for such a policy. An auction does not discriminate in such fashion, but instead discriminates according to the standard of a market-oriented society — ability and willingness to pay. Hence the auction scheme may be seen as a gain in fairness.

If we think there is something good about the present discriminatory scheme, we could use it within an auction system to identify a subclass of people who would be allowed to enter for less than the full amount paid by others — an amount which we would know is more than the special-preference people would pay, given that they would not be among the high bidders. Hence the system would benefit them by giving them a good which is worth more on the market than they are willing to pay for it.

It should also be remembered that if the US admits some poor and unskilled persons by means of a complex system of family ties plus allocation by length of time in the queue, other especially-worthy poor and unskilled persons are implicitly denied admission. There is nothing "fair" or "charitable" in such a system. It would probably be easier to identify and assist the most needy persons if charity were to be given directly, in money, out of admission-fee proceeds, with a consequent increase in total "fairness" and benevolence, no matter how one would wish to define those terms.

So in brief, an auction scheme is not less fair than the present scheme.

Reluctance to ration admission to the US by ability and willingness to pay for it would seem to stem from the same psychological root as does our reluctance to use the market to ration such other "merit goods" as food and gasoline in times of shortage, in contrast to our everyday policy of allocating according to readiness to pay. But in these latter cases the aim of an equal-ration policy is to ensure that everyone in a well-defined population gets the same amount so that none suffers injury to health. The auction plan is closer to rationing health care on the battlefield, where the aim is to try to provide care to those who need it most. But to apply any sort of merit-good principle to immigration is to intermix two objectives at the expense of both (though perhaps with the very purpose of confusing the issue so as to make it easier to attain a hidden objective — fewer immigrants of any kind).

Welfare of the sending countries

What about the loss to sending countries of some of their most productive people? Clearly those countries' residents who will win the auction and emigrate have their welfare improved, because (ex ante) they plan to earn more abroad than at home. And if there are no externalities and no one is injured at home by the migrants leaving, then allowing them to emigrate increases the overall welfare of the sending country prior to the emigration.

If there *are* externalities — for example, the alleged positive externalities derived from physicians (see chapter 14) — and if the US is concerned with not inflicting such externalities upon the sending countries, it can easily compensate the sending countries for the amounts of those externalities with only a small portion of the fees collected in the auction, because it is most unlikely that the externalities are anywhere near the size of the fees that would be paid.

Objections to an auction plan

Some will object: even though the US could best help sending countries with this scheme together with "compensation" for talented émigrés, the US (they say) simply *will not in practice* send the fees abroad, and therefore the scheme will turn out to be exploitative. Perhaps. But this objection leaves the domain of the economic analyst, and enters into the domain of the practitioner of the feasible; let it be argued out there.

One might wonder whether an admission-fee plan would result only in high-skill people immigrating legally, thereby making the US even more inviting than at present for low-skill persons to enter illegally, with the attendant problems of "lawlessness." So it would be. But a guestworker program *in tandem with* an admission-by-fee plan would be a businesslike overall policy, and would avoid the lawlessness problem almost completely. Such a policy would, however, require greater sanctions against any illegals that did come anyway — perhaps most of them high-skill persons — because allowing them to remain illegally would be quite unfair to those who pay high admission fees, and also would spoil the market. If immigration policy were to be put on such a businesslike basis, it would then be less painful than at present to enforce such laws on the books as those that require deportation if the immigrant becomes a welfare burden.

One may also wonder whether such a policy would result in only the very rich being admitted. This need not be so, for three reasons. First, very rich persons may prefer to remain in their home countries because of lack of felt need for economic advance.[4] The absence of revelations of bribes to obtain visas may indicate that this is indeed so. Second, the auction plan could enable persons without liquid assets to gradually repay their admission fee, adjusted for carrying costs, out of future yearly income; it would be collectible along with their income tax, in which case the immigrants need not be rich at the time of the auction. Third, the fee could be set quite low and still yield a profit on each entrant (in fact, a negative fee would break even, given the estimates made earlier in the book).

This scheme would seem to be more advantageous than Bhagwati's scheme mentioned earlier, because there are no complications in collection. Furthermore, by allowing immigrants to bid for places, it would identify those who would most benefit from entrance into the US, and who would most benefit the US. Bhagwati's scheme does not have these properties.

Managerial issues

Interesting management questions arise in connection with an auction policy. For example, should the US attempt to operate as a profit-maximizing monopolist? If so, the profit would be set far above "cost." Such a policy would require some agreement about the best estimate of "cost" − which is discussed in this book.

Another question is whether the same price should be set for all ages and both sexes. As long as policies to deport those who become welfare charges would be enforced, the fee probably could be the same for each married couple irrespective of age. There would probably need to be a different fee for single persons, but I have not yet worked out the logic of such differential fees.

Yet another question is how to estimate demand for entrance. Perhaps this would best be done by adjusting the "quota" from quarter year to quarter year.

If the plan were to aim at maximizing revenue subject to a numerical constraint on the number of immigrants, a price-discriminating lottery would probably be most effective. One method would ask persons to bid for inclusion in the quota, with the persons's actual bid to be paid by each bidder above the quota cut-off. (Because the likelihood of adoption of such a scheme is so low, I shall not pursue theoretical analysis of varieties of such bidding schemes.) Or, it might be decided that it would be unfair to charge different fees to different people, in which case the amount bid by the lowest successful bidder would be paid (noting that higher bidders would be economically more desirable for reasons discussed earlier).

Because of the greater productivity in the US of those who are willing to pay more for the opportunity to immigrate than for those who will not bid as high, the US could surely improve the lot of a larger number of poor persons in the countries of origin than at present by treating the fees as a charity fund for those poor persons, even if only part were sent back. To put it a bit more precisely: specify any number of poor and unskilled immigrants who might be allowed entrance, and estimate their gains by immigration (assuming there are gains, which there might not be). It would be possible for the US instead to admit the same number of high bidders, remit to those poor persons who would otherwise have come the full value of their potential gains in the US, have something left over for US citizens, and also improve the lot of the high-bidding immigrants. Such a procedure would come close to the economist's dream: a "Pareto improvement" in which everyone benefits.

Will the plan ever be politically feasible?

One naturally wonders whether such a policy is so unfeasible politically as not even to be worth discussion. I think not. Furthermore, politically unfeasible schemes often serve as a useful frame of reference for schemes that are more politically realistic at the moment. Furthermore, schemes that seem outlandish when first proposed can later become feasible, as time passes and political and economic water flows under the bridge; the education voucher system is such an example.

Summary of plan

If a country is to ration admission by the amount of human or financial capital that the potential immigrants will bring to invest, why not go even further and simply auction off the right to immigrate, with the proceeds of the auction going to the public coffers?

The policy of rationing admission by sale to the highest bidder embodies many of the best features of such policies considered earlier, such as admission by education and admission by capital investment, without suffering from many of their defects. At the same time it would permit the US to devote at least as much economic resources to charitable welfare as under less market-oriented allocation policies.

The key to the efficiency of an auction system is that individuals are likely to assess their own economic capacities better than can an arbitrary point system; the latter process does not take into account many of the most important characteristics because they are not identifiable with demographic criteria. Those persons who will stake their own money upon correct identification of such capacities are *ipso facto* the best possible bets to be high economic producers in the US.

Recommendation: Adopt an auction plan.

NOTES

1 For more information on the maquiladora program, see: "Mexican factories along the US border succeed despite criticism on both sides," *Wall Street*

Journal, 19 November 1985; Mexican border towns boom, *Washington Post,* 20 April 1986.

2 [T]here is much more agreement among economists than laymen think there is: I sent the first draft of this essay to Melvin Reder, whose credentials include the first modern theoretical paper on immigration way back in 1963. Reder replied that he had been thinking of a similar scheme but had not gotten around to writing it up; he offered his support, and some useful new twists. Then I mentioned it to Mark Rosenzweig, who had been the economics co-director of research for the Select Commission on Immigration and Refugee Policy. Rosenzweig said he had proposed a similar scheme to the Select Commission. Later I sent it to Milton Friedman, because this scheme is so consonant with many of those he has put forth. Friedman replied:

> Re your auction proposal, it does of course appeal to me, but the reason I write back promptly is that I believe this is one of those cases where when competent economists turn their attention to a particular problem, in this case immigration, they are likely to come up with the same solution. Unless my memory fails me, both Gary Becker and Barry Chiswick have suggested the idea of auctioning quotas.

And indeed, Chiswick had suggested a very similar scheme as part of a long paper published in 1982, and Becker has been circulating a preliminary draft on the topic.

3 The qualification "generally" refers to the paradoxical possibility that though by almost any test a larger supply of capital is beneficial in the short run, in the longer run it might have a deleterious effect by reducing the impetus to individuals putting forth vigorous economic activity. This is the argument against foreign aid, of course − a striking apparent contradiction between standard microeconomics and the policy prescriptions of some of the most distinguished microeconomists − and conceivably it might apply also to the human capital that is the subject of this chapter. On the other hand, additional human capital also may have various indirect positive consequences in the long run, as shall be discussed here.

4 Business people leaving the home country − for example, Sweden − to avoid high taxes is not relevant here, because those persons can head for tax shelters, where the lack of earning opportunity is not relevant.

17 Conclusions and Summary of Main Findings

This book analyzes the economic effects upon natives of legal immigrants who have come to the US in order to improve their economic lot. The findings are intended to cast additional light upon a national debate that has been going on for more than a century, and in which there is now high interest: how many immigrants, of what kinds, should the US admit each year? My general conclusion, based on the various analyses and findings, is: more than at present, and chosen more for their economic characteristics and less on the basis of family connections.

Though the general conclusion offered here runs contrary to much public opinion, it is mostly in consonance with the economic literature, and the overwhelming consensus of the most respected American economists agrees, as documented in appendix C.

The findings and conclusions are summarized here in this final chapter. The introduction contains an idealized analysis, plus some reflections that may be relevant to those who may read with an eye to future research.

Immigration Theory and Trade Theory (chapter 2). Contrary to intuition, the theory of the international trade of goods is quite inapplicable to the international movement of persons. There is no immediate large consumer benefit from the movement of persons that is analogous to the benefit from the international exchange of goods, because the structure of supply is not changed in the two countries as a whole, as it is when trade induces specialization in production. Goods that are traded internationally are, in the usual case, produced by workers who are paid much less in the producing country than they could earn in the country where the goods are sold and consumed. The inter-country difference in that labor cost — which can be very great — is shared among the consumer (who pays a much lower price for the traded good than if the good were produced in the consumer's own country) and the employer of the labor which produces the goods (who sells the good for a considerably higher price abroad than if it had to be sold only at home). In contrast, immigrants tend to receive higher wages in the richer country to which they move. The immigrants benefit by the higher wages. But there is little or no immediate gain to the consumers in the new country analogous to the gains when goods are traded internationally.

An example may make the point best: you can hire a driver for a day much cheaper in India than in New York, to your considerable benefit if the driver is competent; the difference in the labor price arises from the different overall relative price structures in poor and rich countries. But if the driver moves to New York and is competent to work there, you will have to pay him/her close to the usual going rate in New York; the driver gains from moving because he/she "owns" himself/herself and obtains the benefits from the use of her/his human capital (which would not be the case if you were to buy a slave). Crucial to the difference between the trade in goods and the movement of people is that the goods which are traded internationally — tires, beer, and autos, for example — can be shipped separately from the persons who produce them. But the services which individuals perform — in driving and in dentistry, say — cannot be moved unless the provider of the service moves (though modern communications does make more possible the rendering at a distance of services such as computer programming, which will reduce the difference in wages between computer programmers in rich and poor countries).

The Size and "Quality" of Immigration (chapter 3). Contemporary immigration is not high by US historical standards. There were 800,000 legal immigrants in peak-year 1980, whereas near the turn of the century, immigration substantially topped the million mark in many years. And the burden of absorbing immigrants was much greater in those earlier times relative to the population size. For instance, immigrants who arrived between 1901 and 1910 constituted 9.6 percent of the population; those who arrived between 1961 and 1970 constituted only 1.6 percent, and between 1971 and 1980 only 2.0 percent. Or consider this: in 1910, 14.6 percent of the population was foreign-born; in 1970 only 4.7 percent had been born abroad, and in 1980 only 6 percent, or approximately 1 person in 17, and this includes those who have been here many years. Amazingly, this "country of immigrants," as the politicians often put it, has a smaller share of foreign-born persons than countries thought to be far more "homogeneous," including Great Britain, Switzerland and France.

As to the "quality" of immigrants, the central economic fact now — and also throughout US history — is that, in contrast to the older US population, immigrants tend to arrive in their 20s and 30s, when they are physically and mentally vigorous and in the prime of their work lives. Immigrants have about as much education as do natives, on average, and this was true even at the turn of the century. Furthermore, immigrants are disproportionally professional and technical persons, a great benefit to the US.

Behavioral Characteristics of Immigrants (chapter 4). Immigrants tend to have especially desirable behavioral characteristics from the economic point of view. Compared to natives, their rate of participation in the labor force is higher, they tend to save more, they apply more effort during working hours, and they have a higher propensity to start new businesses and to be self-employed. They do not have a higher propensity to commit crime or to be unemployed, and (for better or for worse) their fertility rate is not higher.

The Effects of Immigrants Through the Public Coffers – Transfers and Taxes (chapters 5 and 6). Analysis of a large Census Bureau survey shows that, contrary to common belief, immigrants do not use more transfer payments and public services than do natives; rather, they use much smaller amounts in total.

The services that catch the public eye are welfare and Supplemental Security, unemployment compensation, Aid to Families with Dependent Children, and food stamps. Comparing immigrant and native families of similar education and age, there is almost no difference in usage levels. The costs of schooling are somewhat higher for immigrants after the first few years in the US, because their families are younger than native families, on average. But when we include public retirement programs – Social Security, Medicare, and the like – immigrant families on average are seen to receive much less total welfare payments and public services than do average native families.

Summing the categories we find that the average immigrant family received $1404 (in 1975 dollars) in welfare services in years 1–5, $1941 in years 6–10, $2247 in years 11–15, and $2279 in years 16–25. In comparison, natives' receipts averaged $2279, considerably more than the immigrants got during their early years in the US. Furthermore, these early years are especially relevant because rational policy decisions weigh the distant future less heavily than the near future.

The costs of Social Security dominate the entire system of transfers and taxes. Natives get a windfall from immigrants through the Social Security mechanism. By the time the immigrant couple retires and collects, the couple typically has raised children who are then contributing Social Security taxes and thereby balancing out the parents' receipts, just as is the case with typical native families. In this way there is a one-time benefit to natives because the immigrants normally do not arrive accompanied by a generation of elderly parents who might receive Social Security. Admitting additional immigrants may be the only painless way for the US to ease the trade-off between Social Security benefits and taxes that now cramps the nation's economic policies.

If immigrants paid relatively little in taxes, they might still burden natives by way of the public coffers, even with less use of welfare services by immigrants than by natives. We lack direct information on taxes paid, but from data on family earnings we can estimate taxes tolerably well. Within 3–5 years after entry, immigrant family earnings reach and pass those of the average native family, due mainly to the favorable age composition of immigrant families. The average native family paid $3008 in taxes in 1975. In comparison, immigrant families in the US 6–10 years paid $3359, those in the US 11–15 years paid $3564, and those in the US 16–25 years paid $3592. These are substantial differences which benefit natives.

Taken together, the data on services used and taxes paid show substantial differences in favor of natives. If we assume that 20 percent of taxes finance activities that are little affected by population size – for example, maintaining the armed forces and the Statue of Liberty – the difference is an average of $1354 yearly for the years 1–5 in the US, and $1329, $1535 and $1353 for years 6–10, 11–15 and 16–25 respectively, in 1975 dollars. These are the amounts that natives are enriched each year through the public coffers for each additional immigrant family. Evaluating the future stream of differences as one would when evaluating a prospective dam or harbor, the present value of a newly-arrived immigrant family discounted at 3 percent (inflation adjusted) was $20,600 in 1975 dollars, almost 2 years' average earnings of a native family; at 6 percent the present value was $15,800, and $12,400 at 9 percent.

Illegals such as the Mexicans who cross into the US receive little in welfare services due to their status. Representative estimates of the proportions of these illegals using such services are: free medical, 5 percent; unemployment insurance, 4 percent; food stamps, 1 percent; welfare payments, 1 percent; child schooling, 4 percent. Practically no illegals receive Social Security, the costliest service of all. But 77 percent of illegal workers paid Social Security taxes, and 73 percent had federal income tax withheld. Even more telling are the cost–benefit studies which show illegal immigrants paying five to ten times as much in taxes as the cost of the welfare services which they use.

The Use of Existing Physical Capital by Immigrants (chapter 7). New immigrants employ existing plant and equipment capital when they start work, and they use social "demographic" capital such as schools and hospitals previously paid for by natives. Additional capital is required to accommodate the additional people. We wish to know how this use of physical capital by immigrants affects the pockets of natives. The question is best broken down into three kinds of capital — privately owned industrial plant and equipment, publicly owned plant and equipment, and publicly owned demographic capital.

If the private sector of the economy were like the government sector — where a worker's pay may be assumed to equal the full value of what the workers produce, with nothing left over for the owner of the capital — then capital dilution would indeed lower average native income. But in the private sector, theory suggests that an additional worker implies higher earnings by the firm's owners about equal to the loss of earnings by other workers. This tradeoff leaves overall native per-person income in the private sector roughly unchanged (a slight gain to natives) by an additional immigrant.

This tradeoff implies, however, that "workers" suffer as "capitalists" gain. That is, to the extent that the "classes" are separate, there is a transfer from workers' pockets to owners' pockets. But in fact much of our private capital is owned indirectly by "workers" through pension funds, and those same workers obtain part of the gross profit (called "return to capital") by way of the taxes paid on interest and dividends. Hence the loss to the "worker class" is not as great as it may seem to be at first glance.

A capital-dilution effect of some importance occurs in the use of government-owned plant and equipment. In this case there are no benefits captured by the native owners of the capital as there are in the private sector, and hence workers (including immigrant workers) receive in their salaries all the returns to capital. About 8 percent of immigrants work for the government, which translates into a loss to natives equal to about 2 percent of all immigrants' income. Though not trivial, this sum is about the same size as the gain to natives by way of the returns to private capital discussed just above. (We might also note, however, that this 8 percent of immigrants working for the government is only about half the native rate, a difference which has various benefits to natives.)

As to the public capital used by immigrants, we must be concerned with the additional capital outlays needed to equip immigrants — the extra schoolrooms, hospital beds, firehouses, and the like. Not relevant is use of public goods that does not affect natives' use of pocketbooks — looking at the Washington Monument, or riding on a lightly used interstate highway. Furthermore, to a considerable extent we are on a pay-as-you-go basis with respect to capital expenditures: the debt service on past public borrowings covers much of the outlays on new capital. Therefore, through their taxes, immigrants pay "rent" on public facilities. This is an important additional reason why Malthusian capital dilution is not a crucial problem.

For perspective, the negative effect of immigrants upon natives' incomes through capital dilution, mostly for demographic capital, is about one-fourth the size of the positive effect through taxes-and-transfers.

Effects of Immigrants upon Natives' Human Capital Utilization: Technology and Productivity (chapter 8). Though the direct effect upon industrial productivity is hard to nail down statistically, in the long run the beneficial impact upon industrial efficiency of additional immigrant workers and consumers is likely to dwarf all other effects. Some of the productivity increase comes from immigrants working in US industries and laboratories that are at the forefront of world technique. American citizens benefit along with others from a contribution to world productivity in, say, genetic engineering that immigrants would not be able to accomplish in their home countries. Also, the presence of more immigrants means that there are more working persons who will think up productivity-enhancing ideas.

Other increases in productivity due to a larger population – and on these we have solid evidence – come from increased production through learning-by-doing, together with other gains from larger industry scale. Also, increasing the number of customers and workers increases invest-ment, which brings more new technology into use, due to immigrants swelling the population.

There are also less direct effects through human capital changes. The technical level of the persons that a native – call her/him Alpha – works with may affect Alpha's productivity in several conflicting fashions. First, if immigrants have less skill on average than do natives in the same occupa-tion with the same amount of education – and this is likely because people in poor countries almost necessarily have less skill than do persons in the same occupation in rich countries – then even if immigrants who come have average or even better-than-average education, enough of them might drag down the skill levels of the natives they work and interact with. In other words, if there is a huge flood of immigrants from Backwardia to Richonia, Richonia will become economically similar to Backwardia, with loss to Richonians and little gain to immigrants from Backwardia. The effect may therefore be expected to depend in nonlinear fashion upon the proportion of immigrants in such fashion that a few immigrants from Backwardia may have a beneficial effect for other reasons, whereas many may have a deleterious effect for the reason at hand. So even if *some* immigrants are beneficial, a *very large* number coming from poorer countries (that is, numbers that make new immigrants a significant percentage of the workforce, say 10, 20, or 30 percent having come within 5 or 10 years) may have the opposite effect.

Second, and working in the opposite direction, is the stimulative cross-pollenization effect that arises from encounters among people who have different ways of doing things. Though I have not found any systematic evidence on the matter, there is much anecdotal evidence in contemporary society and throughout history that this hybridization effect is important. It should be noted, however, that as with the learning-externality effect, a given immigrant may be expected to make more of a contribution in this fashion when he or she is one of only a few rather than one of many immigrants, because the essence of this effect is that the immigrant be different from those persons he/she works with.

Third, the technical "quality" of casual associations that occur away from the workplace and throughout the society affect a person's skill and productivity. If a large number of technically deficient immigrants were to arrive in a town or country, the productivity of the natives there would likely be negatively affected by this influence.

Effects Upon Natural Resources and the Environment (chapter 9). Immigrants are frequently said to cause a natural resource squeeze for natives. Much of that proposition is demonstrably bunkum. The water and food ingested in the US have been improving in past decades by every reasonable measure of quantity and purity, though the fact is too little known. The air in the US also has been getting less polluted. And over the long run, natural resources have been getting less scarce rather than more scarce, as indicated by the trends in the fundamental economic measure of cost. Additional people do increase resource demand and prices in the short run. But in the longer run, when the system has had a chance to find new sources and substitutes, the result is that resources are typically more available and cheaper than if the temporary shortages had never arisen.

An Integrated Model of Aggregate Effects (chapter 10). Using a simple macro-model and what seem to be reasonable parameters, I estimate the difference between natives' incomes with or without immigrants. When looked at by natives as an investment, similar to such social capital as dams and roads, an immigrant family is an excellent investment worth somewhere between $15,000 and $20,000 to natives, even calculated with relatively high rates for the social cost of capital. (This is in 1975 dollars, to be compared with mean yearly native family earnings of about $11,000 in that year.)

Labor-Market Effects of Immigrants (chapters 11 and 12). The most politically powerful argument against admitting immigrants always has been that they take jobs held by natives and thereby increase native unemployment. The logic is simple: if the number of jobs is fixed, and immigrants occupy some jobs, then there are fewer jobs available for natives.

In the immediate present, the demand for any particular sort of worker is indeed inflexible. In theory, therefore, additional immigrants in a given occupation must have *some* negative impact on wages and/or employment among people in that occupation. There must even be some additional general unemployment while the economy adjusts to additional workers. But we want to know whether the effect will be huge or trivial. To gauge the magnitude of the effect, a model based on queuing theory is constructed, using available estimates on such factors as the average length of time persons who lose jobs remain unemployed. Also discussed in the theoretical section is a model by Harrison suggesting that, to the extent that immigrants consume and purchase even before they go to work, they *decrease* native unemployment, even if immigrant unemployment is observed to be much higher than native unemployment.

Several recent studies have tackled the matter of "displacement" empirically using a variety of approaches. No study has found across-the-board unemployment caused by immigrants, either in the US as a whole or in particular areas of relatively high immigration. And effects on particular groups as surprisingly small or non-existent, even groups (such as blacks and women in California) seemingly at special risk from Mexican immigrants.

In short, immigrants not only take jobs, they make jobs. They create new jobs indirectly with their spending. They also create new jobs directly with the businesses which they are more likely than natives to start.

Concerning wages now: additional persons *outside* of native Alpha's occupation – especially persons with different levels of education – improve Alpha's earning situation because they are complements to her; if, for example, Alpha is a person with much education and skill, she can therefore be better off if there are additional immigrant people of low skill available, as a trained surgical nurse may be more productive if there are additional less-skilled helpers available. Similarly, if Alpha has few skills, Alpha benefits from having additional immigrants of high skill enter the country. Additional persons in Alpha's *own* occupation, however, drive down Alpha's earnings due simply to additional competition. Evidence concerning both the competitive and complementary effects on wages suggests that the effects are small, at least in the US, but competitive effects are observed to drive down some natives' wages – as immigrant physicians worsen the economic position of native physicians (though other persons benefit from lower prices).

Effects upon the Income Distribution (chapter 13). There is no evidence that immigration widens the income distribution in the US.

Effects upon Sending Countries and the Rest of the World (chapter 14). This topic is touched upon briefly because it is outside the scope of the book's main interest. The effect of international migration upon the world as a whole is unambiguously positive because it comprises the movement of factors of production from lower-value to higher-value utilizations. The effects upon the sending countries are theoretically mainly positive, according to conventional static considerations, but such benefits do not seem likely to be realized.

Illegals, and Guestworker Programs (chapter 15). Illegal immigrants tend to have lower-than-average amounts of human capital, and therefore they increase the competition that native unskilled workers face. But the damage to the latter group is far less than is popularly imagined; and the overall effect of the illegals is positive in every manner of influence examined here. Particularly noteworthy is that the immigrants use very small amounts of public services, as mentioned above, both because of their favorable age distribution and because they are afraid of apprehension if they attempt to obtain services. At the same time they pay income and Social Security taxes many times the cost of the services that they use.

Illegal immigrants are not otherwise discussed because they are necessarily quite different from legals in their economic behavior as well as in their background characteristics.

Policy Recommendations (chapter 16). A variety of admission-selection policies are evaluated with respect to their effect upon the standard of living of natives. Policies that discriminate on the basis of economic characteristics, and especially a system such as allocating admission by auction that *self-selects* immigrants according to productive economic characteristics, are especially recommended.

The most general policy issue concerns the total number of immigrants. Taking in immigrants at a rate equal to, or even far above, our present admission rate improves our average standard of living, on balance. American citizens even do well while doing good when admitting refugees. Rather than being a matter of charity, we can expect our incomes to be higher rather than lower in future years if we take in more immigrants. Therefore, increasing the total immigration quota is recommended.

Unlimited immigration is not discussed here as a policy alternative for the US. The reasons are as follows: first and most important, we have little understanding of how many people would choose to immigrate in the shorter and longer run if the door were completely open. At one pole of possibilities is the common fear that US natives would be inundated by tens of millions of immigrants per year, quantities of immigrants proportionately as great as, or even much greater than, the turn-of-the-century rates, which were about 6 times as great as in the 1970s decade. At the other pole is the relatively small number of people − not much more than one million, a large proportion of whom migrate for family rather than purely economic reasons − who are currently registered as applicants for permission to enter the US. Whereas fear on the part of natives pushes upwards the former estimate, the latter figure is pushed downwards by the expectation by many would-be immigrants that it would be a waste of time to apply because admission would not be obtained or would take so long to obtain as to not be worth considering. This is a wide range, and hence any estimate of immigration under an open-door policy must be very uncertain. And we have even less basis for predicting how the *mix* of immigrants by education and skill would change were immigration to be allowed without limit.

A second reason for not discussing unlimited immigration is that we lack empirical evidence to help estimate at which point some of the economic effects that are positive in the broad neighborhood of present admission levels might become negative at immigration rates several multiples of present levels. One such possibility is negative human-capital externalities if immigrants were to lower the skill level. But there are no signs of these constraints operating at present admission levels. A policy of admitting people selectively by economic characteristics such as education would avoid the key theoretical constraint, and would have enormous positive impacts on native income, but whether this is ethically or politically acceptable is another question. Under such circumstances prudence would seem to suggest that any alterations in policy be stepwise and sufficiently close to present levels so that we can feel our way — say increments of a doubling in rate at any one time rather than a greater multiplication of it.

Third, unlimited immigration is unlikely politically, and is a red flag that upsets and arouses many. Literary prudence therefore seems to dictate avoiding discussion of the matter.

Appendix A   Are there Grounds for Limiting Immigration?

This appendix goes beyond economic issues into the more general arena of philosophical and political arguments concerning immigration. The appendix takes up the following question (the answer to which seems self-evident to most persons): is there any persuasive reason for a country to bar any healthy, law-abiding person from immigrating?

Many believe it is in the natural order of things that movement across borders should be limited. But prior to World War I, it was thought uncivilized for nations not to permit free movement, "an improper infringement of personal freedom," according to McNeil (1978, p. xiii); passports did not exist. And arguments about immigration based on "natural rights" all seem to be inconclusive, in part because the concept of rights does not apply to countries as well as it applies to individuals. Therefore, as with most other policies, we turn to judging the matter by considering its consequences.

For many, cultural homogeneity constitutes a reason to limit immigration. Though this is largely a matter of taste, one could investigate the consequences of restrictive policies based on cultural homogeneity for such social issues as economic freedom. But I know of no systematic evidence on the topic, and hence I shall leave it.

The consequence most worried about is that immigrants constitute a welfare burden. This worry usually runs contrary to the facts, however (see chapters 5 and 6), and a variety of policies – many of them already in place – can prevent welfare burden even in most individual cases.

Job displacement is another major concern. But a considerable body of recent research (see chapters 11 and 12) shows that immigrants do not in general have negative consequences on labor markets; rather, the consequences are generally positive. It is true that some particular groups may be injured by a particular group of immigrants. But the issues concerning a negative partial effect in the face of a positive general effect are the same as in the case of trade theory, and hence need not be considered further here.

The difficult questions − and therefore the possible justifications for controlling entry − arise with respect to externalities. Some externalities can be internalized by appropriate tax measures − for example the costs of school buildings and roads. But externalities such as schools having so many immigrant children that native children learn more slowly − an unlikely event, but one which must be considered in principle − cannot be easily internalized (though a voucher system might go a long way). It should be noted that other natives are not barred from entering a community on such grounds, however.

Societies which accept as legitimate that individuals have greater private obligations to those more closely affiliated with them − an effective mechanism for supplying help to those who need it, but one which tends to be suspect by the government in such societies as the USSR, even within the family − might also embody the same kinship principle in governmental actions. But it is likely that while this principle is constructive with respect to personal acts, it is destructive with respect to official action.

The most important externality is alteration in the economic and social system. If a large country were to flood a small country with immigrants for the purpose of taking it over democratically and then changing the system, this would threaten natives' property in their means of livelihood, because economic activities depend upon the social−political system. But such a possibility is quite unlikely. Furthermore, making the right to vote contingent upon citizenship, which is awarded only after some passage of time, might safeguard against this possibility. The same device should help ensure that at least the voting populace share basic civic values, a consensus which many writers argue is crucial for the satisfactory functioning of any society. Perhaps having non-voting residents with (at least at first) different values who might influence citizens − "foreign agitators and revolutionaries" − is a possible objection to immigration, but I do not know of any evidence to confirm that this is ever a realistic danger.

In short, the negative consequences of any level of immigration which is politically imaginable at present are at most speculative, rather than documented. Therefore, a policy which is both prudent and also consistent with these observations would be to increase immigration quotas in a series of increments of significant size − perhaps half a percent, or one percent, of total population at each step − to check on any unexpected negative consequences, and to determine whether demand for admission ever exceeds the supply of places.

Appendix B   Public Opinion toward Immigration

Public attitudes toward immigration certainly influence public policy, though the extent of the influence is unclear. Hence this section presents some facts about that public opinion.

R. Simon studied the major mass-circulation magazine articles on immigration over the past century, and also the available national US public-opinion polls that included questions about immigration, from the earliest polls in the 1930s through 1980 – mainly Gallup, NORC, and Harris surveys. Though the strength of the sentiment has varied, at all times the responses seemed to indicate that Americans were not in favor of more immigration (see table B.1). Fairly typical was a 1977 Gallup poll which asked: "Should immigration be kept at its present level, increased or decreased?" Seven percent said "Increased," 37 percent said "Present level," and 42 percent said "Decreased," with 14 percent "No opinion" (R. Simon, 1985, p. 41). And the widespread opinion among Americans that "most immigrants wind up on welfare" (47 percent, according to a 1986 poll; *New York Times*, 14 July 1986, p. 1) must be noted again.

Harwood interprets the poll data as showing that after World War II there occurred "a significant liberalization – certainly by comparison with the anti-alien restrictionism of the 1920s and 1930s" (1986, p. 202), but increasing restrictionism since then.

Public opinion may have been more negative in 1977 and 1982 than in 1965 and 1973, but the differences are not so large as to constitute overwhelming proof of a trend, given the vagaries of polling techniques and sample sizes. The positive swing toward the earlier levels in the 1986 poll, conducted just before the Statue of Liberty Centennial, may reflect that event and its hoopla, or may simply indicate sampling variation. The techniques of public opinion polls do not allow meaningful significance testing.

Table B.1 Public opinion concerning the volume of immigration

Year	Poll	Question	Response			
1953	NORC	In general, do you think the United States is letting too many immigrants come into this country or not enough?	Not enough 13	About the right number 37	Too many 39	Don't know 11
1965	Gallup	Should immigration be kept at its present level, increased or decreased?	Increased 8	Present level 39	Decreased 33	Don't know 20
1977	AIPO	Should immigration be kept at its present level, increased or decreased?	Increased 7	Present level 37	Decreased 42	No opinion 14
1982	Roper	In recent years, there has been a lot of discussion about the number of immigrants allowed into our country. On the whole, would you say that you would like to see the number of immigrants allowed to enter our country increased, or would like to see the number decreased, or do you think we are letting in about the right number now?	Increased 4	Right number now 23	Decreased 66	Don't know 7
1986	NY Times/CBS News	Exact text not given.	Increased 7	Kept at current level 35	Decreased 49	Don't know or no answer 9

Source: R. Simon, 1985

Another sort of question leaves a different impression, however. Americans have positive feelings toward the immigrants *in their own areas*, and towards the immigrants they know personally. The comparison can be seen clearly in a 1978 poll about Vietnamese immigrants. When asked, "Thinking now about the Indochinese refugees, the so-called 'boat people'; would you favor or oppose the United States relaxing its immigration policies so that many of these people could come to live in the United States?" 32 percent were in favor, 57 percent were opposed, with 11 percent no opinion. But when asked "Would you, yourself, like to see some of these people come to live in this community or not?" 48 percent said "yes," 40 percent said "no," with 13 percent no opinion. There is an interesting split in thought here, with the greater voiced opposition apparently being based upon abstract belief formed by the mass media, and the greater voiced support coming from personal experience with immigrants (R. Simon, 1985, p. 42).

Another indication of lack of consistency in public thinking about immigration is that people look back toward prior waves of immigration with more positive feelings than they have toward the present wave, whenever "present" is, according to R. Simon's study of magazines over the past century. She characterizes American public opinion throughout the century as "The immigrants who came in the past were good folks, but the people who are coming now are scum." For example, an 1888 article in *North American Review* — one of the major magazines of the day — urged curbing immigration because "the population that is coming today is semi-barbarous. They are willing and used to living in filthy crowded conditions," in contrast to immigrants prior to 1860 about whom the author said, "[W]e owe them our greatness as a nation; they gave us brain, bone, and muscle ... they were healthy and good" (R. Simon, 1985, p. 66). Sometimes "the past" means only five years previously, as was the case with the early and late waves of Vietnamese in the 1970s. This viewpoint constitutes an out-and-out logical contradiction, in that each wave of "scum" is a later generation's wave of "healthy and good."

Cafferty et al. made a similar observation:

At all times the restrictionists have counted among their number some of the best minds and some of the most public-spirited citizens of their respective eras. It is only in historical retrospect that their motives have been suspect. Indeed, the restrictionists were often at great pains to distinguish their arguments for restriction from those of previous generations. The argument today, as in the past, is that immigration until now, or until very recently, has been a good thing for our country, but now it must stop, or be sharply curtailed. The restrictionist, in other words, does not draw the line one hundred, fifty, or even twenty-five years in the past; he draws the line in his own time. However, even though he may be cast in the role of villain by immigration historians, the restrictionist has been honest in speaking about one side of the dilemma, namely, the fear of immigration that lurks in all of us. (1983, p. 12)

Governmental policy toward immigration seems to have been more positive than public opinion. This disjunction has existed as far back as records exist, not only in the polls era but also in earlier times, as seen in a survey of magazine articles. The same themes heard now were heard then. For example, in 1890, well-known Congressman Henry Cabot Lodge wrote that "We now have a large population, the ... increase of which is quite sufficient. ... Our labor market ... is over-stocked in many places and that means a tendency toward a decline of wages" (R. Simon, 1985, p. 66). With respect to illegal immigrants, the following appeared in a 1937 issue of *Literary Digest*:

We have within our gates a vast and rather sinister army of aliens who for reasons of their own, thought it best to avoid the officials posted at our port of entry. We are giving millions of them jobs. We are supporting millions more in charity. (R. Simon, 1985, p. 128)

Yet the US did admit immigrants – fewer than might have been desirable, but more than would seem consistent with public opinion.

The fact that public opinion has been, and still is, against immigration in the abstract seems explainable to a considerable extent by what is written in the press and shown on television, in conjunction nowadays with anti-immigration organizations. Consider these results from the June 1986 *New York Times*/CBS News poll. Forty-nine percent of respondents said that "Most recent immigrants are here illegally." That opinion is starkly contradicted by the facts presented by a blue-ribbon study of the Census Bureau in 1980, and even more so by a study published earlier in 1986 by the National Academy of Science. How else can one explain the public being so misinformed than by the frequent repetitions in the press and on television of unfounded estimates of illegal immigration rates, and dramatic accounts of the entries of illegal aliens into the US?

Also, 47 percent of the public said in 1986 that "Most new immigrants end up on welfare," though the average immigrant family receives less transfers and services from the government than does the average native family, and pays more in taxes than the average native family (see chapter 5). Is there any other plausible explanation of the wrong public impression than wrong information being provided by the press?

Another interesting finding of the June 1986 poll is that the proportions who believe that immigration should be decreased among "liberals," "moderates," and "conservatives" are 48 percent, 45 percent, and 57 percent, relatively small differences. The issue of immigration cuts across all political groupings.

It is of some interest to consider who is for and who is against immigration. R. Simon finds that persons with more education and income are consistently more positive toward immigration than are persons with less education and income.

Also relevant is a 1983 poll of 800 black and 800 Hispanic respondents sponsored by the anti-immigration organization Federation for American Immigration Reform (FAIR). FAIR's spokesman claimed that "One of the interesting findings is that Hispanic Americans and black Americans feel about the same way as Americans as a whole on the immigration issue" (Roger Conner, cited by Congressional Research Service, 1984, p. 4). But the Congressional Research Service re-analyzed the data and pointed out that the poll did not interview any non-Hispanic whites, and therefore had no basis for such a comparative statement. CRS then went further and searched their computerized poll data base for other surveys that might allow the comparison at issue. They found that "Generally, the other studies show that Hispanics are less likely to favor measures to restrict immigration than non-Hispanics, but more likely to be concerned with the issue" (p. 4).

The appropriate conclusion, then, is that Hispanics are *not* as likely as are Americans at large to be in favor of restricting immigration, contrary to the statement on the subject widely circulated by FAIR.

I hazard the following generalizations about those who are against immigration:

1 The labor unions have always been the strongest opposition to immigration. And they have enlisted intellectuals who offer apologies for their position.
2 Many intellectuals who worry about greater labor-market competition for poor persons are against immigration. Consider for example this incomprehensible economic logic from Ray Marshall (1984), a professor of economics who also was Secretary of Labor: "Employers arguing that they will 'go out of business' without aliens are really saying that they cannot survive without subsidies. Alien labor willing to work at low wages is a labor subsidy, just as a low interest loan is a capital subsidy."
3 Environmentalists and population-control advocates worry about immigrants increasing the "pressure" upon resources and crowding in nature reserves.
4 Those who, out of a lack of understanding of how a decentralized market economy develops through spontaneous evolution, worry about "chaos" and "loss of government control" oppose immigration. As an example, consider this language from the major force behind the movement for immigration "reform" in the first half of the 1980s, Senator Alan

Simpson: "the first duty of a sovereign nation is to control its border" (1986, p. 7), a view that would startle the Founding Fathers of the US, I believe. Or from Governor Lamm of Colorado: "Can we have today's immigration, virtually out of control, and still remain 'one nation, indivisible'" (1986, p. 1).

5   The most interesting and − aside from the labor movement − perhaps most important category of persons who oppose immigration are those for whom immigrants represent persons of different race and culture. This sentiment need not be race hate or dislike, but can be a taste for maintenance of one's own culture, or for cultural homogeneity. In 1986 Prime Minister Nakasone "said Japan's racial homogeneity has helped it become a more 'intelligent society' than the United States, 'where there are blacks, Mexicans and Puerto Ricans and the level is still quite low'" (*Wall Street Journal*, 13 November 1986, p. 1). The Japanese are extremely loath to admit "gaijin" (foreigners), even as apparently desirable a person as an American business executive who was born and educated in Japan, speaks accentless Japanese, and is married to a Japanese; landlords were so reluctant to have such a person in the neighborhood that it was extremely difficult for him and his family to find an apartment (Fields, 1986). And Prime Minister Margaret Thatcher of Great Britain declared in a television speech that the British fear "being swamped by people of a different culture," and that Great Britain therefore "must hold out the clear prospect of an end to immigration" (Population Reference Bureau, 1978, p. 3). Thatcher's nativist attitude has strongly influenced British policy. Following the deportation of a Sri Lankan refugee, the *Washington Post* reported:

Since assuming office in 1979, Thatcher's Conservatives have gradually whittled down the number of refugees welcomed in Britain by lessening the right of appeal and limiting the right to work .... [B]efore Thatcher took office, Britain was ranked among the top 15 countries as a haven on a refugee-to-population basis. Today it no longer ranks among the top 15 .... In 1987 West Germany received 57,000 applications for asylum, while Britain received only 4,000. (21 January 1989, p. A20)

At least some of this sentiment surely is simple racism, however; there was plenty of evidence of this in the days before the expression of such a sentiment was unacceptable. For example, the intelligence-test movement early in this century fueled the eugenicists who argued that the then-immigrants, largely from Southern and Eastern Europe (many of them Jews), were uneducable and could not be assimilated because "They are morons and imbeciles," as one Doctor of Philosophy put it in a magazine article (R. Simon, 1985, p. 74). Another magazine article statement on the subject by an economics professor:

According to every test made in recent years ... it is evident beyond doubt that the immigrants from Northern and Western Europe are far superior to the ones from Southern and Eastern Europe. The vital thing is to preserve the American race − build it up with Nordic stock: intelligent, literate, easily assimilated, appreciated and able to carry on our American institutes. (R. Simon, 1985, p. 75)

Or a professor of zoology writing in 1919: "First it was the Negroes, then it was the Chinese and Japanese, now it is the Mexicans. Soon it will be the Filipinos" who "bred like flies" and who carried disease (R. Simon, p. 76). In other countries where there is less of a taboo on speaking frankly about the matter, one still hears such views nowadays. This statement was issued by a group of German professors in early 1982:

It is with grave concern that we observe the infiltration of the German nation by millionfold waves of foreigners and their families, the infiltration of our language, our culture, and our national characteristics by foreign influences ...

Biologically and cybernetically, nations are living systems of a higher order, with different system qualities that are transmitted genetically and by tradition. The integration of large masses of non-German foreigners and the preservation of our nation thus cannot be achieved simultaneously; it will lead to the well-known ethnic catastrophes of multi-cultural societies. (*Population and Development Review, viii* (3), 1982, pp. 636−7)

Nowadays, in the US, it is difficult to determine the motivation for opposition to immigration. What does one make of a statement by the governor of Colorado warning that "Ethnic, racial and religious differences can become a wedge; they can grow and eventually splinter a community"? (Lamm, 1986, p. 1).

Here are some speculations about those who are *in favor* of more immigration:

1   Those who wish to bring more of their countrymen from abroad often are in favor. But it should be noted that this impulse often wanes quickly after arrival. As a magazine writer noted in 1914: "Immigrants who came earlier and their descendants have always tried to keep this country for those who were already here and for their kin folk" (quoted by R. Simon, 1985, p. 73).
2   "Cosmopolitans" who take an all-world rather than a nationalistic view.
3   Those who are moved by the putative "US tradition of immigration."
4   Libertarians, on principle with respect to individual rights.

5   Those who worry about refugees.
6   Economists who recognize benefits to the economy as a whole, though seeing that some subgroups might be temporarily hurt.
7   Employers of unskilled labor such as fruit growers.

Native Hispanics and blacks seem to be ambivalent about immigration.

Appendix C Views of Economists and other Social Scientists toward Immigration

STEPHEN MOORE and JULIAN L. SIMON

There is agreement among economists that immigration has had, and has now, a positive effect upon the economic condition of the US. We surveyed those persons who have been president of the American Economic Association, as well as those who have been members of the President's Council of Economic Advisors. In answer to the question "On balance, what effect has twentieth century immigration had on the nation's economic growth?" 81 percent answered "Very favorable," and 19 percent answered "Slightly favorable." (Complete data may be found at the end of this appendix.) None of these top economists said that immigration was "slightly" or "very unfavorable," or felt that he or she did not know enough to answer. This extraordinary consensus belies the public picture of the economic profession as being on both sides of all important matters.

The top economists also are willing to extend their backward assessment into a forward-looking policy judgment. When asked "What level of immigration would have the most favorable impact on the US standard of living?", 56 percent said "more," 33 percent said "same number," and none said "fewer." Only 11 percent said "don't know."

It is instructive to compare the views of persons who are not experts in economic affairs. To the latter question about the level of immigration that would be most favorable for the standard of living, a similar high-level panel of other social scientists – sociologists, political scientists, anthropologists, psychologists, and historians – responded less favorably. Only 31 percent said that more immigrants would be most favorable. It is also startling to find that even though these non-economist social scientists have no expert knowledge of the matter, only 4 percent were unwilling to hazard a judgment and hence said "don't know," an even smaller proportion than the 11 percent among economists. Perhaps the lack of reluctance of such non-experts to express their views on this technical subject outside their fields of special knowledge helps explain why the subject of immigration is as controversial as it is.

For further comparison, consider the polls of the general public (discussed in appendix B) asking a fairly similar question, not about the economic effects of immigration, but the more general "Would you like to see the number of immigrants allowed to enter our country increase, decline, or do you think we are letting in about the right number now?" It cannot be known whether the general public response is mainly based on non-economic or economic factors. But to the extent that economic factors enter in, the reaction of the general public is much more negative, and much less positive, than the assessment of top economists.

(How should we interpret other social scientists giving more positive responses to these economic questions than other Americans – even if less positive than economists? One possibility is that the general pattern of higher education being more associated with a positive view of immigration is being displayed here. Another possibility: world-class tenured professors have relatively little to fear from immigrant job competition. But these are speculations rather than facts.)

We also asked economists about the economic effect of *illegal* immigration. The question was: What impact does *illegal* immigration in its current magnitude have on the US economy?" An astonishing 74 percent of the top economists said that "Illegals have a positive impact." Eleven percent said "neutral impact," and 11 percent said "negative impact," with 4 percent "don't know." This is indeed a striking degree of consensus.

This consensus view about illegals held by top economists certainly is at variance with the point of view expressed by most columnists, editorial writers, and television commentators. And the consensus view of economists is quite different from the view held by other top social scientists. Fifty-one percent of the other social scientists said "negative impact" about the economic effect of illegals, with only 7 percent "don't know", it is likely that the general public is even more negative toward illegals. One can only wonder what motivates this view of economic effects of illegals on the part of others than economists. And I marvel at the lack of uncertainty indicated by the small proportion of non-economists who do not feel qualified to answer.

The discrepancy between the view expressed by the economists and that expressed by the other social scientists and by the lay public fits with a general pattern in which laypersons are more worried by many phenomena than are real experts; nuclear power is a striking example (see Cohen, 1984). And at a meeting of world-class experts on agriculture, minerals, oil, forests, soil erosion, and a variety of related natural resource topics, geographer Fraser Hart observed at the end of the day: "All of us are optimistic about our own subjects, but pessimistic about everyone else's," a clear indication of the negative bias on the part of less-informed persons that pervades discussion of resources and demographic movements.

When we asked the non-economist social scientists about the *non-economic* effects of immigrants, a subject on which they have professional expertise, their judgments are of a different sort. In answer to "What effect has twentieth century immigration into the United States had on the nation's social fabric?" 47 percent said "very favorable," 24 percent said "slightly favorable," 13 percent said "slightly unfavorable," and 9 percent said "very unfavorable," with 7 percent "don't know." And in answer to "What effect has twentieth century immigration into the United States had on the nation's culture?" 59 percent said "very favorable," 27 percent said "slightly favorable," 7 percent said "slightly unfavorable," and 2 percent said "very unfavorable," with 5 percent "don't know."

These assessments by non-economic social scientists of immigration's non-economic effects are quite positive. And here it would seem that – even though such terms as "culture" and "social fabric" may well mean very different things to different people – the social scientists have this expert advice to give to the American public, derived from their scholarly work: lay aside your worries (and claims) about conflict and social tension outweighing the positive social–cultural effects of immigration.

So to sum up: if the best economists understand their subject, immigrants – including illegal immigrants – benefit the economy; they find no economic reason to try not to admit more immigrants, or to prevent the entry of the sort of workers that illegals are, or to get rid of them. This directly contradicts the economic arguments that are given by such organizations as FAIR and The Environmental Fund, which lobby against immigration, as well as the arguments of the labor unions and of such legislators as Senator Alan Simpson. But the views of such well-respected mainstream economists are not reported by journalists, who tend to rely instead upon politicians and interest-group advocates for their print stories and television interviews. And the views of the top economists are seldom heard in the current Congressional debate on immigration.

Table C.1   The full poll results (responses in percentages from a sample of 27 top economists and 55 top non-economist social scientists)

Question:
On balance, what effect has twentieth-century immigration had on the nation's economic growth?

	Economists	Other social scientists
Very favorable	81	51
Slightly favorable	19	31
Slightly unfavorable	–	2
Very unfavorable	–	2
Don't know	–	14

Question:
What level of immigration would have the most favorable impact on the US standard of living?

	Economists	Other social scientists
More	56	31
Same number	33	47
Fewer	0	18
Don't know	11	4

Question:
Do you feel that recent immigrants are qualitatively different in economic terms from immigrants in past years?

	Economists	Other social scientists
More negative impact	7	16
About the same impact	70	60
More positive impact	4	10
Don't know	19	14

Question:
What impact does *illegal* immigration in its current magnitude have on the US economy?

	Economists	Other social scientists
Illegals have a positive impact	74	18
Illegals have a neutral impact	11	24
Illegals have a negative impact	11	51
Don't know	4	7

Question:
What effect has twentieth-century immigration into the United States had on the nation's social fabric?

	Other social scientists
Very favorable	47
Slightly favorable	24
Slightly unfavorable	13
Very unfavorable	9
Don't know	7

Question:
What effect has twentieth-century immigration into the United States had on the nation's culture?

	Other social scientists
Very favorable	59
Slightly favorable	27
Slightly unfavorable	7
Very unfavorable	2
Don't know	5

Question:
Do you feel that recent immigrants are qualitatively different in socio-psychological terms from immigrants in past years?

	Other social scientists
Recent immigrants are less likely to assimilate	36
Recent immigrants are about as likely to assimilate	52
Recent immigrants are more likely to assimilate	7
Don't know	5

Appendix D   Immigration, International Relations, and National Security

It is a truism for many people in and out of government that population growth from natural increase and immigration has an unsettling effect resulting in political instability, war, and revolution, especially in poor countries. And positive effects of immigration upon our international relations are seldom referred to.

The body of scientific literature on population growth and war is thin. But to the extent that there is systematic analysis, I read the conclusion as being that there is no connection between population growth and war or other political instability due to the struggle for economic resources. The classic inquiry into the causes of war is that of Wright, and in his short summary in the *Encyclopedia of Social Sciences* he says:

Population pressure, which produces progressive impoverishment, has had little influence in producing war unless accompanied by increased knowledge of economic differentials and by inciting propaganda.

In sum, studies of both the direct and indirect influence of economic factors on the causation of war indicate that they have been much less important than political ambitions, ideological convictions, technological change, legal claims, irrational psychological complexes, ignorance, and unwillingness to maintain conditions of peace in a changing world. (Wright, 1968, pp. 462–3)

Choucri (1975) concludes that what she calls "demographic" factors sometimes lead to conflict, either violent or non-violent. But her key demographic factor is the *relative* increase in the size of one ethnic group relative to another, rather than *absolute* increase in population size or population density. The importance of this distinction can be seen most clearly by listing the wars that she considers "archetypical cases" of "population dynamics and local conflict." These are: the Algerian War of Independence, 1954–62; the Nigerian civil war; the two wars involving Indonesia;

the conflict in Ceylon; El Salvador—Honduras; and the Arab—Israeli series of wars (p. 135). In my view, none of these are conflicts undertaken to obtain additional land or mineral resources in order to increase the standard of living of the group initiating the conflict. To show that population growth causes conflict, one would need to show that two neighboring countries or groups, *both* of whom are growing rapidly, are more likely to come into conflict than two neighboring countries or groups *neither* of whom are growing rapidly. This Choucri has not shown. As Choucri views the matter, conflict could as easily be caused by one country or group *reducing* its growth rate relative to another country or group, as by one *increasing* its relative growth rate. And in fact many writers have argued that this was the case with France and Germany — that because France's birth rate was so low it induced the French—German wars. Now in the 1980s, Wattenberg (1987) argues that the low US birth rate constitutes a danger vis-à-vis the Soviet Union.

Immigration may also affect our peacetime relationships with other countries and peoples. Hardin and The Environmental Fund offer the ingenious argument that it is really idealistic of the US to keep out immigrants, because doing so allows the US to keep itself strong and therefore able to help the rest of the world; if the US were economically weak, they say, the rest of the world would not have the benefit of its technological contributions. But as long as the US recognizes that admitting the immigrants makes it *stronger* rather than weaker, scientifically as well as economically (and, of course, militarily), this argument — though it is not ethically inconsistent — is seen to be empty.

Permit me to repeat that there is no ethical dilemma. The US does *not* need to balance the gains to others against the sacrifice to itself. Because the US does good for itself at the same time that it does good for immigrants, on balance, we do not need to consider the ethical basis of simply drawing a boundary line around the nation and saying that only those who are lucky enough to be born within the line are entitled to chances that are denied to others for selfish reasons.

Going beyond the economic mechanisms described earlier in the book, immigrants (and their children) can help US export campaigns by speaking foreign buyers' languages and by sharing their cultures. The US worries enough about languages that the federal government funds programs to teach *native* Americans foreign languages for this purpose. One does not require a careful evaluation and an explicit cost—benefit analysis to see how inferior is the latter device compared to admitting immigrants. Consider the following news story:

Guzow, Poland — In the staff dining room of the Guzow Vegetable Experiment Station, Marian Dobrowolski watches, expressionless, as the waitress crosses the bare tiles and sets before him a platter of french-fried potatoes . . .

This is the most important moment in the entire crisis-ridden history of the McDonald's Polish potato project. McDonald's Corp. wants to grow potatoes here; it wants to serve them in its restaurants in Western Europe. The Poles want to grow them. But can they accept the immutable world-wide anti-deviationist standards of the golden french fry? Can McDonald's impose its system on Poland?

That is what Mr. Dobrowolski has come to find out. He was born in Poland 66 years ago. But since 1956 he has lived in the U. S., and for 18 years his office has been on Ronald Lane in Oak Brook, Ill. He is the man from McDonald's. (*Wall Street Journal*, 9 October 1986, p. 1)

Another illustration is found in an article entitled: "Brazil's Japanese population thrives, helps Tokyo forge ties with Brasilia." The article goes on to tell about a

growing community of 800,000 Brazilians of Japanese descent, the largest collection of ethnic Japanese outside Japan. They include farmers, bankers, bureaucrats, engineers and politicians. And they are an important link in ripening financial ties between Brazil and Japan, two of the world's fastest growing economies.

"The Japanese are more cooperative with Brazil in investing and financing than traditional industrial countries. They are very aggressive in international trade. Maybe you could say we have a special relationship," says Ernane Galveas, Brazil's finance minister. (*Wall Street Journal*, 24 September 1982, p. 25)

The personal tie that builds up between countries when there is immigration from one country to the other, even across gulfs of ideology and conflict, is also a political benefit, of course. The Polish–US and Greek–US connections are prime examples. Think how useful it would be to increase such felt connections with China, India, Indonesia, Brazil, and other countries. There is also something of a hostage effect here. (Was it Swift who suggested that a good way to prevent war would be to have the children of the national leaders of hostile countries living in the capital cities of their opponents? Having the adult children study in the opposite-number countries could be a practical step of that sort today. Immigrants can serve a similar purpose.)

References and Bibliography

Abbott, Edith (1931): *Report on Crime and the Foreign Born*, National Commission on Law Observance and Enforcement (Washington, DC: Government Printing Office)

Adams, Walter (ed.) (1968): *The Brain Drain* (New York: Macmillan)

Agarwala, A. N., and S. P. Singh (eds.) (1963): *The Economics of Underdevelopment* (New York: Oxford University Press)

Aigner, D. J., and A. J. Heins (1967): "On the Determinants of Income Equality," *American Economic Review*, 57(1), pp. 175–81

Alchian, Armen, and Susan Woodward (1986): "Reflections on the Theory of the Firm," unpublished typescript (August)

Alonso, William (1975): "The Economics of Urban Size." In John Friedman and William Alonso (eds), *Regional Policy Readings in Theory and Applications* (Cambridge, MA: MIT Press)

Alonso, William, and Michael Fajans (1970): "Cost of Living and Income by Urban Size," mimeo

Anderson, Annelise (1986): *Illegal Aliens and Employer Sanctions: Solving the Wrong Problem* (Stanford, CA: Hoover Institution)

Angle, Paul (ed.) (1954): *The Lincoln Reader* (New York: Pocket Books)

Arnold, Fred, Benjamin V. Carino, James T. Fawcett, and Insook Han Park (1987): "The Potential for Future Immigration to the United States: A Policy Analysis for Korea and the Philippines," unpublished paper given at the Annual Meeting of the Population Association of America, 30 April–2 May

Arthur, W. Brian, and Geoffrey McNicoll (1976): "Samuelson, Population, and the Transfer Effect," mimeo

Bach, Robert L. (1979): "Employment Characteristics of Indochinese Refugees: January 1979," *Migration Today*, 8(3), pp. 10–14

Bachu, Amara, and Martin O'Connell (forthcoming): "Developing Current Fertility Indicators for Foreign-born Women from the Current Population Survey," *Review of Public Data Use*

Bahral, Uri (1965): *The Effect of Mass Immigration on Wages in Israel* (Jerusalem: Falk Project)

Bailyn, Bernard (1986): "Does a Free-born Englishman have a Right to Emigrate?," *American Heritage*, 37(2), pp. 24–31

Baker, Lyle (1986): "Migrants in the Labour Market," Australian Department of Immigration and Ethnic Affairs, [publication] no. 35

Baker, Lyle (1987): "Immigration and Per Capita Investment," unpublished paper given at a conference at Australian National University, 22–3 April

Baker, Reginald, and David S. North (1984): "The 1975 Refugees: Their First Five Years in America," mimeo

Baker, Stephen (1984): "Migrants in the Australian Labour Market, 1972–1983: An Analysis of Participation and Unemployment," Bureau of Labour Market Research, Canberra (September)

Barnett, Harold J., and Chandler Morse (1963): *Scarcity and Growth: The Economics of Natural Resource Availability* (Baltimore, MD: Johns Hopkins University Press)

Bartel, Ann P. (1982): "Location Decisions of the New Immigrants to the United States," mimeo

Basavarajappa, K. G., and Ravi B. P. Verma (1985): "Asian Immigrants in Canada: Some Findings from the 1981 Census," *International Migration Review*, 23(1), pp. 97–121

Bass, Frank M. (1978): "The Relationship between Diffusion Rates, Experience Curves, and Demand Elasticities for Consumer Durable Technological Innovations," Paper no. 660, Institute for Research in the Behavioral, Economic and Management Schools, Purdue University, Lafayette, IN, mimeo

Baum, Barbara M. (1981): untitled mimeo, US Department of State, 5 March

Bean, Frank D., Allan G. King, and Jeffrey S. Passel (1983): "The Number of Illegal Migrants of Mexican Origin in the United States: Sex Ratio-based Estimates for 1980," *Demography*, 20(1), pp. 99–109

Bean, Frank D., B. Lindsay Lowell, and Lowell J. Taylor (1988): "Undocumented Mexican Immigrants and the Earnings of Other Workers in the United States," *Demography*, 25(1), pp. 35–52

Becker, Gary S. (1966): "A Theory of the Allocation of Time," *Ekistics*, 21(126), p. 321

Becker, Gary S. (1976): *The Economic Approach to Human Behavior* (Chicago, IL: University of Chicago Press)

Becker, Gary S. (1987): "A Radical Proposal to Improve Immigration Policy," mimeo

Bell, David A. (1985): "The Triumph of Asian-Americans," *New Republic*, 15–22 July, p. 26

Berry, Albert, and Maria Mendez (1976): "Emigration of Highly Educated Manpower: A Problem for Colombian Educational Policy?" In Bhagwati (1976), pp. 247–76

Berry, Albert R., and Ronald Soligo (1969): "Some Welfare Aspects of International Migration," *Journal of Political Economy*, 77 (September/October), pp. 778–94

Bethe, H. A. (1976): "The Necessity of Fission Power," *Scientific American*, 234(1), pp. 16–18

Bhagwati, Jagdish (1982): "Taxation and International Migration: Recent Policy Issues." In Barry R. Chiswick (ed.), *The Gateway: U.S. Immigration Issues and Policies* (Washington, DC: American Enterprise Institute)

Bhagwati, Jagdish (ed.) (1976): *The Brain Drain and Taxation*, vol. 2: *Theory and Empirical Analysis* (New York: North-Holland)

Birch, David L. (1981): "Who Creates Jobs?," *Public Interest*, 65, pp. 3–14

Birrell, Bob (1976): "How Many Migrants?," *Australian Society*, 22 October

Blau, Francine D. (1980): "Immigration and Labor Earnings in Early Twentieth Century America." In Simon and Da Vanzo (1980), pp. 21–41

Blau, Francine D. (1984): "The Use of Transfer Payments by Immigrants," *Industrial Labor Relations Review*, 37(2), pp. 222–39

Blomqvist, Ake G. (1985): "Unemployment of the Educated and Emigration of Post-Secondary Graduates from the LDCs," *Pakistan Development Review*, 24(3, 4)

Blomqvist, Ake G. (1986): "International Migration of Educated Manpower and Social Rates of Return to Education in LDCs," *International Economic Review*, 27(1), pp. 165ff.

Bloom, David E., and Richard B. Freeman (1986a): "The 'Youth Problem': Age or Generation Crowding?," National Bureau of Economic Research, Working Paper no. 1829 (February)

Bloom, David E., and Richard B. Freeman (1986b): "Population Growth, Labor Supply, and Employment in Developing Countries," Discussion Paper, Harvard Institute of Economic Research (February)

Bogan, Marcos W. (1980): "The Central American Experience in the U.S. Labor Force: Costa Rica and El Salvador, a Preliminary View," Discussion Paper, Istituto de Estudios Sociales de Población, Universidad Nacional, Heredia, Costa Rica

Bogue, Donald J. (1985): *The Population of the United States: Historical Trends and Future Projections* (New York: Free Press)

368   References and Bibliography

Bohning, W. R. (1972): *The Migration of Workers in the United Kingdom and the European Community* (London: Oxford University Press)

Bonacich, Edna, and John Modell (1980): *The Economic Basis of Ethnic Solidarity* (Berkeley and Los Angeles, CA, and London: University of California Press)

Bonacich, Edna, Ivan H. Light, and Charles C. Wong (1977): "Koreans in Business," *Society*, 14, pp. 54–9

Borjas, George J. (1982): "The Earnings of Male Hispanic Immigrants in the United States," *Industrial and Labor Relations Review*, 35(3), pp. 343–53

Borjas, George J. (1983): "The Substitutability of Black, Hispanic, and White Labor," *Economic Inquiry*, xxi (January), pp. 93–106

Borjas, George J. (1985a): "Assimilation, Changes in Cohort Quality, and the Earnings of Immigrants," *Journal of Labor Economics*, 3(4), pp. 463–89

Borjas, George J. (1985b): "The Self-employment of Immigrants," Discussion Paper nos 783–5, Institute for Research on Poverty, University of Madison, WI (October)

Borts, George H., and Jerome L. Stein (1966): *Economic Growth in a Free Market* (New York: Columbia University Press)

Boserup, Ester (1965): *The Conditions of Economic Growth* (London, George Allen and Unwin)

Boyd, Monica (1979): "Immigrants, Income Attainment, and Labour Markets in Canada," unpublished paper given at the Annual Meeting of the Population Association of America (April)

Boyd, Monica (1980): "The Double Negative: Female Immigrants in the Canadian Labour Force," unpublished paper given at the Annual Meeting of the Population Association of America, (April)

Brain, Peter J., Rhonda L. Smith, and Gerard P. Schuyers (1979): *Population, Immigration, and the Australian Economy* (London: Croom Helm)

Bridgman, P. W. (1945): "The Prospect for Intelligence," *Yale Review*, xxxiv (Spring), 444–61

Briggs, Vernon M., Jr. (1984): *Immigration Policy and the American Labor Force* (Baltimore, MD: Johns Hopkins University Press)

Brown, Lester (1974): *In the Human Interest: A Strategy to Stabilize World Population* (New York: Norton)

Browning, Edgar K., and William R. Johnson (1979): *The Distribution of the Tax Burden* (Washington, DC: American Enterprise Institute)

Browning, Mark (1979): "The Effect of Population Growth on Income Growth in LDCs," unpublished paper given at the Annual Meeting of the Population Association of America (April)

Buchanan, James M., and Richard E. Wagner (1970): "An Efficiency Basis for Federal Fiscal Taxation." In Julius Margolis (ed.), *The Analysis of Public Output* (New York: NBER–Columbia University Press), pp. 139–62

Bustamente, Jorge (1977): "Undocumented Migration from Mexico: Research Report," *International Migration Review*, 11(2), pp. 149–77

Cafferty, Pastora San Juan, Barry R. Chiswick, Andrew M. Greeley, and Teresa A. Sullivan (1983): *The Dilemma of American Immigration: Beyond the Golden Door* (New Brunswick: Transaction Books)

Cannan, Edwin (1931): "The Changed Outlook in Regard to Population, 1831–1931," *Economic Journal*, xli (December), pp. 519–32

Caplan, Nathan (1985): "Working toward Self-Sufficiency," *ISR Newsletter* (Spring/Summer), pp. 5, 7

Cardenas, Gilbert (1978): "The Manpower Impact of Mexican Illegal Aliens in the San Antonio Labor Market in the Seventies," mimeo, Pan American University, Edinburgh, TX (March)

Castles, Stephen, and Godula Kosack (1973): *Immigrant Workers and Class Structure in Western Europe* (New York: Oxford University Press)

Cato Policy Report (1986): "Employer Sanctions or Open Borders?," viii(5), pp. 6–9

CENIET (Centro Nacional de Información y Estadisticas del Trabajo) (1982): "Informe final: Los trabajadores mexicanos en los Estados Unidos (Encuesta Nacional de Emigración a la Frontera Norte del Pais y a los Estados Unidos–ENEFNEU)," unpublished paper, Mexico City

Center for the Study of Democratic Institutions (1978): advertising flier

Central Bureau of Statistics, Israel (various years): "Survey on Absorption of Immigrants," Special Series

Central Bureau of Statistics, Israel (various years): "Supplements to the Monthly Bulletin of Statistics"

Chaney, Elsa M. (1977): "The New Immigrant Wave – Colombian Outpost in New York City," *Society*, 14(6), pp. 60–4

Chapman, Bruce J., David Pope, and Glenn Withers (1985): "Immigration and the Labour Market," unpublished typescript

Chapman, Leonard (1976): unpublished paper given at the Annual Meeting of the Population Association of America 30 April

Chenery, Hollis B. (1960): "Patterns of Industrial Growth," *American Economic Review*, 50, pp. 624–54

Chesnais, Jean-Claude, and Alfred Sauvy (1973): "Progrès économique et accroisement de la population, une expérience commentée," *Population*, 28, pp. 843–57

Childe, Gordon (1942): *What Happened in History?* (Baltimore, MD: Penguin), p. 254

Chiswick, Barry R. (1977): "A Longitudinal Analysis of the Occupational Mobility of Immigrants," *Proceedings of the 30th Annual Winter Meeting of the Industrial Relations Research Association, New York City, 28–30 December*

Chiswick, Barry, R. (1978): "Immigrants and Immigration Policy." In William Fellner (ed.), *Contemporary Economic Problems* (Washington, DC: American Enterprise Institute), pp. 285–325

Chiswick, Barry R. (1978): "The Effects of Americanization on the Earnings of Foreign-Born Men," *Journal of Political Economy*, 86(5), pp. 897–921

Chiswick, Barry R. (1979): "The Economic Progress of Immigrants to Form Apparently Universal Patterns." In William Fellner (ed.), *Contemporary Economic Problems, 1979* (Washington, DC: DEL)

Chiswick, Barry R. (1980): "The Earnings of White and Coloured Male Immigrants in Britain," *Economica*, 47(185), pp. 81–7

Chiswick, Barry R. (ed.) (1982): *The Gateway: U.S. Immigration Issues and Policies* (Washington, DC: American Enterprise Institute)

Chiswick, Barry, R. (1984): "Human Capital and the Labor Market Adjustment of Immigrants: Testing Alternative Hypotheses," Discussion Paper no. 7, Migration and Development Program, Harvard University (March)

Chiswick, Barry R. (1985a): "Is the New Immigration More Unskilled than the Old?," Working Papers in Economics no. E-85-6, Hoover Institution (February)

Chiswick, Barry R. (1985b): "Methodological Issues in the Analysis of Immigrant Adjustment and Impact," Working Papers in Economics no. E-85-16, Hoover Institution (June), p. 15

Chiswick, Barry R., Carmel U. Chiswick, and Paul W. Miller (1985): "Are Immigrants and Natives Perfect Substitutes in Production?" *International Migration Review*, 19(4), pp. 674–85

Choucri, Nazli, and Robert North (1975): *Nations in Conflict – National Growth and International Violence* (San Francisco, CA: W. H. Freeman)

Church World Service Immigration and Refugee Program (1983): *Making It on their Own: From Refugee Sponsorship to Self-Sufficiency*, Survey

Clark, Colin (1967a): *Conditions of Economic Progress*, 3rd edn (New York: Macmillan)

Clark, Colin (1967b): *Population Growth and Land Use* (New York: St Martin's Press)

Clark, Robert L., and J. J. Spengler (1979): "Dependency Ratios: Their Use in Economic Analysis." In Simon and Da Vanzo (1980), pp. 63–76

Clodman, Joel, and Anthony H. Richmond (1981): "Immigration and Unemployment," Discussion Paper, York University Institute for Behavioral Research, Downsview, Ontario; revised March 1982

Cohen, Bernard L. (1984): "The Hazards of Nuclear Power." In Simon and Kahn (1984), pp. 545–65

Commons, John R. (1924): *Races and Immigrants in America*, 3rd edn (New York: Macmillan)

Community Research Associates (1980): *Undocumented Immigrants: Their Impact on the County of San Diego*, mimeo (May)

Congressional Research Service (1984): Memorandum to congressional

Hispanic Caucus, from Daniel Melnick, Head, Survey Research Section Government Division on Analysis of the Poll on Attitudes towards Immigration conducted by Lance Tarrance and Associates and Peter Hart, Associates, 27 February

Conner, Roger (1980): "Immigration in the Era of Limits," *Los Angeles Times*, 17 February, part iv, p. 5

Conner, Roger (1982): *Breaking down the Barriers: The Changing Relationship between Illegal Immigration and Welfare*, FAIR Immigration Paper iv (September)

Conner, Roger, and Julian L. Simon (1984): "How Immigrants Affect Americans' Living Standard: A Debate between Julian Simon and Roger Conner" (Washington, DC: Heritage Foundation)

Cooper, Shelley, and Joanne Constantinides (1984): "Working Paper Reviewing the Experience of the Overseas-Born in the Labour Market," Population and Research Branch, US Department of Immigration and Ethnic Affairs (September)

Cornelius, Wayne A. (1976): "Mexican Migration to the United States: The View from Rural Sending Communities," Working Paper, Center for International Studies, MIT

Cornelius, Wayne A. (1977): "Illegal Migration to the United States: Recent Research Findings, Policy Implications, and Research Priorities," mimeo, Center for International Studies, MIT (May)

Cornelius, Wayne A. (1978): "Mexican Migration to the United States: Causes, Consequences, and U.S. Responses," Working Paper, Center for International Studies, MIT (July)

Crewdson, John (1983): *The Tarnished Door* (New York: Times Books)

Cross, H. E., and J. A. Sandos (1981): *Across the Border: Rural Development in Mexico and Recent Migration to the United States* (Berkeley, CA: Institute of Governmental Studies, University of California, Berkeley)

Davie, Maurice R., et al. (1947): *Refugees in America* (New York: Harper & Brothers)

Davies, Gordon W. (1977): "Macroeconomic Effects of Immigration: Evidence from Candice, Trace, and RDX2," *Canadian Public Policy*, 3(3), pp. 299–306

Davis, Kingsley, and Pietronella van den Oever (no date): "Demographic Change and Age Relations in Modern Societies," mimeo, University of Southern California

DeFreitas, Gregory (1986): "The Impact of Immigration on Low-Wage Workers," mimeo

DeFreitas, Gregory, and Adriana Marshall (1983): "Immigration and Wage Growth in U.S. Manufacturing in the 1970s," *Proceedings of the 36th Annual Meeting of the Industrial Relations Research Association* (Madison, WI: IRRA), pp. 148–56

DeJong, Gordon F., Brenda Davis Root, and Ricardo G. Abad (1986): "Family Reunification and Philippine Migration to the United States: The Immigrants' Perspective," *International Migration Review*, 20(3), pp. 598–611

Denison, Edward F. (1967): *Why Growth Rates Differ* (Washington, DC: Brookings Institution)

Douglas, Daryl (ed.) (1982): *The Economics of Australian Immigration*, Conference Papers, Proceedings of the Conference on the Economics of Immigration, 8–9 February

Easterlin, Richard A. (1960): "Interregional Differences in Per Capita Income, Population and Total Income, 1840–1950." In Easterlin, *Trends in the American Economy in the Nineteenth Century* (Princeton, NJ: Princeton University Press), pp. 73–141

Easterlin, Richard A. (1967): "Effects of Population Growth in the Economic Development of Developing Countries," *Annals of the American Academy of Political and Social Science*, 369, pp. 98–108

Easterlin, Richard A. (1968): *Population, Labor Force, and Long Swings in Economic Growth* (New York: NBER), pp. 30–1

Easterlin, Richard A., et al. (1982): *Immigration* (Cambridge, MA: Belknap Press)

Ehrlich, Paul (1968): *The Population Bomb* (New York: Ballantine)

Ehrlich, Paul (1982): Fundraising Letter for Zero Population Growth

Ekburg, Jan (1977): "Long-Term Effects of Immigration," *Economy and Society*, 20(1), pp. 3–22

Ellis, H. S. (1958): "Are There Preferable Alternatives to International Migration as an Aid to Economic Development?" In B. Thomas (ed.), *Economics of International Migration* (London: Macmillan), pp. 347–61

Ethier, W. J. (1984): "International Trade Theory and International Migration," mimeo

Ethier, W. J. (1985): "International Trade and Labor Migration," *American Economic Review*, 75(4), pp. 691–707

Evans, M. D. R. (no date): "Immigrant Entrepreneurship: Effects on Ethnic Market Size and Isolated Labor Pool," Australian National University

Evenson, Robert E. (1971): "The Contribution of Agricultural Research and Extension to Agricultural Production," unpublished Ph.D. thesis, University of Chicago, 1967; summarized in Yujiro Hayami and Vernon W. Ruttan (eds): *Agricultural Development: An International Perspective* (Baltimore, MD: Johns Hopkins University Press)

Fellner, William (1970): "Trends in the Activities Generating Technological Progress," *American Economic Review*, 60(1), pp. 1–29

Fermi, Laura (1968): *Illustrious Immigrants* (Chicago, IL: University of Chicago Press)

Fields, George (1986): "Racism is Accepted Practice in Japan," *Wall Street Journal*, 10 November, p. 23

Findlay, Ronald (1982): "International Distributive Justice: A Trade Theoretic Approach," *Journal of International Economics*, 13(1–2), pp. 1–14

Fischer, Claude S. (1978): "Urban-to-Rural Diffusion of Opinions in Contemporary America, *American Journal of Sociology*, 84(1), pp. 151–9

Flores, Estevan T. (1983): "The Impact of Undocumented Migration on the U.S. Labor Market," *Houston Journal of International Law*, 5(2), pp. 287–321

Fogel, Walter A. (1977): "Illegal Aliens: Economic Aspects and Public Policy Alternatives," *San Diego Law Review*, 15 (December), pp. 63–78

Fogel, Walter A. (1978): Flier of the Center for the Study of Democratic Institutions, Santa Barbara, CA

Francis, Samuel T. (1986): *Smuggling Revolution: The Sanctuary Movement in America*, Studies in Organization Trends, 2 (Washington, DC: Capital Research Center)

Friedman, Milton (1953): "The Methodology of Positive Economics." In Friedman, *Essays in Positive Economics* (Chicago, IL: University of Chicago Press)

Fuchs, Victor R. (1967): *Differentials in Hourly Earning by Region and City Size, 1959* (New York: Columbia University Press)

Gallman, Robert E. (1977): "Human Capital in the First 80 Years of the Republic: How Much Did America Owe the Rest of the World?," *Papers and Proceedings of the 89th Annual Meeting of the American Economic Association, Atlantic City, New Jersey, 16–18 September*, pp. 27–31; also in *American Economic Review*, 67(1), p. 30

Garcia y Griego, Manuel (1983a): "The Importation of Mexican Contract Laborers in the United States, 1942–1946: Antecedents, Operation and Legacy." In Peter G. Brown and Henry Shue (eds.), *The Border that, Joins Mexican Migrants and U.S. Responsibility* (Totowa, NJ: Rowman and Littlefield), pp. 49–98

Garcia y Griego, Manuel (1983b): "Comments of Bustamente and Sanderson Papers and on Research Project ENEFNEU." In Clark W. Reynolds and Carlos Tello (eds), *U.S.–Mexican Relations: Economic and Social Aspects* (Stanford, CA: Stanford University Press)

General Accounting Office (1986): "Illegal Aliens: Limited Research Suggests Illegal Aliens may Displace Native Workers" (April)

"General Eligibility Migrants: Settlement Experience and the Utilisation of Services" (1983), Study Prepared for Australian Population and Immigration Research Program (December)

Gimpel, Jean (1976): *The Medieval Machine* (New York: Penguin)

Glover, Donald R., and Julian L. Simon (1975): "The Effect of Population

374   *References and Bibliography*

Density upon Infrastructure: The Case of Roadbuilding," *Economic Development and Cultural Change*, 23(3), pp. 453–68

Goddard, R. F., L. H. Sparkes, and J. A. Haydon (1984): "Demographic Consequences of Immigration," Committee for Economic Development of Australia and the Department of Immigration and Ethnic Affairs, Publication no. VBPO641 (September)

Goldberg, Howard (1974): "Estimates of Emigration from Mexico and Illegal Entry into the United States, 1960–1970, by the Residual Method," unpublished graduate research paper, Center for Population Research, Georgetown University, Washington, DC

Goldfarb, Robert, Oli Havrylyshyn, and Stephen Mangum (1984): "Can Remittances Compensate for Manpower Outflows: The Case of Philippine Physicians," *Journal of Development Economics*, 15(1–3), pp. 1–17

Graham, Otis L., Jr. (1982): Introduction to R. Conner, "Breaking down the Barriers: The Changing Relationship between Illegal Immigration and Welfare," FAIR Immigration Paper no. 4 (September)

Grant, Lindsey, and John H. Tanton (1981): "Immigration and the American Conscience." In *Progress as if Survival Mattered* (San Francisco, CA: Friends of the Earth)

Greeley, Andrew M. (1976): *Ethnicity, Denomination and Inequality* (Beverly Hills, CA: Sage)

Greeley, Andrew M. (1982): "Immigration in Religio-Ethnic Groups: A Sociological Reappraisal." In Chiswick (1982)

Griliches, Zvi (1958): "Research Costs and Social Returns: Hybrid Corn and Related Innovation," *Journal of Political Economy*, 66 (October), pp. 419–531

Grossman, Jean Baldwin (1982): "The Substitutability of Natives and Immigrants in Production," *Review of Economics and Statistics*, 64(4), pp. 596–603

Grossman, Jean Baldwin (1986): "The Occupational Attainment of Immigrant Women in Sweden," *Scandinavian Journal of Economics*, 3, pp. 337–51

Grubel, Herbert G., and Anthony Scott (1977): *The Brain Drain: Determinants, Measurement and Welfare Effects* (Waterloo, Ontario: Wilfrid Laurier Press)

Hagen, Everett E. (1962): *On the Theory of Social Change* (Homewood, IL: Dorsey)

Hagen, Everett E. (1975): *The Economics of Development* (Homewood, IL: Irwin)

Hall, George E. (1981): testimony before the House Subcommittee on Census and Population, 27 April

Hamermesh, Daniel S. (1979): "Entitlement Effects, Unemployment Insurance, and Employment Decisions," *Economic Inquiry*, 17(3), 317–32

Hamermesh, Daniel S., and James Grant (1979): "Econometric Studies of Labor: Labor Substitution and Their Implications for Policy," *Journal of Human Resources*, 14(4), pp. 518–42

Hamermesh, Daniel S., and Albert Rees (1984): *The Economics of Work and Pay*, 3rd edn (New York: Harper and Row)

Handlin, Oscar (1951): *The Uprooted* (New York: Grosset and Dunlap)

Harrison, David S. (1983): "The Impact of Recent Immigration on the South Australian Labour Market," Report to the Committee for the Economic Development of Australia (May)

Harwood, Edwin (1986): "American Public Opinion and U.S. Immigration Policy," *Annals of the American Academy of Political Science*, 487 (September), pp. 201–12

Hawley, A. H. (1969): "Population and Society: An Essay on Growth." In S. J. Behrman, L. Corsa, and F. Freedman (eds), *Fertility and Family Planning* (Ann Arbor: University of Michigan Press), pp. 189–205

Hayek, Friedrich (1989): *The Fatal Conceit* (Chicago, IL: University of Chicago Press)

Headley, Walter (ed.) (1980): *The Economy and the President: 1980 and Beyond* (Englewood Cliffs, NJ: Prentice-Hall)

Heer, David M. (1979): "What is the Annual Net Flow of Undocumented Mexican Immigrants to the United States?" *Demography*, 16(4), pp. 417–23

Heer, David M., and Dee Falasco (1982): "The Socioeconomic Status of Recent Mothers of Mexican Origin in Los Angeles County: A Comparison of Undocumented Migrants, Legal Migrants, and Native Citizens," unpublished paper given at the Annual Meeting of the Population Association of America

Higgs, Robert (1971): "American Inventiveness, 1870–1920," *Journal of Political Economic*, 79(3), pp. 661–7

Higgs, Robert (1971): "Race, Skills, and Earnings: American Immigrants in 1909," *Journal of Economic History*, 31(2), pp. 420–8

Higgs, Robert (1980): *Competition and Coercion: Blacks in the American Economy, 1865–1914* (Chicago, IL: University of Chicago Press)

Hill, Peter J. (1975): "Relative Skill and Income Levels of Native and Foreign-Born Workers in the United States," *Explorations in Economic History*, 12(1), pp. 47–60

Hill, Peter J. (1976): *The Impact of Immigration into the United States* (Salem, NH: Ayer)

Hirschman, Charles, and Morrison G. Wong (1980): "Successful Minorites: Socio-economic Achievement among Immigrant and Native-Born Asian Americans," unpublished paper given at the Annual Meeting of the Population Association of America (April)

Houstoun, Marion F., Roger G. Kramer, and Joan Mackin Barrett (1984):

"Female Predominance in Immigration to the United States since 1930: A First Look," *International Migration Review*, xviii(4), pp. 908–63

Huddle, Donald L. (no date a): "Raids on Illegals Proved Cheapest, Fastest Way to Help U.S. Jobless, Rice University Economist Finds," press release, Rice University, Austin, TX

Huddle, Donald L. (no date b): "Federal Government is Financing Illegal Aliens on the Job, Rice University Economist Finds," press release, Rice University, Austin, TX

Huddle, Donald L. (1984): "Rice University Economist Blames 'Greedy Employers', Opportunistic Politicians for Delay of Immigration Reform," press release, Rice University, Austin, TX, 3 June

Huddle, Donald L., Arthur F. Corwin, and Gordon J. MacDonald (1985): "Illegal Immigration: Job Displacement and Social Costs," American Immigration Control Foundation

Hugo, Graeme (1983): "Changing Distribution and Age Structure of Birthplace Groups in Australia: 1976–1981," National Institute of Labour Studies Incorporated, Flinders University of South Australia, Working Paper no. 54 (June)

Hugo, Graeme, and Deborah Wood (1983): "Recent Fertility Trends and Differentials in Australia," National Institute of Labour Studies Incorporated, Flinders University of South Australia, Working Paper no. 57

Immigration and Naturalization Service, Western Regional Office (1983): "Illegal Immigration Costs to U.S. Taxpayers" (Washington, DC: INS)

"Immigration in the Era of Limits" (1980), *Los Angeles Times*, 17 February 1980, part vi, p. 5

Inglis, Paul A., and Thorsten Stromback (1984): "A Descriptive Analysis of Migrants' Labour Market Experience," Bureau of Labour Market Research, Canberra (February)

Isaac, Julius (1947): *The Economics of Migration* (London: Routledge and Kegan Paul)

James, William (1962, 1967): *Essays on Faith and Morals* (Cleveland, OH: World)

Jasso, Guillermina (1986): "Whom shall we Welcome? Elite Judgments of the Criteria for the Selection of Immigrants," mimeo

Jasso, Guillermina, and Mark R. Rosenzweig (1982): "Estimating the Emigration Rates of Legal Immigrants using Administrative and Survey Data: The 1971 Cohort of Immigrants to the United States," *Demography*, 19(3), pp. 279–90

Jasso, Guillermina, and Mark R. Rosenzweig (1985): "Estimating the Effects of Experience in the United States on the Occupational Mobility of Immigrants," mimeo (March)

Jasso, Guillermina, and Mark R. Rosenzweig (1986): "Family Reunification and the Immigration Multiplier: U.S. Immigration Law, Origin-

Country Conditions, and the Reproduction of Immigrants," *Demography*, 23(3), pp. 291–311

Jensen, Leif (1987): "Poverty and Immigration to the United States: 1960–1980," unpublished typescript, Department of Sociology, University of Wisconsin, Madison

Jerome, Harry (1926): *Migration and Business Cycles* (New York: National Bureau of Economic Research)

Jones, Eric L. (1981): *The European Miracle* (Cambridge: Cambridge University Press)

Jones, K., and A. D. Smith (1970): *The Economic Impact of Commonwealth Immigration* (Cambridge: Cambridge University Press)

Keely, Charles B. (1982): "Illegal Migration," *Scientific American*, 246(3)

Keely, Charles B., and Ellen P. Kraly (1978): "Recent Net Alien Immigration to the U.S.: Its Impact on Population Growth and Native Fertility," unpublished paper presented to a meeting of the Population Association of America

Keely, Charles B., Patricia Elwell, Austin Fragomen, and Silvio Tomasi (1977): "Profiles of Undocumented Aliens in New York City: Haitians and Dominicans," mimeo

Kelley, Allen C. (1965): "International Migration and Economic Growth: Australia 1865–1935," *Journal of Economic History*, 25(2), pp. 333–54

Kelley, Allen C. (1972): "Scale Economies, Inventive Activity, and the Economics of American Population Growth," *Explorations in Economic History*, 10(1), 35–52

Kelley, Allen C., and R. M. Schmidt (1979): "Modelling the Role of Government Policy in Post-War Australian Immigration," *Economic Record*, lv(149), pp. 127–34

Kelley, Gail Paradise (1977): *From Vietnam to America* (Boulder, CO)

Kendrick, John W., et al. (1976): The National Wealth of the United States (New York: Conference Board)

Kim, Young Yun, and Perry M. Nicassu (1980): *Survey of Indochinese Refugees*, Travelers Aid Society of Metropolitan Chicago, vol. I–V (February)

Kindleberger, Charles P. (1965): *Economic Development*, 2nd edn (New York: McGraw Hill)

Kindleberger, Charles P. (1967): *Europe's Postwar Growth: The Role of Labor Supply* (Cambridge, MA: Harvard University Press)

King, Allan G. (no date): "The Effect of Illegal Aliens on Unemployment in the United States," mimeo

King, Allan G. (1982): "The Effect of Undocumented Hispanic Workers on the Earnings of Hispanic Americans," Workshop on Labor Market Impacts of Immigrants, Racine, WI

Kmenta, J. (1966): "An Econometric Model of Australia, 1948–1961,"

378   *References and Bibliography*

Australian Economic Papers, 5 (December), pp. 131–64

Korns, Alexander (1979): "Cyclical Fluctuations in the Difference between the Payroll and Household Measures of Employment," *Survey of Current Business* (May), pp. 14–44

Kossoudji, Sherrie A. (1986): "The Impact of English Language Ability on the Labor Market Opportunites of Immigrant Men," mimeo

Kossoudji, Sherrie A., and Susan I. Ranney (1986): "Legal Status as Union Membership: Legal and Illegal Wage Rates of Mexican Immigrants," Research Report no. 86–103, Population Center, University of North Carolina, Chapel Hill, NC (October)

Kravis, Irving B., Alan Heston, and Robert Summers (with Alicia R. Civitello, Samvit P. Dhar, Shigeru Kawasaki, Hugues Picard, and Martin Shanin) (1982): *World Product and Income: International Comparisons of Real Gross Product* (Baltimore, MD, and London: Johns Hopkins University Press)

Kritz, Mary M., and Douglas T. Gurak (1976): "Ethnicity and Fertility in the U.S.: An Analysis of 1970 Public Use Sample Data," *Review of Public Data Use*, 4(3), pp. 12–23

Kuznets, Simon (1960): "Population Change and Aggregate Output," in Universities–National Bureau of Economic Research, *Demographic and Economic Change in Developed Countries* (Princeton, NJ: Princeton University Press)

Kuznets, Simon (1967): "Population and Economic Growth," *Proceedings of the American Philosophical Society*, 111, pp. 170–93

Kuznets, Simon (1971b): *Economic Growth of Nations* (Cambridge, MA: Harvard University Press)

Kuznets, Simon (1977): "Two Centuries of Economic Growth: Reflections on U.S. Experience," *American Economic Review*, 67(1), pp. 1–14

Kuznets, Simon, and Ernest Rubin (1954): *Immigration and the Foreign Born* (New York: National Bureau of Economic Research)

Lakshmana, Rao G., Anthony H. Richmond, and Jerzy Zubrzycki (1984): *Immigrants in Canada and Australia*, vol. 1: *Demographic Aspects and Education* (Durham, NC: Institute for Behavioral Research, York University)

Lakshmana, Rao G., Anthony H. Richmond, and Jerzy Zubrzycki (1984): *Immigrants in Canada and Australia*, vol. 2: *Economic Adaptation* (Durham, NC: Institute for Behavioral Research, York University)

Lamm, Richard (1983): "7 Economic Sins Could Turn U.S. into 2nd Class Nation," Christian Science Monitor News Service, in *Champaign-Urbana News Gazette*, 8 August, p. A4

Lamm, Richard (1986): testimony before the Subcommittee on Economic Resources, Competitiveness, and Security Economics of the Joint Economic Committee of the Congress of the United States on the Issue of Immigration, 29 May

Lancaster, Clarice, and Frederick J. Scheuren (1978): "Counting the Uncountable Illegals: Some Initial Statistical Speculations Employing Capture—Recapture Techniques," *1977 Proceedings of the Social Statistics Section*, part 1, American Statistical Association, pp. 530–5

Landes, Elizabeth M. (1980): "The Effect of State Maximum-Hours Laws on the Employment of Women in 1920," *Journal of Political Economy*, 88(3), pp. 476–94

Lane, Chuck (1985): "Open the Door," *New Republic*, 1 April, pp. 7–8

Lane, P. A. (1970): "Immigration and Economics." In Thomson and Trlin (1970), pp. 25–37

Lee, Everett S. (1966): "A Theory of Migration," *Demography*, 3(1), pp. 48ff.

Lee, Ronald (1983): "Economic Consequences of Population Size, Structure, and Growth," *International Union for the Scientific Study of Population Newsletter* (January)

Lesko Associates (1975): *Final Report: Basic Data and Guidance Required to Implement a Major Illegal Alien Study during Fiscal Year 1976*, prepared for Office of Planning and Evaluation, US Immigration and Naturalization Service, Washington, DC (October)

Levine, Daniel B., Kenneth Hill, and Robert Warren (eds) (1985): *Immigration Statistics: A Story of Neglect* (Washington, DC: National Academy Press)

Lewis, William A. (1955): *The Theory of Economic Growth* (London: George Allen & Unwin)

Light, Ivan H. (1972): *Ethnic Enterprise in America* (Berkeley, CA: University of California Press)

Light, Ivan H. (1984): "Immigrant and Ethnic Enterprise in North America," *Ethnic and Racial Studies*, 7(2), pp. 195–206

Light, Ivan H. (1985): "Immigrant Entrepreneurs in America: Koreans in Los Angeles." In Nathan Glazer (ed.), *Clamor at the Gates: The New American Immigration* (San Francisco, CA: Institute for Contemporary Studies Press)

Love, Douglas O. (1978): "City Sizes and Prices," unpublished Ph.D. thesis, University of Illinois

Love, Douglas O. (1982): "City Population Size and Item Prices." In Julian L. Simon and Peter H. Lindert (eds), *Research in Population Economics*, vol. 4 (Greenwich, CT: JAI Press), pp. 83–92

Love, Douglas O., and Lincoln Pashure [J. L. Simon] (1978): "The Effect of Population Size and Concentration upon Scientific Productivity." In Julian L. Simon (ed.), *Research in Population Economics*, vol. 1 (Greenwich, CT: JAI Press)

Lyon, David W. (1977): "The Dynamics of Welfare Dependency: A Survey," Welfare Policy Project, Institute of Policy Sciences and Public

Affairs, Duke University, Durham, NC (Spring)

Maddison, Angus (1982): *Phases of Capitalist Development* (Oxford: Oxford University Press)

Manpower and Immigration (1974): *Three Years in Canada* (Ottawa: Information Canada)

Manson, Donald M., Thomas H. Espenshade, and Thomas Muller (1985): "Mexican Immigration to Southern California: Issues of Job Competition and Worker Mobility," Urban Institute, Washington DC (August)

Maram, Sheldon L. (1980): *Hispanic Workers in the Garment and Restaurant Industries in Los Angeles County* (San Diego, CA: Program in United States–Mexican Studies, University of California)

Marshall, Ray (1978): "Economic Factors influencing the International Migration of Workers." In Stanley R. Ross (ed.), *Views Across the Border: The United States and Mexico* (Albuquerque, NM: University of New Mexico Press)

Marshall, Ray (1984): "Immigration: An International Economic Perspective," *International Migration Review*, 18(3), pp. 593–612

Marty, Martin E. (1978): "Migration: The Moral Framework." In William H. McNeill and Ruth S. Adams (eds), *Human Migration: Patterns and Policies* (Bloomington, IN: Indiana University Press), pp. 387–403

Massey, Douglas S. (1984): "The Settlement Process among Mexican Migrants to the United States: New Methods and Findings" Report prepared for the National Academy of Sciences Panel on Immigration Statistics (June)

Massey, Douglas S. (1986): "Understanding Mexican Migration to the United States," mimeo, Population Studies Center, University of Pennsylvania

Massey, Douglas S., and Felipe Garcia Espana (1987): "The Social Process of International Migration," *Science*, 14 August, pp. 733ff.

McCarthy, Kevin F., and R. Burciaga Valdez (1986): *Current and Future Effects of Mexican Immigration in California* (Santa Monica, CA: Rand Corporation)

McInnis, Marvin (1980): "A Functional View of Canadian Immigration," unpublished paper given at the Annual Meeting of the Population Association of America (April)

McNeill, William H. (1978): "Human Migration: A Historical Overview." In William H. McNeill and Ruth S. Adams (eds), *Human Migration: Patterns and Policies* (Bloomington, IN: Indiana University Press), pp. 11–18

Mera, K. (1970): "Urban Agglomeration and Economic Efficiency," *Economic Development and Cultural Change*, 21, pp. 309–21

Miller, Paul W. (1983): "The Impact of Immigration on the South Australian Labour Market: An Analysis of the 1976 Census," appendix to

Harrison (1983)

Modell, John (1977): *The Economics and Politics of Racial Accommodation: The Japanese of Los Angeles, 1900–1942* (Urbana, IL, Chicago, IL, and London: University of Illinois Press)

Modigliani, Francis (1966): "The Life Cycle Hypothesis of Saving, the Demand for Wealth, and the Supply of Capital," *Social Research*, 33 (Summer), pp. 160–217

Mohr, L. B. (1969): "Determinants of Innovation in Organizations," *American Political Science Review*, 63, pp. 111–26

Morawetz, David (1977): "Twenty-five Years of Economic Development," *Finance and Development*, 14(3), pp. 10–13

Morgan, Larry C., and Bruce L. Gardner (1982): "Potential for a U.S. Guest-Worker Program in Agriculture: Lessons from the Braceros." In Chiswick (1982)

Morrison, Peter A., and Judith P. Wheeler (1978): "The Image of Additional 'Elsewhere' in the American Tradition of Migration." In William H. McNeill and Ruth S. Adams (eds), *Human Migration: Patterns and Policies* (Bloomington, IN: Indiana University Press), pp. 75–94

Morrison, R. J. (1980): "A Wild Motley Throng: Immigrant Expenditures and the 'American' Standard of Living," *International Migration Review*, 14(3), pp. 342–56

Muller, Thomas (1984): *The Fourth Wave: California's Newest Immigrants: A Summary* (Washington, DC: Urban Institute Press)

Muller, Thomas, and Thomas J. Espenshade (1985): *The Fourth Wave: California's Newest Immigrants* (Washington, DC: Urban Institute Press)

Mumford, Stephen (1981): "Illegal Immigration, National Security, and the Church," *The Humanist*, 41(6), pp. 24–30

National Research Council (1985): "Panel Calls Immigration Data 'Woefully Inadequate' to Support Policymaking," press release, 24 June

Neal, Larry (1981): "Interrelationships of Trade and Migration – Lessons from Europe," Paper prepared for the Select Commission on Immigration and Refugee Policy, Appendix B (Washington, DC: Government Printing Office)

Neal, Larry (1983): "Immigration: The West German Case," unpublished typescript University of Illinois, November

Neal, Larry, and Paul Uselding (1972): "Immigration: A Neglected Source of American Economic Growth, 1790–1912," *Oxford Economic Papers*, 24(3), pp. 68–88

Neisser, Hans P. (1944): "The Economics of a Stationary Population," *Social Research* (November), pp. 470–90

Norman, N. (1984): "Economic Impact of Immigration," Australian Workshop on Consequences of Immigration, conducted at the Annual Conference of the International Union for the Scientific Study of Population

Norman, Neville R., and Kathryn F. Meikle (1983): "Immigration: The Crunch Issues for Australia," Committee for Economic Development of Australia, Information Paper no. IP8 (August)

Norman, Neville R., and Kathryn F. Meikle (1985): *The Economic Effects of Immigration on Australia*, vols 1 and 2, Committee for Economic Development of Australia (April)

North, David S. (1979): *Seven Years Later: The Experiences of the 1970 Cohort of Immigrants in the United States*, R&D Monograph no. 71, US Department of Labor, ETA, Washington, DC

North, David S. (1981): *Government Records: What they tell us about the Role of Illegal Immigrants in the Labor Market and in Income Transfer Programs* (Washington, DC: New Transcentury Foundation)

North, David S., and Allen LaBel (1978): *Manpower and Immigration Policies in the U.S.*, National Commission for Manpower Policies, Special Report no. 20 (February)

North, David S., and Marian F. Houstoun (1976): "The Characteristics and Role of Illegal Aliens in the U.S. Labor Market: An Exploratory Study" (Washington, DC: Linton and Company)

North, David S., and Phillip Martin (1980): "Immigration and Employment: A Need for Policy Coordination," *Monthly Labor Review*, 105(10), pp. 47–50

North, David S., and William G. Weissert (1973): *Immigrants and the American Labor Market*, Report of the US Department of Labor under Contract no. 20–11–73–01 (Washington, DC: Transcentury Corporation)

Northage & Associates Pty Ltd (1983): "General Eligibility Migrants: Settlement Experience and the Utilization of Services," prepared for the Australian Population and Immigration Research Programme (December)

Nurkse, Ragnar (1952): "Growth in Underdeveloped Countries," *American Economic Review* (May); reprinted in A. N. Agarwala and S. P. Singh (eds) (1963): *The Economics of Underdevelopment* (New York: Oxford University Press)

Ornstein, Michael D., and Raghubar D. Sharma (1983, revised): "Adjustment and Economic Experience of Immigrants in Canada: An Analysis of the 1976 Longitudinal Survey of Immigrants," Discussion Paper, Institute for Behavioral Research, York University; first published 1981

Orton, Eliot S. (1986): "Changes in the Skill Differential: Union Wages in Construction, 1907–1972," *Industrial and Labor Relations Review*, 30(1), pp. 16–24

Otero, J. F. (1981): "A Labor View of U.S. Immigration Policy," *The Humanist*, 41(6), pp. 39–46

Ozdowski, Sev A. (1985): "The Law, Immigration and Human Rights –

Changing the Australian Immigration Control System," mimeo, Woodstock Theological Center (June)

Parai, Louis (1974): *The Economic Impact of Immigration* (Ottawa: Manpower and Immigration)

Parlin, Bradley W. (1976): *Immigrant Professionals in the United States: Discrimination in the Scientific Labor Market* (New York: Praeger)

Passel, Jeffrey S. (1986): "Undocumented Immigration," *Annals of the American Academy of Political and Social Sciences*, 487 (September), pp. 181–200

Passel, Jeffrey S., and Jennifer M. Peck (1979): "Estimating Emigration from the United States: A Review of Data and Methods," unpublished paper (prepared by the Population Division, US Bureau of the Census), given at the Annual Meeting of the Population Association of America

Patinkin, Don (1959): *The Israel Economy: The First Decade* (Jerusalem: Falk), p. 76

Patinkin, Don (1965): *Money, Interest, and Prices*, 2nd edn (New York: Harper and Row)

Payne, Suzanne (1974): *Exporting Workers: The Turkish Case* (London: Cambridge University Press)

Penner, Rudolph G. (1984): Correspondence, 11 May

Perez, Lisandro (1986): "Immigrant Economic Adjustment and Family Organization: The Cuban Success Story Reexamined," *International Migration Review*, xx(1), pp. 4–20

Perkins, Dwight (1969): *Agricultural Development in China, 1368–1968* (Chicago, IL: Aldine)

Perry, Joseph M. (1978): *The Impact of Immigration on Three American Industries, 1865–1914* (New York: Arno Press)

Perry, William (1899): *Another Essay in Political Arithmetic* (1682). In *The Economic Writings of Sir William Petty*, ed. Charles H. Hull (Cambridge: Cambridge University Press), p. 474

Phelps, Edmund (1966): "Models of Technical Progress and the Golden Rule of Research," *Review of Economic Studies*, 48(3), pp. 251–65

Piore, Michael J. (1975): "The 'New Immigration' and the Presumption of Social Policy," *Proceedings of the 27th Annual Winter Meeting of the Industrial Relations Research Association*

Piore, Michael J. (1979): *Birds of Passage: Migrant Labor and Industrial Societies* (New York: Cambridge University Press)

Poitras, Guy (1980): "The U.S. Experience of Return Migrants from Costa Rica and El Salvador," mimeo

Population Reference Bureau (1978): *Intercom* (May)

Portes, Alejandro (1979): "Illegal Immigration and the International System: Lessons for Recent Mexican Immigrants to the United States,"

Social Problems, 26(4), pp. 426—38

Portes, Alejandro, and R. L. Bach (1980): "Immigrant Earnings: Deter-minants of Economic Attainment among Cuban and Mexican Immigrants in the United States," *International Migration Review*, 14(3), pp. 315—41

Price, Derek de Solla (1975): "Some Statistical Results for the Number of Authors in the States of the United States and the Nations of the World." In *Who is Publishing in Science* (Philadelphia, PA: Institute for Scientific Information), pp. 26—35

Raspail, Jean (1986): *Camp of the Saints* (Costa Mesa, CA: Noontide)

Ravenstein, Edward G. (1889): "The Laws of Migration," *Journal of the Royal Statistical Society* (June), pp. 241—301

Reder, Melvin (1963): "The Economic Consequences of Increased Migra-tion," *Review of Economics and Statistics*, 45, pp. 221

Reimers, David (1985): *Still the Golden Door: The Third World Comes to America* (New York: Columbia University Press)

Reubens, Edwin P. (1978): "Illegal Immigrants and the Mexican Economy," *Challenge* (November/December), pp. 13—19

Ricardo, David (1963): *The Principles of Political Economy and Taxation* (Homewood, IL: Irwin)

Richmond, Anthony H. (1980): *Factors in the Adjustment of Immigrants and their Descendants* (Ottawa: Ministry of Supply and Services)

Richmond, Anthony, and Jerzy Zubrzycki (1984): *Immigrants in Canada and Australia*, vol. 2: *Economic Adaptation* (Institute for Behavioral Research, York University)

Riefler, Winfield (1930): *Money Rates and Money Markets in the United States* (New York: Harper and Brothers)

Rienow, Robert (1981): "Can we Still Close the Gates?" *The Humanist*, 41(6), pp. 14—17

Roberts, K. D., et al. (1978): "The Mexican Migration Numbers Game: An Analysis of the Lesko Estimates of Undocumented Migration from Mexico to the United States," Discussion Paper, Bureau of Business Research, University of Texas, Austin

Robinson, J. Gregory (1979): "Estimating the Approximate Size of the Illegal Alien Population in the United States by the Comparative Trend Analysis of Age-Specific Death Rates," unpublished paper given at the Annual Meeting of the Population Association of America (April)

Rogers, Tommy W. (1969): "Migration Attractiveness of Southern Metro-politan Areas," *Social Science Quarterly*, 50(2), pp. 325—36

Rosenstein-Rodan, P. N. (1943): "Problems of Industrialization of Eastern and South-Eastern Europe," *Economic Journal* (June—September)

Rosenzweig, Mark (1982): "Comment," unpublished paper presented to a meeting of the American Economic Association

Samuel, T. John (1987): "Family Class Immigrants to Canada, 1981–84: Labour Force Activity Aspects," unpublished paper presented to a meeting of the Population Association of America

Samuel, T. John, and T. Conyers (1985): "The Employment Effects of Immigration: A Balance Sheet Approach," unpublished typescript, Employment and Immigration Canada, Ottawa (December)

Samuel, T. John, and B. Woloski (1985): "The Labor Market Experiences of Canadian Immigrants," *International Migration*, 23(2), pp. 225–50

Samuelson, Paul A. (1975): "Optimum Social Security in a Life-Cycle Growth Market," *International Economic Review*, 16 October, p. 530

Saran, Parmatma (1977): "The New Immigrant Wave: Cosmopolitans from India," *Society*, 14(6), pp. 65–9

Schmookler, Jacob (1962a): "Economic Sources of Inventive Activity," *Journal of Economic History*, xxii(1), pp. 1–20

Schmookler, Jacob (1962b): "Changes in Industry and in the State of Knowledge as Determinants of Industry Invention." In National Bureau of Economic Research, *The Rate and Direction of Inventive Activity: Economic and Social Factors* (Princeton, NJ: Princeton University Press), pp. 195–232

Schmookler, Jacob (1966): *Invention and Economic Growth* (Cambridge, MA: Harvard University Press)

Schnapp, John B. (1982): "Soichiro Honda, Japan's Inventive Iconoclast," *Wall Street Journal*, 1 February, p. 15

Schultz, T. Paul (1980): "The Schooling and Health of Children of Immigrants." Appendix D to *U.S. Immigration Policy and the National Interest*, Staff Report of the Select Commission on Immigration and Refugee Policy (Washington, DC: Government Printing Office)

Schultz, Theodore W. (1961): "Investment in Human Capital," *American Economic Review*, li (March), pp. 1–17

Schultz, Theodore W. (1964): *Transforming Traditional Agriculture* (New Haven, CT: Yale University Press)

Schultz, Theodore W. (1978): "Migration: An Economist's View." In William H. McNeill and Ruth S. Adams (eds), *Human Migration: Patterns and Policies* (Bloomington, IN: Indiana University Press), pp. 377–86

Segal, David (1976): "Are there Returns to Scale in City Size?," *Review of Economic Statistics*, 58(3), pp. 339–50

Select Commission on Immigration and Refugee Policy (1981): Staff Report, (Washington, DC: Government Printing Office)

Servan-Schreiber, Jean-Jacques, and Herbert Simon (1987): "America Must Remain the World's University," *Washington Post*, 15 November, pp. 1, 4

Shinn, Eui Hang, and Kyung-Sup Chang (1988): "Peripherization of

Immigrant Professionals: The Case of Korean Physicians in the United States," *International Migration Review*, 22(4), pp. 609–26

Shuval, Judith, et al. (1973): *Adjustment Patterns of Immigrants from the USSR* (Jerusalem: Institute for Applied Social Sciences)

Sicron, M. (1967): "The Economics of Immigration to Israel, 1948–1963," *Proceedings of the World Population Conference, 1965*, vol. 4 (New York: UN), pp. 230–4

Siegel, Jacob S., Jeffrey S. Passel, and J. Gregory Robinson (1981): "Preliminary Review of Existing Studies of the Number of Illegal Residents in the United States." Appendix E to *U.S. Immigration Policy and the National Interest*, Staff Report of the Select Commission on Immigration and Refugee Policy (Washington, DC: Government Printing Office)

Simon, Julian L. (1971): "A Policy to Promote the World's Economic Development with Migration from LDC's to MDC's," *Policy Science*, 5 (September), pp. 110–13

Simon, Julian L. (1974): *The Effects of Income on Fertility* (Chapel Hill, NC: Carolina Population Center)

Simon, Julian L. (1976): "The Economic Effect of Russian Immigrants upon the Veteran Israeli Population: A Cost-Benefit Analysis," *Economic Quarterly*, 23 (August), pp. 244–53 (in Hebrew)

Simon, Julian L. (1977): *The Economics of Population Growth* (Princeton, NJ: Princeton University Press)

Simon, Julian L. (1978): "An Integration of the Invention-Pull and Population-Push Theories of Economic-Demographic History." In Julian L. Simon (ed.), *Research in Population Economics*, vol. 1 (Greenwich, CT: JAI Press)

Simon, Julian L. (1981a): "Global Confusion, 1980: A Hard Look at the Global 2000 Report." *The Public Interest*, 62 (Winter), pp. 3–21

Simon, Julian L. (1981b): "Immigrants, Taxes, and Welfare in the United States," *Population and Development Review*, 10 (March), 1984, pp. 55–69; extracted from Simon (1981b)

Simon, Julian L. (1981c): *The Ultimate Resource* (Princeton, NJ: Princeton University Press)

Simon, Julian L. (1981d): "What Immigrants Take from, and Give to, the Public Coffers." Appendix D to *U.S. Immigration Policy and the National Interest*, Staff Report of the Select Commission on Immigration and Refugee Policy (Washington, DC: Government Printing Office)

Simon, Julian L. (1982a): "A Scheme to Promote the World's Economic Development with Migration." In Julian L. Simon and Peter H. Lindert (eds), *Research in Population Economics* (Greenwich, CT: JAI Press)

Simon, Julian L. (1982b): "How much Welfare and Public Services do Immigrants (and Natives) Use?," unpublished typescript

Simon, Julian L. (1986): "On Aggregate Empirical Studies Relating Population Growth to Economic Development," *Population and Development Review* (forthcoming)

Simon, Julian L. (1987): *Effort, Opportunity, and Wealth* (Oxford: Basil Blackwell)

Simon, Julian L. (1988a): "Trade Theory Throws No Light on Migration," unpublished typescript

Simon, Julian L., and Julie Da Vanzo (eds) (1980): *Research in Population Economics*, vol. 2 (Greenwich, CT: JAI Press)

Simon, Julian L., and Roy Gobin (1980): "The Relationship between Population and Economic Growth in LDC's." In Simon and Da Vanzo (1980), pp. 215−34

Simon, Julian L., and Leslie Golembo (1967): "The Spread of a Cost-Free Business Innovation: The Case of the January White Sale," *Journal of Business*, 40(4), pp. 385−8

Simon, Julian L., and A. J. Heins (1985): "The Effect of Immigrants on Natives' Incomes through the Use of Capital," *Journal of Development Economics*, 17, pp. 75−93

Simon, Julian L., and Herman Kahn (eds) (1984): *The Resourceful Earth: A Response to the Global 2000 Report* (Oxford: Basil Blackwell)

Simon, Julian L., and Douglas O. Love (1988): "City Size, Prices, and Efficiency for Individual Goods and Services," unpublished typescript

Simon, Julian L., and Stephen Moore (1988): "The Effect of Immigration upon Aggregate Unemployment: An Across-city Estimation," unpublished typescript

Simon, Julian L., and Adam M. Pilarski (1979): "The Effect of Population Growth on the Quantity of Education Children Receive," *Review of Economics and Statistics*, 61(4), pp. 572−84

Simon, Julian L., and Richard J. Sullivan (1989): "Population Size, Knowledge Stock, and Other Determinants of Agricultural Publication and Patenting: England 1541−1850," *Explorations in Economic History* 26, pp. 21−44

Simon, Julian L. and Richard J. Sullivan (forthcoming): "A Replication and Extension of Chiswick's Estimate of the Earnings Pattern of Immigrants," *Genus*

Simon, Rita J. (1985): *Public Opinion and the Immigrant* (Lexington, MA: Lexington Books)

Simon, Rita J., and Margo DeLey (1984): "The Work Experience of Undocumented Mexican Women Migrants in Los Angeles," *International Migration Review*, 18(4), pp. 1212−29

Simon, Rita J., and Julian L. Simon (1985): "Social and Economic Adjustment." In Rita J. Simon, *New Lives: The Adjustment of Soviet Jewish*

Immigrants in the United States and Israel (Lexington, MA: Lexington Books)

Sjaastad, Larry A. (1962): "The Costs and Returns of Human Migration," *Journal of Political Economy* (October), pp. 80–93

Smith, Barton, and Robert Newman (1977): "Depressed Wages along the U.S.–Mexican Border: An Empirical Analysis," *Economic Inquiry*, xv(1), pp. 51–66

Solow, Robert (1957): "Technical Change and the Aggregate Production Function," *Review of Economics and Statistics*, 39, 312–20

Soskis, Philip (1966): "The Adjustment of Hungarian Refugees in New York," *International Migration Review*, 2(1), p. 45

Spengler, Joseph (1956): "Some Economic Aspects of Immigration to the United States," *Law and Contemporary Problems*, 21, pp. 236–55

Spengler, J. J. (1958): "The Economic Effects of Migration." In F. G. Boudreau and F. G. Kiser (eds.), *Selected Studies of Migration since World War II* (New York: Milbank Memorial Fund)

Stark, Oded, and J. Edward Taylor (1985): "Testing for Relative Deprivation: Mexican Labor Migration," unpublished Paper, Harvard University

Steinberg, Allen (1981): "The History of Immigration and Crime." Appendix A to *U.S. Immigration Policy and the National Interest*, Staff Report of the Select Commission on Immigration and Refugee Policy (Washington, DC: Government Printing Office)

Steinmann, Gunter, and Julian L. Simon (1980): "Phelps' Technical Progress Function Generalized," *Economic Letters*, 5(2), pp. 177–82

Stevens, Jerry (1978): "Demography, Market Structure and Bank Performance," unpublished paper presented at the University of Illinois

Straight, Michael (1983): *After Long Silence* (New York: Norton)

Stromback, Thorsten (1984): "The Earnings of Migrants in Australia," Conference Paper 46, Australian Bureau of Labour Market Research, Canberra (April)

Stryker, J. Dirck (1977): "Optimum Population in Rural Areas: Empirical Evidence from the Franc Zone," *Quarterly Journal of Economics*, 91(2), pp. 177–93

Sveikauskas, Lee (1975): "The Productivity of Cities," *Quarterly Journal of Economics*, 89(3), pp. 343–413

Taft, Donald R. (1936): "Nationality and Crime," *American Sociological Review*, 1, pp. 724–36

Taher, M. (1970): "The Asians." In Thomson and Trlin (eds) (1970), pp. 38–64

Tandon, B. B. (1978): "Earning Differentials among Native Born and Foreign Born Residents of Toronto," *International Migration Review*, 12(3), pp. 406–10

Taylor, J. Edward (1985): "Selectivity of Undocumented Mexico–U.S.

Migrants and Implications for U.S. Immigration Reform," Urban Institute Policy Discussion Paper PDS-85-4, Harvard University, Cambridge, MA (December)

Taylor, J. Edward (1987): "Undocumented Mexico–U.S. Migration and the Returns to Households in Rural Mexico," *American Journal of Agricultural Economics* (August)

Thomas, Brinley (1954, 1973): *Migration and Economic Growth: A Study of Great Britain and the Atlantic Economy* (London: Cambridge University Press)

Thomas, Dorothy Swaine (1941): *Social and Economic Aspects of Swedish Population Movements, 1750–1933* (New York: Macmillan)

Thomas, W. I., and F. Znanieski (1920): *Polish Peasants in Europe and America* (Boston: Gorlam Press)

Thomson, K. W., and A. D. Trlin (eds) (1970): *Immigrants in New Zealand* (Palmerston North: Massey University)

Thomson, Meldrim (undated): "Amnesty for Illegal Aliens," unpublished typescript

Tiede, Tom (1977): "Aliens: Time to Snuff the Torch?," NEA syndicated column

Tobin, James (1974): "Notes on the Economic Theory of Expulsion and Expropriation," *Journal of Development Economics*, 1, pp. 7–18

Toland, John (1714): *Reasons for Naturalizing the Jews in Great Britain and Ireland. On the same foot with all other Nations. Containing also, A Defence of the Jews Against all Vulgar Prejudices in All Countries* (London)

Topel, Robert (1988): "The Impact of Immigration on the Labor Market." In Richard B. Freeman (ed.), *Immigration, Trade, and the Labor Market*, Summary Report (Cambridge, MA: NBER)

Tulpele, Ashok (1984): "Effects of Alternative Migration Strategies on Government Expenditure," Information Paper no. P12, Committee for Economic Development of Australia, Canberra (August)

United Nations Fund for Population Activity (1979): *Review and Appraisal of the World Population Plan of Action*, UN Population Studies no. 71 (New York: UN Department of International Economic and Social Affairs)

US Congressional Budget Office (1983): Cost Estimate, H.R. 1510, Immigration Reform and Control Act of 1983, 10 May

US Congressional Research Service (1979a): *U.S. Immigration Law and Policy* (May)

US Congressional Research Service (1979b): *A Review of U.S. Refugee Resettlement Programs and Policies* (July)

US Congressional Research Service (1980a): *A History of the Immigration and Naturalization Service* (December)

US Congressional Research Service (1980b): *Temporary Worker Programs:*

Background and Issues (February)

US Department of Commerce, Bureau of the Census (1976): *Social Indicators 1976*

US Department of Commerce, Bureau of the Census (1980): *Money Income of Families and Persons in the United States: 1978*, Series P-60 (June)

US Department of Commerce, Bureau of the Census (1984): *Detailed Population Characteristics*, part 1: *United States Summary*, chapter D, vol. 1, Characteristics of the Population, 1980 Census of Population, PC80-1-D1-A (March)

US Department of Health, Education, and Welfare (1975): Medical Assistance (Medicaid) Finances under Title XIX of the Social Security Act, Publication no. (SRS) 76-03150, NCSS Report B-1 (December)

US Department of Health, Education, and Welfare (1975): "Statistics of Public Elementary and Secondary Day Schools," (Fall)

US Small Business Administration (1984a): *The State of Small Business: A Report of the President* (Washington, DC: Government Printing Office)

US Small Business Administration (1984b): *SBA News*, 2 November

US Social Security Administration (1985): *Social Security Bulletin*, Annual Statistical Supplement

Usher, Dan (1977): "Public Property and Effects of Migration upon Other Residents of the Migrants' Countries of Origin and Destination," *Journal of Political Economy*, 85(5), pp. 1001–26

Van Arsdol, Maurice D., Jr., Joan Moore, David Heer, and Susan Haynie (1979): "Non-Apprehended and Apprehended Undocumented Residents in the Los Angeles Labor Market: An Exploratory Study," mimeo

Victorian Ethnic Affairs Commission, Division of Research and Policy (1983): "Unemployment Issues for Migrant Workers," Working Paper no. 1 (October)

Villalpondo, M. Vic, et al. (1977): *A Study of the Socio-Economic Impact of Illegal Aliens, County of San Diego* (San Diego, CA: Human Resources Agency, County of San Diego) (January)

Wachter, Michael L. (1976): "The Changing Cyclical Responsiveness of Wage Inflation," *Brookings Papers on Economic Activity*, part 1, pp. 115–68

Wachter, Michael L. (1977): "Intermediate Swings in Labor Force Participation," *Brookings Papers on Economic Activity*, part 2, pp. 545–74

Wachter, Michael L. (1980): "The Labor Market Outlook for the 1980s," *Industrial and Labor Relations Review*, 33 (April), pp. 342–54

Warren, Robert (1979): "Alien Emigration into the United States: 1963 to 1974," unpublished paper presented to a meeting of the Population Association of America

Warren, Robert, and Jeffrey S. Passel (1983): "Estimates of Illegal Aliens from Mexico counted in the 1980 United States Census," unpublished paper given at the Annual Meeting of the Population Association of America (April)

Warren, Robert, and Jennifer Marks Peck (1980): "Foreign-born Emigration from the United States: 1960 to 1970," *Demography*, 17(1), pp. 71–84

Warren, Ronald S. (1982): "Immigration and the Natural Rate of Unemployment in Australia," *Journal of Macroeconomics*, 4(4), pp. 449–57

Wattenberg, Ben J. (1987): *The Birth Dearth* (New York)

Weiermair, Klaus (1971): "Economic Adjustment of Refugees in Canada: A Case Study," *International Migration*, 9, pp. 5–27

Weiner, Myron (1987): "International Emigration and the Third World." In William Alonso (ed.), *Population in an Interacting World* (Cambridge, MA: Harvard University Press)

Weintraub, Sidney, and Gilberto Cardenas (1984): "The Use of Public Services by Undocumented Aliens in Texas," Policy Research Project Report, Lyndon B. Johnson School of Public Affairs, University of Texas, Austin

West, E. L. (1963): *Canada-United States Price and Productivity Differentials in Manufacturing Industries, 1963* (Ottawa: Economic Council of Canada)

Will, George F. (1986): "The F Word," *Newsweek*, 26 May, p. 80

Wise, Donald E. (1970): "Bracero Labor and the California Farm Labor Economy: A Micro Study of Three Crops, 1952–1967," unpublished Ph.D. thesis, Claremont Graduate School, Claremont, CA

Withers, Glenn (1987): "Migrants and the Labour Market: The Australian Evidence." In *The Future of Migration* (Paris: OECD), pp. 210ff.

Wood, Deborah, and Graeme Hugo (1983): "Recent Mortality Trends in Australia," National Institute of Labour Studies Incorporated, Flinders University of South Australia, Working Paper no. 55 (July)

Woodrow, Karen A., Jeffrey S. Passel, and Robert Warren (1987): "Preliminary Estimates of the Undocumented Immigration to the United States, 1980–1986: Analysis of the June 1986 Current Population Survey," unpublished paper given at a meeting of the American Statistical Association (August)

Woodrow, Karen A., Jeffrey S. Passel, and Robert Warren (1987): "Recent Immigration to the United States – Legal and Undocumented: Analysis of Data from the June 1986 Current Population Survey," unpublished paper given at a meeting of the Population Association of America

Wright, Quincy (1968): "War: The Study of War." In David Sills (ed.), *International Encyclopedia of the Social Sciences* (New York: Macmillan–Free Press)

Yeager, Leland B. (1958): "Immigration, Trade, and Factor-Price Equilization, Current Economic Content," 20 (August), pp. 3–8

Zazueta, Carlos H., and Rodolfo Corona (1979): *Los trabajadores mexicanos en los Estados Unidos: primeros resultados del la Encuesta Nacional de Emigración* (Mexico: Centro Nacional de Información y Estadisticas del Trabajo, CENIET)

INDEX